Developments in
social skills training

Developments in
social skills training

Edited by

SUE SPENCE

University of Sydney
NSW 2006
Australia

GEOFF SHEPHERD

Fulbourn Hospital
Cambridge
England

ACADEMIC PRESS, INC.
(Harcourt Brace Jovanovich, Publishers)

London   Orlando   San Diego   New York
Toronto   Montreal   Sydney   Tokyo

ACADEMIC PRESS INC. (LONDON) LTD.
24/28 Oval Road
London NW1

United States Edition published by
ACADEMIC PRESS, INC.
Orlando, Florida 32887

British Library Cataloguing in Publication Data
Developments in social skills training.
1. Interpersonal relationships—Study and teaching
I. Spence, S.   II. Shepherd, G
302'.07   HM132

ISBN: 0-12-656620-8
LCCCN: 82-73800

PRINTED IN THE UNITED STATES OF AMERICA

85 86 87 88   9 8 7 6 5 4 3 2

Contributors

M. Bender
London Borough of Newham, 99 The Grove, Stratford, London E15 1HR, England

S. Biggs
London Borough of Newham, 99 The Grove, Stratford, London E15 1HR, England

A. Cooper
London Borough of Newham, 99 The Grove, Stratford, London E15 1HR, England

R. Durham
Department of Psychology, Royal Dundee Liff Hospital, Dundee DD21 5NF, Scotland

S. Frosh
Birkbeck College, Malet Street, London WC1E 7HX, England

L. Fry
4 Sudeley Street, London N1, England

M. Jackson
Department of Psychology, Hollymoor Hospital, Northfield, Birmingham B31 5EX, England

P. Lowe
Department of Psychology, HM Prison Holloway, Holloway Road, London N7 0NU, England

J. Marzillier
Department of Psychology, Warneford Hospital, Warneford Lane, Oxford OX3 7JX, England

J. McGuire
61 Nicholson Road, Sheffield F89 SU, England

S. Morley
Department of Psychology, Fulbourn Hospital, Cambridge CB1 5EF, England

P. Priestley
Peace Close, West Honington, Wells, Somerset, England

G. Shepherd
Fulbourn Hospital, Cambridge CB1 5EF, England

S. Spence
Department of Psychology, University of Sydney, Sydney 2006, New South Wales, Australia

C. Stewart
Department of Psychology, HM Prison Holloway, Holloway Road, London N7 0NU, England

K. Winter
Department of Clinical Psychology, Barnsley Hall Hospital, Bromsgrove, Worcester B61 0EX, England

Preface

Social Skills Training has enjoyed an upsurge of interest in the last ten years. A veritable flood of papers and books have appeared of a practical, theoretical, even a popular kind, describing the approach and attempting to evaluate some of its strengths and weaknesses. The reasons behind all this enthusiasm are easy to understand. Nobody could doubt the central importance of social relationships in all our lives and a new theory, especially one with such an apparent air of scientific respectability, is bound to provoke considerable interest. In addition, the practice of social skills training offers the possibility of combining an educational and technological approach with "softer", more experiential methods. It can literally be, "all things to all therapists". This has proved an almost irresistable combination. But, is it just another fad? Does it just happen to coincide with a number of popular "paradigms"? Or, is there something genuinely new, distinctive and important about the approach? How does it work with particular client groups in specific settings? What are the likely developments over the next ten years? These are some of the questions that we address in this volume. By necessity we have had to be selective. Thus, we have not included any accounts of work with the elderly or the mentally-handicapped and these are specialized areas which must await closer examination in the future. However, we have tried to cover the range of common psychological and psychiatric problems involving adults, children and adolescents. We have also included contributions on what we see to be some of the potentially important growth areas for the future. We selected our contributors because of their extensive experience as practitioners and asked them to concentrate on the practical, rather than the research, issues. The result is, we feel, a rich collection of clinical insights and practical wisdom which we hope will be of value to future practitioners wishing to tackle these kinds of problems. The problems involved here are difficult and complex and they will not yield to solutions which are either easy or simplistic. Nevertheless, we

remain convinced that an empirical approach, combined with a willingness to be flexible and creative, offer the best chances for their solution.

January 1983   *Sue Spence and Geoff Shepherd*

Acknowledgements

We would like to acknowledge the patience and co-operation of all our contributors in the face of difficult and obsessional editorship. We would also like to thank Jean Morgan, Glenna Dixon, Rosemary Marks and Maggie Poland for their careful typing and re-typing of the manuscripts. Emily Wilkinson at Academic Press helped greatly in the initial setting up of the project as did a number of friends at MIND (National Association for Mental Health). Numerous clients and colleagues contributed in ways in which they themselves were often unaware and we sincerely thank them all. More personal feelings of appreciation go to Peter Ellender and Laura Shepherd.

To our parents

Contents

1

Introduction

GEOFF SHEPHERD

Social skills training (SST) is a popular new approach to the assessment and treatment of patients experiencing difficulties in their social relationships. According to its originators it is based on the idea that "some forms of mental disorder are caused or exacerbated by a lack of social competence, and can be cured or alleviated by means of training in social skills" (Trower *et al.*, 1978, p. 1). What is meant by "social competence" in this context? Why is it thought that "some forms of mental disorder are caused or exacerbated" by a lack of it? What is the "social skills" model and what does "training" consist of? What evidence is there that mental disorder can be "cured or alleviated" by means of it? These are the issues to be discussed in this introductory chapter. We will argue that social competence encompasses a much broader concept than that traditionally associated with the social skills model and, only in the light of this broader concept, does the association with mental disorder have any validity. Also, the nature of this association seems to be largely correlational and claims for a true causal connection have yet to be substantiated. The social skills model and the treatment method must therefore be evaluated with regard to this broad view of social competence and may

1

need to be modified accordingly. When we come to consider the question of outcome (see Section I, p. 24) we will see that claims for the demonstrable alleviation of mental disorder through SST are difficult to defend. Claims for "cures" seem frankly extravagant. Let us begin with the first question.

I. WHAT IS SOCIAL COMPETENCE?

The most obvious thought that strikes one in considering this question is that there is no simple answer to it. Social competence isn't any one "thing": it is a number of "things". It can refer to an individual's observed behaviour during a social interaction, how they appear and what they do. It can also refer to their subjective thoughts and feelings, how competent they feel themselves to be. Finally, it can refer to their ability to initiate and sustain social roles and relationships; for example as a worker, a housewife, a parent, friend or lover. Social competence could potentially be defined in any of these three ways, but which would be the best? This is the kind of question which one doesn't want to have to answer. Fortunately, it isn't actually necessary to try. In the past psychologists have tended to cling to the notions of "naive operationalism" (Hempel, 1965) i.e. they have attempted to define highly complex variables by the use of a single measurement operation. Some psychologists, particularly some behaviourists, still stick to this old fashioned idea, but with the increasing acceptance of the concept of "construct validity" we now have a new way of dealing with complex, multidimensional variables.

The notion of "hypothetical constructs" was first introduced by Cronbach and Meehl (1955) and its accompanying method of "convergent and discriminant validation" by Campbell and Fiske (1959). Essentially the idea is a simple one. Hypothetical constructs are explanatory variables whose existence is inferred rather than being directly observed. They are inferred as a result of considering the relationship between different dimensions within the construct and the relationship between dimensions of other related, but conceptually separate, constructs (hence the "convergent" and "discriminant" method). For example, the different dimensions of the construct of intelligence correlate fairly highly together, i.e. they converge within the construct; they are also empirically separate from other constructs such as anxiety or social class, i.e. there is a divergence between these constructs. The network of empirical relationships which defines a construct is known as the "nomothetic net" and the construct hangs, suspended as it were, in the middle of this net.

It doesn't actually "exist" because it isn't directly observable but it is useful to infer its existence in order to account for the observed relationships. It is literally a case of something not existing and therefore having to be invented! This rather mystical idea is the only satisfactory way of conceiving such complex variables as intelligence (Anastasi, 1968), fear (Rachman and Hodgson, 1974; Hodgson and Rachman, 1974) and schizophrenia (Neale and Oltmanns, 1980). It is also a very helpful way of thinking about social competence. Social competence is a set of loosely related dimensions having behavioural, cognitive and performance aspects. They hang together sufficiently closely to suggest that they may have some kind of central common core; however they are not perfectly correlated such that assessments of one would enable us to make accurate predictions about the others.

What implications follow from thinking about social competence in this way? First, it emphasizes the multi-dimensional nature of the concept. We can no longer accept a single measurement as providing an adequate "operational definition". Secondly, it accepts a degree of independence between the different dimensions. They are linked but there may be a degree of "desynchrony" between the component parts (Rachman and Hodgson, 1974). Behaviour may not be at all strongly related to role performance, and cognitions (or role performance) need not necessarily be strongly related to behaviour. In terms of treatment this implies that we should accept each dimension as a potentially separate treatment target. Finally, the idea of a construct of social competence allows us to think about social difficulties in both a general and a specific sense. We are not condemned to being forever preoccupied with the minutiae of social behaviour and yet we still have a framework for thinking about the broader aspect of social functioning, including role performance. With this general orientation in mind, let us now turn to the question of social competence and mental disorder.

II. WHAT IS THE RELATIONSHIP BETWEEN SOCIAL COMPETENCE AND MENTAL DISORDER?

The relationship between social competence and mental health is obviously an important one. Although the use of traditional psychiatric diagnoses can be criticized, the idea that improving social skills might somehow prevent mental illness is a powerful one and probably accounts for much of the appeal of the SST approach. There can be no doubt that many individuals who suffer from mental disorders also show difficulties in their social functioning. This isn't surprising since many of the criteria for making diagnoses of mental disorder are themselves, at least partly, social in nature. Thus, depression is usually characterized by social withdrawal, schizophrenia is manifested by odd or inappropriate social behaviour, and psychopathy involves, by definition, an insensitivity to the reactions of others. There is therefore a degree of tautology in suggesting that mental disorder is strongly associated with social difficulties. The more important question is, can they be sufficiently separated such that we can say anything about a possible *causal* connection? Does a lack of social competence "cause" mental disorder? Or, does mental disorder "cause" a lack of social competence? Or, are they unrelated causally and associated simply because of their joint relation to some third variable, e.g. social class?

These are difficult questions to answer, but their causal implications are critical. If a lack of social competence isn't causally related to mental disorder, then there is little reason to suppose that changing one will have any effect on the other. If both are extraneous effects of some third variable, then perhaps we would be better advised to concentrate on identifying and changing that. In order to decide between these different strategies we need to examine the evidence closely.

As indicated already, individuals suffering from various forms of mental disorder show a range of behavioural, cognitive and performance deficits with regard to their social functioning. Bryant *et al.* (1976) showed that amongst neurotic out-patients, those defined as socially unskilled (according to a number of judges and independent criteria) differed from their more socially skilled counterparts with respect to the performance of a number of discreet behavioural elements, e.g. eye contact, speech volume, etc. Similarly, Rimé *et al.* (1978) found that psychopaths looked more, smiled less and were generally experienced as "behaviourally intrusive". Libet and Lewinsohn (1973) have described the low rates of verbal and non-verbal behaviour in patients with depressive illnesses. Wing (1978) describes the poverty of speech, poor eye contact and lack of use of non-verbal cues which is characteristic of many schizophrenic patients.

These studies appear to demonstrate clear behavioural differences in social interaction which are associated with mental disorders. However, how important these deficits are in *causing* difficulties in social competence (as more broadly defined) remains unclear.

In the same way, Nichols (1974) has listed the common cognitive distortions of neurotic patients with social difficulties. These include a tendency to expect negative social consequences to follow from one's own behaviour and a corresponding tendency to expect disapproval and criticism from others. Depressed patients show characteristically low self-regard in relation to other people, and may also feel helpless and "out of control" (Seligman, 1975). Schizophrenics have perhaps the most bizarre cognitive distortions with regard to their social relationships and these may range from a clear belief that other people are conspiring to harm them, to a total confusion as to what significance a given social interaction might have (Wallace *et al.*, 1980). Once again, the cognitive deficits are clear enough, but how important they are causally is more difficult to tell.

Finally, it is evident that a great deal of attention has been given to the relationship between mental illness and difficulties in social role performance (Kazdin, 1979). Epidemiological studies appear to demonstrate a correlation between high rates of admission to psychiatric services and indices of social isolation and disintegration (Bloom, 1968). Henderson *et al.* (1977; 1978a; 1978b) and Goldberg and Huxley (1980) have shown a strong inverse relationship between the presence of good social supports and various neurotic symptoms in both general practice and community settings. Also, Brown's work, although controversial, seems to suggest the importance of a close emotional relationship for reducing vulnerability to depression amongst women (Brown and Harris, 1978). All these studies confirm the relationship between mental illness and social functioning, but we are still left with the problems of interpreting the nature of this relationship.

Two other sets of studies therefore need to be considered here as they may shed some light on the direction of the causal connections. Brown *et al.* (1962; 1972) and Vaughn and Leff (1976) have examined the effects of various kinds of social interactions within the family, particularly overprotection and criticism, on the symptomatic course of established schizophrenic and depressive patients. These studies suggest that high levels of overprotection and criticism contribute to symptomatic relapse independent of other factors, such as medication or degree of initial behavioural disturbance. Thus, the social interaction problems could be seen as causal. Also, a number of studies by Zigler and Phillips (1961; 1973) and later by Strauss and Carpenter (1972; 1974; 1977a) have examined the significance of early social adjustment for subsequent prognosis and outcome, in mainly schizophrenic patients. These studies are well summarized by Kokes *et al.* (1977) and Strauss *et al.* (1977b). They suggest that premorbid social functioning is a good indicator of subsequent outcome. The lower a person's social "achievements" prior to an illness episode, the worse the likely outcome after the primary symptoms of the illness have disappeared. (These studies also demonstrate that each outcome "system", e.g. work hospital admissions, social relationships, are linked as well as being independent and this linkage suggests a common core of variance which may well be social in origin, see Phillips, 1968; Shepherd, 1980). Because the measures of social competence relate to a period *before* the onset of psychiatric symptoms, these studies can be taken as further evidence for social difficulties causing mental disorder. However, the issue is not entirely clear-cut as there is still the possibility of inaccurate reporting of early social events and the inaccurate dating of the onset of symptoms (Yarrow *et al.*, 1970). Thus, despite a wealth of evidence clearly demonstrating a close *association* between mental disorders and deficits in various aspects of social competence, we are still not in a position to state with any confidence that a lack of social competence *causes* mental disorder. The two constructs are actually so overlapping that it is difficult to see how such an assertion could ever be made. "Third variable" explanations also arise which would enable us to explain the association without there being any necessary causal connection at all. For example, social class has been mentioned, and there are good grounds for supposing that social class contributes causally to both social role difficulties and mental disorders (Dohrenwend and Dohrenwend, 1974). Similarly, underlying physiological or physiochemical processes could explain both the social difficulties and the psychiatric symptoms in schizophrenia (Neale and Oltmanns, 1980).

Unfortunately, the likelihood is that all three possible causal explanations are partly true. Social difficulties do lead to mental disorder, but the converse is also true. Both social difficulties and mental disorder may also be exacerbated by other variables, e.g. social class, physiological arousal. A simple linear model of causality cannot be used and we have to accept that complex interactions exist between a number of different variables. This may seem untidy but it is probably a more accurate view of the reality. We certainly cannot hold to the view that SST even if completely effective would necessarily prevent mental illness. The situation is rather more complicated than that. So, let us now move to consider the social skills model itself and the implications of what we have said so far for the way that SST should be conducted and evaluated.

III. WHAT IS THE SOCIAL SKILLS MODEL?

SST was developed in the United Kingdom mainly from the work of theoretical social psychologists, notably Michael Argyle and his colleagues in Oxford (see Argyle, 1969; Trower *et al.*, 1978). In the USA treatment for social difficulties has been much more closely associated with assertive training, based first on Wolpe's "reciprocal inhibition"

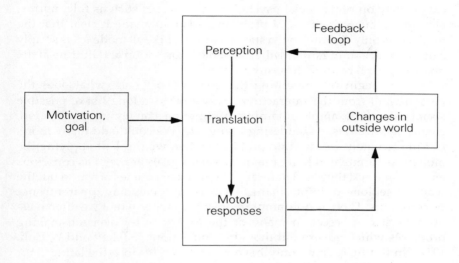

FIG. 1.1 *The Social Skill Model* from Michael Argyle: The Psychology of Inter-personal Behaviour (Pelican Books, 1967), p. 95. Copyright © Michael Argyle, 1967. Reprinted by permission of Penguin Books Ltd

model (Wolpe, 1958) and later on more pragmatic, empirical grounds (Eisler *et al.*, 1973; 1975). We shall concentrate on SST in this country and begin by describing Argyle's original model. This is shown in Fig. 1.1.

The essential feature of the model is an analogy between social interaction and the performance of a motor skill, for example, driving a car or playing a musical instrument. In both cases the behavioural "output" (what the person does) is continually being adjusted according to its effectiveness in achieving a particular goal, for example, success-fully negotiating various road hazards or producing a tuneful melody. This is achieved by a feedback loop which connects the perception of changes in the outside world with the internal mechanisms of defining goals and translating them into appropriate courses of action. Argyle suggested that, in this sense, social interaction shared some of the characteristics of a motor skill and therefore that it might be useful to use this as a framework for analysing social difficulties and perhaps also teaching individuals more effective "skills" to help them overcome their social problems. Interestingly, Argyle did not suggest that the skills model was the *only* way of thinking about social interaction and he drew extensively on other social psychological concepts such as role, norms, etc., in the analysis of social problems. Also, he made it clear that the model was only meant to be "a starting point". Like all models it is simply a useful heuristic organizing the available information and hinting at the possible causal relationships involved.

We can begin by examining the question of goals: what does the person want from the interaction? Argyle offers a long list of possible social goals, for example obtaining information, conveying information, changing attitudes, engendering liking, etc. We could add many more, but immediately we run into problems when we think of applying the model. As formulated here, the individual's goals are seen as conscious and rational and they lead naturally to particular courses of action but the reality is seldom so simple. In the first place, the goals may apparently not be conscious. There is now ample evidence to suggest that we often have little conscious access to many of the higher order decision-making processes which govern out thoughts and actions (Nisbett and Wilson, 1977). Individuals commonly have great difficulty in articulating their goals and when this occurs they may have to be inferred or supplied from outside. The validity of these supplied goals may then be questioned. Goals are often also seen as leading to actions in a straightforward way. Again, this may not be the case in practice. In reality there is seldom a rational, decision-making process whereby the advantages and disadvantages of different courses of action are carefully weighed up. In contrast, there is a confused conflict between different motivational tendencies, the outcome of which is determined by some strange and irrational processes. For example, a patient may tell you most sincerely that he/she wishes to make lasting relationships with the opposite sex. However they evidently find this such a difficult and painful task that they are reluctant to persevere with it. This kind of motivational conflict poses difficulties for a simple version of the model. The model also focuses on goals and motivation in the context of the moment-to-moment interactions, but in practice it may be necessary to consider how social goals operate over much longer time periods. Indeed, only if considered in this light, do maladaptive or distorted patterns of motivation become clear. In terms of goals and motivation then, the model is useful, but it has a number of limitations. These should be borne in mind when we attempt to use it to analyse social difficulties.

Next, we come to the translation/selection stage. Argyle is somewhat vague on how this occurs and suggests that it happens in "the more central regions of the brain". A plan must be selected which seems most likely to achieve the desired goal from a range of possible alternatives and this translation process may be completely unverbalized. There are a number of specific difficulties for psychiatric patients regarding this process. Firstly, the selection of a plan involves making certain predictions about the outcomes of one's own and others' behaviour and, as we have seen earlier, these predictions are often distorted by low self-esteem, "learned helplessness", etc. Secondly, the translation of this plan into action involves the connection of a particular stimulus situation with one of a number of possible responses. The relationship between the stimulus and the response is clearly complex and they may not be at all "compatible". Recent experimental work on the information-processing characteristics of schizophrenic patients suggests that they perform particularly badly on these kinds of complex, incompatible stimulus–response tasks (Hemsley, 1978). It may thus be particularly difficult for them to learn new and complex social strategies. It is certainly one's practical experience that for these kinds of patients any new tasks often have to be broken down into very small units before they can be assimilated. Thus, in terms of translation and selection, the model again focuses our attention on important processes but in practice it needs to be considerably elaborated to deal adequately with the complexities of psychiatric patients.

The pattern of motor responses—what the person actually does—is perhaps the clearest component of the model and considerable effort has been expended on analysing the performance of individual verbal and non-verbal elements, e.g. question-asking, eye-contact, gesture, etc. Interested readers are referred to a useful recent summary by Hargie *et al.* (1981). We shall not describe this work in any detail but a few brief examples may be helpful. In terms of verbal behaviour, question-asking is one obviously important element. Different kinds of questions have different functions and effects. "Open" questions (e.g. "What sorts of things do you like to do?") are useful to begin conversations and to keep them going. "Closed" questions (e.g. "Do you like football?") are good for establishing specific items of information but tend to interrupt the flow of the interaction. Thus, interviewers may be encouraged to progress from "open" to "closed" questions so as to gradually narrow down on specific factual events. On the other hand, those wishing to initiate and sustain relationships may be encouraged to use more open questions with "follow-ups" and perhaps "reflective listening" since these kinds of questions are more likely to maintain interactions.

Similarly, different patterns of eye-contact have been shown to be characteristic of different stages of a conversation. Generally, we look more when we are listening and less when we are speaking. We also tend to look up at the end of an utterance to signal to the other person when it is their turn to speak. During assertive encounters much more eye-contact is made than during other interactions (there is also increased use of gestures and increased voice volume). All these patterns of non-verbal behaviour are quite characteristic and yet they may not be present in those with social difficulties. They may make too much eye contact and be seen as aggressive as a result; or too little and be seen as aloof and unfriendly. They may not vary their pattern of eye contact according to the stage of conversation, or fail to give the appropriate uses to effectively synchronize the interaction. All these problems would tend to lead to a breakdown of social skills but how important are the behavioural elements in determining this?

This is a difficult question. In the first place, we don't have adequate "norms" for social behaviour and thus how do we decide when a particular pattern of eye contact, speech volume or question-asking is abnormal? How "abnormal" does it have to be? We all know people whose social behaviour seems rather "abnormal" and yet who still seem to manage to hold down jobs, make friends, sustain relationships, etc. Of course, there may be some extreme behavioural deficits which are crucial. For example, patients with social difficulties tend not to say very much (Gillingham et al., 1977; Trower, 1980). Obviously, if someone doesn't actually speak, or if you can't hear what they say, or if they never look at you, then they are likely to experience difficulties in their social interactions. However, in general conversations the importance of each behavioural element is probably not so great. There is a large "grey area" of acceptable social behaviour which is much broader than that implied by the social skills model and this conclusion is borne out by the experimental literature. Thus, Arkowitz et al. (1975) and Glasgow and Arkowitz (1975) both failed to find clear-cut behavioural differences in terms of the performance of individual elements between groups of subjects who had either high, or low, frequencies of "dates" with the opposite sex. In Argyle's own work the behavioural differences between skilled and unskilled patient groups were only apparent by comparing extreme groups (Bryant et al., 1976).

It is interesting to note in passing that despite the problems of discriminating between skilled and unskilled groups on the basis of individual elements of behaviour, observers still don't appear to have much difficulty in making a *global* judgement. This has led to one American researcher to comment wryly that, "everyone seems to know what good and poor social skills are, but no one can define them adequately" (Curran, 1979, p. 321). We may suppose that whatever leads observers to discriminate so clearly between skilled and unskilled individuals is not in the performance of individual elements, but concerns more subtle aspects of the interaction. For example, the timing and placement of responses (Fischetti *et al.*, 1977) or the sensitivity of each interactant to changes in the other's behaviour (Trower, 1980). Thus, in Argyle's work the two qualities which correlated most highly with ratings of social skill were complex dimensions of "rewardingness" and "control" (Bryant *et al.*, 1976). These involved encouraging, reinforcing, showing an interest in the other and controlling the interaction in a flexible, sensitive way.

To summarize, it seems that, although the performance of individual behavioural elements may be important at the extremes, and in specific social situations, perhaps their general importance has been over-emphasized. Certainly this does seem to be the case in many SST programmes. Social behaviour is just one aspect of social competence: it is a necessary, but not sufficient, condition.

We come now to consider the effects of social behaviour on the other interactant and their perception of events. As indicated earlier, Argyle saw his model as a starting point and in particular he acknowledged that "the full role of cognitive processes . . . has yet to be delineated" (1969, p. 431). We have already discussed how these cognitive processes may lead individuals to suffer from negative expectations regarding the outcome of their own social actions, or the reactions of others. Indeed, Glasgow and Arkowitz (1975) and Arkowitz *et al.* (1975) found that, although behaviour did not discriminate between their skilled and unskilled groups, self-perceptions did. It often happens that people who do not appear to be particularly unskilled, *feel* themselves to be. These kinds of negative, "stereotype" expectations lead to self-fulfilling prophecies of social failure, these are then reinforced by selective attention and recall of confirming instances and a systematic neglect of the positive evidence. Trower (1981) has discussed in detail how such self-fulfilling prophecies can thus maintain themselves and interfere with progress during treatment. This increasing recognition of the importance of cognitive processes is part of a general trend within behavioural treatments (Mahoney, 1977) and is particularly marked with regard to SST (Yardley, 1979; Wallace *et al.*, 1980). If it is accepted then not only does it have implications for methods of assessment (Shepherd, in press) but also for methods of treatment. These will be discussed in the next section when we consider the SST programmes in the light of our expanded version of the model.

IV. SOCIAL SKILLS TRAINING (SST)

SST is an active, performance-based treatment. The core methods are modelling, verbal instructions, practice (role-play) and homework assignments. It can be done individually, or in groups. The number and spacing of treatment sessions depends on the nature of the clients involved and the aims. The approach of the Oxford group is probably best described in Trower *et al.* (1978) and there are a number of other good "how-to-do-it" manuals available, e.g. Liberman *et al.* (1975); Lange and Jakubowski (1976); Spence (1980); Ellis and Whittington (1981). Elsewhere in this volume our contributors will be describing the problems and pitfalls of deploying SST with specific client groups in specific settings and so at this point we shall confine ourselves to making some general points about the approach.

SST begins with an assessment and this tends to take the form of a short role-play test. The therapist discusses with the patient what kinds of social situations they have difficulty with, e.g. meeting new people, talking to attractive women, standing up to a dominant employer, etc. This is then role-played with another member of the group or a "stooge". The patient may also be asked to complete various questionnaires covering their social anxieties and the range and frequency of their social contacts (see Trower *et al.*, 1978, pp. 138–143). There are a number of limitations to this approach to assessment. Firstly, it overemphasizes the importance of behaviour. As we have already seen, cognitions are particularly important and the cognitive aspects of social difficulties are not assessed at all adequately by standard questionnaires. There are numerous problems with using questionnaires and these have been discussed in detail elsewhere (Shepherd, in press). In this it is proposed that alternative methods should be considered which are based on interviews and "Personal" questionnaires (Shapiro, 1961). These are more individualized and avoid the problem of using vague, general questions. Similar attempts have been made to improve upon questionnaires for the assessment of role performance. For example, Marzillier *et al.*'s (1976) use of "time budgets" and Shepherd *et al.*'s (in preparation) structured "Social Network Interview". Thus, it is important to give due weight to the importance of cognitive factors and role performance and to use assessment methods which will measure these adequately. In the past there often seems to have been an assumption that behaviour is really the only important variable to assess thoroughly.

Secondly, there is a danger that inappropriate treatment targets may be generated. For example, one might concentrate on improving patterns of eye contact when, (*a*) the patient's eye contact is not particularly "abnormal" anyway (see p. 10) and (*b*) they don't look at people not because they don't know "how" to, but because they expect negative consequences to occur if they do, i.e. it is not their behaviour which gives rise to their difficulties but their cognitions. In this case it might seem more useful to attempt to change the latter rather than the former. Similarly, one might be led to focus on building up eye contact when the main problem is that the client has very few opportunities for social contact. They might thus benefit much more from a simple programme of graded task assignment rather than from trying to teach them a new behavioural skill. The general point is that one cannot expect to make a good assessment—and therefore subsequently generate an effective treatment programme—unless one attempts to assess as thoroughly and comprehensively as possible each aspect of social competence that might give rise to difficulty.

Thirdly, the conventional approach to social skills assessment is limited through the "specificity" of social behaviour (Mischel, 1968). Thus, even if behaviour is important in a particular case, there is no guarantee that a role-play test will elicit a valid sample of it. Indeed, there is considerable evidence now to suggest that role-play assessments do not provide a reliable guide to social behaviour in other settings (Bellack et al., 1978; 1979a; 1979b). Although these findings are still somewhat controversial (Wessberg et al., 1979) it is beyond doubt that, wherever possible, direct assessments of social behaviour in "free" social settings would be superior. These measures are difficult to obtain but not impossible (Shepherd, 1977; 1978). They provide assessments which are not only "non-reactive", i.e. they avoid the subject's tendency to simulate a good or a poor performance; they are also a direct measure of the "generalization" of treatment effects, i.e. whether they have transferred from the treatment setting to another setting.

Once the assessment has been completed, then the treatment targets may be set. The conventional approach tends to focus on behaviour, but if cognitive processes seem to be important then some kind of cognitive therapy might be initiated (Morley et al., Chapter 11). Similarly, if the deficit is a simple performance one, then graded task assignment might be used (Falloon et al., 1977). When training a new behavioural response (e.g. asking open-ended questions, making more eye-contact, or increasing voice volume) modelling and shaping, as well as verbal instructions may be used. Thus, if it is not sufficient simply to describe the new response it may be necessary also to demonstrate it. This can be done with prepared video tapes, or using a "live" model (the therapist or another member of the group). If modelling is to be used it is important to direct the observer's attention to that aspect of the model's behaviour which they are meant to be noticing. It is also usually necessary to grade, or "shape", the response gradually so as to maximize the likelihood of initial success. When the client understands what is being suggested, then he/she will be asked to practice in another short role-play. They will then be given immediate feedback, being careful to be positive and encouraging, before giving any criticism. They will then be given the opportunity to practice again. Further practices should be given as necessary and it is important to "overlearn" the new response beyond the first correct performance (Goldstein *et al.*, 1979) as this may help to improve maintenance over time. When the new responses have been successfully learned, it is then crucial to set some kind of "homework assignment" to ensure that there is generalization outside the immediate treatment setting. This is usually a simple, high frequency task. For example, to ask at least one open-ended question in two conversations over the next week, to look at someone and hold at least 5 seconds of eye contact on at least 3 occasions next week, etc. Usually the client is asked to remember or write down how their task went. They may also be asked to give themselves a rating. The results are then discussed at the beginning of the next session. Sometimes individuals may be paired off with one another (the "buddy system") to give mutual encouragement and support for homework assignments.

In general, as we shall see when we come to consider the outcome evidence, SST has not been very successful in generalizing improvements outside the treatment setting and in maintaining them over time. There have been a number of attempts to analyse these problems and a range of solutions have been proposed (Goldstein and Kanfer, 1979; Hersen, 1979; Shepherd, 1980; Wallace *et al.*, 1980). These tend to centre around: (*a*) changing the training conditions so as to make them more realistic (e.g. more use of *in vivo* treatment; "stooges"; etc.), (*b*) changing training techniques so as to build up a stronger initial S-R bond (e.g. by slowing the rate of presentation of information; by "overlearning" followed by "chaining") and (*c*) changing the reinforcement conditions so as to make them gradually approximate real-life (e.g. by "fading" and "thinning" reinforcement). Suggestions have also been made to reduce the "stimulus control" aspects of treatment settings by varying the time, date and personnel involved in treatment (Marholin and Touchette, 1979) and to use cognitive changes as mediators to bring the "transfer gap" (Ellis and Whittington, 1981). All these kinds of solutions have some value; however, the theoretical model proposed in this chapter would dictate a rather different approach to this problem.

If we view social competence as a construct, in the sense defined earlier, then instead of viewing generalization as a problem of transferring responses along a stimulus dimension from "treatment" to "real-life" we would accept that the responses shown in one setting may be quite independent of the responses shown in another. We would then not be surprised that, "there is no evidence that increasing eye contact,

voice volume, or the like, actually affects marital interaction, dating
frequency, level of depression or any other clinically meaningful set of
behaviours" (Bellack, 1979, p. 97). If they are not correlated then there is
little reason to suppose that they would. The implication is that we
should see transfer from behavioural performance to role performance
not as a problem of generalization but as two quite *separate* treatment
problems each requiring a *different* treatment approach (i.e. skills
training and graded task assignment). In a similar way, the problem of
response generalization may not be how to get behavioural responses to
translate into cognitive changes, but how to devise treatment interventions which will affect behaviour on the one hand and cognitions on the
other.

This view of SST as proceeding on the basis of constructing individually centred treatment "packages", with separate therapeutic ingredients
for each identified problem, has been foreshadowed by Marzillier and
Winter (1978). Perhaps it owes most to the individually-centred clinical
approach developed by Shapiro (1970). The theoretical model for social
functioning proposed in this chapter offers a rationale and a conceptual
framework for organizing such an approach. Let us now turn to the
practice of SST with different client groups in different settings and
introduce the first section with a review of the outcome evidence
regarding its effectiveness with adults. The second section will be
preceded by a brief review of the outcome evidence regarding SST with
children and adolescents.

V. REFERENCES

Anastasi, A. (1968). "Psychological Testing". Macmillan, London.
Argyle, M. (1969). "Social Interaction", Methuen, London.
Arkowitz, H., Lichtenstein, E., McGovern, K. and Hines, P. (1975). The
    behavioural assessment of social competence in males. *Behav. Ther.* **6**, 3–13.
Bellack, A. S. (1979). Behavioural assessment of social skills. *In* "Research and
    Practice in Social Skills Training" (A. S. Bellack and M. Hersen, *Eds*). Plenum
    Press, New York.
Bellack, A. S., Hersen, M. and Turner, S. M. (1978). Role-play tests for assessing
    social skills: Are they valid? *Behav. Ther.* **9**, 448–461.
Bellack, A. S., Hersen, M. and Turner, S. M. (1979a). Relationship of role playing
    and knowledge of appropriate behaviour in assertion in the natural environ-
    ment. *J. Consult. Clin. Psychol.* **47**, 670–678.
Bellack, A. S., Hersen, M. and Lamparski, D. (1979b). Role play tests for assessing
    social skills: Are they valid? Are they useful? *J. Consult. Clin. Psychol.* **47**,
    335–342.
Bloom, B. L. (1968). An ecological analysis of psychiatric hospitalisation. *Multivar.
    Behav. Res.* **3**, 423–463.

Brown, G. W. and Harris, T. (1978). "Social Origins of Depression". Tavistock Publications, London.

Brown, G. W., Birley, J. L. T. and Wing, J. K. (1972). Influence of family life on the course of schizophrenic disorders: A replication. *Br. J. Psychiatry* **121**, 241–258.

Brown, G. W., Monck, E. M., Carstairs, G. and Wing, J. K. (1962). Influence of family life on the course of schizophrenic illness. *Br. J. Prev. Soc. Med.* **16**, 55–68.

Bryant, B., Trower, P., Yardley, K., Urbieta, H. and Letemendia, F. T. J. (1976). A survey of social inadequacy among psychiatric outpatients. *Psychol. Med.* **6**, 101–112.

Campbell, D. T. and Fiske, D. W. (1959). Convergent and discriminant validation by the multitrait–multimethod matrix. *Psychol. Bull.* **56**, 81–105.

Cronbach, L. J. and Meehl, P. E. (1955). Construct validity in psychological tests. *Psychol. Bull.* **52**, 281–302.

Curran, J. (1979). Social skills: Methodological issues and future directions. *In* "Research and Practice in Social Skills Training" (A. S. Bellack and M. Hersen, *Eds*). Plenum Press, New York.

Dohrenwend, B. P. and Dohrenwend, B. S. (1974). Social and Cultural Influences on Psychopathology. *Ann. Rev. Psy.* **25**, 417–452.

Eisler, R. M., Hersen, M. and Miller, P. M. (1973). Effects of modelling on components of assertive behaviour. *J. Behav. Ther. Exp. Psychiatry* **4**, 1–6.

Eisler, R. M., Hersen, M., Miller, P. M. and Blanchard, E. R. (1975). Situational determinants of assertive behaviour. *J. Consult. Clin. Psychol.* **43**, 330–340.

Ellis, R. and Whittington, D. (1981). "A Guide to Social Skills Training". Croom Helm, London.

Falloon, I. R. H., Lindley, P., McDonald, R. and Marics, I. M. (1977). Social skills training of out-patient groups: A controlled study of rehearsal and home-work. *Br. J. Psychiatry* **131**, 599–609.

Fischetti, M., Curran, J. P. and Weisberg, H. W. (1977). Sense of timing: A skill deficit in heterosexual socially anxious males. *Behav. Modif.* **1**, 179–194.

Gillingham, P. R., Griffiths, R. D. P. and Care, D. (1977). Direct assessment of social behaviour from videotape recordings. *Br. J. Soc. Clin. Psychol.* **16**, 181–187.

Glasgow, R. E. and Arkowitz, H. (1975). The behavioural assessment of male and female social competence in dyadic heterosexual interactions. *Behav. Ther.* **6**, 488–498.

Goldberg, D. and Huxley, P. (1980). "Mental Illness in the Community". Tavistock Publications, London.

Goldstein, A. P. and Kanfer, F. H. (1979). "Maximising Treatment Gains". Academic Press, New York.

Goldstein, A. P., Lopez, M. and Greenleaf, D. O. (1979). Introduction. *In* "Maximising Treatment Gains" (A. P. Goldstein and F. H. Kanfer, *Eds*). Academic Press, New York.

Hargie, D., Saunders, C. and Dickson, D. (1981). "Social Skills in Interpersonal Communication". Croom Helm, London.

Hempel, D. G. (1965). "Aspects of Scientific Explanation". Free Press, New York.

Hemsley, D. R. (1978). Limitations of operant procedures in the modification of schizophrenic functioning: The possible relevance of studies of cognitive disturbance. *Behav. Anal. Modif.* **2**, 165–173.

Henderson, S. (1977). The social network support and neurosis: The function of attachment in adult life. *Br. J. Psychiatry* **131**, 185–191.

Henderson, S., Duncan-Jones, P., McAuley, H. and Ritchie, K. (1978a). The patient's primary group. *Br. J. Psychiatry* **132**, 74–86.

Henderson, S., Byrne, D. G., Duncan-Jones, P., Adcock, S., Scott, R. and Steele, G. P. (1978b). Social bands in the epidemiology of neurosis: A preliminary communication. *Br. J. Psychiatry* **132**, 463–466.

Hersen, M. (1979). Modification of skill deficits in psychiatric patients. *In* "Research and Practice in Social Skills Training" (A. S. Bellack and M. Hersen, *Eds*). Plenum Press, New York.

Hodgson, R. and Rachman, S. J. (1974). II. Desynchrony in measures of fear. *Behav. Res. Ther.* **12**, 319–326.

Kazdin, A. E. (1979). Sociopsychological factors in psychopathology. *In* "Research and Practice in Social Skills Training" (A. S. Bellack and M. Hersen, *Eds*). Plenum Press, New York.

Kokes, R. F., Strauss, J. S. and Klorman, R. (1977). Premorbid adjustment in schizophrenia: Part II. Measuring premorbid adjustment: The instruments and their development. *Schizophr. Bull.* **3**, 186–213.

Lange A. and Jakubowski, P. (1976). "Responsive Assertive Behaviour". Research Press, Illinois.

Liberman, R. P., King, L. W., Derisi, W. J. and McCann, (1975). "Personal Effectiveness". Research Press, Champaign, Illinois.

Libet, J. M. and Lewisohn, P. M. (1973). Concept of social skills with special reference to the behaviour of depressed persons. *J. Consult. Clin. Psychol.* **40**, 304–312.

Mahoney, M. J. (1977). Reflections in the cognitive learning reand in psychotherapy. *Am. Psychol.* **32**, 5–13.

Marholin, D. and Touchette, P. E. (1979). The role of stimulus control and response consequences. *In* "Maximising Treatment Gains" (A. P. Goldstein and F. H. Kanfer, *Eds*). Academic Press, New York.

Marzillier, J. S. and Winter, K. (1978). Success and failure in social skills training: Individual differences. *Behav. Res. Ther.* **16**, 67–84.

Marzillier, J. S., Lambert, J. C. and Kellett, J. (1976). A controlled evaluation of systematic desensitisation and social skills training for chronically inadequate psychiatric patients. *Behav. Res. Ther.* **14**, 225–239.

Mischel, W. (1968). "Personality and Assessment". Wiley, New York.

Neale, J. M. and Oltmanns, T. F. (1980). "Schizophrenia". Wiley, New York.

Nichols, K. A. (1974). Severe social anxiety. *Br. J. Med. Psychol.* **47**, 301–306.

Nisbett, R. E. and Wilson, T. D. (1977). Telling more than we can know: Verbal reports on mental processes. *Psych. Rev.* **84**, 231–259.

Phillips, L. (1968). "Human Adaptations and its Failures". Academic Press, New York.

Rachman, S. J. and Hodgson, R. (1974). I. Synchrony and desynchrony in fear and avoidance. *Behav. Res. Ther.* **12**, 311–318.

Rime, B., Bouvy, H., Leborgne, B. and Rouillon, F. (1978). Psychopathy and non-verbal behaviour in an interpersonal situation. *J. Abnorm. Psychol.* **87**, 636–643.

Seligman, M. B. (1975). "Helplessness: On Depression, Development, and Death". Freeman, San Francisco.

Shapiro, M. B. (1961). The single case in fundamental clinical psychological research. *Br. J. Med. Psychol.* **34**, 285–298.

Shapiro, M. B. (1970). Intensive assessment of the single case. *In* "The Psychological Assessment of Mental and Physical Handicaps" (P. Mittler, *Ed.*). Methuen, London.

Shepherd, G. W. (1977). Social skills training: The generalisation problem. *Behav. Ther.* **8**, 1008–1009.

Shepherd, G. W. (1978). Social skills training: The generalization problem—some further data. *Behav. Res. Ther.* **16**, 287–288.

Shepherd, G. W. (1980). The treatment of social difficulties in special environments. *In* "Psychological Problems: The Social Context" (P. Feldman and J. Orford, *Eds*). Wiley, Chichester.

Shepherd, G. (1982) Assessment of cognitions in social skills training. *In* "Cognitive Approaches in Social Skills Training" (P. Trower, *Ed.*). Pergamon Press, Oxford. (In press)

Shepherd, G., McGill, P. and Nairne, K. (1982). The Assessment of Social Functioning. II: Social Networks. (In preparation)

Spence, S. H. (1980). "Social Skills Training with Children and Adolescents: A Counsellor's Manual". NFER Publishers, Windsor.

Strauss, J. and Carpenter, W. (1972). The prediction of outcome in schizophrenia: I. Characteristics of outcome. *Arch. Gen. Psychiatry* **27**, 739–746.

Strauss, J. and Carpenter, W. (1974). The prediction of outcome in schizophrenia: II. Relationships between predictor and outcome variables. *Arch. Gen. Psychiatry* **31**, 37–42.

Strauss, J. S. and Carpenter, W. T. (1977a). Prediction of outcome in schizophrenia: III. Five year outcome and its predictors. *Arch. Gen. Psychiatry* **34**, 159–163.

Strauss, J. S., Klorman, R. and Kokes, R. F. (1977b). Premorbid adjustment in schizophrenia: Part V: The implications of finding for understanding, research and application. *Schizophr. Bull.* **3**, 240–244.

Trower, P. (1980). Situational analysis of the components and processes of the behaviour of socially skilled and unskilled patients. *J. Consult. Clin. Psychol.* **48**, 327–339.

Trower, D. (1981). Social skill disorder: Mechanisms of failure. *In* "Personal Relationships in Disorder" (R. Gilmour and S. Duck, *Eds*). Academic Press, London.

Trower, P., Bryant, B. and Argyle, M. (1978). "Social Skills and Mental Health". Methuen, London.

Vaughn, C. E. and Leff, J. P. (1976). The influence of family and social factors on the course of psychiatric illness. *Br. J. Psychiatry* **129**, 125–138.

Wallace, C. J., Nelson, C. J., Liberman, R. P., Aitchison, R. A., Lulloff, D., Elder, J. P. and Ferris, C. (1980). A review and critique of social skills training with schizophrenic patients. *Schizophr. Bull.* **8**, 42–63.

Wessberg, H. W., Mariotto, M. J., Conger, A. J., Farrell, A. D. and Conger, J. C. (1979). Econological validity of role plays for assessing heterosexual anxiety and skill of male college students. *J. Consult. Clin. Psychol.* **47**, 525–535.

Wing, J. K. (1978). "Schizophrenia: Towards a New Synthesis". Academic Press, London.

Wolpe, J. (1958). "Psychotherapy by Reciprocal Inhibition". Stanford Press, California.

Yardley, K. (1979). Social skills training: A critique. *Br. J. Med. Psychol.* **52**, 55–62.
Yarrow, M. R., Campbell, J. D., Burton, R. V. (1970). Recollections of childhood: A study of the retrospective method. *Monogr. Soc. Res. Child. Dev.* **35**, 5 (serial No. 138).
Zigler, E. and Levine, J. (1973). Premorbid adjustment and paranoid–non-paranoid status in schizophrenia: A further investigation. *Abnorm. Psychol.* **82**, 189–199.
Zigler, E. and Phillips, L. (1961). Social competence and outcome in psychiatric disorder. *J. Abnorm. Soc. Psychol.* **63**, 264–271.

SECTION I

Social skills training with adults

PREFACE BY GEOFF SHEPHERD

I. THE OUTCOME EVIDENCE

There have been a number of previous reviews of the evidence regarding the effectiveness of social skills training (SST) with adults. These include Marzillier and Winter (1978), Hersen (1979), Shepherd (1980) and Wallace *et al.* (1980). The present review is based on a detailed consideration of 52 studies on social skills or assertive training conducted with adult psychiatric patients between 1970 and 1980 (Shepherd, 1981, unpublished). This is probably the most comprehensive sample of studies assembled so far. The results may be summarized under a number of headings:

21

A. Subjects

In all, nearly 1200 subjects were involved, however the description of the samples tended to be rather inadequate. In only one case (Liberman *et al.*, 1978) was a standardized diagnostic procedure (the Present State Examination) used. Diagnostic labels were commonly given, but the grounds on which these diagnoses were made were seldom specified. In most cases subjects were simply nominated by staff as being likely to benefit from treatment. In a few instances independent judges were employed to decide on admission to the study (e.g. Eisler *et al.*, 1978) and a range of questionnaires were also used (e.g. the Wolpe-Lazarus Assertiveness Scale, Hersen *et al.*, 1979). There was usually very little information available concerning the subjects' previous social competence, particularly in terms of their social role performance (employment history, early social relationships, etc.). This lack of information concerning subject characteristics is important as it limits the external validity of whatever conclusions may be drawn because it makes inductive inferences difficult. One simply doesn't know the parameters of the particular population which have been successfully treated. Until researchers give much more detailed descriptions of their samples, specific or general conclusions concerning effectiveness will therefore remain unclear.

B. Experimental designs and treatment conditions

About two-thirds of the studies used group designs and about one-third were single cases. In the group designs the most common control groups were "no treatment", various kinds of "placebos" and alternative behavioural treatments. The placebo treatments tended to be rather weak and often lacked credibility (e.g. simple discussion groups). The alternative behavioural treatments were usually simplified versions of SST itself (e.g. modelling alone, verbal instructions alone). In only 4 studies was SST compared with another proven behavioural treatment (systematic desensitization). These were Weinman *et al.* (1972), Marzillier *et al.* (1976); Hall and Goldberg (1977) and Trower *et al.* (1978). There were only 4 studies where SST was compared with an active, non-behavioural treatment (Gutride *et al.*, 1973; Argyle *et al.*, 1974; Rice and Chaplin, 1979 and Monti *et al.*, 1980). Thus, the nature of the experimental controls that have been used restrict our conclusions to the effectiveness of SST compared with no treatment, or perhaps a weak placebo. Its effectiveness in comparison with other active treatments—behavioural or otherwise—has not really been explored.

Regarding the single case studies, the most common design was to use a multiple-baseline. This involves simultaneous monitoring of a number of variables (e.g. eye contact, speech volume, rate of gestures) and then intervening to attempt to influence one of them, e.g. eye contact, while continuing to monitor the remainder. If the intervention specifically affects the targeted variable, one can then argue that a specific effect has been demonstrated. There are various problems with these kinds of experiments (Kazdin and Kopel, 1975). In particular their interpretation rests on two assumptions: (a) that specific interventions will have specific effects, and (b) that non-specific interventions will have non-specific effects. Both of these assumptions may not be justified. Thus, there are quite clear examples where specific interventions have apparently produced quite generalized effects (e.g. Marzillier and Winter, 1978) and whether non-specific interventions can have specific effects awaits further research with better designed placebo interventions.

In addition to the problems of interpretation inherent in the majority of the single case studies, it is also evident that the length of the baseline collected tends to be very short. The establishment of a stable baseline is a necessary prerequisite for judging whether or not an intervention has had any effect. This is especially true where estimation of the size of the effect is based on visual inspection of the data as is nearly always the case. Little is known about the natural variability of social functioning and without adequate baselines, or statistical analysis, it thus becomes very difficult to assess accurately what impact the SST might have had.

C. The nature of treatment

The studies do seem agreed on the basic ingredients of the SST approach. These are the techniques already described in the Introduction, i.e. modelling ("live" or taped), practice (role-play) and homework assignments. Unfortunately, there is much less consensus regarding the number and spacing of treatment sessions. The number of sessions varies from 1–60 and spacing varies from daily to fortnightly. The confounding of amount and intensity of treatment means that the overall length of time for each study varies from a few weeks to a number of months. It is then difficult to know if differences between studies are due to differences between treatments, differences between subjects, or differences between lengths of treatment. For example, Marzillier et al. (1976) used one session per week for 15 weeks and obtained rather poor results. Monti et al. (1980) used 4 sessions per week for 5 weeks and obtained rather good results. There were many differences between these studies, but which were the crucial ones? With such a lack of consensus regarding basic treatment it is difficult to tell.

D. Measures

The commonest outcome measure employed was some kind of behavioural role-play test, this appeared in nearly 90% of the studies. There was also a widespread use of questionnaires and other self-report instruments. This excessive reliance on behavioural tests is unfortunate in the light of the comments made earlier concerning the possible limited overall importance of behaviour and the doubtful relationship between behavioural and other aspects of social competence. Behavioural role plays may also give an unreliable guide to behaviour in other, more natural, social situations (see Chapter 1 and p. 3). Similarly, question-naires provide a very weak method for assessing the cognitive compo-nents of social competence and for obtaining information about social role functioning (see, Introduction p. 1). In about two thirds of the studies there was some attempt to measure "generalization" of treatment improvements. However, this often relied on examining the amount of transfer between trained and untrained scenes all of which were selected from the treatment itself and the pre-treatment assessment. This can only give very weak evidence of the extent to which improvements have generalized to other non-treatment settings. In only about a quarter of the studies was there a genuine attempt to assess outcome by observing social behaviour in some free social situation independent of treatment. The outcome measures have thus been dominated by a narrow behavioural definition of social competence and we have yet to evaluate the effectiveness of SST using a broader concept and more suitable measures.

E. Outcome

We can now turn to the specific question of outcome. From what has already been said it is clear that the conclusions we can draw are limited. As far as the group-based studies are concerned nearly all found SST to be more effective than no treatment. (There were two exceptions, Marzillier *et al.* (1976) and Lauterbach *et al.* (1979)). Comparing SST with placebo, again the active treatment proved generally superior, although one must bear in mind the weakness of many of the placebo controls. Comparing SST with simplified behavioural treatments, it is clear that the full package tends to be the most effective. There was also an additive treatment effect, i.e. the more components the treatment package contained, the more effective it was likely to be. In terms of the effectiveness of single techniques, modelling emerged as probably the most powerful single component, particularly for psychotics (Eisler et al., 1978). Tangible rewards (tokens, etc.) also seemed particularly useful for promoting generalization with this group (Lindsay, 1980). When SST was compared with systematic desensitization the differences in outcome tended to be quite small. As one might expect subjects with prominent anxiety symptoms tended to do best with desensitization (Hall and Goldberg, 1977) whereas the presence of behavioural deficits tended to favour SST (Trower et al., 1978). Apart from these findings, there was very little evidence regarding the influence of individual differences on the outcome of SST. The evidence comparing SST with active non-behavioural treatments, e.g. psychotherapy, tended to produce rather mixed results. In two of the studies there was very little difference (Gutride et al., 1973; Argyle et al., 1974) and in the other two SST appeared to be superior (Rice and Chaplin, 1979; Monti et al., 1980). These results are reminiscent of other outcome reviews with psychological treatments where the differences between treatments have also tended to be rather small (Luborsky et al., 1975; Smith and Glass, 1977).

In the single case studies, the targeted variables did generally show change when the treatment was introduced. However, as indicated earlier, problems in interpretation and the brevity of baseline data made some of these effects rather unconvincing.

F. Generalization

The methods for assessing generalization were weak, but where it was sought, positive evidence was usually found. We can therefore agree with previous reviewers who have suggested that SST "can produce positive changes in social behaviour in the short term" (Marzillier, 1978, p. 124). But, "when the effects were evaluated in situations dissimilar in format from the training sessions, the results were not so promising" (Wallace et al., 1980, p. 57). Unless strong evidence for the generalized effects of SST is forthcoming its clinical usefulness must be limited. It has been argued earlier that such evidence is not likely to be forthcoming until we accept cognitive and social role difficulties as separate problems in their own right, not as problems of generalization from behaviour.

G. Follow-up

Follow-up data were provided in roughly half the studies. The length of the follow-up period varies from 2 weeks to 2 years. Again there was a heavy reliance on behavioural and questionnaire assessment and a considerable amount of missing data. In general the follow-up results tended to indicate that the obtained improvements were maintained. There was also a strong tendency for any differences between treatments to further attenuate.

This seems encouraging, but there is a sense in which follow-up studies may not actually be very relevant. The idea of a follow-up is based on a medical (i.e. intra-psychic) model of disorder. If we believe in the importance of environmental factors in producing and maintaining social difficulties, then we would not actually expect improvements to be maintained unless there were also environmental changes at the same time. (Otherwise we have simply returned the client back to "baseline" conditions). The fact that improvements are sometimes maintained suggests that there may be some kind of cognitive mediation of change. It also suggests that although changes in social role opportunities, although not directly planned, have nevertheless occurred. Maintenance of treatment effects therefore seems dependent upon producing cognitive and role changes and this is probably a more useful way to view it. It is not a simple problem of extending treatment conditions over time. (For a fuller discussion of the logic of follow-up studies in this area, see Shepherd, 1980).

H. Conclusions

The state of the outcome evidence is equivocal to say the least. There are considerable methodological problems which generally make interpretation difficult. There are uncertainties regarding such basic questions as: Who has SST been successfully applied to? How much treatment should be given? How often and for how long? The measures used to evaluate outcome, both in the short-term and regarding immediate treatment effects and in the longer-term regarding generalization and maintenance have been very limited. Nevertheless, SST does seem capable of producing changes which would otherwise not occur.

Of course, there are many unanswered questions. How does SST compare with active non-behavioural treatments, e.g. sensitivity groups or psychodrama? Could stronger evidence for the effectiveness of alternative treatments be obtained if the outcome measures were not so heavily weighted towards detecting changes in behaviour? How would SST compare with a good placebo? What individual differences are important with regard to the outcome of SST? What would happen if a greater attempt was made to match individual differences with treatment strategies? What is the natural variability of social functioning? What kinds of changes might you observe if you took very long baseline periods before intervening? Is it possible to improve the generalization and maintenance of treatment effects by focusing directly on the underlying cognitive mediators of change, or by attempting to change role functioning directly? These issues must all await further research. For the moment, we should probably be interested but sceptical of how significant the demonstrable effectiveness of SST is with regard to "curing or alleviating mental disorder". Let us now turn to current practice and examine some of the practical problems with the SST approach.

II. OVERVIEW OF SECTION I

We asked our contributors to first describe their own particular setting and clients. We also asked them to describe a typical session and how they integrated SST into the general framework of their institutions. We asked them to comment on the questions of individual differences in relation to outcome and what makes a good social skills therapist, as these seem to be neglected topics in the literature. Finally, we asked them to discuss the practical problems and pitfalls of deploying SST in the hope that their experience might forewarn and forearm others.

John Marzillier and Keith Winter begin with a discussion of SST in the context of a general psychiatric out-patient setting. They identify the place of a psychologist working within such a setting and go on to discuss the process of selection and assessment of clients. Throughout their chapter they emphasize the importance of a broad concept of social functioning and in particular they focus on the role of anxiety and other cognitive factors. They describe assessment as an ongoing process of gathering information about a number of different aspects of social functioning from a number of different sources. They also include a valuable discussion of the advantages and disadvantages of individual versus group treatments and a detailed examination of therapeutic "failures".

Robert Durham continues the psychiatric theme by looking at another major group, the long-stay hospital population. He discusses the special difficulties of working with this client group, both in terms of the patients' problems and the staffs'. His particular contribution is a thorough examination of how the traditional SST techniques need to be modified in the light of the specific cognitive and learning difficulties of chronic patients. He also emphasizes the problems for staff and suggests that they should be seen as learning a general therapeutic skill. He stresses that SST is not a panacea and must be integrated within the general therapeutic regime of the setting. This point is also taken up by *Alison Cooper and her colleagues* when considering the last major group of psychiatric clients: long-term patients in the community. They describe the history of trying to set up a SST group and the interplay between the group itself and the organizational characteristics of the setting. They note the need to integrate SST with other therapeutic programmes and like previous contributors they comment on what makes a good social skills therapist. Their work in a community setting probably makes them particularly sensitive to the problems of generalizing and maintaining change and the need to involve both staff outside the group and families.

We then move away from psychiatric patients to consider groups of men and women who have had difficulties with the law. *James McGuire and Phillip Priestley* describe a variant of SST known as "Life Skills Training". This has a broader focus than simply interpersonal difficulties and covers some of the more general role problems (e.g. independent living, employment, etc.) that we have already been discussing. They review the relevant literature and place their attempts to train prison officers to run pre-release programmes within the context of other attempts to help ex-offenders adapt more successfully on leaving prison. McGuire and Priestley examine their outcome data carefully and try to draw out the implications for future training programmes. They discuss in detail the problems for staff in attempting to run therapeutic programmes in what are essentially custodial contexts. This point is also very important for *Phillipa Lowe and Caroline Stewart* who, in the last chapter of this section, are concerned with the problems of women in prison. They describe the history of their particular institution and the advantages and disadvantages of working within a prison setting. In common with previous authors they emphasize the need to combine SST with other psychological treatments so as to adequately meet the variety of individual's needs. They also discuss the issues of selection and the difficulties of running groups in "closed" settings. They also make some important points concerning therapist characteristics and the necessity for therapists to have some experience of the client's sub-cultural norms and values. The chapters do have some common themes, but they may be read separately. An attempt to integrate some of the issues is made in Section IV.

III. REFERENCES

Argyle, M., Bryant, B. and Trower, P. (1974). Social skills training and psychotherapy: A comparative study. *Psychol. Med.* **4**, 435–443.
Eisler, R. M., Blanchard, E. B., Fitts, H. and Williams, J. G. (1978). Social skills

training with and without modelling for schizophrenic and non-psychotic hospitalised psychiatric patients. *Behav. Modif.* **2**, 147–171.

Gutride, M. E., Goldstein, A. P. and Hunter, G. F. (1973). The use of modelling and role playing to increase social interaction among asocial psychiatric patients. *J. Consult. Clin. Psychol.* **40**, 408–415.

Hall, R. and Goldberg, D. (1977). The role of social anxiety in social interaction difficulties. *Br. J. Psychiat.* **131**, 610–615.

Hersen, M. (1979). Modification of skill deficits in psychiatric patients. *In* "Research and Practice in Social Skills Training" (A. S. Bellack and M. Hersen, *Eds*). Plenum Press, New York.

Hersen, M., Bellack, A. S., Turner, S. M., Williams, M. T., Harper, K. and Watts, J. G. (1979). Psychometric properties of the Wolpe-Lazarus assertiveness scale. *Behav. Res. Ther.* **17**, 63–69.

Kazdin, A. E. and Kopel, S. A. (1975). On resolving ambiguities of the multiple baseline design: Problems and recommendations. *Behav. Res. Ther.* **6**, 601–608.

Lauterbach, W., Pelzer, U. and Aniszus, D. (1979). Is social skills training effective in European schizophrenics? *Behav. Anal. Modif.* **3**, 21–31.

Liberban, R. P., Lillie, F., Falloon, I. R. H., Vaughn, C. E., Harpin, E., Leff, J., Hutchinson, W., Ryan, P. and Stoute, M. (1978). "Social Skills Training for Schizophrenic Patients and Their Families". Unpublished Manuscript, Clinical Research Center, Box A, Camarillo, California.

Lindsay, W. R. (1980). The training and generalisation of conversation behaviours in psychiatric in-patients: A controlled study employing multiple measures across settings. *Br. J. Soc. Clin. Psychol.* **19**, 85–98.

Luborsky, Y. L., Singer, B. and Luborsky, L. (1975). Comparative studies of psychotherapies. *Arch. Gen. Psychiatry* **32**, 995–1008.

Marzillier, J. (1978). Outcome studies of skill training: A review. *In* "Social Skills and Mental Health" (Trower *et al.*, *Eds*). Methuen, London.

Marzillier, J. S., Lambert, J. C. and Kellet, J. (1976). A controlled evaluation of systematic desensitisation and social skills training for chronically inadequate psychiatric patients. *Behav. Res. Ther.* **14**, 225–239.

Marzillier, J. S. and Winter, K. (1978). Success and failure in social skills training: Individual differences. *Behav. Res. Ther.* **16**, 67–84.

Monti, P. M., Curran, J. P., Corriveau, D. P., Delancey, A. L. and Hagerman, S. M. (1980). Effects of social skills training groups and sensitivity training groups with psychiatric patients. *J. Consult. Clin. Psychol.* **48**, 241–248.

Rice, M. E. and Chaplin, T. C. (1979). Social skills training for hospitalized male arsonists. *J. Behav. Ther. Exp. Psychiatry* **10**, 105–108.

Shepherd, G. (1980). The treatment of social difficulties in special environments. *In* "Psychological Problems: The Social Context" (P. Feldman and J. Orford, *Eds*). Wiley, Chichester.

Shepherd, G. (1981). "A Review of Social Skills Training With Psychiatric Patients, 1970–1980". Department of Psychology, Institute of Psychiatry, University of London. (Unpublished)

Smith, M. L. and Glass, G. V. (1977). Meta-analysis of psychotherapy outcome studies. *Am. Psychol.* **32**, 752–760.

Trower, P., Yardley, K., Bryant, B. and Shaw, P. (1978). The treatment of social failure: A comparison of anxiety reduction and skills acquisition procedures on two social problems. *Behav. Mod.* **2**, 41–60.

Wallace, C. J., Nelson, C. J., Liberman, R. P., Aitchison, R. A., Lukoff, D., Elder, J. P. and Ferris, C. (1980). A review and critique of social skills training with schizophrenic patients. *Schizophr. Bull.* **6**, 42–63.

Weinman, B., Gelbart, P., Wallace, M. and Post, M. (1972). Inducing assertive behaviour in chronic schizophrenics: A comparison of socioenvironmental desensitisation and relaxation therapies. *J. Consult. Clin. Psychol.* **39**, 246–252.

2

Psychiatric outpatients

KEITH WINTER AND JOHN S. MARZILLIER

I. INTRODUCTION

It seems likely that social skills deficits are frequently a cause of social difficulties and may indeed be implicated in the development of a variety of psychiatric disorders. Upon encountering social difficulties or related psychological disorders, a psychiatrist or general practitioner may decide upon a referral for psychological treatment, at which point social skills training (SST) can be an option considered. Patients are then likely to be seen for assessment either as outpatients at a psychiatric hospital, or in a general hospital clinic, or at the general practitioner's surgery. The recent trend in clinical practice has been for psychologists to see outpatients in health centres in the patient's home town, obviating the need for travel to what are often out of the way and unpopular psychiatric hospitals. The only requirement is a reasonably comfortable, private room since most modern audio or videotape recording equipment is readily portable. Our aim is to describe SST methods which could be applied in this setting and, although the present chapter primarily concerns adult psychiatric outpatients, it is hoped that the methods and problems described will be of interest to other social, psychological and medical agencies involved in the counselling or treatment of adult interpersonal problems.

If one provides a broad definition of SST as the process of teaching people appropriate behaviour for prescribed social interactions, then, even limiting the discussion to adults, it becomes clear that this chapter could fill several volumes. For example, this definition would include the teaching of assertive and caring responses as advocated by Lazarus (1973), the coaching of heterosocial or dating skills (Curran, 1977), teaching patients to control abusive outbursts or rage reactions (Frederiksen et al., 1976), and training parents how to cope with childhood behaviour problems (Bernal, 1969). Although the discussion will touch on some of these issues, the main focus will be on the more typical problems of a person who finds conversation difficult, perhaps cannot find words to say, feels uncomfortable in the company of others, mixes poorly and has few friends or social activities.

II. SELECTION OF PATIENTS

Since our work is mainly carried out in a Health Service setting, our patients are to some extent pre-selected by the general practitioners or psychiatrists who refer them to us. Medical or psychiatric referrals have some advantages and disadvantages over a "walk-in" psychological advice centre. One advantage is that organic conditions or defects can be screened and, where relevant, treated before referral for psychological treatment. Some disadvantages are that the association with psychiatry stigmatizes the patient and may deter him from seeking help and that the involvement of doctors predisposes the patient to view his problem in terms of a medical model, thereby absolving him from the responsibility for behavioural change. The resolution of these problems may have implications for the location of treatment (e.g. home, clinic or hospital) and for the amount of pre-treatment discussion required. It may, for example, be ill advised to proceed with SST with a patient who is convinced that his problems are physically determined and require a medical solution.

In very general terms, three main factors govern the selection of SST as a suitable treatment: (a) the presence of social skills deficits in the context of a psychological problem; (b) that the patient desires change and is motivated to invest time and effort on the problem; and (c) that anxiety symptoms are controlled to the extent that the patient can meet the demands of training.

A. Social skills deficits

The individuals for whom SST is appropriate are often described as "socially phobic", "socially anxious" or "socially inadequate". As previously mentioned, their psychiatric diagnoses can be extremely varied. However, the inclusion of any individual in a programme of SST does not follow from any particular description or psychiatric diagnosis in the traditional sense. Rather, it is determined by a careful behavioural analysis which indicates that poor social skills may be giving rise to psychological discomfort.

It should be emphasized from the outset that social skill is not a unitary concept. It encompasses a wide range of behaviour. Both "speaker" and "listener" skills are involved; for example, the development of conversation content, the timing of an utterance and the appropriate use of eye contact and gesture. Individuals may show a wide variety of deficits or excesses yet be described in the same way, as lacking in social skills.

Just as individuals differ greatly in the degree and type of social skills problem, they will also differ in the degree of associated discomfort. Some people sail through life quite happily ignoring social graces and treading on metaphorical toes. Others are socially skilled, show an adroitness in social timing and flexibility, yet are dissatisfied with their performance. In both of these examples an inability to perceive the effect of one's social behaviour on others, or to perceive oneself accurately may make a significant contribution to the problem. In this context the breakdown of social skill into motor or response skills and into perceptual skills is a useful division (Morrison and Bellack, 1981). It is probably fair to say that perceptual skills have received insufficient attention in the SST literature and that SST in the future will need to examine the value of techniques for improving self-awareness and social sensitivity.

B. Motivation

SST as a form of treatment requires a considerable effort and commitment from the patient if it is to be successful. By comparison, swallowing a pill is relatively easy. Starting with the assumption that the individual is keen to produce changes in behaviour, they must then be not only prepared to devote time to the training or treatment session, but also willing to practise new social techniques in everyday life and, possibly, even to consider changes in their pattern of social activities.

Two motivational problems are commonly encountered. The first of these is the patient who expects treatment by medical magic, by tablet, or by a passive treatment such as hypnosis. If they cannot be persuaded of the applicability of the social skills approach to their problem, then their co-operation is unlikely. The second reluctant patient is the individual who has been referred for treatment by somebody else. For example, a parent may press their son or daughter to seek treatment because they are worried about their offspring's apparent difficulty or unwillingness to mix. In both of these examples behavioural analysis may suggest the appropriateness of SST but, unless the individual concerned is committed to the procedures recommended, then the therapist's effort will be wasted.

C. Control of anxiety

A degree of social anxiety is prevalent in society as a whole and a regular experience for most people. When this anxiety becomes extreme, it incapacitates the sufferer and renders social interaction aversive. If a patient is unable to accept some social interaction as a necessary part of treatment because of excessive anxiety, then he or she is unlikely to learn much from the programme and may well withdraw from treatment.

III. CASE ILLUSTRATION

Brian was first seen by a psychiatrist as an outpatient at the age of 19, four years prior to his referral to a psychologist for a consideration of the suitability of SST or an alternative approach to treatment. At the age of 19, he described to the psychiatrist what was noted as difficulty in dealing with people, both workmates and friends, and fears of becoming a recluse. He was initially diagnosed as suffering from a "phobic anxiety state with associated depression".

A social work report described Brian as the eldest of 6 children, living at home with his parents and working as a labourer in light industry. It mentioned that Brian tended to spend much time in bed, kept to his own company, and was causing concern to his parents on account of his isolation and apparent anxiety about meeting people.

For 15 months Brian received regular psychiatric outpatient appointments, was prescribed a variety of drugs and eventually a course of ECT. In spite of only modest improvement he was discharged. Two and a half years later Brian was again referred for treatment and this time a request was made for him to be seen by a psychologist. A letter from his parents described him as follows: "Brian has tried to get on and mix but he is completely unable to make conversation with anyone. At work be becomes so tense that he cannot work through shaking. He does not even talk at home unless you speak to him. His own doctor said that he would gain confidence as he grew older but, if anything, he is worse. Is there no way he could be helped to face life and work and be able to enjoy life? He seems to get no joy from living and has even talked about killing himself."

Initial interviews revealed that Brian experienced problems in thinking of things to say to people. Further, in describing his own activities, he tended to restrict his account to a minimal number of facts, requiring regular prompting by question. He maintained that this problem had caused him difficulties in forming friendships, that people tended to exclude him from social groups and that he now avoided interaction as the prospect made him nervous.

In so far as there were apparent social skill problems giving rise to anxiety in dealing with others and depression related to the quality of his life, it could be said that a superficial behavioural analysis pointed to the relevance of further assessment of the suitability of SST. Probable targets would be to increase the frequency and length of utterance and to improve the ability to maintain the conversation of others. What of the other factors, motivation and anxiety?

From the letter quoted earlier one might wonder if pressure from Brian's parents had led him to seek treatment. This was no doubt the case. Nevertheless, Brian presented himself as willing to try any treatment which might help him to achieve desired targets. He would like but had never had a relationship with a girlfriend. He would like to be able to strike up acquaintance with workmates. He indicated an interest in sport, particularly horse-racing, and had at some stage wanted to become a jockey. He would like the confidence to approach a riding stable with a view to lessons and to helping out with the care of the horses. These goals were readily agreed between Brian and his therapist and appeared to be realistic. Since Brian was prepared to attend outpatient sessions for an arranged period of time, motivation appeared to be adequate.

Brian's capacity to cope with SST would become apparent at the assessment stage. At least in the early interviews Brian was not overtly distressed and could maintain the interaction. He reported anxiety prior to his appointments and during the interviews and, although this might require attention during the course of treatment, it did not seem to preclude a social skills approach. Brian was not taking tablets or consuming alcohol in order to meet his commitments.

In conclusion, we would say that Brian represents a typical case, originally presenting with a psychiatric diagnosis of phobic anxiety and depression, but in which social skill deficits could be viewed as the precipitating factor. Motivation for treatment was good and it was not considered that excessive anxiety required separate attention prior to embarking on a more detailed assessment with a view to planning an SST programme.

So far we have considered only a few fundamental issues in the selection of SST as an appropriate treatment. The next section will provide a more detailed account of assessment procedures.

IV. ASSESSMENT AND ANALYSIS

One of our major concerns about the use of SST with adult outpatients is that it is often prescribed indiscriminately without an adequate assessment of the patient and his problems. While standard SST courses may be helpful to some patients, there are drawbacks to this "package-deal" approach to therapy. The most obvious drawback is that clinicians may overlook crucial aspects of the patients' problems and assign them to a treatment that is misconceived and inappropriate.

A. The initial assessment

We firmly believe that an extended period of initial assessment is a prerequisite of successful SST. The length of this assessment period will vary depending on the patient and the complexity of the problem presented. It may be necessary to set aside several sessions for the prime purpose of arriving at a comprehensive and thorough assessment of the patient's problems.

The functions of an initial assessment are several. First, the time is needed to understand fully what it is that the patient is complaining of, what "the problem" is. Second, the therapist needs to understand and investigate the patient's social background and current social function.

For example, different strategies may be called for with a patient who is lonely, friendless, unemployed and living alone in a bed-sitter, compared to a patient who holds down a secure job and lives within a supportive family and social network. Third, there is the need to establish a working alliance with the patient. We have found that the establishment of an alliance of trust and confidence is essential to successful SST and several of our notable failures can be attributed to the lack of such an alliance (see Marzillier and Winter, 1982). Finally, the assessment period may be seen as a process of negotiation between therapist and patient with the ultimate aim of arriving at a rational and mutually agreed decision about treatment. Many treatments break down because patient and therapist have very divergent ideas about the aims of treatment. The therapist expects the patient to co-operate with him and work on his problems; the patient sees the therapist as the powerful expert who will give the psychological medicine. It is essential that expectations about treatment are brought out and discussed openly before therapy formally begins.

Currently, we suggest to most patients at the end of the first interview that they see us for a period of assessment lasting between 4 and 6 sessions. We explain that the assessment period is an opportunity for both patient and therapist to gain an understanding of the problem and to arrive at a decision about treatment. It is not uncommon for this decision to be not to proceed with treatment or for the therapist to decide that SST will not be the central therapeutic strategy.

B. Methods of assessment

It has to be acknowledged that much of our assessment of patients' social problems is guided by our subjective judgements about "normal" and "abnormal" social behaviour. To a large extent it is based upon our own social experience and as such it is inevitably limited by the breadth or narrowness of that experience. In order to counter excessive subjectivity on our part we have sought to assess patients' problems in as broad a way as possible using a number of different approaches.

C. The interview with the patient

The largest part of our assessment takes place in the form of interviews with the patient. The interview is important for a number of reasons. Firstly, it is a concise way for the patient to tell us about himself and his difficulties. Secondly, from interviews we get some idea of the patient's perception of the world. The way the patient describes events or his own role in those events may reveal his beliefs about himself and his relationship to others. Thirdly, the interpersonal aspects of the interview are important in developing a good working alliance with the patient and for the patient to assess and get to know his therapist. Finally, the interview can serve as a way of assessing the patient's interpersonal skills albeit in a not very typical social context.

We do not work to a fixed guide or schedule in conducting our interviews. However, we try to ensure that we explore the following areas in some depth:

(a) the problem as presented by the patient;
(b) the origin and development of the problem;
(c) other problems either presented by the patient or as they appear to the therapist;
(d) the patient's childhood and early experiences;
(e) the patient's current and past interpersonal relationships;
(f) the patient's current family and social life;
(g) the patient's current and past occupations;
(h) previous psychological and medical treatments;
(i) the patient's perception of himself and of the prospects for change;
(j) the patient's expectations of psychological treatment.

These are not approached in a fixed order but commonly patients come with a "problem" which can be fruitfully explored in the first interview, and then further investigated as the interviews progress. It is also beneficial to clarify expectations about therapy in the first interview; in some instances patients' expectations about therapy are so discordant with the realities of therapeutic practice that further assessment is fruitless.

D. The interview with a relative or acquaintance

Interviews with relatives, acquaintances, workmates or other significant people in the patient's life can be an invaluable source of information. Such interviews often give a different and interesting perspective on the patient's social problems and can counteract the inevitable tendency of the therapist to see things through the patient's eyes. Sometimes a friend or relative can shed light on a problem. For example, one young man energetically pursued friendships with women but with conspicuous lack of success. He was not unattractive in appearance and was confident enough to seek out women and to chat to them. An interview with a male friend of his revealed that the patient's main problem was excessive seriousness; he never smiled and his line of conversation was ponderous and boring. It was therefore scarcely surprising that most women rapidly lost interest in him. It is good practice to ask all patients for permission to interview someone close to them. Such people may be involved in treatment helping the patient to put into practice what has been learned in the sessions. Furthermore, the therapist can take the opportunity to assess the likely consequences of changes in the patient's behaviour to others in his immediate social life.

E. Behavioural observation

Unobtrusive observation of the patient in a problematic social situation would clearly be an invaluable source of information, but with out-patients it would be an ethically dubious procedure and is, in any event, virtually impossible to achieve. Very occasionally we have accompanied patients on social outings, but there are problems in so doing, not least of which is the blurring of professional and social roles. The alternative that we have adopted is to set up simulated social encounters in our clinic which we record on videotape for subsequent analysis. Sometimes these are role-played interactions but more commonly we set up actual encounters with secretaries, nurses, porters and other personnel around the hospital. Both the patient and the helper are briefed as to the encounter and the recording. Although this makes them somewhat artificial, they are sufficiently realistic to allow us to observe something of the patient's characteristic social style.

The main advantage of observing and recording social behaviour in this way is that we can sample the specific features of the patient's social skills, for example, eye contact, gestures and speech characteristics. In addition, we ask both patient and helper to give us their perceptions of the encounter. This allows us to see how much the patient's perception accords with the other person's and our own. It is quite often the case that the patient's self-perception is distorted. For example, one male patient who reported being shy with women was able to carry out a very successful conversation with a female secretary who found him pleasant and attractive. His shyness and low opinion of himself was not borne out by his behaviour or by the views of another. A further advantage of videotape recordings is that they can be used in treatment in the form of videotape feedback.

F. Self-monitoring

We commonly ask patients to monitor some aspects of their social lives. A very simple form of self-monitoring is in the form of a social diary in which patients record their social activities over a weekly or fortnightly period. In addition, we may ask patients to record their social difficulties perhaps rating their anxiety levels or listing their accompanying thoughts. Self-monitoring is important for a number of reasons. Firstly, it provides a regular and systematic record of events that occur in the patient's life, information that supplements the patient's reports in interviews. Secondly, the degree to which the patient participates in self-monitoring is an index of their motivation in general. If a simple self-monitoring exercise is not completed, then it augurs badly for SST or other form of treatment. Finally, self-monitoring can be seen as the first step in a programme of change which is going to be largely self-directed.

Generally we tailor the type of self-monitoring to the problems that the patient presents. However, we also use standard inventories or rating scales from time to time. Inventories such as the Beck Depression Inventory and Anxiety Checklists are useful in that they provide a quantitative assessment of change which can be used to evaluate treatment effects.

G. The goals of assessment

By the end of the assessment period we hope to have a detailed picture of the patient and his problems. Further, we should begin to have a formulation or analysis of the case, that is, a working hypothesis about what the problems are, how they came about and what function they currently have. The relative success or failure of treatment may be seen as a test of that hypothesis.

The formulation or analysis is conveyed to the patient and a decision about treatment objectives is agreed. By the very fact that he is involved in this process the patient is aware that he must bear some responsibility for change and not sit back and passively receive therapy. Without the active involvement of the patient, SST and other strategies have little or no chance of success.

V. TREATMENT

We do not adhere to a standard treatment format when seeking to help adult outpatients with social problems. The analysis derived from the initial assessment should suggest a number of therapeutic strategies tailored to the individual's problems. For example, in the case of the shy young man mentioned earlier, who perceived himself as more inadequate then he appeared to others, the central problem was seen as a lack of self-confidence allied to the absence of opportunities for meeting people. We successfully treated him primarily by means of videotaped feedback of his conversational skills and by introducing him to an active social club (see Marzillier and Winter, 1978, Case IV). Therefore, the therapeutic strategies illustrated below should be seen in the context of an individually tailored programme of treatment.

A. The management of anxiety

Many of our patients complain of anxiety in social situations and for some it is seen as their primary problem. Where anxiety is intense it is usually necessary for patients to reduce their anxiety as a first step in treatment. It is not very sensible to expect highly anxious patients to participate in a demanding therapy such as SST as the demands of the treatment may increase their anxiety to little good effect. We tend to view the relationship between anxiety and social skills in terms of the inverted "U" curve, in which low levels of anxiety are facilitative of skills acquisition and high levels disruptive. Therefore, patients who experience high levels of anxiety are unlikely to learn anything from SST. It is essential to bring their anxiety level down to manageable proportions.

Various strategies can be adopted to help patients reduce and control their anxiety feelings. But first of all, it is important to be aware of the sources of anxiety and its meaning to the patient. Behavioural analysis may reveal that anxiety is appropriate given the social stresses the patient is undergoing. Although the patient may be helped to control the extent of his anxiety, it will not disappear if it is a realistic response to stress. Only if the source of stress is eliminated will the anxiety be resolved. This was illustrated in the case of a socially anxious man who reported consistently high levels of anxiety at work. These turned out to be related to frustrations and dissatisfactions he experienced in his job. Only minimal relief from anxiety was achieved by anxiety management training; however, there was considerable reduction in anxiety on his being made redundant.

Where anxiety reduction appeared a realistic goal, we have used the following therapeutic strategies:

(1) Establishing a working alliance

The development of a relationship of trust and confidence can help anxious patients to feel at ease during treatment sessions. This in turn will make it easier to tackle social problems directly by SST or similar didactic methods. It is important, therefore, for the therapist to move forward gently with very anxious patients and not to expect rapid therapeutic results.

(2) Muscular relaxation training

Along with many other therapists, we have used progressive muscular relaxation training to help patients control the physical manifestations of anxiety. We have used an abbreviated version of the methods suggested by Bernstein and Borkovec (1973) generally completing deep muscular relaxation training in one or two sessions. We have found that, while most patients can achieve deep relaxation (a procedure carried out when they are on their own) differential relaxation training, which is carried out in actual social situations, is much more difficult and few patients become adept at it. Thus, the notion of muscular relaxation as an active coping skill, while attractive in theory, has proved to be more difficult to implement in practice.

(3) Cognitive methods

Most anxious patients worry about their prospective performance in social situations. We have used a number of cognitive rehearsal procedures to help patients approach social events in a more positive frame of mind. The covert modelling method elaborated by Kazdin (1973) is particularly useful since the patient is instructed to imagine a detailed sequence of activities and is cued in to see himself, or another person, successfully coping with anxiety. In addition to mental preparation for specific events, we focus directly on maladaptive beliefs that may underlie anxiety. For example, where a patient has a tendency to see the negative aspects of his performance, we would seek to make him aware of this tendency and help him to correct it. (For a more detailed discussion of cognitive methods, see Morley *et al.*, Chapter 11).

(4) Graded exposure

Lasting reduction in social anxiety is likely to come from repeated successful performances. Thus, the grading and careful selection of a programme of social activities is an integral part of our treatment. Where possible, these activities are rehearsed in therapy prior to being carried out in reality. This method of graded exposure is applicable to both anxiety reduction and SST since it comprises the important common features of practice and feedback (see below). With some anxious subjects, it may be possible to achieve only limited social targets.

(5) Anxiolytic medication

Since our patients come from either psychiatric or general practice sources, they are commonly taking some form of psychotropic medication. As psychologists, we have generally been averse to the use (and abuse) of such drugs, but there is little doubt that in some instances they are invaluable in reducing the unpleasant somatic effects of anxiety. Recently our approach has been to help the patient use the drugs in a practical manner as part of an anxiety management programme. For example, a graduated programme for the reduction of drugs can be integrated into a graded exposure programme so that the anxiolytic effect of the medication is put to a specific purpose. Ultimately, however, we hope that our patients will learn to do without drugs to control their anxiety.

B. Social skills training

Many of our patients lack the requisite skills to cope with social life. Their lack of confidence in themselves stems from their difficulties in handling a variety of social encounters. For such patients, it is appropriate to train them in social skills. The sorts of skills deficits presented by patients are highly variable but it is possible to discern some common features.

(1) Conversational skills

It is very common for patients to report that they have great difficulty in holding conversations with others. Some report that they can think of little to say and that conversations rarely get started or, if they do, peter out in prolonged silences. Observations of such patients indicate that they often speak in monosyllables, rarely initiate interactions, give away very little of themselves and rarely show any interest in the person they are talking to. In other words, they tend to adopt a passive role, expecting others to make the going. Sometimes specific deficits in non-verbal skills can be seen such as avoidance of eye-contact, the lack of expressive gestures or signs of tension in their posture. Speech can also be hesitant and inarticulate. Where deficits in conversational skills are observed and appear to be a significant factor in the patient's social problems, training in the art of conversation can be of benefit.

(2) *Lack of appropriate assertiveness*

It is scarcely unexpected that socially anxious patients who lack confidence in themselves find it particularly difficult to be appropriately assertive. That is, they are unable to stand up for themselves, handle criticism or deal with people in authority. It is important to help patients in handling a variety of social situations which demand an assertive response. Such situations range from handling an autocratic parent to coping with the intransigence of minor officials.

(3) *Appearance*

Apathy, reduced attention to personal hygiene, and an apparent disinterest in appearance are features of several psychiatric disorders, notably depression. There is a suggestion, however, from some studies that poor appearance may sometimes be a cause and not necessarily a consequence of psychiatric or psychological disorder. Unattractive people, or those with physical deformities, may find socialization difficult. In particular, the formation of heterosexual relationships may be impeded by poor aesthetic appearance and this, in itself, may be a source of anxiety or depression. Although many aspects of appearance cannot be changed, except by surgery, attention to others may make a considerable difference. Making the best of one's appearance could be described as a feature of good social skill and hence its inclusion, albeit briefly, in this chapter. Advice may be given to patients about cosmetics, hair-style, fashion, personal hygiene, skin complaints, weight control and other aspects of personal care. Working in a psychiatric hospital setting may be an advantage insofar as the advice of a beautician, hair-stylist or dietician is usually available. Some therapists may find the subject of a patient's appearance an awkward one to broach. A useful strategy is to begin by asking the patient whether they are unhappy with any aspect of their appearance or physical characteristics. If this subject is tackled at the assessment stage, where perhaps a simple questionnaire listing parts of the body, such as face, hair, eyes, bust, shoulders, hips, etc. could be completed, it will be much easier to return to it constructively at an appropriate stage of treatment. Incidentally, Paredes *et al.* (1969) reported that patients provided with repeated videotape feedback became more careful of their make-up, hair and clothing.

(4) *Friendship formation*

The most common problem that patients present to us is an inability to form friendships. Many of our patients are lonely and friendless, apparently unable to make contact with others. The causes of this problem can be complex and may be due to some of the skills deficits already discussed, for example, poor self-presentation, or lack of conversational skills. In many cases, the patient complains of a lack of opportunity to meet others and perceives social life as bleak and unrewarding. An introduction to social outlets where there are opportunities for making friends can be an important part of SST (see below). In addition, training in the basic and more complex skills in making and maintaining friendships can be of benefit.

Poor conversational skills, lack of assertiveness, difficulties in friendship formation and poor self-presentation are some of the commonest problems we have encountered in our patient population. Other problems occur, such as heterosexual anxiety, lack of humour, difficulties in group settings and relationship problems. Whatever their specific difficulty, we tend to adopt a similar format in our training approach, although the content of the session varies.

(5) *Increasing social activities*

It would seem as though many friendships are made, not during a casual visit to a bar or a disco, but in the course of participation in a structured social activity such as at work, on a study programme, or at a sports club. If the patient already has these opportunities in his repertoire of social activities, it may then be a question of talking over his social contacts, making plans on the elaboration of existing relationships, and checking on the outcome at a later date. In cases where the range of activity is limited, it may be useful for the therapist to be familiar with existing local organisations such as the Housewives' Register, the 18+ Club, Contact or Solo Clubs, and college leisure courses. If known to be reputable, then introduction or computer or video-dating agencies might also be recommended. Where possible, it may help to introduce the lone individual to an existing member of the organization chosen so that they can be sure of at least one familiar face when they attend for the first occasion.

(6) *Social awareness and perceptual skills*

We have suggested earlier that social skill may be divided into perceptual and into motor or response components. So far, our attention has been mostly turned to the motor response in social behaviour, that is to what people say and do during a social interaction. At this point, we would like to emphasize the importance of perceptual skill in assimilating the elements of social situations and thereby deriving a reasonable estimate of our personal social performance and its effect on others. This aspect of social skill has been variously described as social awareness or social sensitivity and defined by Rothenberg (cited in Morrison and Bellack, 1981) as "the ability to accurately perceive and comprehend the behaviour, feelings and motives of others". It is suggested that the manner in which we interpret our impingement upon the social environment may determine our beliefs and expectations about our own social performance. Morrison and Bellack (1981) maintain that insufficient therapeutic attention to these cognitions may explain the limited generalization of newly acquired social skills from the clinic to a natural setting.

In our experience, a set of cognitions indicating low social self-esteem is frequently associated with social anxiety and a low rate of social activity. Sometimes, low self-esteem is a realistic assessment of poor social skills; in other instances, it can only be described as a faulty construction of the individual's social ability. Why is it that a person with good social skills, whose company is enjoyed by other people, should hold such a low opinion of their ability and misinterpret the responses of others? One reason is perhaps that feedback is usually indirect and difficult to evaluate. People seldom tell us that they think about us. For example, those departing from a dinner party or an evening at a friend's house will generally thank their hosts and say they have enjoyed the occasion. Their true feelings may have to be interpreted from more subtle cues such as a yawn, a long face or a raised eyebrow. Could it be that some people have not learned or do not recognize these cues? Or, more likely, if they recognize them, are they sometimes misconstrued?

Of course, it is not only those people with adequate social skills who fail to perceive or judge their social environment with accuracy. There are also individuals with very poor social skills who seem to remain blissfully unaware of the difficulties they create for others. Such people are capable of boring listeners to death, embarrassing others by their rudeness or causing arguments by their dogmatic and inflexible manner. Many such people seem not to recognize the effect they have on others and if they are referred for treatment, it is often at the insistence of another person. We suggest that this problem could also arise from a defect in social perception, but one which results in a faulty positive self-evaluation rather than the more frequently presenting faulty negative self-evaluation.

Morrison and Bellack suggest several possible causes of perceptual defects; a failure to listen, a failure to look, a failure to integrate information, a failure to interpret or decode information, or a tendency to pay attention to irrelevant cues. They recommend an investigation of training in listening or attending, in seeking clarification and in the perception of emotions. Presumably, this would be in addition to the provision of feedback designed to correct faulty negative or faulty positive self-evaluation.

The problem of correcting self-awareness is partially one of providing people with feedback about themselves so that they may acquire a more accurate view of their impact on others. Putting it in other words, they need to develop appropriate cognitions about their social behaviour. In our experience, videotape feedback is extremely valuable for this purpose but does require sensitive clinical judgment as to timing. The therapist should select sections of tape which illustrate good qualities and accompany the replay with verbal feedback emphasizing that the subject appears comfortable, is making an effective contribution, and employing good social techniques. The use of these should be pointed out and socially reinforced, a method described as "focused feedback" by Geertsma (1969). Apart from verbal comments by the therapist, feedback from others, especially from fellow patients in a social skills group, can be reassuring to the subject. With videotape people can see that they don't "stick out like a sore thumb", that their hands do not tremble obviously, or that they are not "giving themselves away".

In dealing with cases of faulty positive self-evaluation videotape feedback has occasionally proved useful as a means of confronting individuals with their failings and thereby seeking to increase their motivation for change.

C. General format of social skills training

Most forms of SST contain the same basic components, discussion, modelling, rehearsal, feedback and task assignment but the specific nature of these components and the way that they are integrated into a training programme varies considerably. In our work with adult outpatients, we have developed a style of SST that reflects the needs of our patient population and the demands of a busy health service setting. Thus we offer a training programme that is generally brief and practically orientated to the social problems the patient experiences. We see patients in small groups and individually. There are advantages and disadvantages to both forms of delivery and we do not favour one method over the other.

(1) *Individual SST*

We have adopted a target or problem-orientated method of individual SST. That is, we gear our training to specific problems that have been identified in the assessment process and to specific targets selected by the patient. Examples of such targets are developing a circle of friends, going out with someone of the opposite sex, talking freely in a small social group, initiating conversations with strangers, etc. It is obviously important to select a target that is relevant to the patient's general problems and realistic. Thus, targets tend to be quite circumscribed. Where a more general target is chosen (e.g. developing a circle of friends), this is further broken down into more discrete steps (e.g. finding a social club or similar environment; introducing oneself; making conversation, etc.). The expectation conveyed to the patient is that SST can help him in achieving a target, but it is his responsibility to implement the skills taught in therapy. Once a target is identified, the skills the patient needs are discussed and, where necessary, modelled by the therapist. The skills may be in the form of discrete micro-skills (e.g. increasing eye-contact; asking questions), or higher-order strategies (e.g. self-disclosure; making conversations), depending on the type and level of difficulties the patient has. The patient is then asked to rehearse those skills in the session, usually in the form of role-played interactions with the therapist, sometimes with another person brought into the session for this specific purpose. Brief sections of social interaction are rehearsed several times until the patient begins to become reasonably adept at the encounter. Continuous verbal feedback is given by the therapist throughout; augmented feedback in the form of audio or videotaped recordings of role-played sessions is given at the end of the session. After each session, a specific and related task is agreed with the patient to be carried out between sessions. At the following session, the patient reports on his assigned task, any difficulties are discussed and repeated skills training given if necessary. Another target may be worked upon in the same way.

The above description is a necessarily simplified account of individual SST. Few patients progress through therapy in such a rational and trouble-free manner. Problems arise at various stages, for example, in choosing a realistic target, in getting the patient to role-play, and particularly in helping the patient generalize the skills learned in therapy to real-life encounters. Most recently we have sought to improve generalization by using existing social resources (e.g. social clubs) and involving other people in the assigned tasks.

There is no fixed time to individual SST; it will largely depend on the patient and his problems. We tend to see patients once weekly for hour-long sessions and anticipate seeing people for between 3–6 months. Sometimes, more intensive therapy is called for, particularly in the initial phases, Feedback we have received from patients in a recent follow-up study of treatment failures indicated that for some people more frequent sessions would have been valued.

(2) *Social skills training in groups*

Social behaviour is itself a group activity and thus the use of small groups in the training of social skills has some apparent advantages over an entirely individually based therapeutic technique. One is the more economical use of therapist time but, equally important, is the opportunity which the group affords for each member to practise newly acquired social techniques with a small cross-section of people who are not members of a helping profession. This asset of a group procedure may be of special value to the individual who perceives his own social performance inaccurately. The opinions expressed by a peer group may add considerable weight to the comment and feedback provided by the therapist.

As with individual SST, a sufficient period of careful assessment and preparation with each patient is an essential pre-requisite. It must be established that the group training procedure will meet the individual's needs by covering the necessary topics. We would only advocate a form of group training which is oriented towards individuals. In other words, individual training is provided within a group framework, allowing patients to learn from one another, to practise conversation together, and even to tackle agreed social activities together outside the clinical setting, for example, a visit to a restaurant, disco or social club. Since some patients will share common problems, excesses or deficits, there may be some saving in therapist time.

In addition to the time spent in the analysis of individual problems, careful forethought is necessary in deciding upon the constitution of a particular group. If the presence of a number of other clients in therapy is to be advantageous, then each must be chosen with at least two considerations in mind:

(1) Will the group provide social situations which are relevant to the individual's difficulty? For example, a young person who had problems in making heterosexual relationships would clearly be better placed in a mixed, rather than a single sex, group.
(2) Will the individual produce particular problems which are likely to disrupt the course of a group programme? For example, the motivation of members is critically important since irregular attendance would seriously disturb the functioning of a small group.

We have found the optimum group size to be between 4–6 individuals with the addition of 1 or 2 therapists. Smaller numbers would undermine the usefulness of the group in that there would be little variation in practice situations. On the other hand, larger numbers would produce extremely lengthy sessions in which each individual spent a relatively small amount of time in conversation practice. We have preferred either single sex groups or groups with a balanced number of males and females, although there may be advantages in putting certain individuals into a sexual minority. A number of other factors may be relevant. For example, range of age and social background. Here again, the nature of specific problem areas should be taken into account in constituting the group.

Working with a small group of 4–6 outpatients, meeting weekly for approximately 10 sessions, the procedure must be carefully planned in advance of each session. Sessions will involve instruction, modelling, rehearsal and feedback, where the general strategy is to prompt and shape an interaction until the cues can be faded out. In this respect, training procedures are similar to those used with individuals, with the additional advantage that the individual's performance in a group situation can be observed and coached. Homework assignments may be set in the group and part of subsequent meetings used for reporting back.

In our groups, two therapists have jointly led each session, allowing them to demonstrate or model aspects of social skill in a dyad. This could only be achieved otherwise on prepared videotape. It also allows for one therapist to clarify instructions or comment made by the other, permits more attentive observation and, in general, facilitates the smooth function of the group sessions. In addition, social reinforcement in the form of verbal approval and encouragement appears to be more "natural" and more effective when it comes from two sides (Sarbin and Allen, 1968).

D. Case illustration: a typical treatment programme

This illustration describes the treatment programme constructed for Brian, whose problem was discussed in an earlier section (see Selection of Patients, p. 32). A period of assessment led to the adoption of the following agreed targets for treatment:

(1) To increase Brian's conversational content or amount spoken.
(2) To increase his frequency of initiating conversation.
(3) To increase the number and range of his social activities.
(4) To make recommendations about his appearance based on a self-perception of "boyishness".
(5) To take steps towards establishing a relationship with a girl.

The first two targets were tackled in an SST group of 3 men and 2 women who met for 10 sessions. Although some aspects of targets (3), and (4) and (5) were considered in the group sessions, these goals were mostly dealt with on an individual basis.

(1) Conversation content was increased by the following method. Homework assignments were set which involved the group participants noting information which could be used in subsequent conversation practice, for example, weather forecasts, news or sports items, TV programmes and, most important of all, personal experiences. Conversational practice exercises would be planned to utilize such information and to provide opportunities for reinforcement. Within the sessions, the therapists may need to provide prompts in the form of questions or reminders or to repeat the same conversational sequence several times, fading out the cues, before achieving a reasonable length of utterance.

(2) Question-asking was modelled as a strategy for initiating and maintaining conversation. Instructions were given to commence an interaction with general questions, using early responses to generate further appropriate enquiries. For example, "Do you live locally?" might be followed by "Do you like this neighbourhood?" or "How long have you lived here?"

(3) Although the group arranged to tackle a number of social excursions together, such as going for a drink, a Sunday morning walk or eating at a Chinese restaurant, and although these events helped to increase Brian's confidence, he needed to make changes in his home social life. Here, the involvement of a brother was valuable as Brian and his brother agreed to visit horse-racing meetings together and occasional discos. In addition, Brian decided to develop his interest in cycling by joining a cycle touring club.

(4) Brian's appearance presented an unusual problem since he was of small stature and "boyish", such that people assumed he was younger than his 23 years. We suggested a change of hairstyle and choice of clothes which produced some improvement. In this instance, Brian's perceptions of himself were probably correct but we feel he derived some benefit from discussing the problem openly.

(5) Finding a girlfriend was a high priority target for Brian and one which he tackled on his own initiative by subscribing to a computer dating organization. In individual sessions we were able to help prepare him for these "assignments" by rehearsing suitable opening sequences, suggesting conversation topics and by considering concluding remarks. Some variety was needed according to the outcome of the evening!

The case of Brian illustrates a fairly typical treatment programme, combining group and individual SST with an examination of self-perceptions and attempts to increase social activities.

VI. OUTCOME, PROBLEMS AND CONCLUSIONS

The outcome of SST depends upon the complexity and severity of the presenting problem, the selection of relevant targets for change, a good working alliance with the patient, the choice of an adequate training procedure and on the response obtained from the use of newly acquired social techniques in the patient's own social environment. Even so, treatment effects can be confounded when several therapeutic strategies are applied simultaneously. Finally, conclusions about outcome will depend on the method and the timing of assessment.

Although specific social techniques such as question asking to initiate conversation or frequency of expressive movements may be observed to change in role-playing or behavioural tests, it sometimes happens that anxiety ratings, mood ratings or indicators of social satisfaction fail to reflect this improvement (Marzillier and Winter, 1978). Thus, SST could be effective in producing immediate and observable changes in social behaviour but not necessarily effective in removing the psychological problem which led the patient to seek treatment. In some instances, the benefit of improved social skills may not become apparent for some months or years after the termination of treatment. For example, a depressed and isolated person may acquire more acceptable social approach behaviours as a result of SST but it may still be some time before they achieve their main objective, finding a partner.

From clinical experience, we would argue that SST is a useful treatment when applied to selected psychiatric outpatients who have deficits in the motor or perceptual element of their social repertoire. An analysis of treatment failures (Marzillier and Winter, 1982) suggested that poor outcome is most likely to be associated with a faulty initial behavioural analysis (the wrong working hypothesis about the problem), poor motivation, a failure to bring excessive anxiety under control, or a failure to produce the desired changes in the patient's social life. This last problem may be due to the lack of generalization of newly acquired social techniques to the natural setting, or to an unpredictable social disaster such as an unmerited snub, put-down, or otherwise unsatisfactory encounter. It would seem to us that the trainer's knowledge of or involvement in suitable groups, clubs or introduction agencies is one way of facilitating generalization and real social change for the patient.

It has also been suggested that poor generalization of SST could be the result of insufficient attention to cognitive variables or to the skills of social perception, whether self or others. Arden and Cappe (1981), for example, discovered that non-assertive subjects could role-play assertion as well as assertive subjects. That they did not do so in everyday life could not therefore be the result of behavioural incompetence but was more likely due to their negative self-evaluation. In similar vein, Bruch (1981) suggests that failure to display assertive behaviour could be ascribed to "interference from negative self-statements" as much as to "a deficit in the terminal skills necessary for the execution of an assertive message". We have recommended improving the accuracy of self-perceptions by means of focused videotape feedback and of training social sensitivity by discussing videotape models and the patient's real-life experiences. Others may feel that the advice of Ellis and Harper (1975) concerned with tackling needs for approval and eradicating "dire fears of failure" is an equally valid approach to the modification of unhelpful cognitions.

Finally, we would repeat our emphasis upon the importance of detailed assessment and individual behavioural analysis. There is inevitable pressure to provide treatments which are cheap and fast, a movement in the direction of computerized SST programmes, package-deal treatments recorded on cassette, programmed instruction booklets and self-help manuals. Some have even wondered whether the one-to-one therapeutic relationship can survive in a nationalized health service. We feel that there is obviously a place for improved technology in the process of SST and it is likely that the use of those methods mentioned may speed the process of acquisition. If the technology is applied to the teaching process *per se*, then more therapist time could be devoted to the initial stages of assessment, the selection of an appropriate treatment strategy and to the prompting which is a necessary part of follow-up if generalization is to occur.

VII. REFERENCES

Arden, L. and Cappe, R. (1981). Non-assertiveness: skill deficit or selective self-evaluation? *Behav. Ther.* **12**, 107–114.

Bernal, M. E. (1969). Behavioural feedback in the modification of BRAT behaviors. *J. Nerv. Ment. Dis.* **148**, 373–385.

Bernstein, D. A. and Borkovec, T. D. (1973). "Progressive Relaxation Training. A Manual for Therapists". Research Press, Champaign, Illinois.

Bruch, M. A. (1981). A task analysis of assertive behavior revisited: replication and extension. *Behav. Ther.* **12**, 217–230.

Curran, J. P. (1977). Skills training as an approach to the treatment of heterosexual-society anxiety: a review. *Psychol. Bull.* **84**, 140–157.

Ellis, A. and Harper R. A. (1975). "A New Guide to Rational Living". Wiltshire Books, Hollywood.

Frederiksen, L. W., Jenkins, J. O., Foy, D. W. and Eisler, R. M. (1976). Social skills training to modify abusive verbal outbursts in adults. *J. Appl. Behav. Anal.* **9**, 117–125.

Geertsma, R. H. (1969). Studies in self-cognition: an introduction. *J. Nerv. Ment. Dis.* **148**, 193–197.

Kazdin, A. E. (1973). Covert modeling and the reduction of avoidance behavior. *J. Abnorm. Psychol.* **81**, 87–95.

Lazarus, A. A. (1973). On assertive behavior: a brief note. *Behav. Ther.* **4**, 697–699.

Marzillier, J. S. and Winter, K. (1978). Success and failure in social skills training: individual differences. *Behav. Res. Ther.* **16**, 67–84.

Marzillier, J. S. and Winter, K. (1982). Limitations of the treatment of social anxiety. *In* "Failures in Behavior Therapy" (E. B. Foa and P. M. G. Emmelkamp, *Eds*). Wiley, New York.

Morrison, R. L. and Bellack, A. S. (1981). The role of social perception in social skill. *Behav. Ther.* **12**, 69–79.

Paredes, A., Gottheil, E., Tausig, T. N. and Cornelison, F. S. (1969). Behavioral changes as a function of repeated self-observation. A controlled study of self-image experience. *J. Nerv. Ment. Dis.* **148**, 287–299.

Sarbin, T. R. and Allen, V. L. (1968). Increasing participation in a natural group setting: a preliminary report. *Psychol. Res.* **18**, 1–7.

3

Long-stay psychiatric patients in hospital

ROBERT C. DURHAM

I. INTRODUCTION

This chapter is concerned with social skills training conducted in a small group setting and constituting one part of the therapeutic activities on a ward of long-stay patients in a psychiatric hospital. The main focus of attention is on the use of such groups to improve the social functioning of that subgroup of the long-stay population who have some conversational abilities, and some realistic possibility of achieving a more independent existence, either within the hospital or in the local community. No attempt is made to describe the use of social skills training techniques in either specialized individual treatment programmes as, for example, in reinstating speech in extremely withdrawn schizophrenic patients; or, in structured social activities, such as games and discussion groups, that are primarily intended for those long-stay patients who have little possibility of discharge but much need of social stimulation and constructive occupation. However, it is hoped that the reader will be able to apply the essential principles of social skills training to all forms of social interaction with long-stay patients, whether or not these occur in the context of a social skills group.

Whereas the prime objective of running a social skills group is to achieve specific treatment goals set for each patient in the group, the group can also be used to achieve goals that are more indirect but which may nonetheless be equally valuable. From the patients' point of view these might include increases in the level of support they receive from the staff, and a greater involvement with their own treatment. From the staff's point of view these might include opportunities to learn new therapeutic approaches to use in their daily interactions with patients, and also opportunities within the group setting to assess regularly the patients' abilities and general functioning. Social skills training in the present context is not solely concerned with modifying specific behaviours of certain patients. More general benefits to staff and patients can be expected to follow from this treatment approach.

It should also be stated at the outset that running social skills groups with long-stay patients in hospital is not an easy task. There are usually a number of obstacles to be overcome, not the least of which is the apathy and very marked learning difficulties of this group of patients. Progress is invariably slow, setbacks are common, and many patients remain in need of continued help and support even when significant improvements in their functioning have taken place. Social skills training, then, is certainly no panacea for the severe social disabilities of people suffering from chronic psychiatric disorder, and what follows does not pretend otherwise. Nonetheless, this type of social treatment can be used to make a clinically valuable contribution to helping long-stay patients learn more adaptive ways of relating to other people and of coping with their disabilities. The achievement of these objectives brings rewards which compensate for the difficulties of working with severely handicapped people in institutional settings.

II. SOCIAL SKILLS TRAINING IN THE CONTEXT OF A LONG-STAY WARD

While it is a truism to state that psychological therapies are always affected by the social context in which therapy takes place, it can take a long while to appreciate the importance of this fact when working in a psychiatric hospital. The nature, goals, effectiveness, feasibility, and even desirability of social skills training with any particular group of long-stay patients will all be markedly affected by the characteristics of the ward environment in which this group of patients lives. Four basic questions need to be asked when the possibility of introducing social skills training is being considered.

A. What is the function of the ward within the system of rehabilitation and resettlement adopted by the hospital as a whole?

Hospitals vary a good deal in the degree to which rehabilitation is organized in a systematic and rational manner. At one extreme some hospitals have a highly organized system which usually involves several wards feeding into one or two predischarge wards; these in turn then feed into day care facilities, group homes, and hostels in the community. In such a system, preferably under the overall responsibility of one consultant, each part of the system has a reasonably well defined function and each member of the team has a clear idea of how he or she fits into the overall plan. At the other extreme some hospitals have no clear rehabilitation policy; there may be a number of different wards, each with a wide variety of patients and several consultants, who may all be loosely engaged in rehabilitation but not in any concerted or systematic manner.

The advantages of an organized system of rehabilitation will be apparent to anyone who has worked in each of the two extremes outlined above. High staff morale, good communications between professions, clear treatment goals, a rational allocation of resources, etc., are all much easier to establish on a ward which has a well-defined place within a wider organizational context. These factors are of particular importance in social skills training, the success of which is very dependent upon ward staff having a clear understanding of the purpose of such treatment and of the importance of their own interactions with patients in achieving individual treatment goals. If such understanding is absent and there is no general concensus among the staff as to the overall function of the ward and how to fulfil this effectively, then social skills training, or any other form of social treatment, will be of little value. Indeed, in such circumstances it will generally be more productive to devote time and energy to promoting a planned system of rehabilitation, than to setting up a social skills group only to see it continuously undermined by staff who lack cohesion and a sense of shared purpose.

B. How is the ward organized?

Social skills training, in common with other forms of psychological treatment on long-stay wards, places considerable demands on ward staff to sustain an active involvement with patients so as to reinforce and maintain any gains that are made in the group sessions. Whether or not these demands are met depends crucially on the manner in which the ward is organized. Experience suggests that psychiatric wards should be organized so as to meet the following needs of the ward staff: psychological support, involvement in decision-making, clearly defined responsibilities, clear communications between staff, and in-service training. The importance of these factors in sustaining staff morale and creating a therapeutic atmosphere is discussed in greater detail by Bennett (1978) and Watts (1983).

C. What social and recreational opportunities are available on the ward?

Some of the interpersonal difficulties of long-stay patients are due not so much to deficits in their social skills but to a lack of opportunity to practise what skills they have. It is difficult therefore to assess a patient's level of social skill, or to help him learn more effective skills if there are no opportunities for him to participate in social activities. Thus, before embarking on social skills training it is important to assess what social activities are part of the weekly routine of the patients on the ward. Are there regular discussion groups on the ward or at occupational therapy?

What evening activities are organized for the patients? How frequently do patients visit the local community to go shopping, visit the pub, go to the cinema, and so on?

If there is an obvious lack of social activities then the first priority on the ward should be to remedy this deficiency. Once social activities are set up it will almost invariably be found that some patients are able to function at a very much higher level than was realized, but that others experience considerable difficulties in even simple social situations. Such information will be of considerable value in selecting appropriate patients for the group and in setting treatment goals.

D. What is the staffing situation on the ward?

Running a social skills group on a long-stay ward is not a method of treatment that can be successfully pursued by one member of staff working alone, whether he or she is a nurse, occupational therapist, psychiatrist, psychologist, or social worker. It is essential that there be at least two members of staff involved for purposes of mutual support, at least one of whom should ideally be a trained nurse so that the work of the group can be integrated into the daily routine of the ward environment. This requirement can be difficult to meet on wards that are severely understaffed or that have chronically high rates of staff turnover, the latter being the more damaging as far as psychological treatment is concerned.

If the group is to be run solely by members of the nursing staff, account must be taken of two important factors. Firstly, because nurses work a rotating shift system, at least three nurses will need to be actively involved in running the group if continuity is to be maintained from week to week. Secondly, the nurses concerned need to be permanent members of the ward staff. Nurses in training or nurses temporarily attached to the ward may be very interested in the group, but they are not in a position to provide the consistent therapeutic interactions with patients, from one week to another, that are necessary to effect change.

The above problems can often be overcome, however, if responsibility for running the group is shared between a psychologist, occupational therapist, psychiatrist, or social worker, and one or two members of the permanent nursing staff. Indeed, this is probably the best solution to adopt if such staff are available and interested. Whatever the outcome it is important that the staffing levels on the ward should be carefully assessed before social skills training is started.

III. SELECTION AND ASSESSMENT

A. Selection of appropriate patients

The initial selection of patients for the group can be based on a broad knowledge of the general characteristics of all the patients on the ward. Once the selection has been made a more detailed assessment of the patients chosen can then be carried out in order to set treatment goals.

All patients in the group should have some basic conversational skills and sufficient motivation to attend a group without excessive amounts of prompting and persuasion from the staff. The selection should be made from those patients who have clear interpersonal difficulties but nonetheless sufficient social awareness to be responsive to other people. Beyond that, the selection should be made on the basis of the patients' ability to work together in a group setting. For purposes of maintaining staff morale, especially with beginning therapists, it is useful to include at least two patients who will participate with little prompting. Conversely, it is unwise to include more than one or two people who are likely to be disruptive or whose attention span is consistently very limited. Sometimes it will be a matter of trial and error in determining which patients are more likely to benefit from the group. Finally, the size of the group should be between 5 and 10 patients.

B. The assessment process

The starting point for a more detailed assessment of each patient should be the question—What interpersonal difficulties does this person have which are preventing him or her from functioning more independently? To answer this question it is best to make careful observations of each patient's behaviour in several different social settings. It is certainly unwise to assume that the behaviour shown by a patient on the ward will also be shown by him or her in the community or at occupational therapy. Some patients are able to change their behaviour in response to the demands of different situations, sometimes in surprising ways. There are several points that need to be borne in mind when making such observations.

Firstly, it is important to avoid using unrealistically high standards when assessing long-stay patients, most of whom have marked interpersonal difficulties in many areas. The aim is not to catalogue every deficit that a person has but rather to understand what particular difficulties are interfering with everyday social functioning. Thus, difficulties such as asking for help, coping with petty frustrations, and keeping psychotic symptoms in check during conversations, are usually much more relevant to the adjustment of most long-stay patients than are difficulties in the finer points of socially skilled behaviour.

Secondly, it is helpful to collect observations in a systematic manner using checklists, rating scales, or questionnaires. Unfortunately, there are no specific measures that are generally agreed to be the best to use. Many of the possibilities are reviewed by Hersen and Bellack (1977). The Social Skills Assessment Form (Fig. 3.1), an unpublished form developed by the author, may be helpful as a general guide to those aspects of the social behaviour of long-stay patients that should be assessed. Its primary purpose is to provide information for setting treatment goals and it is of limited usefulness in evaluating the effectiveness of treatment.

Fig. 3.1

SOCIAL SKILLS CHECKLIST

Resident's name: *Ward:*

Assessment completed by: *Date:*

Please assess the following aspects of the resident's social behaviour in terms of the categories below:

(1) serious difficulty in this area, disturbing to others;
(2) general difficulty in this area, interferes with social interaction;
(3) difficulty in some situations or with some people;
(4) generally appropriate, does not interfere with social interaction;
(5) very appropriate, definite asset.
N.O.—not observed.

Your assessment should be based on observations of the resident's behaviour in a number of different settings over a period of two weeks. Remember to add comments as necessary and to summarize the information at the end.

Non-verbal behaviour	*Category*	*Comments*
1. Facial expression		
2. Eye contact		
3. Body posture		
4. Body movements		
5. Social distance		
6. Tone of voice		
7. Loudness of speech		
8. Speed of speech		
9. Spontaneity of speech		
10. Hesitations in speech		
11. General appearance		

Verbal behaviour	Category	Comments
12. Holding casual conversations		
13. Showing interest in what other people say		
14. Expressing feelings appropriately		
15. Disagreeing with people without getting upset		
16. Keeping symptoms from being intrusive		
17. Asking for help when needed		
18. Accepting compliments		
19. Co-operating with others		
20. Responding to criticism		
21. Other problems (please specify)		
....		
....		
....		

Please also comment on the following:
22. Social supports in the community
23. Friendships in the hospital
24. Degree of social anxiety
25. Response to organized social activities
26. Interest in social activities

Summarize key areas in need of some intervention:

Thirdly, the assessment process should provide some clues as to the causes of each group member's problems. These are likely to be an interaction between a number of different factors. Thus, the psychotic process itself, from which most long-stay patients suffer, typically has a disruptive and disorganizing effect on the ability to attend to social cues and learn new ways of behaving. Many long-stay patients also experience chronically high levels of social anxiety and tend to avoid situations that demand more than minimal participation. Often this is combined with a low tolerance for stress, particularly in regard to the emotional demands of close relatives. The inherent tendency of many patients to be apathetic, withdrawn, and to show disorganized speech (Wing, 1978) may be exacerbated by psychiatric hospitals that provide little social stimulation and few incentives for behaving "normally". Many patients learn from an environment that expects very little of them a tendency to expect very little from themselves. In addition, the side effects of psychotropic medication may inhibit normal social interaction by making patients look or feel awkward or odd, and this in turn may induce a sense of discomfort in other people. The above factors, in combination with premorbid social difficulties, may all be partly responsible for the social deficits observed in any particular patient. Some understanding of the relative importance of these factors to each patient will help to decide on the right balance between teaching basic skills, teaching coping strategies, increasing levels of social stimulation, and providing more adequate incentives for "normal" behaviour. Often such understanding will only come after working with patients in the group for some weeks. Indeed, this will be true of assessment in general, which is always a continuous process of gradually accumulating information about each patient as he or she responds to treatment.

Fourthly, no mention has been made so far of the patients' own feelings about their problems. Is Mrs. X interested in learning how to cope better with social situations? This is a difficult issue in working with long-stay patients, for while every effort should be made to involve them as closely as possible in the assessment process, they are rarely able to articulate their difficulties with much clarity or insight. Simple self-rating scales are sometimes useful in helping patients to focus their attention on the kind of difficulties they experience in social situations. It is important always to try and set treatment goals which are a result of open discussion, and sometimes negotiation, between the group leaders and each patient.

C. Setting treatment goals

Once the information has been collected, 2 or 3 specific treatment goals should be set for each patient. These goals should consist of desired changes in the person's social behaviour that would significantly improve his or her adjustment. They should be realistic, relevant to the person's life, and capable of being understood and remembered by the ward staff and preferably also by the patient himself. They should also be compatible with other goals that may have been set in planning the overall rehabilitation of each patient as discussed by Shepherd (1983).

Examples of treatment goals that might be set are as follows:

(1) Help Mr. X to stop shouting at his father when his father criticises his appearance.
(2) Help Miss Y to learn to listen to other people without constantly interrupting them.
(3) Help Mr. A to speak in a normal tone of voice rather than a whisper.
(4) Help Miss A to keep her delusions from intruding into her conversation.
(5) Help Mrs. B to look at other people when she's speaking to them and smile occasionally.
(6) Help Mr. C to attend the local community centre once a week without being too anxious to join in activities.

IV. TWO "TYPICAL" LONG-STAY PATIENTS

A. Donald is a 29 year old man, hospitalized for 5 years with a diagnosis of paranoid schizophrenia. Preliminary assessment of his social skills showed that a major problem was the way in which his fixed delusion of being followed by a gang of people, interfered with his daily conversations with staff and other patients. His preoccupation with his delusion constantly intruded into his conversation and he was unable to show much interest in other people. Also, he experienced noises in his head which he periodically responded to with outbursts of shouting and banging his ears with his hands, often injuring himself and always disturbing other people. He had difficulty concentrating on activities in occupational therapy and his self-care was generally poor. He frequently responded angrily to supervision and feedback about his poor performance in these areas. He had a close and overinvolved relationship with his mother which discouraged him from learning to be more independent. However, in spite of the above problems he remained interested in ward activities and enjoyed contact with the community.

When first involved in the social skills group Donald was frequently agitated and upset by other people's behaviour, tending to lecture and shout at them in a belligerent manner. His conversation was restricted to topics in which no-one else was interested. One goal of treatment was to help him to disagree with other people and to respond to criticism without getting upset. A series of role-playing exercises in which he had to remain calm and in control of himself when subjected to critical comments was helpful in achieving this goal. A second goal was to help him learn to keep his delusions from intruding into his conversation and to improve his listening skills. Over a period of a year he gradually became much more appropriate and at ease in conversation, and began to appreciate how his angry outbursts affected other people. The social skills training was closely co-ordinated with psychological treatment programmes for decreasing the frequency of his agitated outbursts, improving his performance in occupational therapy, and decreasing his dependence on his mother. He was subsequently discharged to a residential hostel.

B. Jean is a 55 year old woman, hospitalized for over 20 years with a diagnosis of chronic schizophrenia. Assessment of her social skills indicated that her behaviour was variable. For most of the time she was friendly and good humoured, though usually relating to staff in a dependent and childish way, often giggling to herself for no apparent reason, hugging people without warning, and responding to attempts at normal conversation with fatuous and irrelevant comments. At other times she was sullen, withdrawn, and apathetic, requiring a good deal of prompting to maintain a basic level of self-care, and occasionally reacting with verbal abuse when demands were made upon her. She had had virtually no contact with the community for many years, but was generally popular with staff and patients.

Jean required little prompting to attend the group but passively resisted participating actively for several months. Initial treatment goals were simply to reduce the frequency of her inappropriate behaviours such as giggling and making fatuous comments, and at the same time to increase her responsiveness to social cues and her understanding of the social conventions that operated in the world outside the hospital. Jean gradually responded to the demands of the group (principally repeated feedback following inappropriate behaviour and reinforcement of normal behaviour) and to a programme of repeated community trips plus help in establishing a constructive routine of daily activities. After 9 months of active treatment she was considerably more appropriate in her interactions with other people and much more confident about visiting the community. The possibility of her being able to manage in a sheltered hostel was discussed for the first time since her admission to hospital.

V. PROCEDURAL DETAILS

A. Duration and frequency of sessions

Few hospitalized long-stay patients will be able to sustain constructive involvement with a group for longer than 45 minutes, which is about the right length of time for one session. However, it serves no useful purpose to adhere rigidly to this length of time. If a particular session is going well, the time can be extended to an hour. Similarly, if a session is very unproductive it is generally better to stop after half an hour, than to soldier on just for the sake of finishing at a particular time. On rare occasions a combination of adverse circumstances—the group leaders are not feeling well, one of the patients is very disruptive—may make it quite pointless to continue with a session which has only been going for 10 minutes. Finally, the group leaders will need to allocate about an hour and a half of their time to the session as a whole since they will require some preparation time before the group starts and also time to discuss the group at the end of the session.

In deciding how often the group should meet, the following points need to be considered. Firstly, it is not possible to maintain any degree of cohesion or continuity in a group if it meets less than once a week. Secondly, it is usually desirable to meet at least twice a week but only if this can be maintained on a regular basis. It is generally better to meet once a week regularly than twice a week irregularly. Thirdly, the important factor in determining frequency of sessions within the constraints just mentioned, will be the number of staff on the ward who are willing to be group leaders.

B. Number and scheduling of sessions

The positive changes in patients that result from attending a social skills group will come slowly and usually not until the group has become incorporated into the normal clinical routine of the ward. Therefore, there is no fixed length of time that a group should exist. However, the group should not be interminable! All group leaders, not to mention the patients, need a regular break from running the group if they are not to become stale or emotionally exhausted. A good practice is for the group to take a month off every 3 or 4 months, and longer periods may be necessary if the burden of running the group falls mainly on one person's shoulders.

It is important to take a thoroughly business-like approach to the scheduling of sessions. A casual attitude on the part of the group leaders will inevitably transmit itself to the patients and undermine their motivation to attend. Thus, the sessions should start at a fixed time (or times) each week, the details of which, along with the names of patients expected to attend, should be clearly posted on the ward noticeboard. If a session has to be cancelled for some reason, then the group members should, as a matter of simple courtesy, be informed of this fact and the reason for it.

C. Use of technical aids

There are no technical aids that are of essential importance to the success of this kind of group. (Unless one includes in this category the use of a comfortable room which has easy chairs, adequate heating and lighting, and is relatively free from noisy distractions.) However, it is sometimes very helpful to have the use of a blackboard, an audio cassette recorder, and videotaping apparatus. From a practical point of view it is only the videotape which may create difficulties since it is expensive, time-consuming to set up and operate, and requires good lighting to be effective. These factors usually outweigh the benefits of videotape unless the group leaders are fortunate enough to have a videotape system permanently set up in a room which is also a convenient and appropriate setting for running the group.

D. Record keeping

At the end of each session one of the group leaders should record a brief description of the topics covered that day, focusing on the themes that emerged, the active participants, and any homework assignments. An attendance record should also be kept. Such information is best stored in a looseleaf ring binder which can also be used to keep a note of the treatment goals for each patient, details of the syllabus, plus any clinical tips on how particular topics or patients are best approached.

VI. DESCRIPTION OF THE TREATMENT PROCESS

A. The value of a syllabus

The most effective method of deciding on the content of social skills training with this population is to plan group sessions using a syllabus of topics and issues that are of general relevance to all the members of the group. Individual treatment goals can then be pursued within the broad structure that a syllabus provides. The most important advantage of such a strategy is that it encourages the group leaders to focus on topics that would otherwise be neglected or avoided. However, a syllabus should be used flexibly if it is to be of value. It provides a resource on which the group leaders can draw; it should not be slavishly followed at the expense of individual needs. With these caveats in mind, the following topics and issues provide appropriate themes around which any particular group session can be structured:

(1) holding brief conversations;
(2) being a good listener;
(3) giving and accepting compliments;
(4) coping with "crazy" behaviour;
(5) behaving as normally as possible;
(6) getting on with the staff;

(7) expressing feelings;
(8) asking for help;
(9) knowing your rights;
(10) coping with being a psychiatric patient;
(11) stopping yourself jumping to conclusions;
(12) thinking more positively about yourself;
(13) learning to relax;
(14) keeping occupied during the day;
(15) preparing yourself for discharge;
(16) getting on in the community.

It will be apparent from this syllabus that less than half of the topics are strictly concerned with learning social skills in the sense of learning specific ways of behaving with other people. Rather, the topics are broadly concerned with problems and issues which face long-stay patients in hospital, and which often have a negative effect on their social functioning. While the solution to some social difficulties certainly involves the acquisition of specific behaviours (e.g. learning to look interested in what another person is saying), the solution to other social difficulties may involve learning new information (e.g. the whereabouts of the local community centre) or learning to adopt private coping strategies for dealing with distressing experiences (e.g. learning to keep strange thoughts to oneself). All three kinds of learning are usually involved in any particular session, the content of which may vary from a general discussion of, for example, the dangers of becoming too dependent on the staff, to a very specific attempt at skills training in, for example, responding appropriately to the critical remarks of a fellow worker at industrial therapy.

It is helpful to plan topics for the group a month in advance, and to then distribute copies of this plan to the ward staff and members of the group. For example, a typical month for a group meeting twice a week might look like this:

GROUP THERAPY AGENDA FOR MARCH

MEETING TIME: Monday and Thursday afternoons at 3.45 p.m. in the group room
GROUP LEADERS: Joe Roberts and Anne Smith

Date
March 3rd   General discussion
March 6th   Getting on in the community
March 10th   Thinking positively about yourself

March 13th	Trip to shopping centre and local pub
March 17th	Thinking positively about yourself (continued)
March 20th	Getting on in the community (continued)
March 24th	Giving and accepting compliments
March 27th	Giving and accepting compliments (continued)
March 31st	General discussion

In practice it is usually difficult to keep to an agenda because the needs of individuals over-ride the topic planned for a particular session, and because particular topics may take much longer to work through than was anticipated. Nonetheless, the agenda does give some degree of structure to the sessions and is a useful reminder to include excursions into the community as part of the group programme.

B. The basic format

(1) Before the session starts

The group leader and co-leader, together with any observers, should meet briefly before the session starts to discuss the topic for the day, to review the notes made of the previous session, and to remind themselves of individual treatment goals. Since very few long-stay patients will attend a group meeting at the right time and place on their own initiative, some degree of prompting and persuasion by the group leaders and ward staff may be necessary. The degree of prompting needed will be least in a ward in which there is a positive expectation that the patients attend the group, and in which the time and place of the session is clearly communicated to the individuals concerned. Whatever the circumstances it is important that the group leaders share with the ward staff the task of prompting attendance.

(2) During the session

The first task of the group leader is to discuss any unfinished business from the last session and in particular any homework assignments that were made. This will take between 2–15 minutes. The second task, although sometimes by necessity the first, is to find out if there is any immediate problem or personal difficulty that would be suitable for discussion. If there is then it is almost always best to use this as the topic for the session in place of the one that was planned.

There are no hard and fast rules about the best way to organize each session, since different topics, and differences between individuals, require somewhat different therapeutic approaches. Some examples of how various topics can be approached are given below, after which there is a section on useful therapeutic strategies and general guidelines on how to conduct the group. In general, the most important task of the group leader is to encourage the members of the group to talk about and practise ways of coping with situations that they find difficult. At the end of each session it is helpful to summarize the key points that have been made and to set specific homework assignments to be carried out between the sessions.

(3) After the session ends

All staff who attended the group should always meet briefly after the session in order to discuss what took place, to give each other construc- tive feedback, and to make any plans that are necessary for monitoring homework assignments. This time is also important for training pur- poses and mutual support, especially if the session was particularly difficult or frustrating.

C. Three examples of how to structure a session

The following brief notes on useful tips for discussing several rather different topics, will hopefully suffice to give a flavour of the most effective style of conducting the group. It is helpful to build up a file of similar notes for each of the topics in the syllabus.

(1) Being a good listener

Begin by asking if anyone has had the experience of talking to someone who was not listening to what you had to say. If there is no response to this use an example from your own life. Usually several people will say that they have had this experience and found it very frustrating. Use this information to emphasize the importance of listening closely to what other people are saying—we all like to be listened to.

Then ask how each person knows that another person is listening to them. Alternatively, ask how each person knows that someone is not listening to them. Using this information draw up a short list of listening skills and write them on a blackboard or piece of paper. Encourage members of the group to write these down too. Examples might include: looking at the other person, nodding your head, smiling occasionally, asking questions, etc. Remember that most long-stay patients are doing well if they can do some of these things reasonably consistently.

Role-playing is almost certainly the best way of learning listening skills. A good way of doing this is to ask one person to find out something about another member of the group's family background that they did not already know (e.g. where they went to school, what their parents did), just by asking questions and listening carefully. Role-play for 5 minutes, give feedback, and repeat the exercise as necessary.

It may also be helpful for the group as a whole to split into pairs and do this exercise, and then reverse roles. Then ask each person to summarize what their partner had told them about themselves. Some modelling by the group leaders may be necessary.

End by summarizing key points and setting homework assignments.

(2) *Stopping yourself jumping to conclusions*

Begin by suggesting that everyone has had the experience of jumping to some conclusion about something and then finding out they were wrong. Everyone makes mistakes. It is important to realize that this can happen and to try and guard against it. Usually best to give an example from your own life to illustrate this point.

Ask each person to give an example from their own experience of when they misinterpreted something and unnecessarily got upset about it. Then ask each person to say why they jumped to the conclusion they did and what alternative explanations there were for what happened.

In the case of frankly paranoid patients it is best not to focus directly on their delusional system but rather to gradually help them appreciate that their delusional beliefs might possibly not have any basis in reality. The most realistic expectation here is that paranoid patients will begin to entertain the idea that they might be wrong. It is sometimes helpful to get a person who always jumps to the same conclusion (e.g. that no-one likes him) to rate how strongly he believes this on a 0–100 scale. Then gradually encourage him to change his belief (from 100–90–80 etc.) if there is in fact some evidence that some people do like him.

Encourage the group as a whole to practise thinking up alternative ways of thinking about events that individual members of the group have come to some erroneous conclusion about (e.g. list all the possible reasons why someone might have ignored someone else on a particular occasion).

End by summarizing the key points and checking that these have been understood. This topic should be followed up over several sessions in order to be useful.

(3) *Preparing yourself for discharge*

Begin by asking members of the group to talk about their feelings about being discharged from hospital and living in the community again. (If discharge is not a realistic possibility for members of the group the focus of this topic can be changed to increasing contact with the community and learning to live more independently). There will usually be a mixture of anxiety, denial of problems, and misunderstandings expressed by the group. Talk about these in an open, supportive and realistic manner.

Themes such as the following can be used to initiate useful discussion:

(1) What is it like to live in a group home or hostel? Ask members of the group to describe what they know about group homes or hostels. If necessary follow this question up with prompts such as: Who does the shopping? Can you stay in bed all day? Correct any misconceptions and encourage a realistic appreciation of the benefits and difficulties involved in living away from the hospital. If possible ask someone who is familiar with group homes (e.g. a social worker or ex-patient) to attend the group and ask questions.

(2) How do the staff decide if a patient is ready for living in the community? Again, elicit opinions on this subject, and correct any misconceptions. Try and explain as openly as possible how decisions are made. If formal assessment procedures are used, hand out copies of the relevant forms and use these as a basis for discussion.

End by emphasizing the importance of getting out into the community as much as possible, and set homework assignments that include community trips.

D. General therapeutic guidelines

(1) *Sustain a minimal level of active participation*

A vital task of the group leader is to combat the apathy and general inertia that is so characteristic of long-stay patients. In order to do this effectively one must be physically, verbally, and mentally active in devising and executing ways of encouraging the participation of all members of the group in the topic being discussed. Structured exercises, in which members of the group are asked particular questions or given specific tasks to do, are often valuable in this regard. There are several examples of such exercises in the previous section. On some occasions it may be helpful to use exercises that involve the group members leaving their chairs and doing something physically active, even though this is not directly relevant to the task at hand. The simple act of moving around the room may overcome an oppressive inertia that has proved resistant to verbal methods of intervention.

(2) *Create a warm and supportive atmosphere*

The ideal atmosphere to create in the group is one which is warm, informal, and supportive, but at the same time also business-like and task orientated. This is not an easy balance to strike and many group leaders tend to err on the side of being too business-like at the expense of being supportive. In fact long-stay patients are extremely unlikely to learn coping skills in an atmosphere which is insufficiently appreciative of their difficulties. It is important therefore to reinforce attempts at learning even if unsuccessful, to focus on assets as much as on deficits, to use humour whenever possible, and to try and cultivate a style of interaction which is open, non-defensive, positive, and sensitive to the feelings and concerns of group members. Finally, it is worth pointing out the simple but important fact that it is impossible to create the right atmosphere in a group unless people are sitting in a circle reasonably close to each other.

(3) *Establish positive expectations for change*

The group leader must transmit to the patients in the group the expectation that they *can* learn to cope with their psychiatric disability so as to lead a more independent and happier life. To put it another way, the quality of their lives *will* improve even if their psychiatric disorder remains unchanged. For many patients, but not all, such an expectation is realistic although a good deal of patience and perseverance is needed if it is to be realized.

In practical terms, such positive expectations are conveyed by setting realistic goals, encouraging patients to take some risks, reinforcing and prompting normal rather than disturbed behaviour, encouraging contacts with the community, and adopting a positive approach to problem solving. It also means dealing with disturbed, dominating or antisocial behaviour in a firm but understanding manner. The best approach to adopt towards behaviour which is very disruptive is to indicate a willingness to help the person concerned to learn to control his behaviour, but a definite intention to exclude that person from the group if he or she is unresponsive or rejecting of such help.

(4) *Practise coping with difficult situations*

Once a specific problem has been identified in the group, it is helpful to first generate ideas about how to solve the problem from among the patients themselves. There will usually be at least one person in the group who has some ideas about a helpful way to think about the problem or who can model or demonstrate an appropriate way of behaving in the situation. It should be remembered that the patients are usually in a better position than the group leaders to provide a realistic model that is appropriate to their abilities and hence more easily imitated by other patients. In addition, encouraging some members of the group to show other members how to cope with a situation focuses attention on the assets of the patients rather than on their deficits, and encourages mutual support. Only when the resources of the patients are insufficient to solve a problem should the group leaders suggest their own ideas and on occasions model appropriate behaviour themselves.

An effective technique for modelling and practising coping behaviour is role-playing. However, a significant proportion of long-stay patients are extremely resistant to role-playing and generally don't benefit from it even if persuaded to participate. It is most useful with such topics as improving listening skills, learning to be more assertive, and teaching self-control in response to other patients' upsetting behaviour. It should not be used as a routine part of the group but rather as a useful way of tackling certain problems presented by patients who are responsive to this approach.

Some clinicians use as models audio-tapes or video-tapes of people behaving in a socially skilled manner. For example, Goldstein and his colleagues (Goldstein *et al.*, 1976) have developed a comprehensive package of audio-cassettes for use in social skills training with long-stay patients. While these may be effective with some patients whose social skills are at a reasonably good level, there is the danger of such a procedure being much too abstract and presenting as models people with whom many patients find it hard to identify.

(5) *Give clear instructions and feedback*

In most sessions the group leader will need to take an active part in organizing the session and instructing the group members to carry out specific exercises or to behave in certain ways as, for example, when role-playing. Instructions should be clear, direct, and courteous. They should take account of the fact that many long-stay patients are very concrete in their thinking, that is, they often have difficulty in thinking about situations in a complex or abstract manner, and in seeing a situation from someone else's point of view. Long, complex instructions will therefore usually be inappropriate and unhelpful. A useful approach for a group leader to adopt is to check that he has been understood by asking the person he has been talking to to summarize what he has just said. However, this request must be phrased in a gentle and courteous manner or it will be interpreted as being patronizing and rude. Thus, it is better to say "I wonder if I have made myself clear, could you summarize what I've just said", than "What have I just told you?". Those patients who show a chronic inability to remember instructions, or the key points of a discussion, or even the topic being discussed, should be prompted to make written notes to remind themselves.

Providing patients with feedback about their behaviour is an essential aspect of both running a group and creating a therapeutic environment on the ward. The following points are useful as general guidelines:

(1) Be positive more frequently than negative.
(2) Be clear, direct and specific. It is more useful for someone to learn that they "interrupt other people's conversations a lot" than that they are "dominating".
(3) Focus on behaviour immediately after it happens.
(4) Be honest.
(5) Check to see that feedback is understood.
(6) Encourage the members of the group to solicit feedback themselves.
(7) Encourage all members of the group to give feedback, especially positive feedback.

(6) *Give regular homework assignments and follow them up*

Homework assignments work best if they arise naturally out of the topic covered in the session. It is rarely possible or even desirable to give everyone in the group a suitable homework assignment after each session. It is much better to give a few very specific assignments which are followed up than to routinely give each member of the group an assignment after each session. Useful assignments range from asking someone to find out what is showing on the local cinema, to asking someone to practise holding a conversation with one or two specific people. It is always a good idea to try and involve the group members in choosing their own assignments, and it may be helpful to write these down on a 3 × 5 card which the person can carry with him as a reminder. In some cases it will be necessary to arrange for a member of the ward staff to take an active part in helping a patient complete an assignment.

VII. THERAPISTS

A. What makes a good therapist?

The characteristics of a successful group leader have been admirably outlined by Goldstein *et al.* (1976) in the following way:

(1) *General qualities*

(*a*) ability to communicate clearly; (*b*) flexibility and resourcefulness; (*c*) physical energy and enthusiasm; (*d*) ability to work under pressure; (*e*) patience; (*f*) empathy; (*g*) ability to listen; (*h*) interpersonal sensitivity; (*i*) broad knowledge of capabilities and characteristics of patients in the group.

(2) *Specific qualities*

(*a*) knowledge of skills being taught; (*b*) ability to orient patients to material; (*c*) ability to initiate and sustain role-playing; (*d*) ability to reduce and overcome patients' resistance; (*e*) ability to give feedback; (*f*) ability to build group cohesiveness.

Good therapists are essentially those people who, whatever their professional label, are able to use a variety of therapeutic strategies to overcome the problems that arise in motivating, supporting and teaching long-stay patients. Since progress is always slow and usually punctuated by minor and major setbacks, one might add to this generalization the importance of therapists adopting a long-term perspective with regard to the fruits of their labours. In this respect therapeutic work with the long-stay population is a fundamentally different exercise to that of treating neurotic or acutely disturbed psychiatric patients.

B. How should therapists be selected and trained?

Therapists should be selected on the basis of their interest and willingness to learn the necessary clinical skills. Long experience in working with long-stay patients, or in running traditional forms of group therapy, is not necessarily a positive criterion for selection, since such persons may have deeply ingrained habits of interacting with long-stay patients that are basically incompatible with the style of interaction needed in social skills training. Replacing these habits with new ones is not always easy.

Trainee therapists should ideally first be given the opportunity to observe an experienced therapist leading a group for at least half a dozen sessions. He or she should then become a co-leader for several sessions before taking on the responsibility of leading the group. The best approach is one which combines observation, guided participation, feedback sessions, and support.

C. How can other staff and families become involved?

Whenever any member of the group is able to learn more adaptive ways of behaving, it is of course very important that they should be supported and reinforced by other people in their social environment. There is no special way of doing this apart from actively working within this environment to ensure that new skills are reinforced and not extinguished. In practice this may range from meeting with family members, to talking in case conferences, and holding discussions with the domestic staff. The degree to which this is successful will depend on the manner in which the ward is organized as indicated in an earlier section of this chapter.

VIII. EVALUATING THE EFFECTIVENESS OF THE GROUP

The most practical way of assessing the effectiveness of the group is to examine the degree to which individual treatment goals are achieved. This is best accomplished by repeatedly observing the behaviour of each patient in a variety of social situations that are relevant to the goals in question. (It will be recalled that each patient attending the group should have two or three specific treatment goals). For example, if a goal for Mrs. A is to help her keep her delusions from intruding into her everyday conversation, then the frequency and extent to which she does this should be observed in several different situations that form part of her usual daily routine. Similarly, if the goal for Mr. B is to help him disagree with other people without losing his temper, then he should be observed in situations where this is likely to occur, whether this be in the O.T. department, at home with his father, or when getting up in the morning. Such observations can usually be done by the ward staff and other members of the team, as part of the clinical observations that they would routinely make of the patients on the ward, provided of course that they are made aware of the specific treatment goals for each patient. The role of the group leaders is to collect this information and use it, together with their own observations, to come to some sensible conclusion about the effectiveness of the group.

The evaluation process as outlined above is essentially an informal and continuous process of collecting evidence on the progress of each patient in achieving 2 or 3 clearly defined goals. Although simply stated on paper this exercise is of little value in normal clinical practice, and may even be destructive, if the following two points are not borne in mind.

Firstly, the purpose of evaluation is primarily to provide feedback to the group leaders that they can use to make constructive adjustments to the functioning of the group so as to improve its effectiveness. For example, if Mrs. A has made no progress over a 6-month period in learning to keep her delusions from intruding into her conversation, it may be because the therapeutic approach has been inappropriate or inconsistently carried out, or perhaps her behaviour is essentially unmodifiable and a new treatment goal needs to be substituted. It may even be that Mrs. A was a poor choice to join the group and that she should be replaced by Mr. C. The point to be remembered here is that there will always be a number of possible explanations for a particular finding and it is the job of the group leaders to make a judgment on the basis of the available evidence as to which explanation is the most likely, and then to take appropriate action.

Secondly, and this follows from the first point, once the decision to set up a social skills training programme has been made and a group has been established, the important outcome questions to ask should concern specific issues to do with organization, individual goals, staff training and so forth. General outcome questions to do with the overall value to the ward of setting up a social skills group should be asked infrequently, perhaps on a yearly basis, and should involve a comprehensive look at all the possible costs and benefits that are involved. It is not useful, and may be damaging to staff morale, if the group leaders habitually question the value of the group as a whole on the basis of the apparent success or failure of particular group sessions in achieving individual goals.

IX. CONCLUSION

A common thread that has run throughout this chapter has been the importance of integrating the social skills training conducted in group sessions with the daily interactions between staff and patients on and off the ward. Thus, the therapeutic activities during the sessions, far from being a mysterious process occurring once or twice a week in "the group", should be broadly familiar to all persons involved with the ward. Just as the group leaders should use their knowledge of the everyday problems facing the group members to teach them appropriate skills, so should the staff that are involved with the patients each day use their knowledge of what takes place in the group to reinforce and maintain the skills each person has learnt. It is the establishment of this kind of open relationship between all members of the team that is the key to ensuring that treatment gains achieved in the group transfer to the everyday life of each group member and are maintained once social skills training has ended. Teamwork, then, is essential for doing social skills training with this population. The group leaders need to concentrate on developing good working relationships with other staff just as much as they need to develop clinical skills in working with the patients.

Finally, it is important to recognize from the outset that the circumstances for conducting social skills training as described in this chapter will never be ideal. There will always be aspects of institutional care in even the most forward-looking of hospitals that will be detrimental to the therapeutic progress of the group members, and that will frustrate the efforts of the group leaders. Such factors as ward organization and staffing levels are of particular significance in this respect. However, in spite of these difficulties a great deal can still be achieved in improving the quality of life of long-stay patients, and in facilitating the development of a therapeutic environment on the ward that is of benefit to staff and patients alike.

X. REFERENCES

Bennett, D. H. (1978). *In* "Schizophrenia: Towards a New Synthesis" (J. K. Wing, *Ed.*), pp. 211–232. Academic Press, London and New York.

Goldstein, A. D., Sprafkin, R. P. and Gershaw, M. J. (1976). "Skill Training for Community Living: Applying Structured Learning Therapy". Pergamon Press, New York.

Hersen, M. and Bellack, A. S. (1977). *In* "Handbook of Behavioural Assessment" (A. R. Ciminero, K. S. Calhoun, and H. E. Adams, *Eds*), pp. 509–554. Wiley, New York.

Shepherd, G. (1983). Planning the Rehabilitation of the Individual. *In* "Theory and Practice of Psychiatric Rehabilitation" (F. N. Watts and D. H. Bennett, *Eds*). Wiley, Chichester. (In press)

Watts, F. N. (1983). Management of the Staff Team. *In* "Theory and Practice of Psychiatric Rehabilitation" (F. N. Watts and D. H. Bennett, *Eds*). Wiley, Chichester. (In press)

Wing, J. K. (1978). *In* "Schizophrenia: Towards a New Synthesis" (J. K. Wing, *Ed.*), pp. 1–30. Academic Press, London and New York.

4

Social skills training with long-term clients in the community

ALISON COOPER, SIMON BIGGS AND MIKE BENDER

I. THE SETTING

We have been running social skills training (SST) in some form for the last 5 years in an 150-place psychiatric day centre in an East End London borough. The clients catered for tend to be middle-aged, working-class people, with diagnoses of psychosis of a chronic nature. There is a predominance of men. A brief history of how the current organization of social skills has emerged will illustrate the interplay between the organization of the institution and the difficulties in running a group effectively. When the centre was first opened some 6 years ago each member of staff was in charge of a "unit" comprising 15 clients. That member of staff was expected to meet all the needs of all the members of the unit and theoretically a client would progress from the assessment unit, through the centre to the pre-work group, and discharge.

Our initial attempts to set up SST groups were beset by difficulties deriving from this "unit" system. One of our principles is always to include centre staff in the running of groups, with a view to their eventually taking over the groups, rather than the psychologists running groups on their own (Bender, 1976b). However, any commitment of time to a group meant that the staff's unit was left unattended, which at that time was not deemed appropriate. (In the current system clients have free periods, when they may leave the Centre, or spend their time in the community room, where there is a pool table and tea: it is now no longer regarded as necessary to have clients under constant surveillance). At the same time there was increasing anxiety about the way some of the units were operating. One of the units in particular—the one which catered for the needs of withdrawn clients—was referred to as "the silent room". The morale of the staff member was plummeting and clients were exhibiting a reluctance to be admitted to this unit.

In response to this a time-sampling procedure (Hutt and Hutt, 1970) was undertaken of the verbal interactions of 4 clients in each unit, who were comparable in terms of staffs' assessment of their degree of social withdrawal, using the Venables' (1957) scale. These clients were among the 50% lowest scorers in the centre as a whole. Results indicated that clients in the "withdrawn unit" spent significantly less time talking and more time listening than similar clients in other units. This latter observation was important: the clients were not oblivious of activity around them. Moreover, our observation of other clients interacting enabled us to identify certain clients who were "facilitators": they evoked responses from withdrawn clients by virtue of being warm and responsive, without being unduly assertive. As a result of this it was agreed that a number of "facilitating" clients should be transferred to the "withdrawn unit" and that the SST input should be focused on this unit. Clients requiring SST would become members of this unit. Groups would be held in the unit, and the problem of leaving a unit unattended would be overcome.

Alas, our solution failed. While a "facilitating" client can benefit from being helpful in a group of an hour's duration, it was too much to expect of a client to keep it up full-time! Morale plummeted again.

It was in the context of the difficulties described above that the centre was completedly reorganized. Units were disbanded and a curriculum of groups and activities run by the staff was drawn up. Clients now initially attend the centre for a 3-week assessment period at the end of which an individual time-table of activities is drawn up. The client becomes a member of a "tutor group" and the group meets with a particular member of staff for a short session at the beginning and end of every day. This provides a "base" for the client and assists the centre in monitoring changes in his mood or clinical condition. Depending upon the results of the social skills assessment, this timetable may include attendance at the SST groups.

There is no doubt that for some time there was hostility among staff and clients to the idea of SST owing to its association with an unsuccessful attempt to rescue a doomed concept—the "withdrawn unit". On the other hand, the failure did precipitate the reorganization of the centre on lines which permit much greater flexibility and self-determination on the part of the clients. The lesson seems to be that in setting up SST there will always be an interplay between the ideal scheme for training, and the organization of the institution in which it is set. In this instance, there was an impact on the organization of the institution, largely due to the insistence on the inclusion of centre staff in the group.

II. ASSESSMENT AND SELECTION OF CLIENTS

Over the 5 years that SST has been in operation a number of different assessments have been used. (Anyone who would like copies should apply to the authors). Assessment of clients has always been by questionnaire. Questionnaires are, of course, always open to faking, good or bad (Vernon, 1964). To minimize this, the questionnaires are not simply handed out to clients, they are completed in the presence of a member of staff. (In the curriculum, one member of staff has one half-day set aside to assess new clients). The member of staff explains the necessity to fill in the questionnaire with care and consideration, is alert to overly-consistent responses, and can seek further details if in doubt. Assessment results are then discussed at the weekly meeting of the members of staff and psychologists who constitute the social skills team. Results are further scrutinized at the programme planning meetings; this is held at the end of the 3-week assessment period and brings together the results of all assessments prior to drawing up a programme of activities for the client. Thus, there are two formalized opportunities to check on possible discrepancies between the client's self-report and other sources of information, apart from informal discussions among the staff. An attempt was made to undertake behavioural observation of some clients to check on faking. However, owing to the variety among timetables of individual clients, the only standard situations in which clients could be observed were the dining room and the clients' coffee and games lounge. The reaction of clients to observation in these settings indicated that they felt that it was an intrusion upon their privacy, in their free time, and the attempt was abandoned. The form of questionnaire currently in use is a relatively short one, covering 16 skills such as starting a conversation, expressing anger, negotiations and so on. Given that the clients undergo extensive assessment, it was felt important that the social skills assessment focus solely on problems with which the social skills team can help.

Any client who appears to have difficulties in regard to social skills will be offered help provided that: (a) he agrees that he has these difficulties and wishes to work on them; (b) that his difficulties are not due to some condition which would not be responsive to social skills training, e.g. active paranoid delusions; and (c) that he is intellectually capable of coping with the concepts involved. This latter proviso does not usually preclude clients from taking part, for example, clients with IQ's in the 60's have successfully been incorporated, although progress is slower owing to the need to take longer introducing and repeating explanations of the concepts. At times it has been necessary to run two groups: one for the "slower" and one for the "brighter" clients. This helps to obviate discouragement on the part of the former and frustration on that of the latter. With increasing unemployment, moreover, the centre is now admitting young ESN clients, who might have been working in happier times. These clients have social skills difficulties owing to disinhibited behaviour, as opposed to many of the older clients who tend to be over-inhibited. The balance in the current group of these two sorts of difficulties is promoting discussion of the necessity of developing a new group, since the more inhibited clients are becoming overwhelmed.

The problems defined by individual clients are discussed in weekly sessions with their key social skills worker. Clients select the area on which they wish to work, and set themselves "homework" tasks to complete outside the context of the group. Two members of the team conduct these individual sessions on Tuesday afternoon: at the end of the afternoon the members of the group congregate and a provisional plan is devised to cater for the individual target areas in role-play in the second weekly session which is held on Thursday. This structure is elaborated in the next session.

Important points to note are that: (a) whatever form of assessment is used, it should be as economical as possible. Assessment is often uncomfortable for the client, and therefore the client should be able to perceive its relevance; (b) results should be fed back to the client and the client should choose which areas he regards as priorities, rather than being fitted into a "course"; (c) selection of clients should, while allowing as wide a range as possible of clients to participate, be based on the degree to which they are liable to benefit. Including clients of doubtful motivation, or trying to fit social skills into an unsuitable organizational structure, is pointless.

III. PROCEDURAL DETAILS

The SST group takes place twice weekly (Tuesdays and Thursdays). Each session lasts for 1½ hours, which includes about 15 minutes after the session when staff compare notes on the particular events that took place and how clients managed with them. The group consists of 8–10 clients, 2 psychologists and 2 co-workers who are centre staff members. The co-workers see clients in their day-to-day life at the centre and the nearby community. Since different staff are involved on the Tuesday and Thursday sessions, we also have a social skills team meeting for one hour per week so that the staff can co-ordinate their activities across the 2 sessions. They discuss progress and new admissions to the group.

Perhaps the best introduction to this rather complicated set up would be to work through a discussion document originally presented to a "forum" of all the centre's staff. This was intended to familiarize other workers who may interact with group members with the aims and functions of the whole group.

Firstly, a definition was presented:

> The social skills group will focus on assisting clients in the business of approaching and interacting appropriately with other people at a behavioural level. This means focusing on assertive behaviour, general conversation skills etc. Therefore, the group will have a general interest in people who are under—and over—functioning in these areas. The group is not intended for specific phobic reactions, actively psychotic behaviour, inappropriate behaviour induced by drugs, or people who have skills but lack the motivation to use them.

The aim here was to define the areas we felt we could help clients in and to try and ensure appropriate referrals. Otherwise, there may be a tendency for difficult clients, or clients about whom people are concerned, to be referred to the group, when an alternative intervention—for example, medication review might be more helpful. Particular discussion or support groups exist to give clients an opportunity to air these other difficulties and provide help, whilst more specific behaviour problems could be dealt with more directly by desensitization, etc.

> The group will be open, with an 8 week review structure so that targets and programmes are monitored. Referrals for assessment for social skills are welcome from anyone, including those from outside the centre, but the Centre Head must be notified before a client, whose only contact with the centre is social skills, joins the group.
> No-one should be taken into the group without discussion with the co-ordinating worker and tutor taking place.

This part of the document deals with 3 points. Firstly, some of the people referred to the team had been in the centre for some time. Some had been in one institution or another for much of their adult lives. It was important to make sure that the group did not develop norms which inhibited change and merely become rewarding in itself as a place to meet regularly. This is of course, a problem which faces the day centre (or, indeed groups in any institution) as a whole. We felt it was important to give people the capacity to develop their own social relationships rather than just provide a haven from a rejecting social environment. The 8 weeks review, plus regular monitoring of targets was intended to emphasize progress, turnover and an expectation of change. Secondly, we had been receiving enquiries from social workers who felt that some of their clients were in need of SST, but could or would not attend the centre on a full time basis. It was hoped that these people would provide fresh "air" for the clients mentioned above, increase the range of interactional opportunities of group members and help us develop a wider community base. However, this type of referral has not been a very frequent occurrence and this may have something to do with the stigmatizing effect of coming to the centre. The last point refers to ensuring adequate consultation with other staff involved with the client. We have described the structure of selection as it relates to new clients. Clients who have been in the centre for some time may have a "co-ordinating worker". This is a member of the advisory staff, e.g. a psychologist, the teacher or centre social worker. This person has responsibility for ensuring that "difficult" clients, or those whose progress we are especially anxious to follow are adequately monitored. Not all clients have a co-ordinating worker, for example, those who attend the centre for recreational purposes and whose psychiatric condition is quiescent, do not.

Next, the structure was described:

> Tuesday afternoon's session will consist of 1½ hours group time and half an hour co-ordination, and Thursday afternoon 1½ hours group time and an hour for a meeting of the full social skills team.
> In detail, the Tuesday session will include: clarification, charting of progress feedback and role-play, if desirable.
> The Thursday session will include: discussion between Tuesday and Thursday teams on how things went in the Tuesday session, role-play with video-feedback if appropriate, integration and further role-play, and setting of homework targets. There will be outings every six weeks, used as an incentive.

Tuesday's session is attended by one psychologist and co-worker and all the group members. It is aimed to make sure that clients understood the skills role-played on the previous Thursday and related this to their targets. These targets are set individually. Each client is expected to try out skills they have learned in the group in the wider community. It was hoped that clients with similar problems would support and encourage each other in doing this and could then talk about their experiences in the group. This has happened in the case of most group members. Originally it had been intended to split the group up into 3 small groups for target-setting on Tuesdays. However, one member of staff dropped out and the 2 remaining workers ran the group together. Clients reported back on their targets and their results were recorded on wall-charts. This procedure was subsequently abandoned in favour of the clients seeing their key social skills worker individually. This was done for the following reasons: (a) the wall-charts induced a "school-room" atmosphere in the group which both the staff and the clients found uncomfortable; (b) some clients reported privately that they were faking good in reporting back on their targets, as they were reluctant to admit failure or difficulty in front of the whole group; and (c) it was sometimes difficult for the clients to maintain an appropriate level of interest in, and concern for, other clients' progress over the course of an hour. The individual approach overcomes these difficulties and enables a better relationship to develop between client and worker. It also assists in tailoring targets to the client's overall programme aims.

Potential problems deriving from the individual approach are that: (a) clients might "hold back" from discussing problems in the wider group; and (b) dependency on a single worker could develop to such a degree that it inhibits the change which might lead to graduation from the social skills group. The former can be tackled by making sure that clients understand that workers can also bring things for wider discussion when the group congregates at the end of the afternoon, if they are not of a confidential nature. The latter is a problem which we shall explore later.

Where Tuesday's session focuses on the generalization of skills, Thursday's session is more concerned with the practice of particular social behaviours and their integration into more complex sequences of social interaction. The content of Thursday's session is covered in the next section. However, it might be useful at this point to say that once clients have chosen an area to work on and have negotiated targets individual they are expected to bring this information with them to the later sessions and to integrate it into a group dramatic theme. Thus, the content of this skill learning/integration session depends upon targets relevant to the wider community and negotiated by the clients themselves.

Perhaps the most important and sometimes most overlooked aspect of an SST programme is the organization and co-ordination needed to keep things running smoothly. It is necessary to liaise with the rest of the centre and external agencies to co-ordinate feedback for both clients and workers and to maintain consistency between different parts of the team. We have found that the following procedure meets most of these needs:

(1) All newly admitted clients are assessed for social skills problems during the 3 week assessment period.
(2) The results of assessment are discussed at the social skills team meeting held on Thursday and a recommendation is made. A member of the team is designated to attend the Programme Planning Meeting, when programmes are drawn up for new clients, to present the recommendation.

   The social skills team meeting also reviews ongoing individual and group work.
(3) The client may be admitted to the social skills group, individual work may be more appropriate, or may be offered a combination of the two.
(4) The client's progress will be monitored at the team meeting and fed back to other staff in centre case review meetings.*

Points to note in this framework are:

(1) There is a particular need for careful liaison, as only one member of the team is based full time at the Centre.
(2) Clients who need social skills training are not necessarily admitted directly into the group. On occasions, especially if a client is very anxious he/she will be seen on an individual basis initially and introduced gradually into the group. Until recently we had another psychologist in the team who undertook the assessments and individual work. We have now successfully negotiated time for one of our co-workers to take over the assessment function and we, therefore, need only to address ourselves to putting time aside for individual work.
(3) The meetings may seem to occupy a prominent place in the framework, but they are vital to ensure that, for each client in the group, the social skills training input is closely tailored to his overall treatment programme and this is a goal which can only be reached by careful consultation with all staff involved with that client.

In addition, it must be remembered that SST, as indeed any other therapeutic intervention which involves the client confronting his problems, is quite a tough experience. In order to ensure that the client receives maximum encouragement and support, it is essential that the social skills team can count on the backing of other staff in achieving their goals.

* We are grateful to Pat Peart, Shirley Seagrove and Julie Lloyd for their contribution to the Social Skills Group.

IV. A TYPICAL SESSION

The team have found that the most useful basic format for the Thursday skills practice session consists of 3 "rolling" sessions which can be repeated for as long as the group continues: (1) in the first week, the group concentrates upon role playing specific skills; (2) in the second, the skills practiced by individuals or small groups are integrated into a performance by the whole group; (3) finally, a video tape of the second session is shown and discussed in the third session.

A. First session

The first session consists of role-playing specific areas of skill deficit, worked out individually by each client on Tuesdays in relation to their targets. Examples of the skills practiced might be: speaking assertively, listening, supporting another person. Due to pressure of time, individuals usually practice such skills in groups of 3. For instance, an example of a specific skill might be "taking something back to a shop". Once clients have role-played, staff and other clients model more appropriate responses and the original "cast" have another go. As a general rule, the more active clients are encouraged to take part first. This gives the more socially anxious the opportunity to observe others. Whilst this is going on, the rest of the group watches, having been asked to look out for and make suggestions about particular aspects of the strategy used (e.g. eye contact, posture, manner of speech). This whole process would be interspersed with discussion by the whole group. During discussion the group sits in a circle, the staff interspersed among the clients, i.e. not huddled together.

B. Second session

In the second session the individual role-plays described above are integrated into an exercise for the group as a whole. The organization and integration of individual targets into this dramatic exercise is negotiated by everybody taking part. We have found that this approach leads to realistic issues, relevant to the client's own experience being role-played. It also increases client motivation through participation and thus facilitates the generalization of the behaviours being transmitted. The approach also seems to have a positive influence on group cohesion and regular attendance.

A typical session might be "set" in a busy public bar. We all talk about the lay-out of the "scene", who is going to sit where, come in when, and what they are going to do. Each client is expected to spontaneously practice a targeted behaviour somewhere during the performance. The target, therefore, needs to be thought about, introduced and mixed into the flow of the ongoing interaction.

This whole session is videotaped and replayed during the next session. Obviously, consideration needs to be given to the positioning of the camera (as far away as possible) and a restrained use of "zooming-in", so that none of the, sometimes rather unpredictable, action is lost. The emphasis should be on including as much information as possible. rather than creating an aesthetic image. It is often the case that important aspects of the whole milieu are not noticed by the camera-user in the heat of the moment.

C. Third session and the use of video

In the final session the group views the "raw" videotape of the dramatic episode from session 2. The way that clients coped with their targets is discussed as they arise on tape. Before suggesting ways that video feedback can be given it might be useful to point out the ways in which it can uniquely contribute to training and therapy. Firstly, it gives a concrete image which is held separately from the participants' own memories of events. It is therefore less likely to be selectively retrieved and denied to fit what he/she wanted to think happened. This distinctness and distance from the original events also means that people can now see aspects of how they get on with other people other than those which preoccupied them whilst actively taking part. They may, for instance, become more aware of other people's feelings rather than their own particular aims, intentions and needs. Secondly, once on tape, events can be replayed repeatedly to distil more than one level of meaning from the original and emphasize points that the video users might want to make. If particular behaviours need to be emphasized, most equipment also has a stop button which can hold a single frame for about 2 minutes. Both of these points mean that client and therapist can now see their behaviour from the outside, perhaps as other people see them, and can repeat this image to clarify points of misunderstanding or difficulty.

A major problem when using video for the first time, is that the clients may be confronted with a disconcerting visual image of themselves. This "image impact", or "cosmetic shock" can be useful in producing changes in the way that the client presents to other people. However, as some clients expressed apprehension about seeing themselves on tape we felt that the cosmetic shock should be minimized. This can be done by increasing the time between the original event and the feedback session (in this case, one week). The added distance that this approach produces helps clients to concentrate upon the "skill-performing" aspects of the session. One must also be careful when using this technique to focus attention on aspects which can actually be changed, e.g. posture, hand movements, style of dress, etc., rather than those that can't, e.g. signs of ageing, irreversible physical disfigurement, etc.

If video users want to continue with the medium over several sessions they may also find it useful to focus on other "levels" of meaning. This may tend to happen spontaneously anyway. The process may go "downwards" to the "nuts and bolts" of body language and non-verbal behaviour, see Trower et al. (1978). Small bits of behaviour can then be rebuilt into a competent social performance. On the other hand, if one needs to focus "upwards" to the different levels of meaning in a conversation, a reasonably skilled observer of social behaviour can point attention to what your body is saying as opposed to what is being put into words. These, and the more complex aspects of social interaction can often be seen, but may be difficult to explain (Alger and Hogan, 1967; Willener et al., 1976).

As an example of the latter, on one occasion we were discussing dating members of the opposite sex in the group. During the subsequent role-play, a young male member spent a lot of time talking and trying to impress his friend. At the same time his non-verbal behaviour appeared withdrawn and inhibited. When the videotape was fed back, the group discussed the effect the behaviour had on the female members of the group. We managed to persuade him to attempt alternative ways of approaching the situation, e.g. to behave as he would to anyone that he doesn't know very well. This involved being much more sensitive, asking questions and paying attention. The point here was that verbal confrontation and the rejecting cues of the female members were not enough. When the client could see for himself, and when the behaviour was made concrete and was distanced from the original situation which provoked anxiety, he agreed to look at alternative behaviours. Only then could we begin to work on his attention towards cues from others, and the overall impact of the elements of his social behaviour. His underlying lack of self confidence and shyness could then be approached in a relatively safe way and it might then be possible to explore different strategies of interaction which could be learnt using the "nuts and bolts" method.

The degree to which one needs to take the lead using video in this way, would of course depend upon the intellectual ability and social adjustment of the clients involved. Although video may be more useful when putting points across to more inarticulate people, the degree to which one concentrates "upwards" or "downwards", or chooses to be more or less directive, must be expected to depend on the degree of spontaneous insight that different people get from the medium.

In continuing therapy it may also be useful to play back either the visual or the audio channels separately to emphasize the particular sort of communication that one is interested in (Geertsma and Reivich, 1969). When focusing "upwards" this technique could be used to show that there is more than one meaning being communicated. When focusing "downwards" it allows the client to concentrate on one area at a time and master that area rather than getting swamped with a whole mass of social interaction. Of course, if one can decide beforehand to look at, for example, facial movement or hand movement, it might be possible to focus the camera on these areas. If one wants to restrict the record of events to this aspect only, it might even be useful to block out the parts of the screen which are distracting. This may sound a little drastic but in fact it is surprising how much people tend to concentrate on areas other than those which are central.

Then, in the previous example, it was necessary to play back sound and then the video separately and ask him to describe the messages that were being given. In this way the discrepancy between his verbal and non-verbal performance was highlighted. A second way of "interfering" with the raw feedback is to stop it at turning points in the events being taped and provoke discussion on alternative strategies which the participants could have used at that point (Rackham and Morgan, 1977). For example, one group had decided to look at arguments and how to get around them. The scene was then set again. Someone had taken another's chair and things were beginning to escalate into defending the self and attacking the other. The tape was stopped at the point just before things hotted up, and we discussed different ways of dealing with the situation. A tape of an appropriate role-play, or a model-tape can then be played and discussed.

This may be a useful way of associating these alternatives with the preceding events which usually led to aggression. In this situation, model tapes demonstrating skilled interaction were also found to be particularly useful for showing appropriate behaviour. We found that 3–4 minutes was long enough for a model tape but this depends upon the attention span of the client group and the complexity and longevity of the behavioural sequences which need emphasis. It isn't necessary to worry about making an imperfect model tape as imperfect performances often seem to make the point well and don't overawe the viewers. They are also a useful means of stimulating the initial discussion.

Unfortunately at the moment it is difficult to give precise guidelines on when *not* to present video feedback. This depends upon the anxiety of the people involved and the severity of their attempts as shown on the tape. As a general rule we try not to use video with depressed people who tend to select negative aspects of themselves to confirm a negative self image (Biggs *et al.*, 1980). Video is probably most useful with people whose habitual ways of dealing with information involve denial and intellectualization (Nadelson *et al.*, 1977), or who find it difficult to articulate verbal descriptions of social and non-verbal behaviour.

We shall now describe two case examples.

Client A is a 26 year old man. Since his 20th birthday, he has been admitted 3 times to the local psychiatric hospital. The longest stay lasting for 2 months. He had been diagnozed as depressed with schizophrenic symptoms. These have included hearing voices and crawling on the floor "like a snake". Following the last admission it was suggested that he attend the centre, where he has been for the last 9 months. In this time we have not seen these signs of active psychosis. The centre's psychometric team report that he is of normal intelligence and he scores 17 on the Venables (1957) Activity-Withdrawal Scale. This places him in the underactive range.

He was referred to the social skills group because of his withdrawn behaviour. He would spend most of his time sitting curled up in a ball, or asleep in the community room at the centre and made no move to get to know other clients or attend discussion groups. However, he did attend the centre regularly. He saw his social skill problems in terms of being able to start, carry on and end a conversation, expressing anger and apologizing. He had a fairly severe stutter.

In view of this client's withdrawal and lack of motivation to attend other groups, one of the psychologists saw him individually for 8 weeks, after which he agreed to attend the group itself. During this period he practised self-relaxation, and basic communication skills in a relatively safe setting, concentrating on becoming aware of other people's feelings and attitudes in order to reduce his overly self critical introspection. He also attended speech therapy at this time. However, the therapist who was involved felt that progress was unlikely to be made until he developed more self confidence. We agreed to keep in contact and "compare notes" on any progress that this client made in different settings.

The client sat quietly in the group for several sessions and rarely spoke unless he was asked questions. We made sure that he had a minor role in any dramatic sessions and concentrated on helping him to feel part of the group. At this point we aimed to increase his listening and attending skills whilst reducing his anxiety. During feedback sessions he was asked to look out for particular skills in other people's behaviour. As he began to take a more active part in the group we encouraged him to use his non-verbal behaviour to express his feelings, and thus continue non-verbal and verbal expressions whilst concentrating on other people's behaviour. Finally, we asked him to participate in specific role-plays with a small number of people (2–3) and practice the skills that he had been observing.

He has now been attending the group for about 6 months and is participating in the day-to-day social activity in the centre insofar as he actively attends to other people. However, he still waits for others to approach him and rarely takes the initiative in social interaction, except when making specific predictable requests. He says that he now feels more confident and does not avoid situations where he knows that he will have to meet other people. He has recently begun to attend evening classes at a local Technical College. The reports from the Speech Therapist indicate that this client now shows more insight into the existence of communications skills and is more confident in his ability to use them. His stutter has begun to decrease.

Future treatment plans for this client include specifying particular situations which can be role-played and increasing his skills in extended conversation. We also hope to focus on behaviours which are likely to be rewarded naturally, such as asking questions, positive assertion and decision making. We are encouraging group members with similar difficulties to form a support group for journeys into the local community.

Client B is a 20 year old man who was referred to the centre by his Probation Officer following incidents of indecent exposure. He had no previous "history" with Social Service agencies and denied that these incidents had taken place, considering the issue shameful and embarrassing. He seemed to have little understanding of his own and others sexuality. He scored 75 on the Wechsler Adult Intelligence Scale which indicated that he was of dull normal intelligence. A Venables "rating scale for activity withdrawal" score of 35 showed that he was prone to be over-active. There were no signs of psychosis.

At the beginning of his stay, staff reported that he was highly anxious and in need of continual reassurance. It seemed that he had few friends outside the centre. When thwarted in an activity he would respond with an outburst of agression. He would often deny difficulty in social situations, whilst pointing to inflated examples of success in other areas. He saw his social skills problems in terms of expressing anger.

We felt that this client needed a wider repertoire of social skills, particularly in situations which might evoke anxiety or frustration, and his treatment programme should include elements which would help him to articulate and give structure to his social interaction. In particular, we needed to create an environment in which he felt safe enough to explore the implications that his current coping styles had on other people. For the first few sessions he was left to make a role for himself in the drama activities. As far as possible, the team attempted to involve him in discussion and decisions taken by the whole group about how these events could be set up. At the same time he was given targets of a highly specific and concrete nature to perform outside the group. These targets were in the area of conversation skills. We then began to invite feedback from other group members about his behaviour. Specific techniques, such as role reversal and video feedback were also used to focus his attention upon particular areas of dysfunction and as an aid to recognizing and labelling emotional expressions. During this period his treatment programme was largely concentrated upon problem-solving activities and identifying discriminative cues which might lead to misunderstanding. It was important to "set" feedback in such a way that it highlighted the benefits of this strategy consistent with the suggestions concerning feedback made earlier.

As time went on, incidents of frustration decreased, at least within the centre. He had also found himself a place amongst peers of a similar disposition where much of his disinhibited behaviour was accepted, or at least tolerated. At the same time, however, there was little evidence that this had generalized to the home situation where he was increasingly being placed under pressure to find a job. It became clear that contradictions were appearing in his stay in the centre. Were we encouraging this client to stay at the centre, rather than develop contacts in the wider community? How realistic were his parents' aspirations? How far was he blocking further skill development? How far did he need it?

At the beginning of his stay we had concentrated on increasing his feelings of self-worth by participation, increasing insight into the way that others expressed emotion and the effects of his own behaviour. He had been relatively specific regarding the area that he wanted to focus on. Since joining the group his social behaviour had changed within the centre, but was beginning to approach levels of disinhibition which were disrupting other activities in the centre. Eventually, we concluded that his new needs would now best he met elsewhere: firstly, in a more structured "communications group", where skills such as using the telephone, travel and general interview skills could be learned in small steps; and secondly in a discussion group where other means of exploring his current problems were available. This plan was therefore accepted.

This client has now begun to attend a local residents' community centre where has made a few friends. However, the parents were not willing to be included in ongoing casework and he still attends the centre on a regular basis. The local employment situation has deteriorated to such an extent that it is unlikely that he will gain full- or part-time employment.

V. THERAPISTS

Not all staff can teach social skills, whatever their state of text-book knowledge. For example, the "overwarm" supervisor emits a thousand random reinforcers a minute, much of it reinforcing maladaptive behaviour; or, the benevolent authoritarian "let me decide for you, my sick dear". These therapist styles are quite independent of formal qualifications. Truax and Carkhuff (1967) have shown that empathy, congruence and non-possessive warmth are essential ingredients for counselling and that they are unrelated to grades in clinical exams. Perhaps a slightly different list of qualities is needed for the effective practice of social skills, but a similar lack of relevance of professional qualifications almost certainly holds.

The good social skills worker, as with any other type of therapy must:

(*a*) be willing to accept criticism of their work and style;
(*b*) accept interpretation of their own behaviour in terms of their own personality; and
(*c*) have an ability to grasp basic behavioural principles.

Thus, little improvement in their ways of working can be achieved if they adamantly refuse to see that they are over-mothering or over-protecting people. Social skills also aims to work within the scientific, research framework and therefore it is necessary that the worker is prepared to allow his work to be objectively assessed and has some understanding of the aims, purposes and methods of research methodology.

Burden (1981) has suggested the ideal size of team for any psychological project is 2, and we would think this is the correct size for the social skills *face-workers*. Additionally, they must have somebody to talk to and discuss their work and that person should sit in on some of the sessions to see how things are going. The merit of keeping the actual workers to 2 is that this allows the formal training to be relatively easy to organize in terms of time-tabling and does not diffuse the skills so thin that "everyone in this centre teaches social skills". It should be emphasized that the need for a small specialist team does not contradict the point made earlier that everyone in the institution must be aware of the approach used by the team and be minimally sympathetic to it. Otherwise generalization is not going to stand any chance.

Selection of SST therapists depends on the qualities outlined above, plus a willingness to be flexible not only in terms of personality, but also in terms of time. *In vivo* assessments of clients' competence, such as going out for a meal, or to the pub, cannot always be fitted into standard working hours. A final attribute is that they should have some commitment to stay in the same job for say, a year, minimum, since it will take up to 6 months or even longer to make them good social skills workers and it is rather disheartening, both for clients and those working with them if they move on too quickly. While this is less of a problem in the present economic climate, it may well be worth thinking about taking somebody who is slightly less potentially capable but is more likely to stay longer in the centre, rather than someone who will be on the first bus to a better job should the opportunity arise.

As regards the training of therapists, there are a number of points to note:

(1) If possible, use video, so that staff can see their non-verbal behaviour. Where this is not possible, a combination of advisory staff sitting in and the use of audio is quite powerful. However, do not get hooked on the idea that if you haven't got a video then you are doing second rate social skills.
(2) The aim must be for the advisory staff to create maximal trust between him/herself and the "face"-workers. She/he will not always be there when crises arise and will need to be able to get a reliable and self-critical account later to be able to draw out lessons for next time. It is obviously also important that the "face"-workers have a supportive and trusting relationship between themselves.

    A lot of time must be spent looking at the personalities of the workers, including the advisers and building up the trust. Once this is done, it may be quite useful to have staff and advisers rating each other's performances on a simple checklist.
(3) Get the clients to rate their progress toward the goals they have chosen to work on at given intervals as a form of feedback to the staff.
(4) As described above, the clients define the areas they want to work on themselves. There is now evidence from the work of Lazare *et al.*

(1975) that the "consumer approach" is useful in preventing dropping-out from treatment. It also ties in with the point made earlier about excluding clients who really do not care whether they are socially skilled or not. The group sessions themselves can be regularly rated on simple consumer dimensions such as utility, interest, enjoyment. This will give some feedback as to how the therapists are functioning.

(5) Besides the regular reviews of progress by the social skills team, there should be regular case reviews of the clients' general progress involving all staff. This, as well as promoting generalization, is also a useful training format. It allows the workers to see how their work is fitting into the general context.

We have discussed in some detail the importance of, and ways of achieving, the involvement of other staff in a SST programme. So far, however, we have not looked at the involvement of families. We can all tell social skills horror stories of the inapplicability of SST without careful consideration of the family context. For example, the young man who was carefully trained to offer to make the tea at home only to be told by his father to pack it in as it was his (the father's) job. The pseudo-professional status of family work can be seen in many day centres/hospitals which admit the "patient" and then after fully assessing him (in the family's eyes, firming up the diagnosis) send out a family worker to place his problems in a family context. Not surprisingly, he often comes running back to the centre talking about uninsightful (i.e. non co-operative) families. If we are considering the family's reactions as important to social skills, we need to have an assessment and treatment system which treats the family as the unit of concern, not the unit of treatment. No one likes being called ill, especially when they haven't asked to see the doctor and especially when it is not a doctor that comes to see them but some young woman from the welfare.

If the family is the unit of concern, the crucial assessments need to be done *before* anyone is admitted to the centre. You have to get the family to a stage where they can see that there is a common problem to which they are all contributing. Only then can you take one member out for a specialist treatment and one is surprised how often other family members benefit from activities outside the home (luncheon clubs, craft activities, discussion groups, etc.) in the same centre as their son is getting his social skills training in. It may also be better if social skills sessions are not in day centres/hospitals but in less stigmatizing places, such as social work offices, GP surgeries and further education classrooms. The involvement of families brings us back to the point about flexibility about working hours. It is not acceptable to define as "unmotivated" a family member who is not prepared to lose 2 or 3 hours' pay to be there when you want to visit. On the other hand, it may be decided that it would be better not to involve the family. For example when the aim of the treatment programme is to enable the client to become more independent and make his own decisions. In any event, a visit to the family must only be undertaken with the permission of the client.

We have found that working with less intellectually competent clients, where progress is slow and repetition necessary, can be draining on the enthusiasm of the most committed staff. Consequently with such clients it may be helpful for staff to have a "break" from the group at intervals, to try and prevent staleness. Alternatively the whole group may have periodic breaks, to allow the team time to review the programme and consider innovations.

VI. OUTCOME AND GENERALIZATION

The question of outcome is best restricted to what is going on in social skills. In terms of social skills, 2 sets of measures are needed:

(1) Did the person achieve the goals that were set in the group?
(2) Did they generalize?

The first question we tackle by getting the clients to repeat their initial assessment at intervals and by examining the results closely with the clients. Clients also have progress books, used in the individual sessions. By reporting back on homework in terms of a simple scale (very difficult/difficult/average/easy/very easy) a graph can be drawn up. The clients seem to find this helpful so long as this is done on an individual basis, rather than in the group. The second question is more important. We have found it easier to obtain reliable information from families (using the Rating of Behaviour in Social Situations) than from the staff. Family memberships tend to stay constant, while staff change; and we have found inter-staff reliability to be practically nil. What one staff sees as withdrawal, another staff sees as being polite. Thus, we have tended to rely on the client's report as to his progress, backed up by the observations of a number of staff as to his general behaviour in the centre, and on outings outside the centre. Initially devised as reinforcement for participation in SST, these outings also provide a useful opportunity to observe the client's behaviour regarding bus-conductors, unhelpful shop assistants, etc. Outings also provide an opportunity for the clients to receive feedback which is often more realistic than that available in the Centre, where there is a tendency for staff and clients to tolerate inappropriate behaviours. On a recent outing to a pub, when 2 or 3 of the clients' voices became progressively raised and horse-play developed, a member of the public enquired of them whether it was "their age or their mental ability" which accounted for their behaviour. This feedback was much more powerful than any of our discussions or video feedback!

At risk of labouring the point, the co-operation of the other staff is vital if skills learned in the group are to generalize outside it. For example, while teaching a client who is hesitant to tackle authority figures, another staff cuts straight across him, and without so much as a word of apology, talks to that staff member, perhaps pausing only briefly to comment unfavourably on the client stalking off swearing. What hope of encouraging this client to approach a member of the public if he gets this response in the supposedly considerate environment of the centre? One final point about involving other staff: a sure way to alienate staff is to be over-concerned with confidentiality. As a general rule, clients in the centre are assured of confidentiality *only* in terms of information being discussed only among persons involved in his treatment programme. Confidentiality about what happens in a group is seen as unhelpful; it prevents adequate liaison between staff and makes intelligent comment on the work of the group impossible. Of course there is a need for confidentiality when somebody is discussing highly intimate details of their life, but social skills training is not the right place for this. Thus, if you have to be confidential about your social skills group, you are in fact not running a social skills group, but a "watered-down" therapy group. Of course, we are not saying that feelings and experiences do not have to be discussed in social skills groups, but they should be discussed in such a manner as to allow other staff to be informed about their general drift.

Once skills are learned and generalized, they may need "topping up". For this, it is important that the group be an open one, so that a client may be re-admitted quickly if he needs preparation for a particularly daunting experience—role-playing appearing at a DHSS tribunal, for example. You might even consider an "old social skills boys group". Remember, the golden rule that over-learning never does any harm. You may well want to continue getting feedback from clients on a skill that caused them difficulty which they can now do with ease, long after they had started to do it with ease. As in all anxiety problems, regular exercise of a potientially difficult skill is essential.

VII. PROBLEMS AND SOME HINTS ON SOLUTIONS

We have discussed a variety of pitfalls which may beset a SST programme, or other therapeutic endeavours for that matter. Central to most of them seem to be the amount of support and constructive criticism one can expect from colleagues.

If possible, work in teams so you're not not isolated from feedback and from a bit of political power. Two people are harder to deter than one. Try to get an outside person who can listen intelligently and make hypotheses that you can take or leave but can be worked on. Research your work so that it may convince some of the more interested but sceptical staff. If you haven't the time, contact the local psychologists at the nearest college, hospital or university: they may well find a student to do it for you. To convince staff on the therapeutic side, try to familiarize yourself with the total programme of the clients in your group so that your work feeds in to that of the other staff. They will then be pleasantly surprised how your work on his behaviour enables the clients to participate more in other sessions run by other staff. This may help in generating interest and support for your work. Find out who's doing similar work in nearby centres to give yourself a wider perspective so that what you call socially skilled behaviour is not at odds with the cultural norms in the area from which your clients come.

However, these hints may be of no use at all. It may be a case of "if the ground isn't right, don't waste your seeds". As we described in the introductory section, compromises tend to have an accelerating effect and the group's function can move further and further away from the ideal as time passes. It may then be better to concentrate your efforts elsewhere or to tackle the philosophy of the institution head-on.

VIII. REFERENCES

Alger, I. and Hogan, P. (1967). The use of videotape recording in conjoint marital therapy. *Am. J. Psychiatry* **123**, 1425–1430.

Baekeland, F. and Lundwall, L. (1975). Dropping out of treatment: a critical review. *Psych. Bull.* **82**, 738–83.

Bender, M. P. (1976a). Mental health services in Newham, with special reference to the Worland Centre. Modified version of a paper at the London Hospital, April 7th.

Bender, M. P. (1976b). "Community psychology". Methuen, London.

Biggs, S., Rosen, B. and Summerfield, A. (1980). Video feedback and personal attribution in anorexic depressed and normal viewers. *Br. J. Med. Psychol.* **53** **(3)**, 249–254.

Burden, R. (1981). The educational psychologists as instigator and agent of change in schools: some guidelines for successful practice. *In* "Reconstructing Psychological Practice" (I. McPherson and A. Sutton, *Eds*), pp. 45–51. Croom Helm, London.

Geertsma, R. and Reivich, R. (1969). Auditory and visual dimensions of self-observation. *J. Nerv. Ment. Dis.* **148**, 210–223.

Henny, L. (1978). "Film and Video in sociology". Media Studies Program, Utrecht.

Hutt, S. J. and Hutt, D. (1970). "Direct Observation and Measurement of Behaviour". Thomas, London.

Kennard D. and Clemmey, R. (1976). Psychiatric patients as seen by self and others: an exploration of change in a therapeutic community setting. *Br. J. Med. Psychol.* **49**, 35–53.

Lazare, A., Eisenthal, S. and Wasserman, L. (1975). The customer approach to patienthood. *Arch. Gen. Psychiatry* **32**, 133–137.

Rackham, N. and Morgan, T. (1977). "Behaviour Analysis in Training". McGraw-Hill, London.

Trower, P., Bryant, B. and Argyle, M. (1978). "Social Skills and Mental Health". Methuen, London.

Truax, C. B. and R. R. Carkhuff, (1967). "Towards effective counselling and psychotherapy". Aldine, Chicago.

Venables, P. H. (1957). A short scale for measuring activity-withdrawal in schizophrenics. *Ment. Sci.* **103**, 197–199.

Vernon, P. E. (1964). Personality assessment: A critical survey. Methuen, London.

Willener, A., Milliard, G. and Ganty, A. (1976). "Videology and Utopia". Routledge and Kegan Paul, London.

5

Life skills training in prisons and the community

JAMES McGUIRE AND PHILIP PRIESTLEY

I. INTRODUCTION

Social skills training (SST), strictly defined, refers to a collection of methods which can be used to help individuals behave more appropriately and effectively in interactions with others. It is designed, in the majority of cases, for those whose social reactions fail to reach a norm; whose behaviour can be described as being in some way marked by a "deficit" or lack of skill. It employs a specific set of techniques, such as *modelling* (demonstration and imitation of proficient social performance), *practice* (repetition and gradual approximation towards desired goals), and *feedback* (instruction and/or reinforcement related to the degree of progress someone is making); and it is focused for the most part on skills, like the use of bodily signals or the fluency of speech, which could be characterized as the "elements" or "building blocks" of more complex social behaviour. Used in this form, SST is identified most closely with psychiatry; and has been applied quite extensively in the clinical field (e.g. Trower, *et al.*, 1978), though it has also been used to help a variety of other groups, for example to give training in heterosocial skills, or in assertiveness (Bellack and Hersen, 1979). In a different vein, SST has been employed to help trainees acquire "professional" interpersonal skills required in a number of occupations (Ellis, 1980; Hargie *et al.*, 1981; Ivey and Authier, 1978; Priestley and McGuire, 1983).

A variant form of SST, which has developed as an outgrowth of it, is known as *life skills training*. Though using similar methods, this differs slightly from SST in that it is usually concerned with more complex kinds of skill which might be called for when dealing with everyday situations in which "survival" is at stake. "Survival" as used here does not denote some dramatic life-or-death struggle, but refers simply to the kinds of encounter in which an individual must strive to maintain his or her standard of living—by securing a job, asserting rights, managing money, "coping with the system"; or will end up worse off than before.

In this chapter, we want to describe a project, funded by the Home Office Research Unit between 1975 and 1978, which tested the usefulness of this kind of training with groups of adult male offenders in custodial and non-custodial settings. The "custodial" settings in this case were two prisons, Ranby and Ashwell; the "non-custodial" setting was the Day Training Centre, Sheffield, an alternative to prison run by the probation service. The aims of the project were to set up special "release courses" in the two prisons and develop a programme of "social and remedial" education in the Day Training Centre; and to monitor the running of these courses and evaluate their overall effects.

In practical terms, a life skills training session would approach the problem of helping individuals act more effectively in some sphere of their lives by deploying methods which are parallel to those used in SST. Some encounter—be it a job interview, attempt to resist sales pressure, or effort to calm down a potentially inflammatory situation—would be examined in detail; the merits of various strategies for handling it would be discussed; individuals might try a number of ways of negotiating it in a series of role-plays; and others would comment on whether these would be likely to succeed or whether the performance needed to be further polished. Partly as a consequence of the kinds of issues to which it is addressed, and partly because of the areas in which it has been developed, life skills training would supplement this basic diet of interaction training with a number of other ingredients.

One of these would be information; an "input" of facts regarding the law, leisure opportunities, the job market or whatever other data were relevant to the problem under discussion. The concept of "life skills training" emerged from work with socially disadvantaged groups, as part of a number of compensatory education programmes in North America; hence, the groups at whom it was aimed were often very badly informed about the operation of the world around them. Associated with this, life skills training also aims to foster the growth of what are known as "problem-solving" skills—a range of competencies, such as fact-finding, decision-making, analysing the consequences of actions, or generating alternative courses of action, which are indispensible for the solving of many of life's difficulties whether large or small. Thus training of this kind deals not only with the behavioural components of a skill, but also with the cognitive processes which (presumably) underlie it.

Programmes founded on life skills training or analogues of it have been shown to be effective for helping the socially disadvantaged to make more of their lives, solve their problems more effectively, and see themselves in a more positive light. Results on these lines have been reported from an evaluation study of the Saskatchewan Newstart life skills project (Saskatchewan Newstart, 1973). This project, directed at groups of disadvantaged adolescents and adults, took the form of a series of "life skills courses", each lasting several weeks, in which a total of 295 individuals took part between 1969–1973. The courses, for which a substantial quantity of back-up resource materials was produced— including manuals, slides, audio-tapes, films and a variety of other teaching aids—all followed a similar format in which a number of key "life skills" (such as fact-finding) were first developed, and then applied to a number of "life areas" (job, family, leisure, community) in which it was expected they would prove useful. The course content therefore extended from fairly simple exercises with limited aims, such as "Seeing oneself on video", to much more elaborate activities running over several sessions, concerned with topics like "Solving a financial crisis" or "Raising a family alone". Evaluation of these courses, and comparisons made between their graduates and others on a "control" course of straightforward basic education, proved favourable to the life skills courses both on post-test and follow-up criteria (Warren and Lamrock, 1973).

Other projects employing methods akin to those tested in the Saskatchewan study have produced similarly encouraging results. The work of Spivack and his associates (Shure, 1980; Spivack, et al., 1976), which assessed the value of training in problem-solving skills with several different groups, has suggested that psychiatric patients, juvenile offenders, and various other populations can benefit from a series of exercises which deal directly with quite complex kinds of problems and social situations.

Although only a few studies so far have reported on the possible applications of SST with offender groups, the broad indications are that its effects can be beneficial. Research work has shown that SST can be used successfully to improve the conversation skills of delinquent girls (Maloney *et al.*, 1976), the basic communication skills of adolescent male offenders (Spence and Marzillier, 1979), and the job interview performance of delinquent boys (Braukmann *et al.*, 1974). It can help "egocentric" juvenile offenders to appreciate other people's points of view through participation in role-play (Chandler, 1973), and can contribute to the general social adjustment of adolescent offender groups (Sarason and Ganzer, 1973; Thelen *et al.*, 1974). It can help adults to restrain their abusive verbal outbursts (Frederiksen *et al.*, 1976), and can assist alcoholics who want to learn to refuse drinks (Foy *et al.*, 1975). SST can also enable delinquent youths to negotiate conflicts with their parents more successfully (Kifer *et al.*, 1974), and it can boost young offenders' self-esteem and sense of self-control in the short-term (Spence and Spence, 1980). Encounters with police, which many young offenders find difficult and handle badly (Piliavin and Briar, 1964) can be dealt with more constructively following SST (Werner *et al.*, 1975). Finally, SST can prove valuable for helping sex offenders to cope more appropriately with social situations, and to feel more relaxed in the company of others (Burgess *et al.*, 1980; Crawford, 1976).

It would be surprising if no questions remained unanswered considering the modicum of research that has been conducted to date. One major query concerns the durability of gains made in social skills training sessions, with the results of some researchers (e.g. Spence and Marzillier, 1981) suggesting these lack any real persistence. Another issue is whether training effects are generalized to behaviours other than the "target" or to social settings other than the training session (Shepherd, 1978; Spence and Marzillier, 1981). Yet in the Chandler (1973) and Sarason and Ganzer (1973) research cited above, long-term follow-up studies (after 18 months and 3 years respectively) showed that those who had participated in social skills sessions were less likely to *re-offend* than their counterparts in placebo and control groups.

Taking the modest success of SST in helping offenders to alter some aspects of their social behaviour; and given the encouraging results of life skills training in aiding individuals towards solution of their real-life problems, it seemed worthwhile to look at the potential of a "life skills package" for work with offenders in this country. The project described here was intended to explore this possibility. This project was not an "experiment" with placebos, no-treatment controls, etc., in the normal sense of the word. The research was developmental and action-oriented in nature, and had to comply with the day-to-day demands of the prisons and Day Training Centre (DTC) in which it was housed—a central question of the project being whether activities of this type *could* be carried on in these sorts of places. Evaluative material was gathered both while the project was in progress and afterwards.

Although comprising a single project, the prison and DTC courses differed somewhat in terms both of content and style of operation, and are best described separately. A fuller account of the whole project is given elsewhere (Priestley *et al.*, 1982).

II. RELEASE COURSES IN RANBY AND ASHWELL

Prisons in this country have a long tradition of preparing prisoners to resume their lives in the outside world, via vocational training and work-release schemes on the one hand, and the ministrations of prison welfare or probation officers on the other. There have also been spasmodic attempts to provide routine pre-release courses, typically consisting of set-piece lectures by representatives of social security and other helping agencies, followed by question-and-answer sessions. There is hardly any evidence to suggest that these schemes have been effective, either in their more limited aims of equipping discharged prisoners to compete more effectively in the labour market and to settle into the community; *or* in their more global but sometimes understated ambition of reducing rates of criminal reconviction (Bottoms and McClintock, 1973; Soothill, 1973). There is, in fact, virtually no evidence for the effectiveness of *any* conventional "penal treatment" method in reducing offence rates (Brody, 1976).

The "release courses" to be outlined here were distinctive in two ways. Firstly, they sought to introduce an element of social and life skills training into the preparation of the prisoner for life in the community; and secondly, it was proposed that basic-grade prison officers be trained to act as tutors on full-time courses incorporating these methods. A number of obstacles lay across the path that led from the formulation to the achievement of these objectives.

The first hurdle was simply the magnitude of the problems which face the newly released prisoner. In a very short period following release he or she must resume broken relationships with family and friends, or establish new ones where this is not possible; must find accommodation and work; and must negotiate the serpentine procedures that surround the payment of social security benefits. These tasks, difficult enough for many ordinary citizens to order to their own satisfaction, are all the more so for the ex-prisoner, who begins the race burdened with special handicaps. Some of the latter derive from the legal and extra-legal disadvantages of the convicted criminal, but others have to do with the personal attributes of offenders and with the nature of imprisonment itself.

Offenders in general, and prisoners in particular, do not lend themselves to easy classification, but there are a number of well documented factors related to the likelihood of individuals becoming detected delinquents. They are male rather than female; usually young, urban, and working class; and they personify in their lives many of the classic indices of social and psychological deprivation (Rutter and Madge, 1976; West and Farrington, 1973). These include poverty; poor accommodation; bad health; criminal parents, siblings and peers; and fragmented or non-existent work records. Although many delinquent careers fade away with advancing age, there are some offenders whose personal characteristics appear to interact with the penal and prison environment in a way that makes them progressively less able to lead independent lives of their own. The extreme form of this condition has been labelled "institutional neurosis" (Barton, 1966).

Another difficulty confronted this project in the shape of the uniformed prison officer. Since 1963 it has been the official policy of the Prison Officers' Association to press for the involvement of its members in "welfare" or rehabilitative work within the prison system (Prison Officers Association, 1963). The immediate response of the Prison Department to this initiative at the time it was made was to set up a joint working party with the Association on "The role of the modern prison officer". This working party has been in session ever since without visible effect on the roles of more than a handful of "modern" prison officers. Most recruits to the prison service are attracted to the work because of its security and the high wages which extensive overtime makes available. Advertising, selection, and basic training for the service reflect the essentially disciplinary nature of the officer's ordinary duties (Thomas, 1972).

A third set of problems derived from the institutional matrix in which both officers and prisoners find themselves locked (Zimbardo, 1973). The cloven social structure of the contemporary prison has long historical roots and mirrors a state of enduring hostility between captors and captives; between officers and prisoners; between "screws" and "cons". Recent staff militancy has aggravated these divisions and lent a keener note to the prisoner's complaint that "all screws are bastards" (Priestley, 1980).

Finally, prisoners tend to resent theories of criminal causation and the reformatory practices they promote which insist that offenders are in need of psychiatric attention (Boyle, 1977). Life skills methods, in stressing the role of the subject in the definition and amelioration of personal deficits, promised one possible answer to this difficulty. Coupled with this, there was also evidence from the United States that "naive" or briefly-trained agents (as an alternative to "therapists") are capable of implementing sophisticated approaches to personal change— with results that challenge those obtained by qualified and experienced workers (Gartner, 1971; Goodman, 1972).

Given these difficulties then, the question which this research asked and attempted to answer was; "Can either or both of these innovations (social/life skills training in the hands of prison officer tutors) be made to work in the context of the English prison system?". Facilities for testing this proposition were requested at Dartmoor and Dorchester, both West Country prisons; but by processes which only keen students of administrative routines will fully appreciate, we were offered Ranby and Ashwell, both in the Midlands. Ranby, a category "C" security prison, houses 400 or so prisoners in billet-style huts within a secure fence erected around a former army camp. Its workshops are equipped for the production of woodwork and for electromechanical assembly, and the prison provides a number of training courses in the building and construction trades. Ashwell, also a former army camp accommodating 400 men, is an open prison with no perimeter security, which does not normally accept prisoners convicted of sexual or violent offences.

A. Preparation and staff training

At the commencement of the project, materials of various kinds which appeared appropriate to the problems of the departing prisoner were assembled, piloted, and used to form the basis of a "curriculum" addressed to such difficulties as finding and keeping work, managing money, handling personal relationships and so on. Throughout the duration of the project, materials were constantly being developed or borrowed from elsewhere, and retained or discarded according to the reactions they evoked amongst prisoner groups.

Also at this stage, a number of decisions were made about the overall organization of courses. It was decided that courses would be for 12 prisoners at a time; that attendance would be voluntary; that each course would be advertized in the prisons, and all those leaving within specified dates (usually covering a 3-month interval) would be eligible to attend. It was also decided that where there were more than 12 applicants, the officers would select from amongst them. Two officers would run each course. The length of the courses was initially envisaged as 12 weeks, but this subsequently proved too daunting a prospect for officers and research workers alike.

The next phase of the work was the training of prison and probation officers in the use of course materials. The agenda for the staff training course—especially for the prison officers who had no previous social work or teaching experience—was a formidable one, covering basic skills in interviewing, teaching, and leading group discussions. In addition, the prospective course tutors were asked to assimilate the basic ideas and methods of SST, including the use of role-play and videotape recording; to become reasonably adept in the use of vocational guidance materials; and to master a variety of assessment and testing techniques. Two training courses for staff were held, the first of 6 weeks in late 1975, the second of 5 weeks a year later. They were attended by 13 officers from Ranby and Ashwell prisons, and by 2 probation officers from Sheffield Day Training Centre. The courses themselves were intended, at least in part, to be an analogue of the courses the staff would subsequently run with groups of prisoners and probationers. They adopted a "skills training" approach for learning how to interview, teach, and run groups. This comprised an examination and demonstration of each skill followed by instruction, role-play and practice; observational and video feedback on performance; followed by more rehearsal and practice. As a project, the officers were also asked to plan and run a one week release course for prisoners in other establishments than their own.

B. Release course membership

During the "experimental" period from January 1976 until the end of December 1977 the trained officers ran 11 courses at Ranby, and 8 at Ashwell. They varied in length from 1–10 weeks, but the majority were of 4, 6, or 8 weeks' duration, with the modal length being 6 weeks. The courses lasted 5 days per week full-time—starting at 8.00 am and continuing till the end of the prison working day at 4.30 pm. Applicants for courses usually formed between 20–50% of those eligible. The men who were accepted by the officers—132 at Ranby, and 92 at Ashwell—appeared to be typical of the wider populations from which they were drawn.

They tended to be men in their twenties, of average age around 28. More than half of their current convictions were for property offences, either burglary, theft, or handling. Significant minorities at Ranby had been convicted of violence (13·6%) or taking vehicles (11·4%), and almost 1 in 5 of the Ashwell men (17·4%) had been convicted of fraud or deception. They were serving, on average, sentences of just over a year—13·6 months at Ranby, 16·3 months at Ashwell; and had substantial previous criminal histories, with 10·0 previous convictions at Ranby and 7·6 at Ashwell. Their intelligence levels as measured by the AH2 test were distributed normally around a mean of 56·30 at Ranby (n = 108) and 49·93 at Ashwell (n = 86). Given the age distribution of these groups, a surprisingly low proportion of the prisoners were married. At Ranby, 33·1% of the sample were married men, 48·4% were single and 18·5% separated or divorced. At Ashwell the corresponding figures were 37·8%, 33·3% and 28·9% respectively.

Although release courses were at the outset based on some assumptions about the nature of the problems men would face after discharge, a more systematic sampling of prisoners' own perceptions of these was obtained from a survey of 250 men in 3 prisons—Ranby; Ashwell; and Walton (Liverpool), a large local prison. The most prominent of their problems, as anticipated, turned out to be that of securing *employment* (mentioned by 82·8% of the sample); followed by *family* problems (45·2%), *accommodation* (44·4%), *people* (37.2%), and *money* (37.2%). Smaller proportions of those surveyed referred to problems such as *social security, getting into trouble, personality, drink, police*, and so on. These are precisely the problems addressed by the methods of "life skills training" developed by Saskatchewan Newstart and other North American projects.

C. Course content and organization

The curriculum which was assembled to help prisoners tackle these and allied difficulties with more confidence and competence contained a variety of exercises, which fell into two main categories. In the first were items which assisted individuals to take stock of themselves and their problems—broadly speaking, assessment and self-assessment materials. Amongst them were pencil and paper techniques along a continuum of sophistication from open-ended brainstorming and sentence-completion exercises to the Rotter Internal-External Scale and the Cattell 16PF. Supported by peer interviews, group discussion, the use of video and other more active and conversational methods, these were all designed to provoke a process of self-scrutiny which would hopefully help course members to pinpoint aspects of their problems which they could try to solve before release.

The second major category of materials were those which were thought useful for helping course members to achieve some kind of learning gain—whether in terms of information, attitudes and feelings, or behaviour. For example, course members might want to find out more about some aspect of employment or welfare rights; might want to become more confident or less anxious about some situation beyond release; or might want to get better at negotiating with officials, handling encounters with police, or coping with family and friends. Informational needs were met by more or less traditional means of instruction—speakers, printed matter, films, etc.,—supplemented by "information-search" projects and a constant but less formal exchange of ideas between course members. Attitudes and feelings were explored most commonly through group discussion. The course officers eschewed "sensitivity training" and other "groupwork" methods as unsuitable for prisoner groups. Attitudes are in any case inextricably interwoven with behaviour; and both were approached in release courses by a common strategy based on social skills methods—including role-play (modelling and rehearsal), the use of feedback from observers and on video, and critical incidents analysis. Role-playing can, as some research has suggested, have as much of an impact on attitudes as on behaviour (Culbertson, 1957). Video feedback can, as other work has shown, influence individuals' self-image as well as their social performance (Griffiths and Gillingham, 1978).

As the courses progressed, two other elements were added to all these specific techniques to form what emerged as a general "problem-solving" framework. These were, first of all, exercises for helping individuals to isolate targets or goals they wished to pursue during courses or after exit from prison. Personal objectives were elicited in interviews with course officers; in written formats such as an "objectives checklist"; through the use of video "predictions" ("Where I will be in 6-months' time"); and via the universal medium of group discussion. The final addition to the curriculum consisted of methods for evaluating the work that was being undertaken on courses. During the last session on Friday afternoons, prisoners were asked to evaluate the preceding week's activities; they were also asked to record a set of comments on video at the end of a course. Information of this sort, originally intended for research purposes, also proved valuable for helping individual prisoners to monitor their own progress towards the achievement of personal goals. The sequencing of SST and other exercises in a "problem-solving" framework is described more fully elsewhere (Priestley et al., 1978).

The introduction of a full-time course incorporating methods like the foregoing into a prison is, not unnaturally, viewed with great circumspection by its potential consumers. Before any of the materials could be used with groups of serving prisoners it was necessary to establish with them the conditions under which courses were to operate. Prisoners were, to begin with, suspicious not only of the officers but also of the exercises they were being asked to engage in; and were particularly concerned with the uses to which information divulged in a course would be put. To allay these perfectly justifiable fears, assurances were given at the outset that any information generated during course sessions was to be regarded as confidential—in the sense that it would not be entered in official prison records, or communicated to any third party without the express consent of the individual concerned. It is not clear how these assurances were received at the time they were made; but as groups coalesced, as prisoners were allowed (and encouraged) to keep their own "files" of all course materials, and it became clear that confidences *were* being respected, both group discussions and responses to assessment exercises appeared to become both more free and more frank.

Whatever their length, the earlier courses at Ranby and Ashwell all adopted a similar overall structure; they would begin with assessment (lasting for anything between 2 days and 2 weeks), move on to setting objectives (both short- and long-term), and then devote the remainder of the time to whichever problems—work, rights, police, drink—were foremost in the minds of the members of that particular group. But as weekly evaluations revealed what prisoners saw as a surfeit of pencil-and-paper measures in the early parts of courses, the officers began to spread assessment methods more evenly throughout the timetable.

The composition of a typical timetable for one week of a release course is illustrated in Table 5.1. This is the timetable for the second week of a 4 week course held at Ashwell prison in the autumn of 1977.

The unifying theme which ran through the week's activities was self-presentation and communication, with particular reference to job search, but glancing briefly at "offending" and at relations with police. The programme was filled out with films and two sessions of gym. But in addition to this programme of group activities, there were also a number of parallel individual sessions in which officers worked with prisoners on a one-to-one basis—discussing their problems in more depth.

The motive force for most of the week's proceedings was provided by role-play and the use of video for recording and observing behaviour. Video was used for "whispers"—recording the successive distortions of a message as it is passed from one person to another; for self-presentations in which individuals recorded a brief talk and had their performances evaluated by the rest of the group; and for appraising and training behaviour in a number of role-play exercises, associated principally with

TABLE 5.1

Timetable for one week of a release course at Ashwell

	Session 1	Session 2	Session 3	Session 4
Monday	Interaction with police: self-ratings	Film: "Edna The Inebriate Woman"	Cartoon strip and discussion	Video version of "Whispers"
Tuesday	Self-assessment of job search skills	Jobs ads plus letters of application	Gym ———— Film of personnel manager	Interview practice with video feedback
Wednesday	Job-search simulation: applying to be a caretaker	Video playback of simulation	"Faces" a set of slides of human faces	Discussion on "first impressions"
Thursday	Role-play of work situation —"On strike money"	Gym ———— Film: "Somebody else not me"	Offence behaviour: "Take and drive away"	Free-period project time
Friday	Self-presentation; prepare and video a 3-minute talk	Video playback with self-ratings and discussion	St John's Ambulance; first aid demonstration	Weekly evaluation/ discussion

work. Video was received as a mixed blessing by serving prisoners; most, after initial trepidations and the customary shock of seeing themselves for the first time, took to it with enthusiasm and benefitted visibly from its use. A few looked upon it as merely an extension of the police computer and refused steadfastly to appear on it. Besides its compelling stimulus-value, the video proved to be enormously educational in the "social skills" sense of the word.

In some prison courses, one day was spent on "interaction training" as such. This was intended primarily to enable prisoners to identify any kind of social encounter which they found difficult to handle, and to examine and practice different approaches to it. The day would begin with some general discussion of the ways in which people influence each other socially; and this would be followed by some simple exercises in non-verbal communication (e.g. identifying and modelling postures) based on suggestions of Argyle (1975) and Falloon *et al.* (1974). Next, a short 25 item checklist would be used to help group members pinpoint situations they found difficult to handle. Some of these would be looked at in detail and ideas obtained from the group as a whole on how to cope with them more satisfactorily. On other occasions, a "group problem-solving" format was used: some cards describing awkward social situations were distributed, and group members were asked to read their cards and say how they would deal with the situation described.

The most elaborate exercise used in these sessions was "critical incidents analysis". The group members were asked to form 3 or 4 smaller groups, and each of these was asked to make a short video tape—lasting say 2–3 minutes—depicting a difficult encounter in which one of its members had been involved and which he had dealt with badly (with subsequent unfortunate effects). The prisoners were asked to imagine that they were doing an "action replay" of the incident as it might be seen on a TV sports programme. The video-tapes thus produced were then used to generate suggestions as to how the incident might have been better handled: on playback, the tape would be stopped at various points and group members invited to propose alternative courses of action that would have had less unfortunate consequences.

D. Results

Two hundred and twenty-four prisoners attended release courses at Ranby and Ashwell during 1976 and 1977. Their responses were continuously monitored in an attempt to gauge the acceptability and utility of the course contents. The most immediate test lay in whether those prisoners who had volunteered to take part continued to attend courses (they were free to leave at any time). Less than a dozen men either left of their own accord or were removed compulsorily by officers before the conclusion of their courses. The remainder—the overwhelming majority—gave what amounted to a passive vote of confidence in the ability of basic grade prison officers to run social-skills-oriented courses. More active evaluations paid direct tribute to the work the officers had done. "After the first hour of the course" said one man, "that wall that was going to divide me and those screws ceased to exist".

Prisoners claimed that they had enjoyed their courses and found them useful in a number of ways. Perhaps the most vital of these to men on the verge of release from the dependent environment of the prison was the increase in self-confidence which the majority of them reported. "I was scared stiff of going out, but now I've got self-confidence" was how one man expressed it. More systematic confirmation of these feelings emerged from the weekly evaluation sheets filled in by all course members. They were asked to rate their degree of confidence on five-point scales with regard to *finding work*, sorting out their *accommodation* problems, and dealing with *social situations*. On most courses these ratings described an ascending curve of confidence as dates of discharge drew nearer (Priestley *et al.*, 1982).

Specific gains were reported in the areas of *self-knowledge*—"In all honesty, it's made me see myself as I really am"; *understanding others*—"I've found out a lot about other people—not to judge them from first impressions"; *improved personal relations*—"It's helping me to mix and talk to other people"; *self-control*—"I've learned a few things like holding your temper and not just getting stuck in"; and *finding work*—"It's helped me to present myself to an interviewer".

Prisoners were not, of course, unanimous in their judgements. A few condemned the whole enterprise as pointless and personally futile; others said they had enjoyed or found beneficial only certain parts of a course, and yet others were critical of poor material, poorly organized and presented. So far as possible the officers attempted to meet (non-abusive) criticism with substantive improvements in course content and delivery. The officers also reported gains and losses of their own from the work, "I've had more job satisfaction in the last six weeks", one of them claimed, "than in the last six years in the service". On the other hand, all the officers had to confront and surmount the hostility of their colleagues, together with a mixture of inert and outright resistance to the conduct of the courses from more senior uniformed staff. At the beginning of the research the combined impact of some of these forces almost brought the project to a halt. But the courses survived, and the best of them were characterized by the creation of an atmosphere in which the ordinary rules, roles, and relationships of normal prison life were set aside in favour of mutual cooperation, hard work and good humour.

Inside the two prisons then, there was a clear degree of success in achieving some of the aims of the research; but the crucial test of the methods lay not inside an institutional classroom, but in what happened to men after release.

Following their progress in the community proved difficult. However, about two-thirds of the ex-course members remained in contact, by some means or other, with the officers who had run their courses—an indication of the extent to which the traditional enmity between the two groups had been breached. Unfortunately such feedback was not sufficiently systematic to permit more than very tentative conclusions about the transfer of learning to real-life situations.

Data gathered from letters and returned follow-up forms; from interviews; and from discussions and ratings made at two follow-up meetings held in Nottingham and attended by ex-prisoners from as far afield as the Isle of Wight and the Orkneys, confirmed and amplified the message of evaluations obtained inside the prisons. Men described how they had used what they had learnt on courses to obtain special needs payments from social security; to find work—in one case after 13 years of voluntary unemployment; to get on better with members of their families; to moderate their drinking; and to control their aggressive behaviour. Despite these reported gains, a subsequent check on the criminal re-convictions of course members showed that approximately 40% had appeared in court again by August 1978—almost exactly the same proportion as amongst a random sample of non-course members (who were similar to course members on standard criminological criteria) released from the two prisons over the same period. However the data were manipulated (which they were considerably) it proved impossible to demonstrate statistically significant differences between course members and their non-course contemporaries in terms of overall reconviction rates, time elapsed to re-offending, or the seriousness of offences as reflected in the sentences they attracted. There was however one significant finding; significant both statistically and for the direction in which it pointed the conclusions to be drawn from this research. This was that former course members at Ranby, where one in three of the population had present or previous form for violence, were *less* likely to be re-convicted after release for offences involving violence than prisoners who had not been on courses (p < 0·05). The numbers involved were small and must be seen as indicative; but they may suggest that if re-offending is to be the criterion by which interventions with offenders are to be judged, then *offending* behaviour must form part of the "curriculum" that is employed with them. This does not mean that social or life skills training—to help individuals to find work, or manage their personal relationships—should be abandoned; many goals, perfectly desirable in themselves are self-evidently worth pursuing whether or not they have pay-offs in terms of re-conviction. To test whether social or life skills methods might influence re-offending, they would have to be applied directly to the social situations which surround the commission of offences. In release courses, the issue of personal violence was often dealt with directly; a factor which may have been responsible for the subsequent drop in violent offences amongst members of the Ranby group.

III. PROGRAMME DEVELOPMENT IN SHEFFIELD DAY TRAINING CENTRE

Day Training Centres (DTCs) are alternatives to prison. If they were not available, the offenders who are sent to them would receive prison sentences; and a majority of those who attend the four existing DTCs (in London, Liverpool, Pontypridd and Sheffield) have previously served prison sentences. Under the 1972 Criminal Justice Act, which sought to reduce the prison population by creating a range of non-custodial options to it, an individual whose offence would customarily warrant a prison sentence may, if the court sees fit, be placed on probation and required to attend a Day Training Centre for a period not exceeding 60 days. Consequently in 1973–74, four experimental DTCs were set up, to act as hosts for the fortunate few who could thus be "diverted" from custody. Beyond the simple instruction that they prepare a course of social and remedial education for their incoming trainees, these centres were given little guidance as to the kinds of regime they ought to establish. The Sheffield centre, during the first few years of its life, adopted a group-centred orientation and attempted to become a "therapeutic community" modelled closely on the lines of the work carried out by Maxwell Jones (Clark, 1974). In 1975, however, it sought a change of direction; and became closely associated with the Ranby and Ashwell "release-course" project which has just been described, thus forming a third site in which the methods of life skills training could be explored.

The aim of this segment of the project, as at the prisons, was to develop, test, and evaluate a skills training package which would hopefully help offenders on probation at the Centre get better at solving their problems—and perhaps be less likely to commit offences as a result. Related to this aim was the overall question of whether a course of sufficient interest and relevance could be run in a setting in which all the pressures it was trying to counter—including more or less continuous opportunities to get into trouble—were operating in such close proximity.

The process by which Sheffield DTC came to base its programme on the use of social and life skills training methods was a gradual one. Over a period of several months during 1976 the content of the centre's 12-week course steadily assimilated more materials and methods of a "life skills" nature. Since 1977 it has focused its activities on three interlinked aims: first, to help those who attend to find out more about themselves and their problems; second, to build up their confidence; and third, to help them acquire the ability to solve problems by themselves and to make decisions about their own lives on the basis of what they have learnt.

The actual running of a DTC course is a fairly exacting business. During the period of the research described here courses ran from 8.30 in the morning till 4.30 in the afternoon, 5 days a week, for 12 weeks (this has since 1980 been shortened to an 8-week course in order to accommodate more individuals per year). Within each working day there were only $4^{1}/_{2}$ hours of "contact time" (since 1980, increased to $5^{1}/_{2}$), or formal sessions; though extrapolated over a 12-week interval this is equivalent to a probation order lasting many years. Groups of probationers—with between 7 and 10 members at a time—arrived in the centre at 6-weekly (now 4-weekly) intervals. Each group was run by a staff probation officer and an ancillary worker who were responsible for the overall planning, organizing and execution of a course. However, the precise contents of the central weeks of each course were determined by group members themselves.

A. Day Training Centre goups

In the normal course of events, offenders are referred to and recommended for Day Training by probation officers in the local probation area; and offenders themselves must consent to a DTC order before it can be made. Since the alternative is likely to be a sojourn behind bars, consent is in most cases readily given. Nevertheless, almost half of those who are recommended for DTC and who also consent to it are subsequently sent to prison or borstal.

The individuals who attended Sheffield DTC during the period of this research were—as far as can be judged in terms of standard criminological indicators—fairly representative of the "petty recidivist" population which forms a substantial proportion of all those in British prisons at any one time. Some background data gathered on the 1977 intake of men (n = 66; until 1979, the centre did not admit women) may serve to convey an impression of the typical DTC trainee. The average age of this group was just over 30 with a range from 18–55. Their mean number of previous convictions was 9.75 (S.D. = 6·63). Their offences included the normal range of transgressions that might be expected in such a sample, with the most frequent previous offence categories being theft (29·8% of all offences committed by the group), burglary (25·8%), fraud (7·8%), car theft (7·2%), and violence (6·9%). Not surprisingly given these records, 82% of the 1977 intake had already been in prison, and all but one of the remainder had received a sentence of borstal or detention. Half of the group were single—a high proportion given the age distribution—and the incidence of divorce and separation (23% of the group as a whole) was also high. All had extremely unstable work records; most had been unemployed for many months prior to their entry to the DTC. Finally, literacy problems were fairly common amongst these individuals; though this cannot be stated with any accuracy since they were not "tested" in any way. Also—again an impression unsupported by statistical detail—many of them suffered from various forms of ill-health, and 6 were permanent invalids.

The problems which these men brought to the DTC—which it was the centre's first task to discover, included most of those that might be anticipated amongst a low-income, disorganized, offender group. In any single group of trainees at the DTC, 9 out of 10 will have employment problems (and might even be labelled with the official tag of near-worthlessness, "unemployable"); more than half will have major financial worries; a quarter or so will have family or accommodation problems; and there will in addition be a variable number of very heavy drinkers, and of violence-prone, or of extremely diffident and withdrawn individuals. The hazards and frustrations of inviting such a group to work together, disclose their difficulties to each other, and subsequently take part in role-plays, video sessions, or self-perception exercises, can well be imagined.

B. Course organization

The course programme in which these individuals participated had 3 phases:

Weeks 1–4: After a number of introductory sessions over the opening days of a course, most group activities focused on the process of *self-assessment*. Using a variety of methods with varying degrees of formality, this was designed principally to help individuals to get to know themselves and each other better, and to stimulate them to think about aspects of their lives which for the most part they were unlikely to have examined before. This led, during the fourth week of a course, to a number of sessions in which group members (usually in the company of their probation officers from outside the DTC) *set targets* for themselves, both for the rest of their time at the DTC and after they had left. This first segment of a course was planned beforehand by the centre staff.

Weeks 5–8: The exact content of the central weeks of a course was determined by course members, and depended on which issues were of most concern to them. The programme for these weeks was therefore planned jointly by staff and course members during the earlier weeks.

Broadly speaking, the main focus of this period was on *learning* in which-ever problem areas were given priority by a group; which could include social behaviour, money, rights, alcohol, violence, accommodation, police, drugs, courts, personal relations, attitudes to sex, family problems, leisure, and many specific topics subsumed by these general headings. It was during this part of a course that the emphasis on "life skills" was made most explicit.

Weeks 9–12: The final section of the course was concerned mainly with work; with helping group members review their previous job (or unemployment) histories, assess their work skills and preferences, and engage in actual job search. Included in this phase were a number of visits to various local work places; occasional pieces of community work carried out by group members; and a series of roleplay and other exercises concerned with the skills of securing work. Those who managed to find a real job, and whose attendance at the DTC had been regular, were allowed to leave the centre after their tenth week.

The "social skills" component of the course, which to a certain extent ran through all three phases, consisted of a number of different kinds of exercises. It was rarely possible to follow a textbook-style training sequence and social skills methods were almost always integrated with other elements of the "curriculum". This usage of SST also differed from conventional practice in that, as with the prisoner groups, individuals' "treatment targets" were self-determined; they were geared completely to their own problems and personal goals. The social/life skills ingredients of the course included:

(1) Several pencil-and-paper assessment exercises, e.g. person perception (individuals rate themselves and others on scales); the *Life Skills Checklist* (Saskatchewan Newstart, 1973); or the *Skill Survey* (Goldstein *et al.*, 1976).
(2) Video self-presentation exercises, e.g. where individuals give talks on video (or describe their "best points"), and rate their performance on playback.
(3) Games and simulations with a social training aspect, e.g. "broken squares"; "whispers"; a simulated TV news broadcast, etc.
(4) Street interviews: the group draws up a list of questions on a topic of interest and puts them to members of the public (recorded on a portable video machine).
(5) Job interview training: a sequence of role-plays which form a "successive approximation" to real job interviews.
(6) Role-plays of difficult social situations (with and without video playback), e.g. conflicts at work and at home; lending and borrowing

money; courtroom scenes; encounters with police; violent incidents; talking to members of the opposite sex; making social security claims, etc.

The direction in which these and related exercises were developed was determined predominantly by what would be acceptable to groups whose members were inclined to be apathetic and easily distracted. They were also often, initially at least, very poorly motivated; disenchanted with any official attempts to help them with their problems and, on occasion, sullen, uncooperative or openly hostile. In addition, rather than being designed to provide systematic training in basic skills or pre-scribed features of social behaviour, the exercises were intended to give individuals a general boost in their all-round social confidence.

C. Results

What were the effects of this exploration of a life skills training package in Sheffield DTC? The evaluative material summarized here is based on the reactions of 123 men who attended the centre between January 1976 and March 1978, comprising 17 separate "intake" groups. These results were collated from: an analysis of attendance records over the period; interviews with the men; ratings of course activities, self-confidence, etc., made on specially prepared evaluation sheets; statements made by a number of ex-probationers at a follow-up meeting; and replies of probation officers to a follow-up questionnaire on their perceptions of individuals who had attended the centre.

(1) Attendance

The most direct kind of testimony as to the success or failure of a programme like the one developed in Sheffield is the extent to which it can hold the attention of its "target" audience and induce them to turn up every day. Those who have experience of working with offenders on a non-formal basis will recognize the kinds of pressure which operate in this situation and the recalcitrance of individuals long accustomed to "dropping out" of things—out of school, out of jobs, and ultimately in some cases out of society. In DTCs, probationers who fail to attend regularly can be taken back to court and may end up in prison, yet this risk of imprisonment does not deter them from absenting themselves any more than it deters them from committing offences in the first place. In the period prior to the advent of a life skills course in Sheffield, attendance was often very poor and the drop-out rate from the course very high. During the period of this research, however, there was a marked improvement in both of these indicators.

Completions: As far as the attrition rate is concerned, it is useful to compare the proportion of group members who succeeded in completing the required 60 days at different stages over the two-and-a-quarter years during which the life skills programme was being set up. While amongst the first 4 intake groups, the average proportion of "completions" was 63·5%, amongst the last 4 groups (out of 17) it was 85·7%. A plot of the numbers of men in consecutive groups completing the course reveals a steadily rising curve (Priestley *et al.*, 1982).

Absenteeism: A more striking index of the improved capacity of the centre to sustain group members' interest is obtained by examining the pattern of absenteeism and the way it changed over 17 successive groups. Figure 5.1 charts the rate of unexplained absence (any absence from the centre not arranged or accounted for, in terms of illness, court appearances, job interviews, etc.) group by group. It also compares it with absenteeism rates amongst the last cohorts of men to attend the DTC before the inception of a life skills programme. If the rudimentary index of whether or not someone is there tells us anything about levels of interest or motivation, then the DTC's "appeal" to its consumers seemed to increase markedly over this two-and-a-quarter year period.

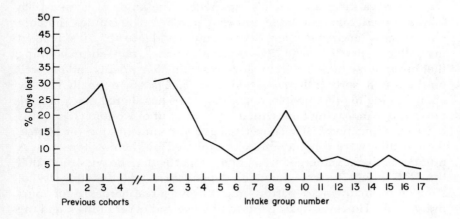

FIG. 5.1 Rates of unexplained absence.

(2) *Reactions to the course*

Given that the "staying power" of course members seems to have been affected by the centre's gradual changeover to life skills, what were their other reactions to it? During the progress of the research, a lot of information was gathered from probationers in the centre about their views of the kinds of activities on offer. This was accomplished through informal discussion; through interviews with some course members just before they left the centre; and via the use of a weekly evaluation sheet which asked for ratings of the usefulness of various sessions.

Social confidence: Group members were also asked, as in the prisons, how confident they felt about finding work and dealing with social situations after they left the centre. Also as at the prisons, these "confidence ratings" showed gradual increases from one week to the next. Ratings of social confidence for the first seven weeks of group 15, for example (expressed in terms of a percentage of maximum confidence), are typical:

Week:	1	2	3	4	5	6	7
% Confidence:	72·0	72·2	80·0	86·0	74·0	80·0	88·2

Although data of this kind are not normally considered very reliable, the fact that a similar pattern emerges from courses spread out over a two-year interval does suggest some common factor is at work.

Verbal comments: Interviews with DTC trainees during the last week of their stay tended to support the view that they found attendance at the centre a rewarding, and useful, experience. The kinds of gains which they reported can be classed under a number of headings, notably *self-confidence* and *motivation*: "It's built my confidence up", "It's changed my outlook"; *practical help*: "I've sorted my finances out—the main thing that brought me here. I've come to terms with all my debts and I'm well on the way to sorting them out"; *interpersonal gains*: "normally I'm shy about talking to other people, being in groups has altered that"; and *job prospects*: "I'm leaving here with a job. I was out of work for 18 months before coming here". There were negative comments too, of course, though they were considerably outnumbered by the positive ones. A number of themes emerged from them; in particular, the possibility that the DTC might foster a habit of dependence, and that the lack of stimulation following departure might prove a real hardship for some individuals. However, taking the confidence and other ratings, and the verbal comments together, it is possible to assert that the DTC did have a generally favourable impact on its course members, in helping to "get them out of the rut" as one expressed it.

(3) *Follow-up*

The next major question, naturally, is whether these beneficial effects were sustained after course members had left the DTC behind. Some data pertinent to this question were gleaned from a follow-up meeting held in Sheffield towards the end of the research period. As amongst the ex-prisoner groups, this tended to endorse what those present and others had said while they were in the centre itself: that they felt more confident, were better able to find and keep jobs, and that they attributed significant changes in their lives to the time they had spent in the DTC.

Probation officers' questionnaire: To obtain a fuller picture of the progress of DTC ex-clients after they had left, a follow-up questionnaire was sent to the probation officers who continued to supervize them in the field (Day Training is, as was mentioned above, only part of a longer probation order). Of 118 questionnaires sent out, 94 (79·6%) were returned. The replies tended to corroborate what probationers themselves had said about the effects DTC attendance had had upon them.

Perceived gains: The main object of the questionnaire was to discover whether probation officers agreed with their clients about the kinds of gains they had made through being on a life skills course. A substantial majority of the respondents (67·0%) said course members had benefitted from the experience, a much smaller proportion (22·4%) thought their clients had not benefitted and a few (10·6%) could not decide. Asked about any specific changes they could see, probation officers echoed the statements of trainees themselves: "He has greater levels of self-awareness, more confidence, and broader horizons"; "He benefitted by realizing that he had control over his life and actions"; "He does not react to things as violently or impetuously as before"; "It enabled him to avoid prison for two years—the longest period of freedom since childhood".

Field POs were asked in another question to rate any changes they perceived in a number of prescribed categories: *confidence*; *ability to find work*; *ability to communicate*; and *ability to solve problems*. The most salient gains reported were in terms of self-confidence and ability to communicate; apparent gains in problem-solving ability were less marked, and job-finding was rated lowest of all, with almost half of the group (48·6%) rated as having made no gains at all.

Work records: Paradoxically, when probation officers were asked about the work histories of their clients since they had emerged from the DTC, their replies proved more encouraging. A quarter of the sample (24·5%) had been in stable employment since leaving the centre; and a further sixth (17·0%) had been in casual employment. Both of these figures suggest a marked change in the work patterns of a sizeable number of ex-DTC trainees. Although the largest single proportion (35·1%) remained predominantly unemployed, and a sixth (18·1%) have returned to prison, these results—covering intervals between 6 months and 2 years since individuals had left the centre—indicate that there has been a significant shift in the employment patterns of those who attended DTC. There is evidence to suggest that the DTC's effectiveness in helping individuals to find jobs has improved further since this survey was undertaken. Thirty-seven (64·9%) of the 57 course members who left the DTC between April 1978 and April 1979 had jobs to go to on their departure—jobs which they themselves had found while still at the DTC (Burney, 1980).

Re-offending: The most sought-after outcome of any "intervention" in the criminological field is that it should have some influence on reconviction rates. As regards the present research, no direct evidence can be adduced concerning this since there was no "control" group with whom the DTC group could be compared. Some tentative suggestions can however be made. Forty-nine of the 94 offenders who attended the centre during 1976–78 and on whom follow-up information is available had been in trouble again (some while they were still at the centre), giving a crude re-offending rate ot 52·1%. Comparing this with the *expected* re-conviction rates for men in their twenties and thirties with an average of 10 previous convictions, extrapolated from the HMSO publication *The Sentence of the Court*, this would appear to be slightly better than the 60% of those who would have re-offended following a sentence of imprisonment. It is interesting that another follow-up study carried out by the DTC (Burney, 1980) over a one-year period (trainees between April 1977 and May 1978 followed up in May 1979) produces a figure that is better than the post-prison re-conviction rate by an equivalent amount—34% as opposed to 42%. It has been suggested that the Sheffield programme may have more impact on re-offending rates than that of other DTCs (Burney, 1980).

Taken separately, none of the foregoing pieces of evidence may be convincing in itself; but cumulatively, they point to the conclusion that the life skills course as implemented in Sheffield DTC achieves its aims in altering the self-attitudes and social behaviour of those who take part in it.

IV. RESULTS OVERALL

It is not possible, in considering the overall effects of life skills training in the project just described, to disentangle the precise contributions made by different methods and exercises. The work described was developmental in nature and did not conform to a standard "experimental" design. Nevertheless some conclusions can be drawn. The results have in general been positive, in that they show (*a*) that life skills training can be used in custodial and non-custodial settings, by workers who are not trained therapists or teachers; (*b*) that these methods are viewed approvingly by both those who use them and those who participate in them; (*c*) that they do have beneficial effects in terms of the confidence, future employment, and other aspects of the lives of trainees. But the results also support the view this this kind of training is specific in its effects. Courses were addressed to job-finding, money management, dealing with social situations, and other topics seen as problems by trainees. In so far as it has not been possible to show any clear-cut (and significant) effects on re-conviction, this may suggest that SST will only affect this variable if methods are tailored closely to the interpersonal contexts of offence behaviour (McGuire and Priestley, 1983).

Whether the results of painstaking research justify it or not, social and life skills training methods are coming to be used more and more commonly in everyday practice—in work with offenders (Fawcett and McKeever, 1979; Howe, 1979), in schools (Hopson and Scally, 1981; McGuire and Priestley, 1981), and in youth and community work (Ellis and Barnes, 1979; Youth Opportunities Development Unit, 1979). Though this may in most cases be far removed from the original "clinical" version of SST, it has nevertheless been inspired by it. The primary reason for the recent expansion in the use of these methods seems simply to be that they provide a way of working that is more attractive to staff groups and more lively, interesting and purposeful for participants.

V. ACKNOWLEDGEMENTS

We would like to thank Rosemary Barnitt, Mary Edwards, David Flegg, Valerie Hemsley, and David Welham, research associates on the project described in this chapter; the prison officers and probation staff who took part in the research; and all of those who participated in the prisons and DTC.

VI. REFERENCES

Argyle, M. (1975). "Bodily Communication". Methuen, London.
Barton, R. (1966). "Institutional Neurosis". John Wright, Bristol.

Bellack, A. S. and Hersen, M. (*Eds*) (1979). "Research and Practice in Social Skills Training". Plenum, New York.

Bottoms, A. E. and McClintock, F. H. (1973). "Criminals Coming of Age". Heinemann, London.

Boyle, J. (1977). "A Sense of Freedom". Canongate, Edinburgh.

Braukmann, C. J., Fixsen, D. L., Phillips, E. L. and Wolf, M. M. (1974). An analysis of a selection interview training package for predelinquents at Achievement Place. *Criminal Justice and Behaviour* **1**, 30–42.

Brody, S. R. (1976). "The Effectiveness of Sentencing". Home Office Research Study No. 35. HMSO, London.

Burgess, R., Jewitt, R., Sandham, J. and Hudson, B. L. (1980). Working with sex offenders: a social skills training group. *Br. J. Soc. Work* **10**, 133–142.

Burney, E. (1980). "A Chance to Change: day care and day training for offenders". Howard League for Penal Reform, London.

Chandler, M. J. (1973). Egocentrism and anti-social behavior: the assessment and training of social perspective-taking skills. *Dev. Psychol.* **9**, 326–32.

Clark, D. H. (1974). "Social Therapy in Psychiatry". Penguin Books, Harmondsworth.

Crawford, D. A. (1976). A social skills treatment programme with sex offenders. Paper presented at the SHRU Conference on Sex Deviance, London. Mimeo: Broadmoor Hospital.

Culbertson, F. M. (1957). Modification of an emotionally held attitude through role playing. *J. Abnorm. Soc. Psychol.* **54**, 230–233.

Ellis, J. and Barnes, T. (1979). "Life Skills Training Manual". Community Service Volunteers, London.

Ellis, R. (1980). Simulated social skill training for interpersonal professions. *In* "The Analysis of Social Skill" (W. T. Singleton, P. Spurgeon, and R. B. Stammers, *Eds*). Plenum, New York.

Falloon, I., Lindley, P. and McDonald, R. (1974). "Social Training: a manual". Psychological Treatment Section, Maudsley Hospital.

Fawcett, B., Ingham, E., McKeever, M. and Williams, S. (1979). A social skills group for young prisoners. *Social Work Today* **10**, 16–18.

Foy, D. W., Miller, P. M., Eisler, R. M. and O'Toole, D. H. (1976). Social-skills training to teach alcoholics to refuse drinks effectively. *J. Studies Alcohol* **37**, 1340–1345.

Frederiksen, L. W., Jenkins, J. O., Foy, D. W. and Eisler, R. M. (1976). Social-skills training to modify abusive verbal outbursts in adults. *J. Appl. Behav. Anal.* **9**, 117–125.

Gartner, A. (1971). "Paraprofessionals and their performance". Praeger, New York.

Goldstein, R. P., Sprafkin, R. P. and Gershaw, N. J. (1976). "Skill Training for Community Living". Pergamon Press/Structured Learning Associates, New York.

Goodman, G. (1972). "Companionship Therapy". Jossey-Bass, San Francisco.

Griffiths, R. D. P. and Gillingham, P. (1978). The influence of videotape feedback on the self-assessments of psychiatric patients. *Br. J. Psychiatry* **183**, 156–161.

Hargie, O., Saunders, C. and Dickson, D. (1981). "Social Skills in Interpersonal Communication". Croom Helm, London.

HMSO (1969). "The Sentence of the Court. A Handbook for Courts on the Treatment of Offenders". HMSO, London.

Hopson, B. and Scally, M. (1981). "Lifeskills Teaching". McGraw-Hill, London.

Howe, P. (1979). Intermediate Treatment: The development and operation of a "social skills" group. Mimeo, The Barton Project, Oxford.

Ivey, A. E. and Authier, J. (1978). "Microcounselling". Charles C. Thomas, Springfield, Illinois.

Kifer, R. E., Lewis, M. A., Green, D. R. and Phillips, E. L. (1974). Training predelinquent youths and their parents to negotiate conflict situations. *J. Appl. Behav. Anal.* **7**, 357–364.

Maloney, D. M., Harper, T. M., Braukmann, C. J., Fixsen, D. L., Phillips, E. L. and Wolf, M. M. (1976). Teaching conversation-related skills to pre-delinquent girls. *J. Appl. Behav. Anal.* **9**, 371.

McGuire, J. and Priestley, P. (1981). "Life After School: a social skills curriculum". Pergamon Press, Oxford.

McGuire, J. and Priestley, P. (1983). "Offending Behaviour: skills and stratagems for going straight". Batsford, London (In press).

Piliavin, I. and Briar, S. (1964). Police encounters with juveniles. *Am. J. Sociol.* **70**, 206–214.

Priestley, P. (1980). "Community of Scapegoats: the segregation of sex offenders and informers in prisons". Pergamon Press, Oxford.

Priestley, P. and McGuire, J. (1983). "Learning to Help: basic skills exercises". Tavistock, London (In press).

Priestley, P., McGuire, J., Flegg, D., Hemsley, V. and Welham, D. (1978). "Social Skills and Personal Problem Solving". Tavistock, London.

Priestley, P., McGuire, J., Barnitt, R., Flegg, D., Hemsley, V. and Welham, D. (1982). "Social Skills in Prisons and in the Community". Routledge and Kegan Paul, London. (In press)

Prison Officers' Association (1963). The Role of the Modern Prison Officer. *The Prison Officers' Magazine*, November, 330–333.

Rutter, M. and Madge, N. (1976). "Cycles of Disadvantage". Heinemann, London.

Sarason, I. G. and Ganzer, V. J. (1973). Modelling and group discussion in the rehabilitation of juvenile delinquents. *J. Counsel. Psychol.* **20**, 442–449.

Saskatchewan Newstart (1973). "Life Skills Coaching Manual". Training Research and Development Station, Department of Manpower and Immigration, Saskatchewan.

Shepherd, G. (1978). Social skills training: the generalization problem—some further data. *Behav. Res. Ther.* **16**, 287–288.

Shure, M. B. (1980). Real-life problem solving for parents and children: an approach to social competence. *In* "Social Competence: Interventions for Children and Adults" (D. P. Rathjen and J. P. Foreyt, *Eds*). Pergamon Press, New York.

Soothill, K. (1973). "The Prisoner's Release". George Allen and Unwin, London.

Spence, A. J. and Spence, S. H. (1980). Cognitive changes associated with social skills training. *Behav. Res. Ther.* **18**, 265–272.

Spence, S. H. and Marzillier, J. S. (1979). Social skills training with adolescent male offenders: I: Short-term effects. *Behav. Res. Ther.* **17**, 7–16.

Spence S. H. and Marzillier, J. S. (1981). Social skills training with adolescent male offenders: II: Short-term, long-term and generalised effects. *Behav. Res. Ther.* **19**, 349–368.

Spivack, G., Platt, J. J. and Shure, M. B. (1976). "The Problem-solving Approach to Adjustment". Jossey-Bass, San Francisco.

Thelen, M. H., Fry, R. A., Dollinger, S. J. and Paul, S. G. (1976). Use of video-taped models to improve the interpersonal adjustment of delinquents. *J. Consult. Clin. Psychol.* **44**, 492.

Thomas, J. E. (1972). "The English Prison Officer since 1850". Routledge and Kegan Paul, London.

Trower, P., Bryant, B. and Argyle, M. (1978;. "Social Skills and Mental Health". Methuen, London.

Warren, P. W. and Lamrock, L. A. (1973). Evaluation of the life skills course. *In* "Readings in Life Skills" (D. S. Conger, *Ed.*). Training Research and Development Station, Department of Manpower and Immigration, Saskatchewan.

Werner, J. S., Minkin, N., Minkin, B. L., Fixsen, D. L., Phillips, E. L. and Wolf, M. M. (1975). Intervention Package: an analysis to prepare juvenile delinquents for encounters with police officers. *Criminal Justice and Behaviour* **2**, 55–84.

West, D. J. and Farrington, D. P. (1973). "Who Becomes Delinquent?". Heinemann, London.

Youth Opportunities Development Unit (1979). "Social education in informal settings: case studies of practice within the Youth Opportunities Programme". National Youth Bureau, Leicester.

Zimbardo, P. G. (1973). The Mind is a Formidable Jailer: a Pirandellian Prison. *The New York Times*, 8th April.

6

Women in prison

PHILLIPA LOWE AND CAROLINE STEWART*

I. THE SETTING

This chapter concerns social skills training (SST) with women in Holloway Prison and to set it in context some description of the prison and its population is required. The original Holloway was built on the radial

---

* The views expressed in this chapter are the authors' and do not necessarily represent those of the Prison Department, Home Office.

model, a design imported from America during the Victorian era which has tiered wings radiating like the spokes of a wheel from a central area. Many male prisoners are still housed in prisons of this type but by the mid 1960s the view was being expressed that women prisoners with their small numbers and special needs should be accommodated in a modern building which reflected current attitudes to imprisonment. One of these attitudes concerned the nature of the female offender. The very small proportion of offenders who were women and the current sexual stereotypes led to the conclusion that crime is a predominantly male preserve. Women who committed crimes were perceived as "odd" and possibly "mad" and the observed disturbance of many women prisoners added weight to this view (Gibbens, 1971; Goodman and Price, 1967; Prins, 1980; Walker, 1968). The new prison was therefore designed on a medical treatment model. At the planning stage in the late 1960s the female prison population was under 1000 and had been static for a number of years (Home Office, 1971). There was no reason to believe that the number of women appearing before the courts would drastically change and it was thought that the number of women in prison would reduce rather than increase as more non-custodial alternatives became available to those who were "normal" and more treatment opportunities became available to those who were "abnormal". The New Holloway was therefore designed to hold no more than 550 women in single room accommodation. Many treatment and training resources were built in and the open design with its green areas and walk-ways reflected the intention to create a rehabilitative and therapeutic institution.

By 1977 when the first part of the new prison was ready for occupation, a very different picture was emerging of the female prison population. The number had increased considerably and the trend was upwards. (Home Office, 1978; Smart, 1977). Attitudes towards female offenders were also beginning to change. Terrorism had appeared on the scene with a not insignificant proportion of women involved and women also appeared to be becoming implicated in other major crime. Women's lives were now resembling those of men in many areas and perhaps crime was no exception. The incompetent rootless and disturbed woman prisoner was still there, but delinquent criminal types were now appearing in sufficient numbers to rule out the future redundancy of female prisons. Holloway Prison in the 1980s is not regarded as a solely medical establishment, nor even as a primarily rehabilitative institution. Many of the tasks are those of a remand centre and local prison, holding people for the courts and, when they are sentenced, moving them on as quickly as possible to prisons elsewhere so that there is room for the next batch of remands. The only sentenced women who remain in Holloway are those who are too psychiatrically disturbed to go elsewhere, those allocated to the Mother and Baby Unit and those selected for the Therapeutic Unit (a group-work community). A few also stay because they are engaged on essential work in the prison. The population is therefore a transient one, the women often unsure of their immediate future. The longer term residents may have quite severe problems of personality and social adjustment and are often emotionally very volatile.

The use of behavioural techniques with offenders is well established (Braukmann et al., 1975; Davidson et al., 1974) and of these SST has become an increasingly popular method both inside and outside prison (Cullen, 1980; Grayson, 1980; Spence, 1979; Spence et al., 1979). It has been utilized in Holloway for a number of years, both before and after the move to the new premises. The faulty behaviour patterns of many of the inmates, as evidenced by the way in which they organize their free lives, as well as by the way they cope, and fail to cope, with prison gives plenty of scope for this kind of training. The organization and attitudes of the prison, which retain some therapeutic philosophy, make it possible to withdraw women from other duties for training sessions. However, the high turnover of the prison's population has implications for treatment as inmates may not stay long in the prison and the length of their stay may be unpredictable at the outset. Those allocated to the prison's Therapeutic Unit can confidently be expected to stay in the prison long enough for a programme to be devised for them, but for many others there is not time to embark on a lengthy, scientifically controlled form of treatment. With these people it may more often be a case of crisis intervention, with a few sessions devoted to tackling one presenting problem. Pragmatism rather than clinical rigour tends to be the key-note.

Prison as a setting for treatment has both advantages and disadvantages. The client population's presence is guaranteed, but their good will is not. They are thrown into many difficult situations with other people which provide suitable material for the practice of social skills, but there is an element of artificiality in the situation and many skills cannot effectively be practised in this setting. The highly structured environment provides good framework for regular sessions, but the heavy presence of authority can be inhibiting to both trainers and trainees. However, this level of authority is an inevitable feature of prisons and can often be put to good effect as a central problem with many inmates is the way they respond to the people who control their lives. Thus, the problems are not such as to outweigh the relevance and feasibility of this type of training (Cullen, 1980). For many prisoners a term in prison may well be their first opportunity to be free of their normal pressures and to take a cool look at their situation. The drug addict and alcoholic may have unclouded brains for the first time in many years and the victim of violent personal relationships may be for the first time without physical fear. For some people, prison is the beginning of a change process.

II. ASSESSMENT AND SELECTION OF CLIENTS

A wide range of different types of problem behaviours may present themselves for which SST is seen as an appropriate strategy. A combination of techniques may be used in any particular case (Marzillier *et al.*, 1978). SST may be accompanied by, for example, systematic desensitization, contingency management, group therapy, counselling or a more didactic, information giving approach (as in the Jobs Course). The problem behaviours which we may be concerned with can be classified as follows:

A. Problem behaviour which is directly related to the woman's offence

For example, the control of anger and aggression in response to provocation in a woman who is serving a sentence for an offence of violence. The aim of treatment is to teach her control of both her aggressive feelings and behaviour and to teach appropriate assertiveness.

B. Problem behaviours which may underlie a woman's offending but which in themselves are not criminal

In this group we are concerned with the "inadequate" woman, often of limited intellectual capacity, who lacks many of the social and life skills to provide for herself as an independent individual in outside society. Prison acts as an "asylum" and for some the offences, often such as criminal damage, are seen as a deliberate attempt to be arrested and to be returned to prison. SST aims at teaching some of these very basic social and life skills. She might be a shy and anxious woman, who drinks heavily to enable her to face people. Her excessive drinking has led to a variety of criminal activities such as shoplifting, theft of drink and getting into fights. SST combined with a desensitization hierarchy, aims to overcome her social fears and teach her the skills she feels she lacks.

C. Problems in coping with prison life

An example here is the quiet and under-assertive woman who is unable to say "no" to the other women who want to borrow things from her. The object of SST is to help her to be more assertive when saying "no", but to do so in a reasonable way which would be found acceptable by the other women.

D. Problems resulting from being in prison

In this case it might be a woman coming to the end of a long sentence feeling increasingly anxious about her discharge, and especially about meeting "normal" people again, making friends, talking about things other than prison life. A desensitization hierarchy with SST aims to give her practice at the social skills she fears she has lost while in prison.

There are three main ways in which SST is used in Holloway (a) with individual referrals, (b) as part of the Jobs Course and (c) with women in groups on the Therapeutic Unit.

(1) Individuals

Individuals selected for SST are usually referred by prison staff of various grades but may sometimes present themselves. The reason for the referral is couched in terms of an immediate problem, prison-related or outside world-related. The decision to undertake a social skills programme is made at a later stage with the informed consent and, hopefully, eager acceptance of the individual concerned.

Treatment targets for individuals are generally selected according to individual needs. When a person has been referred or has referred herself the reason for the referral may be markedly different from the problem which is eventually tackled. Prisoners often bring themselves to the notice of staff for reasons which are far removed from those with which they really require help. This may be because they have difficulty in articulating the real problem or because they wish to present a more acceptable area of concern for initial contact. In some cases the therapist may need to help the prisoner towards a perception of the most pressing problem but in SST, perhaps more than in other therapies, there needs to be a basic agreement between client and therapist about what is being dealt with and the way in which it is done. Staff may refer a woman as a result of a minor prison crisis or out of concern about the way in which she deals with prison life. The presenting problem may be the one that is tackled immediately but assessment of the person may suggest that there are other deficits which should be examined. Many women who come to prison conduct their social and interpersonal lives in very faulty ways, but the strange, crowded and authoritarian atmosphere of the penal institution throws up its own problems which most of us would no doubt experience if incarcerated. These problems may be of the most immediate concern to the prison and help should be given. However, there could be more pay-off in tackling the woman's underlying problems and not just the ones created by being in prison. SST in prisons therefore generally arises out of a variety of types of referral and treatment targets gradually unfold rather than being delineated at the outset.

(2) *The jobs course*

The jobs course is open to all women in the prison. It is advertised on a generally displayed notice which offers training on the various aspects of seeking, applying for and keeping a job. The woman is interviewed by the course co-ordinator who discusses with her which of the ten items available would be of most value to her. While she is given some guidance, it is very much left to her to define her own needs.

(3) *Groups*

Those who join the social skills group are already members of Holloway's Therapeutic Unit and the SST which they receive towards the end of their stay is an integral part of the unit's activities. This unit tackles a variety of presenting problems and utilizes both group work and individual counselling. Selection is therefore for the unit as a whole and not for this particular aspect of its treatment. When a new social skills group is selected, usually comprising those who have 3–4 months left of their sentences, the skill survey (Priestley *et al.*, 1978) is given to them by the therapists who run the course. Each woman is then interviewed so that the course can be explained and further problem areas elicited from her. Before each course begins the names of its members are given to the weekly main group of the therapeutic unit and comments invited about their social skills needs from unit members as a whole. The ensuing discussion gives rise to material which can be used in various group activities as well as on the social skills course. Staff also give their view of the women's needs which can be drawn from their observations of the way in which they conduct their daily lives on the prison unit.

The targets can be set more clearly in advance with these women than with individual referrals as they are already well known to the therapists, their officers and their peers, but it is by no means unusual for these to change as the course proceeds and new issues arise.

Treatment goals as far as the women are concerned with their varieties of styles and abilities may be massive or minimal for example ranging from a whole new approach to a marital relationship on the one hand, to the ability to answer a question on the other. The therapist needs to select targets which are high enough to make demands of the prisoner, but not so difficult that they would discourage her. It is possible that within the same group a very sophisticated social skill may be being taught to one while another is helped with some basic linguistic or posture problem. Because of this, it is fortunate that prisoners can sometimes show a marked sensitivity towards each other, especially if they are living together in the context of a therapeutic unit. When this sensitivity is lacking the therapist's role becomes an extremely difficult one. Treatment targets are obviously set in relation to the social and cultural environment to which the inmate will return on release. Because of the wide range of these and the limitations which are set on any therapist's knowledge the women must be responsible for the details of their own targets to a large extent. This is quite appropriate as anything which leads to a degree of self determination in a prison, with its regimentation and organization of each detail of the individual's life, is to be welcomed.

III. A TYPICAL CLIENT

1. A B was a 30 year old woman serving a 6 month sentence for making hoax telephone calls regarding planted bombs. This was her first prison sentence though she had previous convictions for hoax calls. She had a history of a disturbed home background and by her own account (and confirmed by reports) she had been unwilling to leave her home on her own since the age of 12. Generally she looked after the house while her parents went out to work but, during periods of depression she did not do this, taking to her bed instead. This caused arguments with her parents, at the end of which she would rush out of the house and make her hoax calls. A B was referred because of her disturbed behaviour while in prison. She was very depressed and repeatedly scratched and cut her arms. She refused to leave her room and would not talk to anyone, preferring to sit huddled up in a corner in her room.

A combined approach was used as her depressive behaviour and her social isolation seemed inter-related. Her history suggested that she would be lacking in many social skills as her main social contacts had been members of her family and therefore her opportunities for learning had been limited. A hierarchy of targeted behaviours was drawn up, the main aim being to get her out of her room, to increase her contact with the other women and the staff on her Unit and eventually to get her to participate in other prison activities she had previously avoided, e.g. to eat in the dining room. She was seen daily initially and a goal was set for each day. This might be spending a fixed time out of her room with her therapist, or approaching a member of staff to ask for something. In the latter instance, much time would be spent modelling and coaching her on what to say. Great enthusiasm on the part of the therapist and masses of praise for each goal achieved was an essential part of the programme. As she progressed more complex tasks were included, e.g. buying things in the prison shop. Several sessions role-playing with the therapist preceded the *in vivo* practice. As her discharge approached, she expressed fears about going back to her socially isolated state when she returned home. She also seemed uncertain about going shopping, using buses, asking people for directions, etc. Day release was arranged and she spent some time practising these activities, again being coached by the therapist who at first modelled for her and then increasingly let her manage situations on her own. Progress and improvement was measured in two ways: firstly, there was an obvious change in her mood, reflected in the absence of periods of time spent huddled in the corner of her room, absence of self-injury, and the observation of a more lively, smiling woman. Secondly, her social contact increased. She moved into a dormitory and reported that she had made friends with the women there.

2. C D was a 38 year old woman serving a life sentence who had spent many years in prison. She originally referred herself for SST as she wished to learn why her social interactions in the prison were so often regarded as aggressive and challenging when she felt that she was being nothing of the sort. Thus, she suspected that her style was faulty and she wished to examine it and possibly to change it. The work was undertaken jointly by a psychologist and a prison probation officer and the areas examined using role-play and VTR feedback were conversational style with other inmates, making requests of staff and expressing anger appropriately. Both she and the prison staff dealing with her gave good feedback of her progress during this period. After a gap of a few months, she returned to the therapists for help in coping with parole interviews, as she was now being assessed for release. This area was tackled as any other interview training would have been, looking at self-presentation and the giving of information. It was not felt that this coaching gave her an unfair advantage as the intention was simply to give her the

confidence to do her best. It is perhaps indicative of the success of these sessions that she was subsequently given a release date for some time hence. Most of this period was to be spent in an open prison to prepare her for the outside world and it was decided to use her last few weeks in Holloway to help her make this transition. She was extremely fearful of her first steps outside the prison and the programme was designed to overcome these fears. Every few days she was taken out of the prison by a therapist and a prison officer to undertake a task of carefully graded difficulty. The first one involved sitting for half an hour in the public library next door, the last one was to be a day trip to the crowded West End of London for shopping and a visit to the cinema, during which she would be responsible for the money and the general organization of the day. In between, it was planned to introduce her gradually to shopping, eating out, interacting with the strangers and taking more and more responsibility for these expeditions. The gradual increase in difficulty of the items ensured that she coped confidently and happily at each stage. She subsequently settled well at the open prison.

IV. PROCEDURAL DETAILS

A. Individual referrals

The women are seen on their own as a rule, though occasionally two may be seen together if their needs are complementary or similar. There is flexibility in the number of sessions and their length. Women may be seen daily, weekly or monthly; and for periods of 15 minutes up to 1½ hours depending on what it is felt she can cope with. The baseline level of ability is generally far more limited than in the groups (see below) and the emphasis is therefore on much more basic and fundamental social skills, e.g. posture (to avoid the institutional shuffle), conversational skills (many of the women have great difficulty in talking to the other women and making friends), and expressing feelings and frustrations verbally rather than physically. Sessions may take place in the Psychology Department (where the therapeutic unit group and the jobs course also are held) but also may take place on the woman's unit (i.e. her living quarters) or perhaps in her place of work. The procedures adopted are the standard ones and include definition of the problem, identification of target behaviours, arriving at agreement about these with the woman herself, use of standardized exercises and role-plays, VTR, feedback from the client and therapist, coaching and modelling and practice. Additionally, we combine SST with other techniques such as relaxation.

Many of the problems that bring women to our attention are concerned with their behaviour in prison and so initially the emphasis of our intervention will be on this. The difficulties experienced in prison often reflect problems outside and inevitably in later sessions our attention will turn to these "outside" problems when the immediate "inside" needs have been met. When it is appropriate and practically possible, we arrange for a day's parole and take the women out of the prison to give them the chance of some real-life practice. Most commonly these outside sessions have involved going shopping, use of public transport, asking directions, handling money, and eating out. These trips out may seem low key to those working in a community setting, but when working in a prison they represent a very significant development which may go some way to help bridge the gap between prison experiences and life outside. This is an essential aid to generalization (Shepherd, 1978) and very necessary if our work is to have any long-term relevance to the prisoners. The provision of home leave for women serving over 18 months gives a very useful opportunity for the woman to practice in her home environment the skills she has been learning in prison. It can also be useful for identifying additional problems which can be tackled during the last few weeks of her sentence.

B. Jobs course

Sessions in the jobs course may be run with groups or with women on their own depending on how many at any one time have asked to do a particular part of the course. There are 10 options on offer which are as follows: vocational guidance, vocational testing, job finding (use of newspapers, job centres), telephoning, form filling, interviewing, physical presentation, money and taxes, how to keep a job and finding a job (this was not an SST item, but an interview with the local Employment Liaison Officer). Women can do any or all of the options. The women are usually seen only once for any item, but repeated sessions are possible if the woman requests it. The same SST procedures are used as for individual referrals.

C. Groups

The Therapeutic Unit group is a course of 8 weekly sessions of 1½ hours each, with between 4 and 6 members. The organization of each session

varies as the course progresses, the initial sessions being more structured. The aims of the course and the methods that will be used are
re-explained. Simple structured exercises provide the main content of
these sessions where the aim is to make the participants more aware of
their own behaviour in social situations. Examples of these exercises are
taking turns to look bored and interested when talking in pairs and
listening games. The group leaders have a pool of exercises from which
they draw and their selection of any particular ones will be influenced by
their advance knowledge of the women in the group. An attempt is made
to include exercises which will illustrate points of particular importance
to individual participants as well as general points of relevance to all.
These early sessions also allow time for the therapists to discuss with the
course members which of their needs and problems they would like
included in later sessions and identifying common areas of concern. The
women are invited to examine situations or incidents occurring currently
in the prison and also those concerning their lives outside. It is frequently
noted that there are many parallels between the way they describe how
they handle (or mishandle) situations inside prison and how they handle
them outside. Drawing out these parallels can prove useful in increasing
the credibility of social skills training in a prison, which at times is seen
as being rather artificial and unconnected from "real life".

The first sessions are also designed to give the women the opportunity
to overcome what is at times considerable self-consciousness and
embarrassment at role-playing and seeing themselves on the video.
Women who are very anxious can usually be persuaded to play a
"supporting role" for someone else, after which they feel happier about
role-playing their own situations. Some women refuse to be filmed at the
first session. This is accepted and it is generally the case that later on in
the course, she herself will ask to go on the video, or will respond to gentle
persuasion from the therapists or the other women. In some cases we may
use VTR very sparingly, or not at all. It would be counter-productive with
those who have a very low level of skills or with those who are
preoccupied with a physical problem, e.g. obesity.

Subsequent sessions aim to find a balance between the areas that the
leader feels could usefully be worked on and the problems the women
themselves have identified. Typically, the therapists suggest a particular
area as the subject of a session. This might be being assertive, expressing
anger, giving or receiving praise, asking for help or a favour, saying "no",
explaining they have been in prison, apologizing, compromising and
being interviewed. Course members are then asked to give examples
from their own experiences of any difficulties they may have had in these
areas. If, as not infrequently happens, a woman feels she has had no

difficulties handling any of these situations, she will be invited to demonstrate her strategy to the others. This may result in a good model of how to handle an incident, but it may also prove a useful learning exercise for the woman herself who afterwards may feel that her way of doing things was not in fact the most effective. She may then be given the opportunity to try a different approach.

Once the subject matter for each session has been agreed upon and each group member has decided which incident or events they want to work on, there follows a series of role-plays which are generally filmed, followed by feedback on performance, coaching and modelling by the therapists and possibly the other women, repeated role-plays for practice, and further feedback from the therapists. Feedback from the woman herself about how she felt trying something different is seen as an essential element as well, the assumption being that she is only going to adopt a new style of behaviour if she feels comfortable with it. Also, in many instances a woman's feedback on her own performance, has more impact on her than feedback from anyone else. (The tendency to be highly self-critical and negative must be watched for and counteracted by the therapists). Feedback from the other group members is also encouraged and is highly influential, and as the therapeutic unit women generally display a certain sophistication of social skills, can be very pertinent and telling. Coming from peers, it also has a credibility the therapists may sometimes lack due to the difference between being a prisoner and being a member of staff. But the women can be over-protective of each other or can collude with each others' delinquent style. The therapists need to watch out for this and prevent it if possible.

V. THERAPISTS

Two therapists work together on our sessions whenever possible. This is so that one person can operate the camera when video is used and equally importantly so that there is some mutual support for therapists. We have often been aware that even a small group of female prisoners can feel like a crowd and this is especially the case when youngsters, such as borstal girls, are involved. To plan, organize, control, role-play, encourage and lead feedback would be a difficult and exhausting job for one person. The exception would be when one was working with an individual who could not cope with more than one therapist and in a case such as this the second worker might well be introduced as part of the treatment.

The qualities of a good social skills therapist in a women's prison must be much the same as those of a good therapist in any other setting, but certain attributes are particularly desirable given the high level of energy and the low self esteem of many of the women with whom we deal. Those who have worked with both male and female prisoners often comment that the women are far less passive in their acceptance of what is done with them and far more challenging of the authority with which it is done. The practical implications of this is that the therapist must be able to retain a high level of enthusiasm at all times, must be prepared to join in and put herself at risk of ridicule and must recognize when it is appropriate to be very directive and when to "soft-pedal". When dealing with groups there may be a very considerable range of ability among the women present, intellectual, social and emotional, and this has to be recognized and dealt with appropriately. The effective therapist will make good use of the abilities by asking them to act as models in situations where they are known to be competent and by acknowledging the usefulness of this feedback of other group members. This should be done in such a way that any suggestion of favouritism is avoided. In the case of more limited members, care must be taken to give them experience of success, however small, as another failure to someone whose life is a catalogue of failures may be more than they are prepared to tolerate.

It would be reasonable to assume that social skills with prisoners at least implies a captive client group with whom to work, but this is not necessarily the case. If interest or goodwill is lost it is simple enough for the woman to opt out and either remove her physical presence or her co-operation. How this is tackled depends on whether the woman is being seen individually or as a member of the group. If she is being seen on her own efforts are made to deal with her objections and to persuade her to participate, but if she still refuses she is allowed to withdraw from treatment. On the other hand if she is a member of the group, her refusal is not accepted in this way as attendance at these sessions is an integral part of the therapeutic unit's activities. It may be appropriate to discuss her unwillingness in the social skills session, though this obviously withdraws time and attention from others. Alternatively, she could be seen on her own at another time to find out what her objections are and to deal with them. It may be that she feels particularly concerned about demonstrating her weaknesses in front of others, and usually a private discussion of her fears or an opportunity to practice on her own will reassure her sufficiently to bring her back into the group. If this still fails, the matter becomes an issue for discussion at the community meeting. By this stage the other unit members will have views about her attempts to opt out of a unit activity and would want her to examine this problem in terms of her general difficulties with trusting others or risking change. In fact it is much more likely that a woman will not refuse to attend but will spend the whole session demonstrating her unwillingness by either being unresponsive or by actively undermining the attempts of others. This is very disheartening to the rest of the group and the therapist must then use her skill to counteract the negative input. The fun of active participation as well as its practical benefits in terms of improved skills should be emphasized. Concentration and enthusiasm can be shortlived with our population and the skilled therapist is therefore one who can keep the tempo high by using a variety of methods and activities. Care should be taken to avoid communicating weariness and disillusion, however strongly they may be felt at times, and the therapist must be prepared to be questioned repeatedly on the rationale of the procedure and to be able to persuade others of its relevance. Ultimately success may well rest on the strength of personality of the therapist.

Experience suggests that a firm, even bossy approach has more pay-off than one which goes along with the immediate preferences of the inmate and this is not easy for a therapist whose preferred style is non-directive. An assertive style is especially important when dealing with a group, though as is the case in most prison situations, confrontation should be avoided and the leaders should be sufficiently sensitive to know when a member can be persuaded or cajoled no further. If the support of other group members can be won, group pressure can often succeed where leadership fails. While the therapist must obviously have some firm belief in the social skills model in order to operate in a convincing manner, a too narrow, purist approach can often be less effective than one which allows for a mixing of therapeutic approaches. For example, it may be necessary to deal with the "prison business" before getting down to considering ways of coping with a family or employment situation. Those living in a closed community quite naturally are overwhelmingly concerned with the day-to-day matters which affect their lives. Some of these matters can be used as material for the session while others cannot and they have to be dealt with and put aside before it is possible to concentrate on the relevant issues. An effective therapist should therefore be prepared to mix counselling and advice with social skills, perhaps moving from one to another as necessary.

As well as flexibility, the accomplished prison worker should be a good source of information about different life styles and habits. When interview skills are being taught, for example, it may be necessary in the course of one morning to role-play a college lecturer, a supermarket manager and a computer expert, with equal aplomb and technical skill. When examining a tricky domestic or social situation recognition must be given to the variety of cultural and social circumstances from which prisoners are drawn. Perhaps more than with any other groups, the therapist must take pains to avoid being judgmental and applying her own social standards, which may not be appropriate to the client group. One woman had been refused service in a hamburger bar and dealt with this by damaging the restaurant and assaulting its manager. The problem which she brought to the group was to find a way of dealing with her anger and humiliation such that it would not result in her arrest should the situation arise again. The cool, sophisticated approach which was modelled for her and which she reproduced looked excellent on the video film but she rejected it as totally inappropriate. She then did a role-play which was full of abuse and obscenity. Although this was unacceptable by normal standards, she was delighted as she had succeeded in expressing her anger verbally rather than physically. The therapists had to accept this as a successful outcome.

To run social skills training effectively in prison it is probably necessary to be a member of the prison's staff rather than a visitor or a sessional worker. A full understanding of prison life gives an awareness of the preoccupations of the client group as well as allowing for the informed use of prison incidents for role-plays. All prison therapy is heavily dependent on the co-operation of the discipline staff, who have daily contact with the women and experience at first hand their problems with authority and with their peers. Prison officers can provide base-line data before treatment starts, can encourage "home work" tasks on the unit and can help to monitor the outcome of therapy. It is important that officers are fully informed of what problem the woman is working on as it is with them that she is likely to try out her new skills for the first time. A good prison therapist is therefore one who can work co-operatively with others and who is sensitive to the prevailing prison climate. This has implications for the selection of social skills trainers in prison, who would probably be drawn from specialist staff who had a fair amount of experience in the prison situation. In-service training courses are run for those prison psychologists interested, but the best grounding comes from first acting as co-therapist and video operator and then being thrown in at the deep end!

Working with prisoners probably gives the least opportunity of any group of involving families of clients. Family members are not readily accessible and many of them may feel antipathetic to work being done by prison staff. However, Holloway probably provides better opportunities than many prisons for making outside contacts and, while this has rarely been done in a social skills context, it is not uncommon to set up family therapy sessions in the prison or to take inmates to their homes to discuss problems with the family. On one occasion a future husband was invited into the prison and the inmate and the therapist explained to him the social skills training work which had been done and showed him video films which illustrated it. The intention was that once she was released, he would take over responsibility for ensuring that she continued to exercise her new found skills. Her correspondence after release suggested that this was the case.

VI. OUTCOME

A traditionally accepted measure of success is long-term changes in social skills which have generalized outside the prison. In Holloway, this sort of outcome evaluation is not very feasible, nor is it necessarily thought to be the most appropriate outcome measure. Holloway has a very transient population and this means there can be no guarantees that a woman starting a programme will still be in the prison to finish it. The safer assumption is in fact that she will not, and the programme is organized accordingly. This means that it really is not feasible to attempt to set up the sort of experimental design of treatment and control groups, of random allocation, etc., which would be necessary for a conventional follow-up study. However, in institutions which have a more settled population, a more controlled and rigorous approach to evaluation is possible and an example of this is current work at Bullwood Hall Borstal for girls (Cullen, 1980). We have made some attempts to collect information about our clients after discharge. These have included sending questionnaires to the Probation Officers of borstal trainees who did the jobs course and collating the large amount of informal information received in the prison about women who have been on the therapeutic unit. These women are in frequent contact with the unit through letter or by 'phone. They are also allowed to return to groups to report on their progress. However, it is difficult to assess the reliability of this information and this questions its scientific value as an outcome measure. Even when a piece of information is known to be correct it is sometimes difficult to assess whether it is good news or bad news. Getting married may be good news if it indicates stability, but bad news if it is known that the woman has not divorced her previous husband! As far as was possible, the information received was categorized as good, bad or "neutral", and it was found to be evenly distributed into these three categories. Unfortunately, few conclusions can be drawn from this.

We have tended to concentrate on other measures of outcome which we consider are more appropriate to the types of referrals we see. Firstly, we are referred women who are having difficulties in one way or another in coping with being in prison. Our interventions are evaluated by examining changes in these women's behaviour in prison. The main sources of this information are our own observations, feedback from staff and from the women themselves. Secondly, when we work with the women on the therapeutic unit we are working with those who are undergoing a much more wide-ranging treatment, and social skills is one element of a general treatment package. The wider aims of that unit are to produce changes in attitudes and general "style" in women who may have different presenting problems (to do with drugs, alcohol, violence, persistent criminality for example) but share a wish to change and a belief that they have little control over their lives. The primary aim is to teach them specific social skills, It is also hoped that by doing SST, they will learn to control their behaviour and see the effect that behaving differently may have on other people. Thus, they will no longer feel the passive victim of circumstances and of their habitual behaviour patterns. Changes in the women's behavioural style and in their attitudes are the main outcome measure, though it may be difficult to define whether these changes are due to SST itself or the total experience on the Therapeutic Unit. The sources of information about changes are as for individual referrals but additionally we get comments from the main community meeting. Feedback from the women themselves takes the form of "consumer satisfaction" ratings. This involves filling in a 5 point rating scale on interest, enjoyment and usefulness. A satisfied customer does not ensure new learning or its generalization, but it would seem a necessary component to motivate the women to try out their new skills in different settings. On the whole, the sessions are received well and found relevant.

VII. PROBLEMS

The problem of the artificiality of the prison environment as a setting for SST has already been touched upon. Total institutions have the effect of intensifying and dramatizing minor issues and people's immediate concerns which they bring forward as role-play material may not be totally relevant to their normal lives. The concerns of freedom may pale into insignificance besides the day-to-day pressures of institutional life, and it may be hard for people to put themselves in imagination back into their normal roles. Simple matters become difficult in prison and difficulties evaporate. Communication becomes a problem and much prisoner energy is put into getting others to do things on their behalf, but earning a living and fending for oneself are no longer issues and it is possible to assume a state of child-like dependence. Perhaps most significant is the relative inaccessibility of the outside world for "home-work" tasks. Some women may be debarred by their legal status or their state of mind from any excursions outside the prison. However, it is not difficult to get permission to take low security risk sentenced women out of Holloway to practice skills, but the amount of time available for such outings is naturally limited by practical considerations. When a person has been in prison for even a short space of time a trip out can be an overwhelming experience, sometimes exciting, sometimes frightening, and it would not be wise to cram in too many novel events. There is little opportunity therefore for a comprehensive programme of practice in the outside world. Within the limits of imprisonment we find that there are opportunities for highly realistic work. As noted earlier, the problems which the women have outside are often mirrored in prison and incidents and relationships in Holloway are not necessarily dissimilar to those outside. These can be used for *in vivo* practice. Examples are coping appropriately with authority and dealing with anger and frustration. We are less able to provide practice in the area of family relationships and its day-to-day social situations such as going to the pub. It is in recognition of this that the social skills programme concentrates on the areas which best relate to prison and can be practised in this environment. We therefore make a point of giving women homework tasks. Doing the homework can be made easier if the help of another prisoner is enlisted. In Holloway there is some acceptance of the idea of women helping each other with their problems and not infrequently room-mates agree to do this. On the therapeutic unit staff have organized room changes with this in mind.

An overriding problem affecting any type of treatment in prison is the basic conflict between security and rehabilitation. The best interests of each are usually served by attitudes, behaviours and arrangements which are diametrically opposed and the provision of some sort of appropriate compromise can be taxing to staff and confusing to inmates. Those sent to prison must adapt somehow to the prisoner role and though there is a variety of possible styles for this they usually involve some element of resistance to authority. Indeed, many offenders come to prison with a hostile attitude to authority already well ingrained. This inhibits them against accepting prison staff as treaters and trainers and any desire to change may well be suppressed as being too close to the goal of the penal system. The stigma of mental illness also operates strongly in prison, probably because of the low social status of offenders and their need to find a lower group to look down upon, and there can be resistance to being considered "a suitable case for treatment".

All these problems have a bearing on the generalization and maintenance of treatment goals. (Huff, 1981). In considering generalization, there is first the issue of the learning that is gained in the treatment room being applied on the prison unit and, then of prison learning generally being applied to life in free conditions. It is possible to assess the amount of generalization to prison situations through feedback from the staff and the woman herself. Follow-up to assess maintenance is not impossible but is made very difficult by the prison tradition against continuing contacts after discharge. The woman herself may not wish for further contact, even if she feels that she has gained from her prison experience, as prison to many ex-inmates is something to be set firmly behind them. Some prisoners who have co-operated well with treatment may lose any further interest in behaviour change once they have left the institution, as their problems may be socially defined and therefore more distressing to others than to themselves. Aggression is an example of this type of problem behaviour. It is strongly disapproved of in the prison and the woman might thoroughly accept the need to eradicate it, but once in her usual setting with her usual contacts the behaviour might simply become an acceptable way of life once more.

In view of this, it is perhaps surprising how much informal contact is kept by ex-Holloway women. Many look back on aspects of prison life, particularly certain individuals with appreciation and nostalgia. In this way some knowledge can be gained of their present life and even occasionally some impact be made upon it. Permission can be sought for a member of staff to visit an ex-inmate to give support. This would be done in the context of general assistance and advice rather than as a purely social skills intervention. Attempts have been made at "postal-therapy", the ex-inmate filling in and returning forms which monitor a certain behaviour, but the discipline and motivation required for this particular type of follow-up is beyond most ex-inmates. A more realistic way of continuing treatment is to refer the women elsewhere after release and this has occasionally been done. However interest by the woman in the continuation of treatment may not survive her release and the nature of many ex-prisoners is such that making and keeping appointments is an overwhelming difficulty. An illustration of this is that while for a number of years a room has been available in Central London where members of the Holloway Psychology Department could meet ex-clients on neutral territory involving neither a difficult visit to the prison nor to the home; it has never yet been used. Even if more follow-ups were demanded, it would not be easy to devote much time to this sort of work as the needs of other inmates are always pressing and institutional tasks must have priority.

A prison with a history of orientation towards treatment is obviously easier to run a social skills programme in than one which has defined its role in a more limited way. Holloway provides opportunities for therapeutic contacts with prisoners, but may sometimes place obstacles in their way. These are more likely to be due to institutional constraints, such as staff shortages, than to lack of staff co-operation. Staff are generally helpful, though they may sometimes unwittingly undermine treatment. For example, if a woman with severe deficits is given homework tasks staff may be tempted to give her too much help or may be over-generous in their appraisal of her performance. They may also fail to appreciate the need to treat individuals differently, for there is a strong prison tradition of equality of treatment. This is generally a positive feature of imprisonment but the prison therapist sometimes suggests that it is set aside in the interests of the individual. For example, a case might be made for a series of trips out of the prison for a woman facing particular difficulties on discharge. Such concessions could not feasibly be made for every woman. We must also take into account that staff bring to the job varied experiences, skills and expectations and that they operate in strikingly different ways. This has obvious implications as it will affect the way officers react to women with problems and those trying out new behaviours. It is therefore necessary to take time to explain and discuss what is planned for a particular woman before treatment gets under way.

Ethical issues take on a new dimension in prison and some would say that treatment should not be attempted in an institution in which security and coercion are a primary feature. It has often been pointed out that consent is an uncertain commodity in a non-voluntary situation and that treatment in prison can never be undertaken for entirely pure motives. These arguments have some attraction, but most people who work in prisons would be loath to give up the opportunity for helping those who wish to change. Without this element of progress and hope, penal institutions would be dreary places and would probably become unacceptably repressive. Prison workers in helping inmates to develop must therefore undertake this task with sensitivity to the prison environment and to the subjects' needs. When consent is sought for any programme care must be taken to ensure that it is informed consent and a full explanation must be given of what is entailed. Because social and cultural standards vary so widely between the various members of the total prison community, care must be taken by the treaters not to impose their own standards on the client group. These could be inappropriate and value judgements should be avoided where possible. But a treatment philosophy which aims towards teaching the behaviours which work best according to the clients' own definition could also have its pitfalls. Society would be rightly disapproving of prison treatment which turned inmates into more polite thieves and more plausible defrauders. This issue, as with so many pertaining to prison, requires balance and sensitivity.

VIII. CONCLUSIONS

The issues outlined above apply to all psychological treatments in prison. SST is perhaps one of the most easily adapted and readily accepted methods. It has considerable face validity in the institution because it comes across to staff as being practical and relevant. The sort of problems it helps with and the methods used can be clearly described and easily understood by staff who may be unfamiliar with more technical treatment language.

The trend generally is for an increasing number of professional groups to be involved with SST. This is also the case in Holloway, where both the Probation and Education Departments are becoming interested in this sort of work. Unfortunately, it has not been possible to involve prison officers more actively as therapists, as has happened in life skills programme with male offenders. This is a development which we in Holloway would welcome. We envisage that our SST work will continue and increase, perhaps leading to more involvement with our colleagues in other departments.

We would also like to expand our efforts to include staff training where we have already made some preliminary incursions, such as practising for promotion interviews and helping new staff handle unfamiliar prison situations. Given the resources, the potential applications for SST in Holloway are very considerable.

IX. REFERENCES

Braukmann, C. J. and Fixsen, D. L. (1975). Behaviour Modification with Delinquents. In "Progress in Behaviour Modification" (M. Hersen, R. M. Eisler and P. M. Miller, Eds), Vol. 1, pp. 191–231. Academic Press, New York.
Cullen, E. (1980). "Social Skills Training for Female Borstal Trainees". Home Office, London. (Unpublished)
Davidson, W. S. and Seidman, E. (1974). Studies of Behaviour Modification and Juvenile Delinquency. Psychol. Bull. 81, 998–1011.
Gibbens, T. C. N. (1971). Female Offenders. In "Contemporary Psychiatry" (T. Silverstone and B. Baraclough, Eds). Headly Brothers, Ashford.

Goldstein, A. P. (1978). Teaching Aggressive Adolescents in Prosocial Behaviour. *J. Youth Adolescence* **7**, 74–92.

Goodman, N. and Price, J. (1967). "Studies of Female Offenders". Home Office Research Unit, Her Majesty's Stationery Office, London.

Grayson, D. (1980). "Social Skills Training Survey". Home Office, London. (Unpublished)

Home Office (1971). "Report on the Work of the Prison Department, 1970". Her Majesty's Stationery Office, London.

Home Office (1978). "Report on the Work of the Prison Department, 1977". Her Majesty's Stationery Office, London.

Huff, G. (1981). "Social Skills Training: A Critique". Home Office, London. (Unpublished)

Marzillier, J. S. and Winter, K. (1978). Success and Failure in Social Skills Training: Individual Differences. *Behav. Res. Ther.* **16**, 67–84.

Priestley, P., McGuire, J., Flegg, D., Hemsley, V. and Welham, D. (1978). "Social Skills and Personal Problem Solving". Tavistock Publications, London.

Prins, H. (1980). "Offenders, Deviants or Patients". Tavistock Publications, London, New York.

Sarason, I. (1978). A Cognitive Social Learning Approach to Juvenile Delinquency. *In* "Psychopathic Behaviour: Approaches to Research" (R. D. Hare and D. Schalling, *Eds*). Wiley, Chichester and New York.

Sarason, I. and Gauzer, V. J. (1973). Modelling and Group Discussion in the Rehabilitation of Juvenile Delinquents. *J. Counselling Psychol.* **20**, 442–449.

Shepherd, G. (1978). Social Skills Training: The Generalization Problem. *Behav. Ther.* **8**, 1008–9.

Smart, C. (1977). "Women, Crime and Criminology". Routledge and Kegan Paul, London.

Spence, S. H. (1979). Social Skills Training with Adolescent Offenders. *Behav. Psychotherapy* **7**, 49–56.

Spence, S. H. and Marzillier, J. S. (1979). Social Skills Training with Adolescent Male Offenders: 1. Short term effects. *Behav. Res. Ther.* **17**, 7–16.

Walker, N. (1968). "Crime and Punishment in Britain". 2nd Edition. Edinburgh University Press, Edinburgh.

SECTION II

Social skills training with children and adolescents

PREFACE BY SUE SPENCE

I. INTRODUCTION

A. Historical background

Despite a considerable body of evidence to demonstrate a relationship between the level of children's social functioning and their long-term adjustment, there has been surprisingly little effort put into the development of children's social skills (Combs and Slaby, 1977; Van Hasselt *et al.*, 1979). The school curriculum typically focuses on the teaching of academic skills and the development of interpersonal skills tends to be left as an incidental by-product of the system, hoping that an adequate level of social functioning can be achieved through parental influence. Unfortunately, this optimism is often misplaced. Many children experience poor peer relationships, have few or no friends and find it difficult to handle the complicated interactions involving adults such as teachers or parents. Many of the interactions which children engage in require extremely sophisticated social skills, such as those needed in making friends, dealing with teasing or bullying, asking for help, or dealing with a wrong accusation. Given the lack of attention given to their development perhaps it is not surprising that many children fail to acquire these complex skills.

The past 10 years has shown an increased interest in the teaching of social skills to children and adolescents. This interest however has mainly been in the remediation of interpersonal problems that are already established, for example with children who are found to be socially withdrawn or isolated, or those who respond aggressively to conflict situations. There are still very few programmes in which social skills are actively taught as part of the educational curriculum, in order to prevent the development of social problems. Historically, attempts to teach social skills with young people have developed from three separate backgrounds; modelling/imitation studies, problem-solving approaches and traditional skills training/assertive training programmes. Although each approach differs in terms of the teaching components, they all generally reflect the notion of social learning theory. Each approach assumes that social behaviour is learned, and can therefore be taught, given an appropriate learning experience.

Many of the early attempts to improve children's social functioning made use of modelling techniques. These studies primarily focused on the teaching of friendship making skills (e.g. O'Connor, 1969; 1972; Evers and Schwarz, 1973) and helping behaviours (Staub, 1971; Yarrow, 1973). The children were generally required to watch films or peer models engaging in appropriate social responses. Short-term improvements were found for socially isolated children in terms of increased frequency and quality of peer interactions and helping behaviours in pre-school children. The use of imitation learning was therefore found to be an effective method of teaching interpersonal skills, at least in terms of producing short-term improvements. The second approach, namely problem-solving stemmed from the work of D'Zurilla and Goldfried (1971) which stresses the importance of cognitive factors in social functioning. Children need to be able to identify the existence of problem situations and generate alternative solutions. They need to be able to work out the likely consequences of different responses and pick the behavioural response likely to be the most successful. This type of problem-solving approach has been extensively developed for use with children by Spivack and Shure (1976) and implemented successfully by researchers such as Allen *et al.* (1976). The final approach that has influenced the teaching of interpersonal functioning has been the specific Social Skills Training approach (SST) based on the work of Argyle

(1969) and Wolpe (1958). Although both approaches combine the use of methods such as instructions, discussion, modelling, role-play, feedback and behavioural tasks, the focus of training is slightly different. The Argyle approach has tended in the past to emphasize the teaching of very specific, micro-level skills such as eye contact, posture, tone of voice, or social distance (see Chapter 1). On the other hand, the assertive training approach developed from Wolpe's early work has tended to focus at a slightly higher level, teaching more complex strategies of responding such as how to refuse unreasonable requests or handle conflict situations. In practice, the two approaches are hard to separate. Although many early studies tended to focus on the teaching of very simple skills with children such as eye contact or listening skills (e.g. Bornstein *et al.*, 1978; Calpin and Kornblith, 1979; Spence and Marzillier, 1979) this seems to have been primarily for research purposes, in order to demonstrate that specific skills can be taught. In practice most programmes now seem to accept the need to train both the basic social skills and the more complex strategies of responding, as the following chapters in this section will demonstrate. Indeed it is gradually becoming evident that social skills training programmes for children and adolescents are developing progressively, to incorporate the methodologies given by the various perspectives. The following chapters will provide examples of the way in which the teaching of problem-solving skills can easily be incorporated into the traditional social skills training approach.

B. Outcome studies

There have been several extensive reviews of the use of SST techniques with children and adolescents (e.g. Combs and Slaby, 1977; Spence, 1979; Van Hasselt *et al.*, 1979). There is now quite a substantial body of research literature and perhaps it is easiest to focus separately on child populations presenting different problems.

(1) Studies with socially withdrawn, isolated, unpopular or unassertive children

Early studies which attempted to enhance the social behaviour of isolated, withdrawn or unassertive children tended to focus on increasing the frequency of interaction by reinforcing the children's attempts at interaction (Hartup, 1965). This type of approach is unlikely to be of lasting value to children unless they already interact in an adequate way. Simply increasing quantity, if the *quality* of interaction is poor, is not likely to help the child make friends. Indeed, if an unskilled child tries more often to approach peers in an inappropriate way, even more problems may result (for example, they may be more frequently rejected, rebuffed or taunted for their efforts). An early attempt to improve the interaction skills of socially isolated children was reported by O'Connor (1969). Six children who were identified by their teachers as being long standing social isolates were shown a short film in which an initially withdrawn child engaged in progressively more complex social interactions with peers. A control group of 7 children observed film unrelated to peer interactions. Behavioural observations of the children in the classroom taken immediately after the film indicated that those children who had seen the modelling film showed a marked increase in their frequency of interaction. This increase was not shown by the control group. Subsequently teachers' ratings showed that only 1 of the 6 children in the modelling group continued to be rated as socially isolated. The benefits of similar modelling films have since been confirmed by other studies such as O'Connor (1972) and Evers and Schwarz (1973). The evidence to date however only shows that modelling films can produce short-term changes and it remains to be shown whether such improvements can be maintained for any length of time.

Coaching procedures involving instructions, practice games and feedback have also been found to produce improvements in social interaction. Oden and Asher (1977) assigned 33 socially isolated children to either a coaching group, a peer-pairing method, or a no treatment control group. In the peer pairing condition, the children were assigned a partner who was non-isolated to play with in a games session. The results of sociometric assessment showed that only the children in the coaching condition made significant pre- to post-training gains, as being rated as desirable playmates.

More complex SST procedures have been used to reduce social isolation and lack of assertion by several investigators. Bornstein *et al.* (1977) reported 4 single cases of children who were identified as unassertive from behavioural observation. Improvements in the performance of specific skills such as eye contact and audibility were found along with improvements in overall assertiveness as measured by role-play tests. There was no attempt however to assess whether the benefits generalized beyond the training setting to natural interactions. Whitehill (1978) did try to assess for generalization and found that SST was successful in improving the conversation skills of 4 socially isolated children. Improvements were found in both the training settings and real-life situations as measured by sociometry, teacher ratings, observation of role-plays and naturalistic observation of play and classroom interactions. Although the study showed generalization of benefits to natural settings, these changes were not maintained at 8 weeks follow-up.

It seems then that SST can produce immediate improvements in social functioning with isolated, withdrawn and unassertive children. But, much more research is needed before a conclusion may be drawn as to whether programmes can be developed that lead to long term gains.

(2) *Studies with aggressive children*

Previous research has shown that aggressive children are often unpopular with their peers and tend to elicit anti-social responses from their peers (Patterson, 1976). Patterson *et al.* (1975) suggest that if highly aggressive children are left untreated then the problem is likely to persist, as the consequences of their aggressive acts may lead to reinforcing events, such as adult attention or peer responses. Bornstein *et al.* (1978) therefore stressed the need for intervention at an early age with aggressive children. They suggested that certain aggressive children may be deficient in basic social skills and would therefore benefit from social skills training. Four highly aggressive inpatient children were trained in eye contact, appropriate tone of voice and requests for new behaviour, according to a multiple baseline design across behaviours. Training consisted of instructions, modelling, prompting, behaviour rehearsal and feedback. Each child was assessed before, during, and after training using a series of role-play tests. Measures of each target behaviour and ratings of overall assertiveness were made from each videotaped role-play. The results demonstrated an improvement on each of the target skills following the onset of the relevant phase of training and an increase on assertiveness ratings. The improvements were maintained at the 2- and 4-week follow-up for all subjects, but for only two of the subjects by the 24 week follow-up. The carry over effect to the generalization (untrained) scenes was also minimal with 2 of the subjects. These results demonstrate noticeable individual variations in response to training and suggest that SST may be of lasting benefit to some individuals but not others. Further information relating to individual difference characteristics would be useful in order to identify those individuals most likely to benefit from SST.

In a similar study, Calpin and Kornblith (1979) carried out a social skills training programme with 4 boys, aged 9–11 who were emotionally disturbed, aggressive inpatients. The same series of role-play assessment scenes to Bornstein *et al.* (1978) were used before, during, and after training. Measures were taken of target skills, such as expressions of affect, requests for new behaviour and overall social skill performance.

Calpin and Kornblith trained each skill sequentially in a multiple baseline across behaviours technique. Training consisted of instructions, modelling behaviour rehearsal and videotaped feedback. The results showed that improvement occurred on all target behaviours following the relevant phase of training and there was also an increase on the general rating of social skill performance for all subjects. There was also evidence of a carry over effect to the generalization scenes and maintenance at the 3 month follow-up for 3 of the 4 subjects. Both the Calpin and Kornblith (1979) and Bornstein *et al.* (1978) studies failed to assess the benefits of SST in real-life, day-to-day, interactions and this limits the conclusions that can be drawn. SST does seem to be effective in improving the performance of basic social skill components, but whether this leads to more successful social interaction is therefore questionable.

Goldstein *et al.* (1978) have also attempted to apply a form of SST known as Structured Learning Therapy to aggressive adolescents. The authors stressed the role of social skill deficits in the maintenance of deviant behaviour, particularly aggression. Several studies carried out by the team and their research students support the view that structured learning therapy can be effective in enhancing interaction performance with aggressive adolescents. However, Goldstein *et al.* (1978) fail to provide details as to the assessment measures used during evaluation, which obviously limits the conclusions that can be drawn. This paper is particularly useful in that it points out the need to programme for the generalization of training effects and suggests several methods of achieving this. These include: appropriate selection of targets and homework tasks, increasing the range of trainers and the range of training situations.

In conclusion, the data relating to the use of SST techniques with aggressive children is encouraging at first sight, but once again further studies are necessary to investigate the long-term, generalized benefits in real-life situations.

(3) *Studies with young offenders*

A third category of problem children to which SST has been applied are juvenile offenders. Initial studies (e.g. Sarason and Ganzer, 1973; Thelen *et al.*, 1976) tended to assume that all juvenile offenders were deficient in social skills and should therefore benefit from SST. However, more recent attempts have questioned this assumption and selected only those juvenile offenders who have been shown to experience interpersonal problems (e.g. Spence and Marzillier, 1981).

A series of studies from the Achievement Place Programme in Kansas,

USA reported the successful training of a wide range of basic social skills. Single case research designs were used to show that SST could produce improvements in basic conversation skills (Maloney et al., 1975; Minkin et al., 1976) heterosexual social skills (Braukmann et al., 1973) interview skills (Braukmann et al., 1974) and police encounter skills (Werner et al., 1975). The finding of short-term improvements in specific social skills such as eye contact and listening skills has also been confirmed by Spence and Marzillier (1979). It remains to be shown whether such changes can be maintained and carried over into interactions in everyday life. Similarly this type of single case approach has tended to focus on whether SST can successfully produce improvements in skills, rather than whether any subsequent changes in offence behaviour occurs.

Other, more detailed training programmes have focused on teaching more complex interaction skills. For example, Sarason and Ganzer (1973) reported an extensive research programme which is one of the few studies to assess the effect of training on subsequent offending. One hundred and ninety-two male, first offenders were randomly assigned to 3 groups, an SST group, a discussion group and a no treatment control group. The SST procedure involved the modelling of appropriate behaviour by adult students showing a variety of problem situations. The boys were then asked to imitate the correct behaviour as closely as possible during role-play. They then received audio or videotaped feedback. Sessions took place in groups of 4, over 14 one hour periods. The discussion group received an equivalent level of input but simply discussed the same social problems dealt with in the SST group. The no-treatment comparison group merely received the standard regime of the institution. The results showed positive changes in attitude (such as shifts towards internal locus of control) positive changes in behaviour and less recidivism over the 3 year follow-up for both discussion and SST groups, compared with the no treatment group. There were no significant differences between the 2 treatment conditions, which suggests that the improvements could have resulted from either increased adult attention, or discussion of information about ways of handling difficult social situations.

Since the Sarason and Ganzer study, several other major projects have been reported. Shoemaker (1979) reported successful improvements in assertive responses with juvenile offenders in a cottage home setting. Ollendick and Hersen (1979) found SST to produce significant improvements on behaviour measures during role-play (e.g. eye contact, latency of response and aggressive contact). Higher points earned during the institutional programme were also found for the SST group but these benefits were not found for either the discussion or no treatment control groups. Both these studies however failed to determine the durability of the effects or whether there was any influence on future offending.

A recent application of SST has been with juvenile offenders and their parents. This is an important development in view of the evidence that maladaptive family interaction patterns seem to be a primary factor in maintaining adolescent offending (Alexander, 1973). Improvements in interactions between parents and children have been shown following SST procedures in terms of communication and negotiation skills (Alexander and Parsons, 1973; Kifer et al., 1974). Alexander and Parsons (1973) trained a variety of family interaction skills, such as increased levels of reciprocal communication, more equal communication between family members and greater requests for clarification and feedback. These responses had previously shown to differ in the families of young offenders compared to the patterns of responding in non-offender families (Alexander, 1973). The effects of training family interaction skills was compared to the effects of client centred therapy and no treatment. Forty-six families were randomly assigned to each of these groups, and were then followed-up over a 6–18 month period. The results showed that the interaction skill training procedure which involved modelling, prompting, practice and reinforcement, produced a significantly lower recidivism rate than the client centred or no treatment procedures. Perhaps most important was the finding that families who did not show any change in interaction patterns within the assessment setting also demonstrated minimal reduction in recidivism. This supports the notion of an association between family interaction patterns and persistent juvenile offending. These results are encouraging as they suggest that SST procedures may be of benefit to the families of young offenders, if not with the adolescents themselves.

A similar study was reported after Kifer et al. (1974) in which 3 pre-delinquent youths and their parents were trained to negotiate conflict situations. An SST approach was used to train negotiation skills using a multiple base-line design across subjects. The assessment of negotiation skills within the training setting throughout the programme demonstrated an increase in performance following the introduction of training for each subject. In addition to the use of the learned responses within the clinical setting, this study can be commended for attempting to determine whether the training effect generalized to the home situation. Unfortunately, the measure used involved the assessment of responses during discussion of problem situations rather than the family's response to spontaneous conflicts. A greater percentage of negotiation behaviours occurred after training on this measure, but the absence of an untreated control group prevents the conclusion being drawn that these improvements were specifically due to the training procedure. This study also failed to investigate the durability of training effects. In reviewing studies in which SST has been applied with young offenders it would seem that positive changes in social behaviour can be produced in the short-term. Whether these improvements are maintained and generalize to everyday life situations remains to be shown conclusively and perhaps most importantly, it remains to be seen whether SST can produce reliable and marked reduction in future offending.

(4) Studies with children in ordinary schools

Several studies have been reported recently in which social skills training methods have been applied to children without specific problems, either for preventative purposes or to facilitate the development of skills. Two interesting studies have been reported in which attempts were made to increase pro-social helping behaviours with young children. In the first study reported by Staub (1971) the effectiveness of an "induction" method was compared to role-play techniques in teaching helping and sharing behaviours.

Staub hypothesized that helping behaviour is influenced by the extent to which a child can empathize with others, and that empathy can be increased by reverse role-play techniques. In addition, helping behaviour is also influenced by the extent to which the child has the skills and knowledge to enable him or her to help. Seventy-five kindergarten children were randomly assigned in pairs to either role-play, induction, role-play plus induction, or a control (non-helping role-play) condition. In the induction procedure an adult described situations where a helping response was required and discussed ways in which help could be given. In the role-play condition, pairs of children role-played alternately being the victim and the helper in a variety of problem scenes. Staub found that children in the role-play condition demonstrated significantly more helping responses towards a distressed child and shared sweets more with others immediately after training, whereas this increase was not found with the control procedure nor after induction. The induction procedure however, did lead to a slight increase in helping responses towards an adult. The effects were maintained at the 5–7 day follow-up.

A similar study was reported by Yarrow et al. (1973) using live adult models in order to teach helping behaviours to young children. In the group, adults demonstrated helping responses using symbolic situations such as pictures or games, in addition to real life problems. The models described their own actions during the demonstrations using the word "help". Two days after training a significant increase in helping behaviours was found on the symbolic tests, independent of whether the children had previously had a highly nurturant relationship with the adult model. However, there was less increase in real life helping situations which brings into question the generalizability of the training effects. Thus, the 2 studies suggest some promise in the teaching of pro-social behaviours with young children but it would be useful to investigate the effects of combining both the modelling and the role-play methods as the benefits could well be enhanced.

A slightly different approach to the development of pro-social behaviour has been taken by Spivack and Shure (1976, 1978). These researchers attempted to develop a 10 week programme aimed at facilitating social adjustment with young children, primarily as a means of preventing secondary mental health problems. The programme aims to teach problem solving skills to young children so that they can develop their own alternative solutions to interpersonal conflicts. Many of the components of the teaching package relate to those used in social skills training. Social conflict situations are enacted using stories, games, puppets and role-play in order to teach children to identify problems, generate alternative solutions and look at their consequences in relation to the problem. The children are then encouraged to practise the different alternatives using symbolic methods and are given feedback according to their performance. This type of approach stresses the role of the individual in selecting alternative ways of responding, with less emphasis on the individual having the skills necessary to carry out the response successfully. Many of the components of the Spivack and Shure package are highly suitable for inclusion in social skills training programmes. However, evaluative research is needed regarding the benefits of this social problem solving approach before the effectiveness can be accepted.

Allen *et al.* (1976) have attempted to evaluate the preventative benefits of a social problem solving approach with young children. They stressed the need to try and modify social systems rather than simply trying to modify the behaviour of the children presenting problems. The school is viewed as a major source of influence upon the behaviour of children and is therefore in an ideal position to teach a variety of social and self-help skills in addition to purely academic skills. Allen *et al.* began their programme by preparing the teachers and school system for the implementation of a social problem solving curriculum. Teachers from regular schools were trained extensively in methods of teaching social problem solving skills. The children were then selected on the basis of teachers' ratings of social withdrawal and isolation. These judgements were then validated by means of observations of social interaction frequency, over a 5 week period. Thirty children aged between 3 and 7 years were confirmed as being social isolates and were then allocated to either a treatment group of 20 children or a no treatment control group of 10 children. The groups were matched according to frequency of social interaction. The treatment group then received instruction in problem solving techniques and viewed modelling films over a 4 month period, under the guidance of class teachers.

Post-training evaluation showed a significant increase in the problem solving skills of the experimental group but not in the control group. An increase in the frequency of social interaction was also found for the experimental group after training which almost brought them to the levels of non-isolates. This effect was not found for the control children. Unfortunately the study did not report any long-term follow-up data. The measures of problem-solving skills used also tended to involve response to stories or questions rather than behavioural observation of real-life problem-solving ability. The generalizability of training effects is therefore rather questionable. Thus, it would seem that a social problem-solving approach may offer promise both as a method of remediating social interaction problems and as a method of reducing the likelihood of secondary problems related to social inadequacy, but there are still some doubts concerning its effectiveness.

A final study to be discussed in this section is the attempt to increase the assertive behaviour of elementary school children reported by Michaelson (1978). In this study, 80 elementary school children were randomly selected from 2 schools and assigned to either 8 hours of assertive training, 16 hours of assertive training, 16 hours of social studies with the trainers, or no contact. The children were not selected on the basis of any behavioural problems and were attending regular schools. The assessment of progress involved a children's questionnaire, a staff questionnaire and the Rathus assertiveness scale (revised for children). Assessments were made before and after training and at the 4 week follow-up. Training took place on a class basis, with 20 children in each group, and involved instructions, modelling, behavioural rehearsal and discussion. The assertive responses focused on compliments, complaints, refusals, requesting favours and asking for explanations. The results showed a significant increase on the children's self-report questionnaire, for both treatment groups at post and follow-up assessments. This was not found for the control groups. There were no differences on this measure between the 8 and 16 hour assertive training groups. The 16 hours training was found to produce better results than the other groups on the teacher's questionnaire at the 4 week follow-up, but no differences were produced on this measure immediately after training. Michaelson

concluded that 16 hours of training produced more stable and generaliz-
able results than 8 hours training. The results are encouraging in that they
suggest some short term benefit of a skills training procedure of this type
with young children. However, further studies are still required, involving longer term follow-ups and better measures of generalization, (e.g.
peer sociometric ratings) before conclusions can be drawn as to the
benefits of assertive training methods within a regular class-room
setting.

The research on SST involving children in ordinary schools again
seems to underline its promise as a preventative approach. However, as
before the data relating to normal children can be criticized in that
adequate attempts have not been made to assess the durability or
generalizability of training effects.

(5) *Summary of research findings*

This review of the literature relating to SST with various child populations suggests that the technique offers promise as a method of teaching
interpersonal skills. As with the development of many new techniques,
there has been an initial burst of enthusiasm towards its application.
However many of the studies to date have been marred by inadequacies
in their design. Few have carefully evaluated the long-term, generalized
effects of training, particularly in terms of significant changes in social
behaviour in everyday life. Much more research using carefully designed
single case experimentation or group designs is required before valid
conclusions can be drawn as to the long-term generalized benefits of
training. There are clearly many other questions that need to be
answered. It would be useful to investigate different ways of increasing
the transfer of training effects from the training setting to the community.
Similarly, it would be helpful to know which children are most likely to
benefit from SST and how therapists could identify these individuals.
Finally, it is worth noting the problems produced by the lack of a
generally accepted definition of "social skills". Few of the studies
available to date provide a clear indication of how they define socially
skilled behaviour and this has often led to confusion in the selection of
targets for training.

For example, several studies have selected clients for training without
any initial assessment to demonstrate social skills deficits (e.g. Bornstein
et al., 1978; Calpin and Kornblith, 1979). Thus, there has been a tendency
to assume that individuals who engage in certain types of problem
behaviour, such as aggression or offending, *must* be deficient in social
skills. This is a questionable assumption. There is also often a rather

arbitrary selection procedure in deciding which skills to train, again reflecting a lack of research into the valid components of socially skilled behaviour. Although the orientation of this book is primarily practical, it is important to discuss the empirical evidence with the state of the art. There is a danger of SST being seen as a "treatment for all ills" as is often the case with a new approach. The data shows that this is clearly not the case and that practitioners should proceed with caution, carefully evaluating their efforts at every stage.

C. Summary of Section II

In reviewing many of the social skills training programmes carried out to date with children and adolescents, it is clear that the exact methods used in the assessment and training of social skills varies considerably, according to the client group and training situation. We were interested to explore in greater detail the exact ways in which SST methods and assessment procedures have developed with various child-client groups in the UK.

The authors were asked to describe their settings, clients, assessment and selection procedures, training methods, along with a range of practical considerations and the problems they had encountered in the process of setting up SST programmes. *Stephen Frosh* in Chapter 7 opens this section by describing a project in which SST has been developed with infant school children in a class-room setting. He discusses the importance of using SST as a preventative approach, in order to prevent later difficulties. Children who experience peer difficulties are identified early on in life and selected for SST within the school curriculum. In addition to outlining the SST procedures used, this chapter provides an interesting discussion of the practicalities involved in health-care professionals working within the school system.

In Chapter 7, *Mary Jackson* describes a SST programme with much older children who have been referred to an adolescent, psychiatric out-patient clinic. In order to overcome many of the problems of working in a clinical setting, such as difficulties in achieving generalization and labelling effects, she has developed a community based programme in a youth club setting. She outlines an extensive assessment procedure and a great deal of valuable information on techniques that can be used in training with young people. Carrying out the sessions in a community based setting overcomes many of the difficulties described in Chapter 9 by *Sue Spence* working with adolescent offenders in a residential institution. Difficulties in selecting relevant targets and programming for

generalization are obvious limitations which emerge from this programme. The chapter, however, provides extensive discussion regarding
assessment procedures and the practicalities of working with boys who
are often extremely disruptive and lacking in motivation to change.

The client groups involved in the three chapters differ considerably
and the methods of teaching social skills have therefore been adapted
accordingly. Similarly, the type of skills selected for training also vary
markedly according to the age and type of presenting problems of the
children. Various common themes, however, can be seen to recur
throughout and will be expanded in the final conclusions.

II. REFERENCES

Alexander, J. F. (1973). Defensive and supportive communications in normal and
    deviant families. *J. Consult. Clin. Psychol.* **40**, 223–231.
Alexander, J. P. and Parsons, B. V. (1973). Short-term behavioural intervention
    with delinquent families: Impact on family process and recidivism. *J.
    Abnorm. Psychol.* **81**, 219–225.
Allen, G. J., Christy, J. M., Larcen, S. W., Lockman, J. E. and Selinger, H. V. (1976).
    "Community Psychology and the Schools". John Wiley, London.
Argyle, M. (1969). "Social Interaction". Methuen, London.
Bornstein, M., Bellack, A. S. and Hersen, M. (1977). Social skills training for
    unassertive children: A multiple-baseline analysis, *J. Appl. Behav. Anal.* **10**,
    183–195.
Bornstein, M., Bellack, A. S. and Hersen, M. (1978). "Social skills training for
    highly aggressive children in an inpatient psychiatric setting". University of
    Pittsburg. (Unpublished)
Braukmann, C. J., Maloney, D. M., Phillips, E. L. and Wolf, M. M. (1973). The
    measurement and modification of heterosexual interaction skills of pre-
    delinquents at achievement place. Unpublished Master Thesis. University
    of Kansas.
Braukmann, C. J., Maloney, D. M., Fixen, D. L., Phillips, E. L. and Wolf, M. M.
    (1974). Analysis of a selection interview training package for pre-delinquents
    at achievement place. *Crim. Just. Behav.* **1**, 30–42.
Calpin, J. P. and Kornblith, S. J. (1979). Training aggressive children in conflict
    resolution skills. University of Pittsburg. (Unpublished)
Combs, M. L. and Slaby, D. A. (1977). Social-skills training with children. *In*
    "Advances in Clinical Child Psychology" (B. B. Lahey and A. E. Kadzin, Eds),
    Vol. I, pp. 161–201. Plenum Press, New York.
D'Zurilla, T. J. and Goldfried, M. (1971). Problem solving and behaviour
    modification. *J. Abnorm. Psychol.* **78**, 107–26.
Evers, W. L. and Schwarz, J. C. (1973). Modifying social withdrawal in preschool-
    ers: The effects of filmed modelling and teacher praise. *J. Abnorm. Child
    Psychol.* **1**, 248–256.
Goldstein, A. P., Sherman, H., Gershaw, N. J., Sprafkin, R. P. and Glick, B. (1978).
    Training aggressive adolescents in pro-social behaviours. *J. Youth Adol.* **7**,
    73–93.

Hartup, W. W. (1965). Peers as agents of social reinforcement. Young Children **20**.

Kifer, R. E., Lewis, M. A., Green, D. R. and Phillips, E. L. (1974). Training pre-delinquent youths and their parents to negotiate conflict situations. *J. Appl. Behav. Anal.* **7**, 357–364.

Maloney, D. M., Harper, T. M., Braukmann, C. J., Fixsen, D. L., Phillips, E. L. and Wolf, M. M. (1975). Teaching conversation-related skill to pre-delinquent girls. *J. Appl. Behav. Anal.* **8**.

Michelson, L., Wood, R. and Flynn, J. (1978). Development of an assertive training programme for elementary school children. Paper presented at the Association for Advancement of Behaviour Therapy.

Minkin, N., Braukmann, C. J., Minkin, B. L., Timbers, G. D., Timbers, B. J., Fixsen, D. L., Phillips, E. L. and Wolf, M. M. (1976). The social validation and training of conversational skills. *J. Appl. Behav. Anal.* **9**, 127–139.

O'Connor, R. D. (1969). Modification of social withdrawal through symbolic modelling. *J. Appl. Behav. Anal.* **2**, 15–22.

O'Connor, R. D. (1972). Relative efficacy of modelling, shaping, and the combined procedures for modification of social withdrawal. *J. Abnorm. Psychol.* **79**, 327–334.

Oden, S. and Asher, S. R. (1977). Coaching children in social skills for friendship making. *Child Dev.* **48**, 495–506.

Ollendick, T. H. and Hersen, M. (1979). Social skills training for juvenile delinquents. *Behav. Res. Ther.* **17**, 547–555.

Patterson, G. R. (1976). Follow-up evaluations of a programme for parents' retraining their aggressive boys. Canadian Psychiatric Association Journal.

Patterson, G. R., Reid, J. G., Jones, R. R. and Conger, R. E. (1975). "A Social Learning Approach to Family Intervention". Vol. I. Castalia, Eugene, Oregon.

Sarason, I. G. and Ganzer, V. J. (1973). Modelling and group discussion in the rehabilitation of juvenile delinquent. *J. Counselling Psychol.* **5**, 442–449.

Shoemaker, M. E. (1979). Group assertion training for institutionalised male delinquents. *In* "Progress in Behaviour Therapy with Delinquents" (J. S. Stumphauser, Ed.). Charles C. Thomas, Springfield, Illinois.

Spence, S. H. (1979). Social skills training with adolescent offenders: A review. *Behav. Psychoth.* **7**, 49–57.

Spence, S. H. and Marzillier, J. S. (1979). Social skills training with adolescent, male offenders: I. Short-term effects. *Behav. Res. Ther.* **17**, 7–16.

Spence, S. H. and Marzillier, J. S. (1981). Social skills training with adolescent, male offenders: II. Short-term, long-term and generalised effects. *Behav. Res. Ther.* **19**, 349–368.

Spivack, G. and Shure, M. B. (1976). "Social Adjustment of Young Children. A cognitive approach to solving real life problems". Jossey Bass, London.

Spivack, G. and Shure, M. B. (1978). "Problem Solving Techniques in Child Rearing". Jossey Bass, London.

Staub, E. (1971). The use of role playing and induction in children's learning of helping and sharing behaviour. *Child Devel.* **42**, 805–816.

Strain, P. S. (1977). An experimental analysis of peer social initiations on the behaviour of withdrawn preschool children: Some training and generalization effects. *J. Abnorm. Child Psychol.* **5**, 445–455.

Thelen, M. H., Frey, R. A., Dollinger, S. I. and Paul, S. C. (1976). Use of video-taped models to improve the interpersonal adjustment of delinquents. *J. Cons. Clin. Psychol.* **44**, 492.

Van Hasselt, V. B., Hersen, M., Whitehill, N. B. and Bellack, A. S. (1979). Social skill assessment and training for children: An evaluative review. *Behav. Res. Ther.* **17**, 413–439.

Werner, J. S., Minkin, N., Minkin, C. J. and Bonnie, L. (1975). Intervention Package: An analysis to prepare juvenile delinquents for encounters with police officers. *Crim. Just. Behav.* **2**, 22–36.

Whitehill, M. B. (1978). A conversation skills training programme for socially isolated children: an analysis of generalization. Unpublished master's thesis, University of Pittsburgh.

Wolpé, J. (1958). "Psychotherapy and Reciprocal Inhibition". Stanford University Press.

Yarrow, M. R., Scott, P. M. and Waxler, C. Z. (1973). Learning concern for others. *Devel. Psychol.* **8**, 240–260.

7

Children and teachers in schools

STEPHEN FROSH

I. WHY TEACH SOCIAL SKILLS?

The momentum of the "Social Skills Training (SST) for children" movement over the last decade or so has been very considerable, giving rise to
a substantial literature and to widespread interest amongst professionals
working in psychology and in education. Whilst Stephens' (1980)
prophecy that "Teaching socially desirable behaviour will no doubt be
the Zeitgeist of the next decade" (p. vii) should be treated with considerable caution, there is little sign of this interest abating, and the research
and clinical possibilities to which SST gives rise appear profound
enough to sustain it for some time to come. To a degree, this upsurge in
SST work with children is a derivative of work on the social interactions
of other populations (e.g. Trower *et al.*, 1978), but there are also 2 major
lines of developmental research which provide a rationale for the
movement. In the past, most attention has been devoted to the ways in
which children become "socialized" by the learning experiences to
which adults (primarily their parents) introduce them, with relatively
little work being carried out on the role of peer relationships in child
development. Nevertheless, the research evidence that is available strongly
suggests that the experiences children have with one another are enormously important, providing the context and impetus for the development
of a whole range of skills and capacities which may be rather different
from those generated by interactions with adults. Hartup (1980), for
example, lists "aggressive and sexual socialization, the development of
moral values and the development of sociability" (p. 282) as some areas
which are probably profoundly influenced by experiences with peers.

In addition to evidence on the positive value of good peer relationships, it has been shown several times that children who have difficulties
in this area are a very "high risk" group for the development of other
problems. Asher *et al.* (1977) present evidence that children who have
poor peer relationships are more likely to drop out of school, be later
identified as juvenile delinquents, and have mental health problems in
later life. Roff *et al.* (1972) found a high positive correlation between
delinquency and low peer-acceptance scores obtained 4 years earlier.
Cowen *et al.* (1973), in an 11 year long study, found that peer ratings of
popularity were better predictors of later psychological problems than
any other measure. Rutter (1979) has argued that having poor peer
relations in childhood is a good predictor of adolescent maladjustment
and Cartledge and Milburn (1978) have summarized evidence suggesting
that poor social skills are related to impaired cognitive and academic
performance. Taking all this into account, Asher *et al.*'s (1977) conclusion
seems tenable: "The consequences of low peer acceptance may be more
severe than the consequences of low achievement" (p. 33).

Evidence that peer problems are associated with later psychological difficulties does not necessarily imply any aetiological connection: the notion that peer problems *cause* psychological ones in any simple way is much too crude to do justice to the enormous variability that exists in children's patterns of development. Similarly, it is important not to overstate the case for SST: just as peer problems are not the only cause of wider psychological difficulties, so social skills deficits are not the only sources of interpersonal problems. Thus, many personal, situational and background factors (intelligence, race, success in class, parental marital discord, etc.) have a part to play in determining a child's friendship status (Asher *et al.*, 1977; Miller and Gentry, 1980). Again, it may be that social isolation and withdrawal is constructive and necessary at times (Oden, 1980). Nevertheless, the *use* that a child makes of his or her personal characteristics and environment must be of some importance, and it is this that is referred to as "social skill". The clearest analogy is with problem-solving: given an interpersonal situation, does a child have a number of alternative courses of action ("solutions") which he or she can take, or is he or she tied to narrow, rigid and perhaps self-destructive modes of behaviour, such as aggression? To the extent that SST aims at increasing a child's repertoire of possible actions within an interpersonal setting, then it will always be of value, irrespective of the other determinants of the child's psychosocial state.

This rationale for SST with children suggests that such work may be of use in preventing later difficulties, and hence it should be widely accessible. Along with the enormous evidence that is available on the importance of carrying out behavioural programmes with an eye to the settings for which they are intended (e.g. Wahler *et al.*, 1979) it is clear that the appropriate place for implementation of SST is in the schools. Additionally, if the child's teachers can be utilized as social skills trainers, then the power and reach of SST programmes will be enormously enhanced. It is around the possibilities for classroom-based SST work, incorporated into the teachers' repertoire of techniques, that this chapter is based. Most emphasis will be on pre-adolescent children, but the general principle that SST should be carried out in the relevant environment for the client is a broad one, applicable elsewhere.

II. SCHOOL AS A SETTING FOR SST

A. Involving schools in SST

Schools are often suspicious of mental health interventions, sometimes with good reason. Frequently, experiences of alienating and mystifying psychiatric jargon, poor explanations of treatment plans and inadequate support for teachers working under stress are the salient memories with which a school staff will greet a psychological professional. Perhaps as an indication of the relatively small amount of attention that has been paid to this issue, information on how to maximize the chances of establishing and maintaining good relations with school staff is very hard to come by. Some advice is offered by Allen *et al.* (1976), who provide "Guidelines for consultant survival in a school system" (pp. 41–42) centring around communication, collaboration, enjoyment and feedback; not a bad list of some essentials of social skills, as it happens. Not wishing to repeat their detailed suggestions here, it need only be added that a kind of "problem-solving" procedure based on clear and practical discussions of general and specific elements of the intervention is important. General discussions should centre around the aims and progress of the SST programme, and should incorporate support from colleagues for those teachers who are actually involved. More specific discussions could deal with the situations that have arisen during SST and the possible ways in which these could be approached. This is not just a cosmetic recommendation: the school staff are clearly more expert than any outside professional when it comes to the system within which, and the children with whom, they work; active incorporation of their ideas into the SST programme is thus likely to increase its effectiveness.

B. School and classroom characteristics enhancing social skills learning

Once access to a school is achieved, there are certain situational characteristics which may have an influence on the ease with which peer-intellectual skills can be learnt by children. While there are hardly any definites in this area, the following suggestions may provide a guide to some aspects of school and classroom functioning which might repay attention.

(1) *Size and stability*

In general terms, the number of children in a school and in each of the classes it contains may have an impact on the quality of a child's social experiences. For example, large classes and schools may provide a greater variety of such experiences; smaller classes, on the other hand, may allow more opportunities for participation in activities, and hence may encourage children to become more engaged in social interactions (Asher *et al.*, 1977). On another level, children who attend schools in which there is a high turnover of children or staff are at a disadvantage when it comes to making friends (Asher *et al.*, 1977); not surprisingly, high-turn-over schools are also linked to child psychiatric disorder (Rutter *et al.*, 1975). Finally, whether a school is open-space or more traditional in design has no demonstrated impact on social skills, although open designs may make for more mutual friendships and a happier "social climate" in the class (Miller and Gentry, 1980).

(2) *Classroom resources and organization*

While poorly-equipped classrooms are unlikely to be good places to learn anything, it is not true that the more resources there are the better. For instance, Smith and Connolly (1976) showed that, with nursery children, removing play objects from class resulted in the children increasing their social interactions, establishing larger groups, and operating less frequently as "loners". Greater levels of sharing and creative establishment of activities were also observed when materials were withdrawn (Gump, 1980). The *type* of available activities also influence the kinds of social interaction which may occur: for instance, Charlesworth and Hartup (1967) found that dramatic play activities provided more opportunities for positive social interactions in young children than did table play.

With slightly older children, one way of encouraging social activity in class is to structure work around a cooperative learning programme. A particularly intriguing example of this is provided by Blaney *et al.* (1977), who organized fifth-grade pupils into "small interdependent learning groups". Each child taught the other members of the group a portion of the work assigned to them, with the material divided into as many parts as there were children. "In essence", the authors report, "the students put their knowledge together in a jig-saw-puzzle fashion, each child having a piece of knowledge that no-one else in the group had" (p. 123). At the end of 6 weeks, children in the co-operative groups showed higher self-esteem than controls and liked groupmates better than classmates. Other researchers (e.g. Hertz-Lazarowitz *et al.*, 1980) have confirmed that children taught in cooperative small groups become more cooperative on judgmental and behavioural measures. Finally, the more diverse social experiences that are available in class, the more different social strategies are likely to be learnt (Oden, 1980).

In summary, certain aspects of school and classroom functioning make the learning of social skills either more or less easy for children, and to some extent these aspects are amenable to change. In the next sections, an outline of procedures for assessing the quality of a child's social functioning is given, plus a more precise account of those social skills that might be important in a classroom setting.

III. ASSESSMENT AND SELECTION OF CHILDREN FOR SST

The particular procedures used in any psychological intervention depend crucially on the kinds of information required—that is, on a series of questions which may be asked about the particular group under study. For children in schools, the principle questions concerning social interaction centre around teachers' perceptions ("Which children do teachers regard as having peer problems, and why?"), peer perceptions ("Which children are isolated from, or rejected by, their peers?"), interpersonal activity ("What behaviour is characteristic of this or that child who is disliked by peers and/or selected by teachers as having problems?"), social knowledge ("What do the children know about solving interpersonal problems?") and characteristics of the class ("What is the level of friendship in this class? What is the usual social behaviours of children in their class like?"). Obviously, there may be several alternative sources of information that bear upon these questions; in this section, a brief account will be given of 4 such sources which are almost certain to be of value: teacher questionnaires, sociometry, observations of behaviour, and cognitive tasks.

A. Teacher questionnaires

In any work in schools, obtaining the views of teachers about children is an important first step. Not only are teachers the adults with the most direct knowledge of how children behave in their school, but their opinions and attitudes may influence their own behaviour, and hence the children's learning environment. Thus, even if a teacher's opinions about a particular child should prove to be totally inaccurate (e.g. he or she declares a child to be unpopular when that child turns out to be everybody's best friend), they are still of significance. Questionnaires, which are basically a form of structured interview, allow a teacher to express his or her views on the child while also imposing certain constraints in an attempt to increase the chances of these views being accurate.

Various published questionnaires have been used in social skills research, most of them fairly general screening devices derived from work carried out with other interests in mind. For example, Frosh and Callias (1980) used Rutter's (1967) questionnaire as a measure of the child's overall level of adjustment; others have used Walker's (1970) Problem Behaviour Identification Checklist, which includes measures of acting-out, withdrawal, distractability, disturbed peer relations and immaturity (Cartledge and Milburn, 1980). A more specific measure of social adjustment is described by Spivack and Shure (1974), which samples three factors (difficulty in delaying gratification, proneness to emotional upset, social aggressiveness) and gives scores on inhibition, impulsiveness and "problem-solving ability". While all these scales have established reliability, they tend to refer only indirectly to social interaction, and hence may not always be relevant measures of those behaviours in which an individual SST practitioner has an interest. In these circumstances, Cartledge and Milburn's (1980) advocacy of checklists specially constructed to suit particular interventions is probably appropriate.

Various other comments about teacher questionnaires are in order. Firstly, they are often difficult for teachers to complete, especially if they do not quite seem to capture the problem; it is therefore important that teachers are allowed to write freely about each child if they so wish. Secondly, the validity of teacher ratings is not always very good (Van Hasselet et al., 1979); however, Greenwood et al. (1977) review studies indicating that teachers can be much more accurate about child behaviour than they are usually given credit for, particularly when asked to make specific judgements about children whose behaviour is extreme. Green et al. (1980) have recently established quite impressive validities for teacher reports, and the lesson is quite clearly that the more specific and behaviour-oriented the questionnaire, the more accurate it is likely to be. Finally, it is worth noting that questionnaires may represent a form of teacher-training in their own right, sharpening up teachers' awareness of social development and peer-interaction difficulties in their children.

B. Sociometry

Sociometric assessment, which involves obtaining reports from children concerning their views of their peers, is an essential component of any analysis of social skill. Two main forms of sociometry predominate in the SST literature. The first is the *nomination* method, which simply involves asking children who their best friends are (positive nominations) or if there are any children in their class whom they dislike (negative nominations). Variations on this method include specifying the number of children to be selected, specifying the situation ("Who do you like working/playing with?") and using photographs to circumvent memory problems. The nomination method has the advantage of being easy to carry out, and of distinguishing between 2 different types of children with peer problems: (a) isolated children, who tend to be passive, withdrawn and anxious over social interactions, and who typically receive no positive or negative nominations (Hymel and Asher, 1977); (b) rejected children, who receive several negative nominations and who tend to be aggressive. It is the rejected children whose problems are most likely to continue (Combs and Slaby, 1977). Nomination methods are also good for measurement of reciprocity and identification of cliques (Oden, 1980). Disadvantages of nomination procedures include their relatively low stability over time (Asher et al., 1979) the ease with which they are influenced by situational variables (Frosh and Callias, 1980) and the likelihood that little information will be provided on the many children in a class who receive few acceptances or rejections. The second major sociometric method is the rating scale, in which every child in a class is asked to rate every other one according to how much they like playing or working with them. This procedure has several advantages (Van Hasselt et al., 1979): (a) each child is rated by all of his or her classmates, providing an enormous amount of information on friendship patterns; (b) the rating scale incorporates positive and negative criteria automatically; (c) children are not easily overlooked; (d) rating methods have high correlations with nomination methods, as well as correlating with more external variables (e.g. observations of behaviour), suggesting that more, and more valid, information is obtained. Finally, Asher et al. (1979), using a 3-point scale based on allocation of children to pictures of either a happy, neutral or sad face on the basis of how much they are liked, have shown that the rating procedure is highly reliable over time for children as young as 4 years old. Thus, rating procedures are more generally useful than nomination ones; however, they are relatively laborious to carry out and do not discriminate as easily between isolated and rejected children.

Some additional points may be made about sociometry. Firstly, in addition to information on the popularity of particular children, much other data is provided, for instance on the level of friendship in a class, or on whether specific children have positive or negative outlooks on others. Secondly, reciprocal choices are more likely to indicate stable friendships than are unilateral choices (Busk et al., 1973). Thirdly, few studies have been able to show any systematic relationship between sociometric and observational data; thus, while it is possible to pick out popular, isolated or rejected children, a more fine-grained analysis of how these children behave is required in individual cases.

C. Behavioural observations

Observations of a child's actual behaviour in class are a vital element in the development of any SST programme. An enormous variety of different observational schedules can be used, from simple counts of one behaviour of especial interest "how many times does he hit another child during a science lesson?") to complex coding systems based on coverage of large numbers of different types of behaviour (e.g. Gottman, 1977). These different systems all have their uses, but one or two general points can be made. First, the importance of observing at least some behaviours cannot be over-emphasized: teacher reports may be inaccurate, sociometry may be too nonspecific. Secondly, observations have often been uninformative either because the categories used have been too broad (Green *et al.*, 1980) or irrelevant to the children or SST programme concerned (Frosh and Callias, 1980). Finally, training teachers to carry out systematic observations may be a powerful SST technique in its own right, alerting them to the specific social acts of children in their class.

While it is being stressed that the particular observational system to be used depends on the setting, children and purposes one has in mind, the kind of categories that might be of interest can be illustrated by reference to the author's own system, used with children aged between 5 and 7 in fairly informal classes. Observations are made every 10 seconds, with the child's behaviour being coded in one of the following categories (inter-rater agreements average about 80%): (*a*) playing with others (active involvement in cooperative play); (*b*) solitary (constructive activity alone); (*c*) talking (talking or listening to another child, without other interaction); (*d*) zonked out (dreaming, staring aimlessly, passively watching others); (*e*) distractability (playing about, interfering); (*f*) transitional (between activities, waiting for teacher, getting materials); (*g*) aggression (physical or verbal abuse at a child); (*h*) grown ups (positive, negative or neutral interactions coded separately); (*i*) other.

D. Problem-solving tasks

In addition to observing what a child does, it is also important to ascertain what he or she knows. Whilst much work has used Piagetian-type egocentrism tasks (e.g. Chandler, 1973), it is Spivack and Shure (1974) who have offered the most coherent series of tasks, for use with young children as well as older ones. Their research indicated that problem-solving abilities such as being able to imagine alternative solutions and to conceptualize means and obstacles in moving towards a goal, were important across all age groups. For young children, their measures of these skills are the Preschool Interpersonal Problem-Solving Test (PIPS) and the "What Happens Next?" game. The former tests the child's ability to think alternative ways in which a child in a story can get a chance to play with a desired toy which another is using, and also ways in which he can avert the wrath of his mother for some misdemeanour. The "What Happens Next?" game involves the child in generating endings for stories involving interpersonal conflicts. In various studies the usefulness of these measures has been established, and they have the advantages of being relatively non-moralistic (quantity rather than quality of alternatives is scored) and interpersonally relevant.

Role-playing procedures can also be used to assess a child's knowledge of social skills. One example is the Behavioural Assertiveness Test for Children (e.g. Bornstein *et al.*, 1977) which comprises several interpersonal encounters in which the child must act out a response. However, the external validity of role-play measures is uncertain (Van Hasslet *et al.*, 1979). Finally, Gottman *et al.*'s (1975) "Making Friends" procedure in which the child is asked to pretend that the assessor is a new child in school with whom he wishes to make friends, may give some indication of the child's knowledge of social skills, although not, of course, of whether he tends to use them in class.

IV. WHAT ARE SOCIAL SKILLS?

Before moving on to a description of SST techniques, it is worth pausing to consider the nature of the skills one is interested in training. Much of the evidence concerning which attributes of children are important for social success comes from investigations of the correlates of high or low peer status rather than from experimental manipulations of children's levels of skill; hence, there can only be approximate guidelines given as to which skills will be relevant to any individual case.

In line with the "problem-solving" perspective taken in this chapter, the term "social skills" is not being used to refer to particular acts, but to a general capacity to generate alternative courses of action and to select between them when faced with an interpersonal encounter (cf. D'Zurilla and Goldfried, 1971). Many of the ideas upon which this perspective is based derive from the work of Spivack and Shure (1974), whose data on the cognitive correlates of children's problems has already been alluded to. In summary, socially successful children appear to have at their command more potential techniques for negotiating difficult (and everyday) interpersonal situations. The processes involved here include sensitivity to when problems occur, ability to imagine alternative courses of action and sensitivity to the consequences of actions and to cause and effect in behaviour (Spivack and Shure, 1974, p. 20).

In addition to the general notion of social skill as problem-solving activity, there are also some more specific guidelines available for conceptualizing the differences between socially successful or unsuccessful children. For example:

(1) Children who are highly accepted by their peers tend to score well on measures of sensitivity, responsiveness and generosity in peer interaction—they give attention and approval often, greet others, show affection, and so on (Combs and Slaby, 1977; Hartup *et al.*, 1967).

(2) Children who are not much liked by others, but are not particularly disliked, tend to be withdrawn, passive and anxious (Gottman, 1977).

(3) Children who are actively disliked by others tend to be agressive, and to be locked in a vicious cycle whereby their aggression makes them rejected, which in turn reduces the possibilities of learning alternative modes of interaction. In this way, they become more and more reliant on aggression as their only social "skill". Interestingly, socially successful children can be aggressive when the situation calls for it (Combs and Slaby, 1977); the difference is that the unskilled child has no alternative.

(4) Children who are well liked are better at seeing things from the point of view of others; disliked children tend to be relatively more "egocentric" (Gottman *et al.*, 1975).

In summary, the general aims of SST with children are to increase the number of strategies for interaction at their command, and to communicate guidelines on how to choose between them. With any one child, however, one might wish to use a more circumscribed goal based on some of the correlates of social status outlined above.

A. Case study

Donna was a 5 year old child in a play-oriented, open-space designed classroom. At the start of the intervention, her teacher gave her a score of 25 on the Rutter (1967) scale for teachers, which placed her well within the maladjusted range; on Spivack and Shure's (1974) questionnaire she had high scores on all 3 factors of difficulty in delaying gratification, proneness to emotional upset and social aggressiveness. Sociometrically, no child in Donna's class named her as a friend, and 3 children picked her as the child they most disliked. Donna's sociometric rating score was the lowest in her class, 1·53 (the mean for the class was 2·21, derived from the three-point scale of Asher *et al.*, 1979). Some weeks of baseline observations in class showed Donna's behaviour to be highly variable, although it was clear that she spent most of her time in solitary activity, either constructive or passive. When SST was instituted, Donna proved to be a bellicose and moody child with whom to work, although there were times when she was cooperative. Problems with her often centred around sharing and her inclination to dominate games through aggression and shouting. The SST work concentrated on encouraging her to lower her voice and use effective verbal formulae for obtaining the things she wanted. While Donna was not always willing to try the suggested techniques, she did use them on occasions, to good effect. At the end of the intervention, Donna was still nobody's best friend, but her sociometric rating was now nearly average for her class (2·24, mean for class 2·33). Her teacher rated her as improved on all of the Spivack and Shure factors, although she still scored highly. Behaviourally, slightly more of Donna's time was spend interacting positively with other children.

V. PROCEDURES FOR SST IN SCHOOLS

A. In-class social skills training

Retaining the primary purpose of constructing an SST procedure which is of use to a teacher as part of his or her everyday repertoire of techniques, the first procedural question concerns whether SST should take place inside the class or in a withdrawal setting. There are obvious advantages to withdrawal work: the setting is under relatively close control, with few distractions and the resultant possibility of ordered, coherent and predictable SST programmes. Some interesting work has been carried out in this way: for example, Oden and Asher (1977) took isolated children out of class to coach them individually in social skills, while Frosh and Callias (1980) formed small groups of problem children to work with in a withdrawal setting. However, while withdrawal work is relatively easy to carry out there are some significant drawbacks, the most important of which centres around the issue of generalization of therapeutic effects to the classroom. In line with much other behavioural work, Cartledge and Milburn (1978) review data on behaviour durability to argue that responses developed in one specific setting or at one time will not automatically transfer to, or persist within, settings and occasions with different characteristics. For example, Wahler (1975), in a detailed study of 2 boys, showed that changing behaviours at home resulted only in unpredictable changes at school. Frosh and Callias (1980) found that various aspects of their withdrawal procedure militated against generalization—for example, use of a small group compared to the larger class setting, use of children from different school classes in the same group, and use of adults other than class teachers as social skills trainers. Arguments of this kind make it clear that the withdrawal setting may be rather different from the environment in which one hopes the child's social behaviour will change, and hence that more powerful effects may be possible if a way can be found to work directly in the classroom. This makes good sense, too, in terms of the preventive framework around which this chapter is constructed: if teachers are to use SST techniques as part of their activity in class, then these techniques must be employed in class at an early stage in the programme. For these reasons, the rest of this chapter will focus on the details of a potential classroom-based SST intervention, based on the experience of the author and other researchers and practitioners.

B. Parameters of intervention

(1) Groups

In-class work will often involve large groups of children, but it is recommended that the initial intervention involves no more than 4 children, and fewer are conceivable.

(2) Frequency and duration of sessions

Given the hectic nature of classrooms, especially with young children, sessions should be brief but frequent. Ten-minute sessions 3 times a week is a reasonable schedule for young children; older children may be able to tolerate longer sessions, but intensive, coherent, time-limited work is crucial.

(3) Materials

As the aim is to make the SST procedure realistic, the groups should be centred around work or play activities that are conventional in the classroom—for instance, working together on a drawing, helping each other with work, playing a cooperative game. In general, the more the situation can be structured so as to encourage the children to interact with one another, the better.

(4) Other children

It is certain that other children in the class will make demands on the teacher while the SST session is going on. To some extent (not always, of course) this can be capitalized upon by involving these childen in the SST itself, either as participants (e.g. offering or receiving help from group members) or as on-lookers to whom comments about the group's activity can be directed. This has the advantage of creating new interpersonal situations for the group members to negotiate.

Having presented a broad context for an SST programme, the next section will detail some actual training techniques, followed by an account of how they might be applied in class.

VI. TRAINING TECHNIQUES

SST techniques of relevance in this context are those that can be applied in the free-flowing and often energetic context of the classroom. With children up to adolescence, the principle building-blocks around which most programmes have been constructed are reinforcement, modelling and coaching.

A. Reinforcement: rewarding desired behaviour

Given the voluminous evidence that teacher-supplied contingencies such as attention can be effective controllers of children's behaviour (Cartledge and Milburn, 1978) and that such contingencies are often misapplied so that children may actually be rewarded for an inappropriate social behaviour (Combs and Slaby, 1977), it is not surprising that many workers have looked to reinforcement as a possible method of changing social behaviour. Most work has been carried out with socially withdrawn children rather than rejected ones; nevertheless, the effectiveness of reinforcement in increasing or improving social interaction is quite impressive. Allen *et al.* (1975), for example, worked with groups of "socially ineffective" fourth and fifth-graders, rewarding them for interaction inside and outside the group, and demonstrating sociometric gains which were sustained 5 months later. Grieger *et al.* (1976) increased levels of cooperative play amongst kindergarten children when peers reported friendly behaviour and the children received badges or praise from peers, and Slaby and Crowley (1977) shaped up similar behaviour in young children by instructing teachers to attend to as many instances of verbal cooperation as possible. Several single-case studies have shown the power of adult contingencies applied to the child or to his or her peers (Strain and Timm, 1974).

It is clear that the controlling effect of adult and peer contingencies is a powerful source of social behaviour change; there are, however, limitations. For one, reinforcement relies on the occurrence of the desired behaviours, and is a clumsy way of training new skills (Combs and Slaby, 1977). Secondly, a concentration on increasing the amount of social behaviour (a common goal of such studies) may be inappropriate if the child is unskilled (Oden and Asher, 1977). Thirdly, the durability of treatment effects is questionable (Van Hasslet et al., 1979), and it is likely that shaped behaviours fade away when the adult contingencies that established them cease. Hence, the use of reinforcement of desirable social behaviour is not recommended in isolation from other training methods, but is obviously a useful component of the SST procedure.

B. Modelling: demonstrating desired behaviour

While the usefulness of modelling as a teaching procedure has been established for some time, it was the work of O'Connor (1969, 1972) that pointed to its potential for SST. O'Connor (1969) constructed a 23 minute film consisting of 11 episodes in which a child successfully entered a group of other children, with a narrator drawing attention to the child's relevant behaviours. A single showing of this film increased isolated children's social interactions to the level of non-isolates, and O'Connor (1972) showed this effect to be more rapid and stable than that produced by reinforcement. This finding was replicated by Evers and Schwarz (1973) and by Keller and Carlson (1974), while Yarrow et al. (1973) used an effective live modelling condition in which adults showed and verbalized helpful behaviour in a classroom setting.

Modelling is clearly a powerful procedure, of great promise not only because of its impact but because of the ease with which it can be carried out. Predictably, however, there are problems. Firstly, it is likely that the children used in the O'Connor studies were only mildly problematic (Van Hasslet et al., 1979). Secondly, a failure to replicate O'Connor's (1969) result by Gottman (discussed by Van Hasslet et al., 1979) casts doubt on their generality. Finally, when one examines the effective components of the modelling procedure, the most powerful one is almost certainly the way the model (or the narrator) draws the child's attention to the social skill being illustrated, and provides information on its utility. This verbal commentary is almost exactly what is meant by the next technique, coaching.

C. Coaching: providing guidelines for behaviour

Coaching refers to procedures based on providing the child with a
behavioural role, letting him or her practice, and then giving feedback.
The seminal study in this area is that of Oden and Asher (1977), who
coached third and fourth grade socially isolated children along the
following lines: (*a*) instruction from an adult in a skill (e.g. how to join in
a game; (*b*) playing a game with a peer to practice the skill; (*c*) a post-play
review session with the coach. Each child received 6 such play sessions
over a 4 week period; assessment showed that the coached group
increased on play (not work) sociometric ratings significantly more than
controls, and had maintained this improvement one year later. There
were, however, only non-significant changes on friendship nomination
scores and on observed behaviours. While there have been failures of
replication (e.g. Hymel and Asher, 1977), support for the efficacy of
coaching carries from other workers (e.g. Gresham and Nagle, 1980;
Bornstein *et al.*, 1977; Whitehill *et al.*, 1980). Once again, however,
impressive data with rejected and aggressive children is lacking;
nevertheless, the congruence of the coaching procedure with a problem-
solving framework is encouraging, and initial results are promising.

D. Classroom application

To illustrate how the various SST techniques can be applied in a
classroom setting, a short extract from a training document for teachers is
reproduced below. The procedures suggested derive from Frosh and
Callias' (1980) adaptation of Oden and Asher's (1977) work, and are
geared to use within the time-limited structures described in the
previous section. Two basic categories of technique are used, continuous
commentary and problem-solving.

(1) *Continuous commentary*

The best way to generate new ideas for children and to guide their
behaviour constructively seems to be to talk constantly about what is
going on. This talk should be positive, focusing either on things that are
going well in the interaction, or on courses of action that would be good
to try. It thus encompasses the twin attributes of *praising* children for
successful interactions and of *coaching* them in possible alternatives. It
has been found in the past that the best way to keep this commentary
going is not to talk too directly to the children, but to talk *across*

them—either at other children or at another adult. In this way, the talk does not intrude on the children's activity, but is still picked up by them. Thus "Did you see how Ann waited her turn?" may be more effective than direct comments to the children themselves. The idea is to provide the children with guidelines and suggestions enabling them to generate new ways of acting and to choose between the possibilities open to them.

(2) *Problem-solving*

If the session breaks down, for instance because of a fight or dispute, then the best technique is to stop everything and ask the children to sit still for a moment. While this is difficult for them, over time they get better at it as they learn the expectations surrounding them. The next step is two-pronged: (1) *problem-identification*: encouraging answers to the question "what went wrong,"—e.g. "he wanted to go first, and so did I"; (2) *solution-generation*: "what would have been a good thing to do?". This can provoke useful verbal answers for children to work on, but will more often require the teacher to engage in modelling. This involves pretending to be one of the children involved in the dispute and, with the aid of another adult or even another child, *acting out* a possible solution to the problem. After this, the children intially involved in the difficulty should be asked to try out the solution for themselves.

Note that the concentration throughout these procedures is on monitoring of the children's activity with immediate feedback and suggestions concerning alternatives that are available. Along with the behavioural potency of the modelling component, the commentary involves encouragement of the use of verbal formulae, which have been shown to have considerable self-regulatory power (Meichenbaum, 1979). Thus, the procedures encompass many of the elements of behavioural technology which appear to be most effective in producing therapeutic change (social reinforcement, immediate feedback, participant modelling, problem-solving, verbal regulation of behaviour) within a package that has practical utility in the classroom setting.

VII. TEACHERS AS THERAPISTS

A. Teacher skills

Throughout this chapter, emphasis has been placed on making the child's teacher the social skills trainer. In line with the whole "social skills" orientation, being a good trainer ("therapist") is not seen as being a matter of possessing certain personality characteristics, but of the appropriate utilization of some specific skills. In addition to the SST techniques outlined in the previous section, it is possible to point to a few more general skills that might help a teacher become an effective trainer; the following is not an exhaustive list, but a personal one.

(1) Organization

The way in which a class is organized is particularly important when the teacher is devoting his or her attention to a small number of children for the purposes of SST. At these times, some arrangement whereby children work in small, cooperative groups (see Section II) is both a valuable way of encouraging the class to continue functioning and a good SST structure in its own right.

(2) Observation

An essential requirement of effective SST is careful observation of a child's actual behaviour at relevant times and in relevant situations. Mastering of formal aspects of the observational technology, such as time or event-sampling, is always useful, but the crucial point is that the teacher should learn to focus on what the child *does*, so that the chances of the SST programme dealing with real problems are maximized.

(3) Reinforcement

Many studies attest to the power of attention and praise from teachers as consequences for pupil behaviours (Sherman and Bushell, 1975). Almost as many have shown that teachers, by attending to undesirable behaviours, may sometimes shape and maintain the very activities they would like to eliminate (Cartledge and Milburn, 1978). Control over the way social reinforcement is dispensed is thus very important, in general terms and for effective SST.

(4) Commentating

The coaching procedure advocated here requires continuous verbal commentary from the teacher. This a demanding process in which the teacher must focus on what is happening in the group, imagine alternative courses of action, and verbalize this material so that it can generate guidelines for the children's behaviour.

(5) *Modelling*

As with the coaching procedure, the crucial elements in modelling are that the teacher focuses on the relevant problem, verbalizes the strategy being employed to overcome it, and displays actively the processes involved in putting this solution into practice—i.e. that the problem-solving *process* is demonstrated as well as the result.

B. Training teachers as therapists

Very much the same principles apply to training teachers in SST techniques as to training the children themselves. Emphasis is placed on problem-centredness: that is, the construction or identification of concrete situations in which SST is appropriate. Thus, in the author's work, as well as general discussions of principles, a "resource person" (a psychologist or teacher who has already carried out SST work) runs early sessions of an in-class SST programme in conjunction with the teacher, demonstrating to him or her the application of previously discussed techniques. Gradually, the "resource person" withdraws from sessions, so that the teacher progresses from observation of the SST procedures, to participation, to control. This design aims to leave the teacher with the skills and confidence to continue with SST long after the psychologist or adviser has left—and hence to maximize its preventive possibilities. Additionally, discussion and feedback of information and ideas with other members of staff in a school is an important way of maintaining interest and support for the long-term aims of the intervention.

VIII. EVALUATING OUTCOME

In terms of prevention, evaluation of the effectiveness of the SST programme is a difficult procedure, in that the goals are long-term and rather general ("healthy adolescent functioning", etc.) and may be influenced by many factors other than the programme itself. In any event, a programme user will quite properly wish to have more immediate measures of whether or not the SST has been useful: he or she will not wish to wait 10 years before deciding whether it is worth persevering with the techniques. Fortunately, it is possible to specify short-term goals which are compatible with the long-term aims; clearly, with respect to children one is concerned with improving the quality of their social functioning; with respect to teachers the aim is to encourage effective utilization of SST techniques in an everyday setting.

A. Children

Formal assessment procedures for evaluating children's social functioning were described in Section III. Here, what must be reiterated is that specific outcomes of interest will be peculiar to any individual child; nevertheless, the following checklist may be useful in outlining some of the ways in which changes in social behaviour can be assessed:

(1) Teacher's view (derived from questionnaire and interview): does the teacher recognize any improvement in the child's interpersonal skills?
(2) Children's view (derived from sociometry): has the child improved his or her friendship status?
(3) Social interactions (derived from observations of behaviour): have any characteristic problematic social behaviours of the child, such as extreme passivity or aggression, been reduced in frequency *and* been replaced by more creative modes of social activity?
(4) Cognitive skills (derived from problem-solving tasks): has the child increased his or her knowledge of alternative courses of action when faced with interpersonal encounters?

B. Teachers

This chapter has emphasized the importance of training teachers as SST personnel. Possible ways of assessing the success of this enterprise include:

(1) Teacher's views (derived from interviews): although the accuracy of a person's report on changes in his or her own behaviour is open to doubt, the teacher's opinion on the usefulness of SST and his or her competence to carry it out should not be neglected. At the very least this will indicate whether the work is likely to be continued once the formal programme has ended—an important evaluative criterion.
(2) Teacher actions (derived from observations of behaviour): does the ratio of social to non-social instruction by the teacher increase? Are specific SST techniques such as modelling and coaching used in class? Specific observational systems to measure the occurrence of particular behaviours can be constructed in the same way as those for children, described in Section III.
(3) Levels of friendship in the class (derived from sociometry): changes in the levels of friendship in a class, measured by the average sociometric ratings given and received by children, are quite a good

indicator of the quality of social functioning in that class, and hence reflect in part on the skills of the teacher.

(4) Improvements in target children (derived from multiple sources of assessment): does SST carried out by the teacher help the children at whom it is directed?

Clearly, many factors might influence all these assessment areas. Nevertheless, if a teacher views SST negatively, shows no changes in behaviour, has a class where friendship levels decline and where problem children do not increase their skills, then the programme obviously needs alteration. If the converse is true, then one can, at the very least, be optimistic.

IX. CONCLUSION: PROBLEMS AND PROSPECTS

As a counterbalance to over-enthusiastic advocacy of SST in all circumstances, it is perhaps as well to finish a chapter such as this with some words of caution. The first is a general point: the sources of children's problems are multiple, often chronic, frequently intractable, and often outside the professional range of even the most broad-minded mental health worker. While problem-solving notions of increasing the range of behavioural alternatives open to children when facing interpersonal (and other) situations are of general utility, it cannot be claimed that SST is a panacea for all childhood ills. Unfortunately, while a child's skills might increase, if the situations he or she has to face are universally destructive then no SST programme will make more than a marginal difference to that child's life. The second point, which is linked, concerns the thorny issue of generalization—the maintenance of treatment gains across time and settings. Despite the advantages of in-class SST programmes carried out by teachers, it must be recognized that difficulties of generalization still remain. Not only do playgrounds and out-of-school play settings differ from classrooms, but classes vary enormously, and a child whose skills have been developed by an alert teacher may lose them when moved into a more rigid environment. Which is another way of saying that the SST programme must reach out to other staff members in addition to teachers directly involved and that the ideas must be spread across a school if children's gains are to be maintained.

Generalization considerations raise the third difficulty: that of encouraging and maintaining staff interest in the project. Offering support and help to hard-pressed teachers will usually be welcomed, but a programme that demands the investment of time and effort on their part relies also on showing results. For this reason, it is suggested that interventions centre, at least initially, on teacher-identified problems: effective resolution of these will almost certainly store up a bank of goodwill which might help the programme overcome difficult times. This is in addition to the frequent consultation with staff that is an important element in any kind of school-based work.

There are, then, difficulties with SST work in schools which partly explain the relative paucity of impressive therapeutic results. Nevertheless, evidence concerning the importance of peer relationships for children's development, plus data on the therapeutic potential of specific techniques, plus alertness to problems of generalization and the potential of work in school settings, all provide an impetus for SST and a promise of future success. In the end, one is attempting to construct a method of early intervention which is practical and powerful and which will have a long-term positive impact on children; whatever the difficulties, the attempt seems worth making.

X. REFERENCES

Allen, R. P., Heaton, R. and Barrell, M. (1975). Behavior Therapy for Socially Ineffective Children. *J. Am. Acad. Child Psychiatry* **14**, 500–9.

Allen, G. J., Chinsky, J. M., Larcen, S. W., Lochman, J. E. and Selinger, H. V. (1976). "Community Psychology and the Schools". Lawrence Erlbaum, New Jersey.

Asher, S. R., Oden, S. L. and Gottman, J. M. (1977). Children's Friendships in School Settings. *In* "Current Topics in Early Childhood Education" (L. Katz, Ed.). Ablex, Norwood, New Jersey.

Asher, S. R., Singleton, L. C., Tinsley, B. R. and Hymel, S. (1979). A Reliable Sociometric Measure for Preschool Children. *Developmental Psychology* **15**, 443–4.

Blaney, N. T., Stephen, C., Rosenfield, D., Aronson, E. and Sokes, J. (1977). Interdependence in the Classroom: A Field Study. *J. Educ. Psychol.* **69**, 121–8.

Bornstein, M. R., Bellack, A. S. and Hersen, M. (1977). Social Skills Training for Unassertive Children: A Multiple-Baseline Analysis, *J. Appl. Behav. Anal.* **10**, 183–195.

Busk, P. L., Ford, R. C. and Schulman, J. (1973). Stability of Sociometric Responses in the Classroom. *J. Genet. Psychol.* **123**, 69–84.

Cartledge, G. and Milburn, J. P. (1978). The Case for Teaching Social Skills in the Classroom: A review. *Rev. Educ. Res.* **1**, 133–156.

Cartledge, G. and Milburn, J. F. (1980). "Teaching Social Skills to Children". Pergamon Press, New York.

Chandler, M. J. (1973). Egocentrism and Anti-Social Behavior: The Assessment and Training of Social Perspective-Taking Skills. *Devel. Psychol.* **9**, 326–332.

Charlesworth, R. and Hartup, W. (1967). Positive Social Reinforcement in the Nursery School Peer-Group. *Child Dev.* **38**, 993–1002.

Combs, M. L. and Slaby, D. A. (1977). Social-Skills Training with Children. In "Advances in Clinical Child Psychology" (B. B. Lahey, and A. E. Kazdin, Eds), Vol. 1. Plenum Press, New York.

Cowen, E. L., Pedersen, A., Babigian, H., Izzo, L. D. and Trost, M. A. (1973). Long-Term Follow-up of Early-Detected Vulnerable Children, J. Cons. Clin. Psychol. 41, 438–446.

D'Zurilla, T. and Goldfried, M. (1971). Problem Solving and Behavior Modification. J. Abnorm. Psychol. 78, 107–129.

Evers, W. L. and Schwarz, J. C. (1973). Modifying Social Withdrawal in Preschoolers: The Effects of Filmed Modelling and Teacher Praise. J. Abnorm. Child Psychol. 1, 248–256.

Frosh, S. J. and Callias, M. M. (1980). Social Skills Training in an Infant School Setting. Behav. Psych. 8, 69–79.

Gottman, J. M. (1977). Toward a Definition of Social Isolation in Children. Child Dev. 48, 513–517.

Gottman, J. M., Gonso, J. and Rasmussen, R. (1975). Social Interaction, Social Competence, and Friendship in Children. Child Dev. 46, 709–718.

Green, K. D., Forehand, R., Beck, S. J. and Vosk, B. (1980). An Assessment of the Relationship among Measures of Children's Social Competence and Children's Academic Achievement. Child Dev. 51, 1149–1156.

Greenwood, C. R., Walker, H. M. and Hops, H. (1977). Issues in Social Interaction/Withdrawal Assessment. Exceptional Children 13, 490–499.

Gresham, F. M. and Nagle, R. J. (1980). Social Skills Training with Children: Responsiveness to Modelling and Coaching as a Function of Peer Orientation. J. Cons. Clin. Psychol. 48, 718–729.

Grieger, T., Kaufmann, J. M. and Grieger, R. M. (1976). Effects of Peer Reporting on Cooperative Play and Aggression of Kindergarten Children. J. School Psychol. 14, 307–313.

Gump, P. V. (1980). The School as a Social Situation. Ann. Rev. Psychol. 31, 553–82.

Hartup, W. (1980). Peer Relations and Family Relations: Two Social Worlds. In "Scientific Foundations of Developmental Psychiatry" (M. Rutter, Ed.). Heinemann, London.

Hartup, W., Glazer, J. A. and Charlesworth, R. (1967). Peer Reinforcement and Sociometric Status. Child Dev. 38, 1017–1024.

Hertz-Lazarowitz, R., Sharan, S. and Steinberg, R. (1980). Classroom Learning Style and Cooperative Behavior of Elementary School Children. J. Educ. Psychol. 72, 99–106.

Hymel, S. and Asher, S. R. (1977). Assessment and Training of Isolated Children's Social Skills. Paper presented at biennial meeting of the Society for Research in Child Developments, New Orleans, Louisiana.

Keller, M. F. and Carlson, P. N. (1974). The Use of Symbolic Modelling to Promote Social Skills in Preschool Children with Low Levels of Social Responsiveness. Child Dev. 45, 912–919.

Meichenbaum, D. (1979). Teaching Children Self-Control. In "Advances in Clinical Child Psychology" (B. B. Lahey and A. E. Kazdin, Eds), Vol. 2. Plenum Press, New York.

Miller, N. and Gentry, K. W. (1980). Sociometric Indices of Children's Peer Interaction in the School Setting. In "Friendship and Social Relations in Children" (H. C. Foot, A. G. Chapman, and J. R. Smith, Eds). Wiley, Chichester.

O'Connor, R. D. (1969). Modification of Social Withdrawal through Symbolic Modelling. *J. Appl. Behav. Anal.* **2**, 15–22.

O'Connor, R. D. (1972). Relative Efficacy of Modelling, Shaping and the Combined Procedures for Modification of Social Withdrawal, *J. Abnorm. Psychol.* **79**, 327–334.

Oden, S. (1980). A Child's Social Isolation: Origins, Prevention, Intervention. *In* "Teaching Social Skills to Children" (G. Cartledge and J. F. Milburn, *Eds*). Pergamon Press, New York.

Oden, S. and Asher, S. R. (1977). Coaching Children in Social Skills for Friendship Making. *Child Dev.* **48**, 495–506.

Roff, M., Sells, S. B. and Golden, M. M. (1972). "Social Adjustment and Personality Development in Children". University of Minnesota Press, Minneapolis.

Rutter, M. (1967). A Children's Behaviour Questionnaire for Completion by Teachers: Preliminary Findings. *J. Child Psychiatry* **8**, 1–11.

Rutter, M. (1979). "Changing Youth in a Changing Society". Nuffield, London.

Rutter, M., Yule, B., Quinton, D., Rowlands, O., Yule, W. and Berger, M. (1975). Attainment and Adjustment in Two Geographical Areas: III: Some Factors Accounting for Area Differences. *Br. J. Psychiatry* **126**, 520–33.

Sherman, J. A. and Bushell, D. (1975). Behavior Modification as an Educational Technique. *In* "Review of Child Development Research" (F. D. Horowitz, *Ed.*), Vol. 4. University of Chicago Press, Chicago.

Slaby, R. G. and Crowley, C. G. (1977). Modification of Cooperation and Aggression through Teacher Attention to Children's Speech. *J. Exp. Child Psychol.* **23**, 442–458.

Smith, P. K. and Connolly, K. J. (1976). Social and Aggressive Behaviour in Preschool Children as a Function of Crowding. *Biol. Soc. Life* **16**, 601–620.

Spivack, G. and Shure, M. B. (1974). "Social Adjustment of Young Children". Jossey-Bass, San Francisco.

Stephens, T. M. (1980). Foreword. *In* "Teaching Social Skills to Children" (G. Cartledge and J. F. Milburn, *Eds*). Pergamon, New York.

Strain, P. S. and Timm, H. A. (1974). An Experimental Analysis of Social Interaction between a Behaviorally Disordered Preschool Child and Her Classroom Peers. *J. Appl. Behav. Anal.* **7**, 583–590.

Trower, P., Bryant, B. and Argyle, M. (1978). "Social Skills and Mental Health". Methuen, London.

Van Hasselt, V. B., Hersen, M., Whitehill, M. B. and Bellack, A. S. (1979). Social Skills Assessment and Training for Children: An Evaluative Review. *Behav. Res. Ther.* **17**, 413–42.

Wahler, R. G. (1975). Some Structural Aspects of Deviant Child Behaviour. *J. Appl. Behav. Anal.* **8**, 27–42.

Wahler, R. G., Berland, R. M. and Coe, T. D. (1979). Generalization Processes in Child Behavior Change. *In* "Advances in Clinical Child Psychology" (B. B. Lahey and A. E. Kazdin, *Eds*), Vol. 2. Plenum Press, New York.

Walker, H. (1970). "Problem Behavior Identification Checklist". Wester Psychological Services, Los Angeles.

Whitehill, M. B., Hersen, M. and Bellack, A. S. (1980). Conversation Skills Training for Socially Isolated Children *Behav. Res. Ther.* **18**, 217–225.

Yarrow, M. R., Scott, P. M. and Waxler, C. Z. (1973). Learning Consideration for Others. *Devel. Psychol.* **8**, 240–260.

8

Adolescent psychiatric outpatients

MARY JACKSON

I. INTRODUCTION—DESCRIPTION OF SETTING

Typically, anyone working with an adolescent psychiatric outpatient population would encounter their clients initially in a hospital setting. Usually the referral would come from a psychiatrist or associated profession. The most obvious and available setting, therefore, in which to conduct social skills training (SST) would be the hospital. This is generally the place where the therapist is based, where the therapist has facilities at his/her disposal, where the videotape equipment is housed and where the adolescent will be expecting to come. However, there are serious disadvantages to the use of hospital premises for such a venture:

(1) There is a large amount of negative "stigma" involved in regular visits to a publicly acknowledged psychiatric setting for treatment. It is often the case that adolescents are reluctant to attend for this reason alone or, at least, wish to keep such visits a secret. The stigma involved (for example, being teased by peers) may be worse than that involved with the initial problem. Also, the negative stigma would make it very difficult to establish training as a positive event.

(2) The hospital setting is obviously a clinical one. As such it is far removed from the natural setting and hence the setting in which social difficulty occurs and in which social skills are needed. Ideally, treatment should be carried out in the natural environment or in settings which closely approximate the natural environment, so that the problem of transfer of training from the training to the application setting may be reduced. This is rarely feasible so that practitioners have had to investigate ways in which the problem of transfer may be diminished. Goldstein (1977) in drawing from learning theory points out some methods which have been found to enhance transfer of training from the training setting to the natural (application) setting and one important factor is the similarity between training and application setting.

(3) Shepherd (1980) advocates that social performance be studied both at the level of social interaction and at the level of social integration and quotes correlational evidence to suggest that the two go hand in hand. When running SST groups, trainers invariably encourage their group members to practise the skills being trained outside the training setting in actual social situations. Such practice is rarely performed and one reason for this is because socially inadequate people tend to avoid social situations and social integration generally. Therefore, if one is to spend time training social interaction skills one should also concentrate on social integration skills to ensure that

adolescents are getting ample opportunity both to practice the skills trained and to obtain the social reinforcement needed to maintain the skills.

Ideally, therefore, SST for adolescent psychiatric outpatients would be conducted in as naturalistic a setting as possible. One way in which this may be attempted with an adolescent population is by setting up a special social skills training youth club. (SSTYC). This should be in a building outside the hospital (and unrelated to it) where there are facilities for both youth club and SST activities. The present chapter offers some guidelines as to the methodology and procedures involved in the setting up and running of such a club.

II. ASSESSMENT

A. Referral system

When setting up a SSTYC group for adolescent psychiatric outpatients the first point to consider is how to get referrals. Most psychiatric settings are run according to a multi-disciplinary team approach where any discipline may refer an adolescent patient but where the psychiatrist maintains overall medical responsibility. It may be possible to go outside this setting and take referrals directly from general practitioners or social workers in the field, but whoever the referral agents are it is important that they are aware of the facility being set up so that they can make the appropriate referrals. Also, it may be necessary to extend the referral agencies to include people who are more likely to come across socially inadequate adolescents (for example: careers officers, school counsellors, etc.). Here are some guidelines to follow:

(1) Ensure that the referral agents are aware of the facility being set up and know the population for whom it is intended.
(2) Ensure that adolescents are referred for "social assessment" rather than for SST. This makes the task easier if the referral is not appropriate.
(3) Ensure that there is medical cover. If a consultant psychiatrist is not involved, then ensure that the GP is informed and has agreed for the adolescent to receive this type of "treatment".
(4) Inform the referral agent of your decision.

B. Introducing the concept of social skills

During the first interview it is often difficult to establish a smooth, balanced interaction because of the adolescent's inhibitions and low speech level. It is therefore advisable to introduce an assessment early on in the interview which can be administered verbally, thereby giving the adolescent a chance to settle down while maintaining certain levels of social interaction. It is highly unlikely that adolescents will have any understanding of the concept of social skills, let alone whether or not they are socially skilled. One very good way in which to introduce them to this concept is to go through a questionnaire which covers the various aspects of social skill. Administering such a questionnaire verbally also allows the interviewer to pinpoint social difficulties. One questionnaire which covers a wide range of problem areas is "The Social Problem Check List" (Rowe, 1980), which is a modified version of the List of Social Situations Problems which was compiled by Spence (1979) for use with delinquent boys.

The types of problems covered in the questionnaire can be seen to fall into 8 categories: problems with adults; lack of assertiveness; lack of basic skills; embarrassment; problems with friends; problems with members of the opposite sex; problems with strangers; problems with temper control.

At the end of administering the questionnaire the interviewer can then explain that the items in the questionnaire are the types of behaviours which constitute social skills.

C. Selection of targets

When selecting targets for treatment it is important that the adolescent takes an active part in the decision-making process as to the target problems which need attention as well as possible solutions to these problems. Thus, after completing the social problem check list each adolescent should be asked to select and define 4 problem areas with which they would most like help. This should be done in conjunction with the interviewer so that the problems and solutions arrived at will be as specific and behavioural as possible and also to ensure that desired solutions are not too far out of line in terms of feasibility and social acceptability. For example:

(1) If an adolescent states that he would like more friends, the interviewer would then ask him how he might make more friends. The

adolescent may then go on to explain that he finds it difficult to talk to people if he doesn't already know them. The interviewer should then attempt to discover whether the adolescent has difficulty initiating such a conversation, keeping a conversation going, engaging in appropriate eye contact, etc.

(2) An example of the feasibility/social acceptability problem might be when the adolescent states that he would "like to be strong enough to fight the two lads who keep bullying him at school". Here, the interviewer would have to work through the entire problem with the adolescent in an attempt to point out the undesirable consequences of such a goal. Also, the interviewer should ask the adolescent why he thought he was bullied, did he want to be bullied all the time, what sort of reactions might prevent future bullying, etc., until a solution desirable to the adolescent and the interviewer could be arrived at, which is both feasible for training purposes and socially acceptable.

Once the 4 target problems have been identified, the adolescent may be asked to rate them for level of difficulty on a 1–5 point scale.

D. Social self esteem

Although social self esteem does not give precise information for the formulation of treatment programmes there is some evidence to suggest that this type of measure discriminates between psychiatric and normal adolescents (Kiff, 1980). It is possible that such a measure may also discriminate between adolescents with and without social difficulty. In this programme, a Social Self Esteem Questionnaire was used, compiled by Spence and Spence (1980).

E. Integration measures

The importance of social integration for successful social functioning has already been mentioned. Some suggestions as to ways in which this can be measured are:

(1) Social activities (Rowe, 1980)

This measure is a modified version of the one developed by Marzillier (1975) for use with adults. It consists of a list of 20 social activities found to be common among normal adolescents. The person is required to state whether or not he has engaged in these activities over the last 3 months. This procedure yields a "range of social activities" score.

(2) Social contacts (Rowe, 1980)

This assessment attempts to measure the number of friends an adolescent has by defining friends as people "he has been with socially on at least two occasions in the last three months". This measure is once again a modified version of the one developed by Marzillier (1975) for use with adults.

(3) Social diary

As a third measure of social integration, a social diary form may be used. This gives information as to the frequency of social activities and contacts. The week may be divided into 11 leisure periods, that is 7 evenings and the mornings and afternoons of the week-end. Adolescents are required to fill in what they were doing and who they were with for each leisure period for one week. From this a frequency of social activities score and a frequency of social contacts score may be derived.

F. "Significant other" measures

Thus far the emphasis has been on adolescents' self report of difficulty. It is obviously important to find out how the adolescent perceives himself but it is also important to investigate whether these perceptions are accurate. It could be that the adolescent is perceiving himself in a very negative light where others perceive him positively, and *vice versa*. Such information is valuable for treatment in terms of the adolescent's perception skills.

(1) Parents

In order to gain information about the accuracy of adolescents' self report, parents may be asked to fill in the same self-report measures. More general information may also be collected about how the child is functioning at home. One questionnaire used for this purpose is the Parents Questionnaire (Jackson, 1981).

(2) Teachers/employers

It may also be beneficial to collect information from teachers/employers as these people are likely to be with the adolescent for a large part of the day and are therefore in a position to observe general behaviours and behaviour changes. Such information also gives clues as to whether there is any transfer of training to the school/work situation.

(3) *Referral agents*

One way of ensuring that the referrals are appropriate is to use a Referral Form which may also serve as an assessment measure. This form could be completed again after training to measure changes which have taken place and could give information as to the general psychiatric condition of the adolescent. One form which has been used for this purpose is The General Clinical Rating Form (Rowe, 1980).

(4) *Friends*

Another way of finding out how the adolescent is functioning is to ask him to nominate a peer to rate his performance. This could give valuable information as to how peers perceive their behaviour. One problem with this, however, is that many socially inadequate adolescents have no such person whom they could nominate.

G. Direct behavioural measures

(1) *Direct observation*

As Bellack *et al.* (1978) point out: "*In vivo* observation is presumed to be the best (if not the only) strategy for securing meaningful data about client functioning". However, there are numerous problems involved in attempting to do this (see Bellack *et al.*). There are also ethical issues involved in observing people in natural settings without their knowledge. This does not mean that researchers and therapists should stop trying to find ways in which this can be done but they should certainly be aware of the problems and difficulties involved.

(2) Videotape measures

Because of the difficulties involved in direct observation, behaviour role-play tests have been widely used as an alternative. However, the single-response behaviour role-play test, although offering standardized techniques for measurement, is highly contrived and it is dangerous to assume that a subject's response in this situation is closely related to his responses in the natural situation. Firstly, the subject is only allowed one response whereas an encounter in the natural environment may continue for a number of responses. Secondly, one cannot assume that the subject responds as if the situation were real. Thus, the more realistic the role-play test the better. The author's chosen preference is therefore a conversation test where the subject is asked to hold a 3 minute conversation with a stooge. If the emphasis is on peer relations, then the stooge should be of the same age and sex as the subject. This may be done using other group members but certain problems arise in that two socially unskilled adolescents trying to interact with one another makes the whole affair exceedingly difficult. Ideally, one should employ a socially skilled adolescent and train him/her to respond in a standardized way: this procedure has been used by Jackson (1981) where the instructions to the stooge were:

> Be friendly, do not make your answers too long but do not give one or two word answers. Do not ask any questions unless there is a silence in which case count to ten slowly then ask a question. Also:
>
> (1) When the subject introduces him/herself, you must pretend you didn't hear him/her and say "I'm sorry, I didn't hear you. What did you say your name was?".
> (2) When the subject asks you to give him/her a game of table tennis later, you must make an excuse like "I'm sorry, I've twisted my ankle and I can't play games that involve running around".
> (3) At the first convenient point ask the subject to "Tell me more about yourself".

The stooge received 10 practice trials with the therapist prior to both pre and post assessment. The instructions to the subject (client) were:

> "We want you to hold a friendly conversation with X. You will find that X is friendly but it is up to you to:
>
> (1) Start up the conversation by introducing yourself.
> (2) Keep the conversation going.
> (3) End the conversation after 3 minutes when the buzzer sounds.
>
> Also, at some point during the conversation you must
>
> (4) Ask X if he will have a game of table tennis later on.
>
> Do you understand—do you have any questions?"

The subject was then asked to repeat his task assignment to the test administrator to ensure that he understood what he should do. If he could not do this the instructions were read out to him again until he could repeat his task assignment correctly.

Once this interaction has been videotaped there are a number of behaviours which can be studied, that is—number of initiations, number of questions, amount spoken, eye contact, attention feedback responses, number of smiles, posture, facial expression, clarity of speech, speed of speech and speech content (see Spence, 1979). Also, one can rate specific target responses, for example: starting up the conversation, introducing self, keeping conversation going, ending conversation, requesting a game of table tennis, repeating name, accepting refusal of a game of table tennis and telling others about self (see Jackson, 1981).

H. Selection of targets

Having selected 4 targets together with the adolescent, further targets may be selected for treatment after analysis of the videotape measures. It may be that some of these targets overlap with the ones already selected by the adolescent but this should not be assumed to be the case. The adolescent should be aware of these extra targets selected and should know how and why they were selected.

I. Assessment in the training setting

Valuable information can be gained from observation of the adolescent in the group setting, particularly if the setting is a social one. The SSTYC is an ideal setting in which to attempt direct behavioural observations and it is certainly possible to identify larger problem areas such as: bullying, inability to deal with teasing, isolated behaviour, refusal to take part in games, provocation, interruptions, etc. Such problems can be identified in the first few sessions and can be incorporated into the treatment programme. The therapist may, for example, start off the fourth session by saying to Joey—"Have you noticed that you get teased a lot by the other kids here?"

Joey: "Yes, it really gets on my nerves".
Therapist: "Why do you think you get teased so much?"
Joey: "Because they know it upsets me, I suppose".
Therapist: "How do you think they know?"
Joey: "Well, because I shout back and come and tell you about it".
Therapist: "Yes, that's right. Well, this week I want you to try to ignore it and talk about something else or talk to someone else."
Joey: "Yes, well, I'll try".
Therapist: "I'll be watching to see how you get on. O.K.?"
Joey: "O.K."

III. TYPICAL CLIENTS

It is likely that the vast majority of adolescent psychiatric outpatients would benefit from some form of SST. Trower *et al.* (1974) distinguished two types of social inadequacy–primary inadequacy, when there is a lack of appropriate skills either through failure to learn or through learning inappropriate skills, and secondary inadequacy, where clients have the skills within their repertoire but are unable to use them because of some primary problem such as anxiety. However, as these authors point out, it seems that these categories overlap somewhat and a large number of individuals can be seen to have characteristics of both types of inadequacy.

Problems which may be seen to be associated with social difficulty in the adolescent psychiatric outpatient population are numerous, such as social anxiety, social phobia, social withdrawal and school refusal, behaviour problems, aggressive problems, temper problems, stealing, anorexia nervosa, retarded physical development (especially in boys), and a general lack of self confidence and low self-esteem. Here are some examples of clients who would probably benefit from social skills training:

A. Case 1, Muriel

Muriel is 16 years of age and lives at home with her mother and younger sister. She gets on well with both her mother and sister. She is an intelligent girl and always did well at school. She has 8 "O" levels and is hoping to go to a college next year to study for her "A" levels. She is at present on a government training scheme, working in an office. Muriel was referred because of her high anxiety level and her inability to mix socially. She finds it difficult to travel on buses, go shopping and go out to public places. At such times she feels very anxious. She believes that people are staring at her, that they know how anxious she feels and that she is making a fool of herself. She has always found it easier to get on with adults and had no friends at school. The other girls at school would sometimes tease her about her weight (she is overweight), her academic success and her good relationships with teachers. When interacting with her peers Muriel stares at the floor, mumbles quietly and says very little. She sits in a hunched up position and has a permanently miserable facial expression. Sometimes she laughs during pauses. This laugh is because she is embarrassed but it often appears as if she is laughing at the other person. From her behaviour with adults, however, it is clear that Muriel has all the skills necessary for successful social performance within her repertoire. Muriel is only unable to use these skills when she feels anxious. This anxiety is related to her peer group (it is these people whom she avoids when travelling on buses and going to public places). She maintains that her peers do not like her and whenever a peer approaches in a friendly way she perceives this as hostile, believing that they are trying to mock her. She reacts accordingly, and is ultimately ignored by them.

B. Case 2, Stephen

Stephen is 17 years of age. He lives at home with his parents and is an only child. He is of average intelligence. He left school at 16 and has worked in a factory ever since. At school he had one friend whom he sometimes saw at week-ends. Since leaving school he has lost contact with this friend and has been unable to make any new friends. He goes out occasionally to the shops, to football matches or to the cinema. All these activities are either alone or with his father. Apart from these outings he stays at home, he does little to help around the house and spends much of his time model making. Stephen became more and more unhappy. At weekends he would spend most of his time in bed. He would stay away from work frequently with colds and headaches. He no longer spent time making models. He could see no point in life and altogether presented as a very depressed and unhappy young man. Stephen says he does not know what his problem is. He would like to have more friends but cannot understand why his aims in this direction have been unsuccessful. When interacting with others Stephen has a blank facial expression, he speaks in a monotone voice and says very little. He never asks questions and gives monosyllabic answers. When asked a question he always takes a long time to answer. He never initiates conversations with others.

C. Case 3, Joey

Joey is 14 years of age. His parents, who are both teachers, were divorced 3 years ago and he now lives at home with his mother, stepfather and elder brother. He and his brother argue constantly and his mother claims that Joey is usually the cause of these arguments. Joey's parents have always regarded him as a problem and describe him as "extremely demanding". They have also expressed concern that he is underachieving at school. However, psychometric assessment indicates that Joey is of average intelligence and that this is adequately reflected in his school work. This is in contrast to his brother who is doing very well at school and is of above average intelligence. Joey was originally referred to a psychiatrist because of stealing and management problems, both in school and at home. Joey has been caught stealing on numerous occasions and if he wasn't caught in the act of stealing, he was caught in the act of spending or bribing. With regard to management problems, Joey persistently interrupted people, constantly got into fights, and seemed to be unable to avoid trouble, or at least had no desire to avoid it. Joey is a slightly built, blond haired, bespectacled youth who looks younger than he is. He is verbally fluent and very well spoken. He has attended various evening clubs but has always failed to make friends. Social assessment indicates that Joey has all the basic skills within his repertoire. However, in an attempt to make friends he interrupts constantly and offers sweets and money to the people he is trying to befriend. When teased by other kids he retaliates by boasting or eventually threatening that he will "tell on them" and get them into trouble, and ultimately Joey does just this.

The 3 case histories presented illustrate a wide range of problems which require some form of SST. It is important to remember, however, that it may be necessary for the adolescent to receive some other form of treatment before, during or after SST. Considering the case of Joey, for example, it would seem that his parents have had, and indeed still have, inappropriately high expectations of Joey and his performance at school. It is likely that he has failed to receive attention and social reinforcement because of this and it would probably be necessary for some form of family therapy to be carried out at the same time as social skills training.

IV. PROCEDURAL DETAILS

A. Factors relating to the group

(1) Size of group

Obviously the size of the group is limited by the facilities and staff available, but in order to get a good Youth Club atmosphere a number in the region of 12–16 would be advisable with three or four regular members of staff.

(2) *Homegenous v. heterogenous problem groups*

The question here is whether one should aim for a group of members with the same problem (homogenous) or a group of members with different problems (heterogenous). In practice, it would be difficult to achieve the former, especially with a small group and the most one could hope for would be similarity of problems. However, a heterogenous group, especially with larger numbers, has many advantages. For example, it ensures that members interact in the group, which may not be the case if the members were all socially anxious or socially with-drawn. Also, live peer models have been found to be more effective (see Bandura, 1971) and if there were no members in the group with ability in the skill being trained then the therapist would have to model or use a videotape model.

(3) *Age range*

It is not necessary for all members to be the same age but certainly a 16 year old girl might feel insulted to be placed with 12 year old girls. It is wise to remember that younger girls and older boys is a better mix than *vice versa*. Practical experience in running this type of group indicates that 3 years would be the maximum age range.

(4) *Duration of sessions*

When running SST groups for adolescents, the preferred session duration seems to be about an hour. The Youth Club which the author is running starts at 5.30 and continues until 8.30 p.m. giving a total time of 3 hours. Within the youth club the more formal SST session lasts between 30 minutes and 1½ hours, the point here being that flexibility is essential. The arranged length of the SST session is 45 minutes but as trainers will know, sessions vary considerably, and when important issues are raised, and have not been fully dealt with, it is beneficial to take extra time to deal with these issues if members are still interested and participating. This is another advantage offered by the SSTYC approach where taking extra time presents no problem.

(5) *Frequency of sessions*

Some shy adolescents feel extremely threatened by the thought of attending the club despite the fact that it is both small and specialized. The first hour of the first session is difficult for them but usually by the end of the evening they have settled down well. It is necessary at the outset to obtain some form of commitment from the members to attend regularly. This sometimes presents a problem. If the club was run twice a week it may be exceedingly difficult to get this commitment initially. Also, as the club runs for 3 hours, 2 sessions a week may be difficult to arrange. However, once the adolescent has settled into the club it is hopefully much more likely that he will be prepared to attend more frequently and will enjoy doing so. It would be possible to run such a club as an open group where new members can join at any time and where individuals leave when they have attained their pre-specified goals. However, one could envisage a situation where members would not want to leave and possibly refrain from achieving all goals in order to stay. Generally, therefore, it is advisable to run the club on a weekly basis for a limited period of about 16 weeks and to establish links with local youth club leaders so that arrangements can be made to transfer members to these local clubs at the end of the SSTYC. This important, firstly so that the members do not become dependent on the SSTYC and also so that they can maintain the level of social integration which has been achieved by attending the SSTYC.

(6) *Equipment*

Standard youth club equipment, such as a table tennis table, and a billiard table would be an advantage but they are not essential. The planning of the sessions is far more important and there are many games which are very enjoyable and which require no equipment at all. Perhaps the most important items are records and a record player, as the music helps to create an easy going, relaxed atmosphere for the members. Videotape equipment can be useful, but once again it is not essential. The most important use of video is for pre- to post-assessments. If video equipment is going to be used at the club then a portable video set would be advantageous.

(7) *Visitors*

There tends to be a certain amount of interest in any new approach and it is likely that referral agents, students and other therapists will want to visit the club. Here the important factors to bear in mind are:

(1) Does the adult know any of the adolescents? If so, then it is necessary to ask the adolescent whether he or she minds X coming along to the club one week—it is after all the adolescent's club.
(2) Will the adult fit into the club? There are steps which can be taken to increase the likelihood that they will fit in. For example, by stressing the casual nature of the club, the need for casual dress, and explaining that anyone attending must take an active part in all games and activities to avoid the "watching" approach.
(3) Is there a danger of having too many adults in the club at any one time? This may be avoided by ensuring that all visits are made by appointment only.

B. Explanation of treatment

It is important that the SSTYC is introduced to both the adolescent and his parents as a recommended approach which is likely to be of benefit. It will be necessary to explain that it is a less formal type of treatment which aims to help adolescents with their particular problems. The adolescent and his parents should be prepared to take part in the assessment before and after SSTYC attendance. With regard to the use of video, there is an interesting article by Christian (1981) which points out the fact that there are, at the present time, no relevant laws which can be referred to on this issue. A great deal of caution is therefore necessary. It is important to ensure that the adolescent and his parents are fully aware of the fact that video will be used, when it will be used (for example, pre- and post-assessment, training sessions, etc.), why it will be used (for training, for research, for teaching other disciplines) and who will see it (for example, other club members, other colleagues, etc.). It is important to specify how long the videotape recordings will be kept. It may also be necessary to point out that it is difficult to conceal the identity of the person on the videotape recording. If anyone objects to the use of the tape for teaching, then there must be agreement that the tapes will be wiped clean at the end of the training and evaluation period. It is advisable to have a printed consent sheet with explanatory details about the video. Parents or adolescents (if they are over 16 years of age) should then sign this consent sheet but should be allowed to retract consent at any time. Finally, some form of contract of agreement as to treatment should be drawn up. Parents, adolescents and therapist should sign this. The contract of agreement should specify: (1) acceptance of SSTYC as a recommended form of treatment; (2) agreement to attend the SSTYC regularly; (3) agreement to take part in the assessment battery which has already been explained by the therapist.

V. DESCRIPTION OF A TYPICAL SESSION

A. Importance of structure

Members respond best when the club has a definite structure, especially in early sessions when they do not know each other very well. It is important that within this structure there is provision for "free time" when members need to take the initiative for social interaction. It is also important that the structure is flexible and modifiable, depending on the various situations which arise. A suggested structure would be as follows:

5.30–6.00   Free time
6.00–6.15   Group games (e.g. Killawink, Buzz, etc.)
6.15–7.00   Formal SST
7.00–7.15   Group games (e.g. Football)
7.15–7.30   Coffee time
7.30–8.00   Free time
8.00–8.30   Group games (e.g. Yes and No, In the Manner of the Word, etc.)

B. Reinforcement system

It is necessary to establish high levels of motivation at the outset as more often than not when adolescents attend their first session they come reluctantly and will often have very low levels of motivation. It is important that adolescents are: (a) motivated to attend the SSTYC; (b) motivated to participate in the SSTYC activities; (c) motivated to learn the skills being trained, and (d) motivated to use the skills trained.

It is unlikely that the first requirement will be fulfilled unless members enjoy the sessions. It is therefore necessary to establish the youth club as both positive and reinforcing. On a more specific level, there should be ample opportunity at the club for members to receive reinforcements (for example, positive attention, social reinforcement, and also, if possible, more tangible reinforcements).

One way in which tangible reinforcers could be used would be to incorporate an ongoing points system into the session, and to award prizes to the members who have earned the most points at the end of the evening. This would mean that points could be awarded for club attendance, participation in youth club activities, learning social skills and using social skills. The problem here, however, is that some members are brighter and/or more able than others and would therefore more easily earn points. This problem may be overcome by using individual targets. These may be specified at the beginning of the evening for each member. For example:

(1) Muriel's targets

 (*a*) to take her coat off at the beginning of the evening; (*b*) to sit up in the chair, keeping her back straight.

(2) Joey's targets

 (*a*) not to shout back and retaliate when teased by other group members; (*b*) not to boast about his father and his chemistry experiments during group activities.

(3) Stephen's targets

 (*a*) to initiate a conversation with another member during free time; (*b*) to ask questions during group activities.

Thus, Joey and Stephen would not earn points for taking their coats off at the beginning of the session because they have no difficulty doing this. Muriel, on the other hand, has difficulty taking her coat off and would therefore earn a pre-specified number of points for successful completion of this behaviour. Obviously, the targets should not be too difficult for the individuals concerned and should be selected gradually according to their levels of difficulty. That is, during early sessions less difficult targets should be selected but once these have been achieved and maintained, more difficult targets may be chosen.

C. Using formal SST methods

(1) General governing principles

During the more formal SST part of the evening, structure is again important. Therapists would be well advised to have a rough plan for each session. Also, when training social skills it is important to train the general governing principles underlying the skills. For example, when training conversation skills the general governing principles might be:

(1) Greet other. Look, smile, say "hello".
(2) Identify attitude. If positive, continue. If negative, stop.
(3) Ask some general questions—"how are you", "how's work/school", "what have you been doing lately".

Ask some specific questions—these questions should be related to the answers received from general questions; for example—"when are your exams", "what are you doing when you have left school", "what was the party like last week-end".

(4) Answer any questions—avoid one or two word answers and give a little extra information.
(5) Volunteer information about yourself.
(6) Close conversation. Take control of the conversation, give excuse or reason for leaving, say for example—"It's been nice to see you, I must go now as I have to catch my bus". "See you soon".

The general governing principles for conversation skill may be further subdivided into:

(1) Starting up a conversation
(2) Keeping a conversation going
(3) Ending a conversation.

The length of time spent on training particular skills will depend on the level of skill within the group. It may be necessary, for example, to spend a session on each subsection of the conversation skill plan and a fourth session on the complete package.

(2) *Discussion and instructions*

The session usually starts with a general discussion about the skill being trained. It is best if the group members can be encouraged to suggest particular strategies rather than being told by the trainer. As these strategies are discussed it is useful to write them up on a wall chart or blackboard.

(3) *A poor role-play*

It is unlikely that all the important points will be covered in the first discussion so that a "poor" role-play by therapists would be one way of helping members to identify important issues.

(4) *Modelling*

At this stage a conversation incorporating the general governing principles which have just been discussed should be modelled. It is preferable that the model is an adolescent, and if there is no member who would perform this task adequately, a pre-recorded role play by an adolescent model from outside the group could be used. Another point to remember is that a coping model is more effective than a mastery model (see Bandura, 1971).

(5) Role-play

At this stage members are asked to role-play a conversation. The situation should be specified as precisely as possible and should be as realistic as possible. Members may be asked to recall a conversation which they found difficult and to specify the details of the situation as precisely as possible. If group numbers are large, members may be split into pairs to practice their role-plays. At this stage the therapists should supervize each pair in turn, giving feedback as necessary.

(6) Feedback

Feedback should be given in a positive way and because of this it is important that the therapist maintains overall control of any feedback given. In order to avoid negative feedback being given by group members the therapist may ask specific questions about a particular member's performance. It is often necessary to point out behaviours which members didn't do, or perhaps behaviours which they performed inappropriately. However, this may still be done in a positive and non-threatening way. For example—"Yes, Stephen, that was very good, you looked at Joey, you smiled, you faced him and you asked a relevant question, but perhaps next time you could speak up a bit more just to make sure Joey hears what you have said". Feedback may also be given in the form of videotape recording playbacks. It is important at this stage to point out the dangers involved in the use of this procedure. Firstly, because feedback should be positive, the recording must be carefully edited to ensure that only successful social performance is played back to the member concerned. This is often very difficult to do. Also, adolescents (especially females) often have low self-esteem, low self-images and negative body images. Therefore, even the most successful social performance would be viewed negatively by such a member when played back on video. If adolescents do not like going on video it may well be an indication that they find video playback aversive. They should therefore never be pressurized to take part in this aspect of training. It has been found useful to introduce video into the group by allowing the members to take turns in using the camera and to experiment with recording.

(7) *Reinforcement*

Reinforcement in the form of positive feedback, attention, praise and points should be used throughout the session for both effort and achievement. However, each member should understand that reinforcements are received for their own improvements and not for doing better than other group members.

(8) *Behaviour rehearsal (practice)*

Once a particular skill has been trained it is necessary for members to practice the skill in relevant situations. Practice should take place during the SST session initially. Following this members should be encouraged to practice the skill in the youth club and in social situations outside of the setting. Points may be awarded during the youth club sessions for appropriate and successful use of a skill.

(9) *SST in the form of a game*

Thus far the importance of structure and reinforcement have been emphasized and the use of the traditional training techniques have been discussed. There is, however, another important technique which rarely appears in the SST literature, which is game playing (that is, introducing an element of games into the SST). It has been stressed throughout that members should enjoy the training and one way in which this may be achieved effectively is by game-playing. For example:

The ball game. Group members sit round in a circle and are only allowed to talk when they hold the ball. They are only allowed to stop talking when they have passed the ball to someone else and to do this they have to "hand the conversation over". This game may be used for asking general and specific questions, for answering questions, for volunteering information about self and for changing the subject. The rules may be altered accordingly.

Guess the attitude. This game may be used for facial expression, voice intonation or both. Pictures, tape recordings, videotaped role-plays or role-playing by group members may be used. The game is useful in that it trains members to identify the attitudes of others during conversation, as well as training them to convey attitudes and emotions to others. There should be a list of attitudes provided for members to choose from.

Getting out of a conversation. Two people are in conversation, one person has the task of keeping this person in conversation, the other person must try to get out of the conversation in a friendly way. The therapist shouts "Now" and from this point the second person tries to get out of the conversation as quickly as he can. Someone times his performance with a stop watch. Each member has two attempts and the winner is the person who obtains the biggest improvement (in terms of time) between his/her first and second attempt. Also, any member whose performance is rated as unfriendly by the group is disqualified. The rules for a friendly performance must be specified at the outset.

It is possible for many social skills to be trained by use of games. It is important, however, that members do not compete with each other for points but with their own previous performances. In this way members may see themselves succeeding and a good group atmosphere is likely to result.

D. Social skill enhancement games

The Youth Club session is divided into "free time" and "organized time". During organized time it is necessary for the therapist to supervize some form of group activity. Obviously there are many group activities to choose from, but given that the club has been set up specifically to train social skills, the activities should be selected according to the extent to which they may be seen to be enhancing social skill. There are many group games which fulfil this criterion and games may also be developed or modified to do so. When selecting and implementing games, it should be remembered that the purpose is to involve the members in observation of or participation in some sort of social interaction in an enjoyable and non-threatening way. Examples:

(1) *In the manner of the word*

This is a miming game. One player leaves the room while the others decide on a particular adverb (for example: quickly, angrily, etc.). The player is then called back in and asks one of the others to perform a task "in the manner of the word". He may ask a player to perform a task as many times as he needs in order to guess the adverb correctly.

(2) *Killawink*

Each player is given a card. The player who receives the only joker given out is the "killer". The cards are held face downwards by the players after they have looked at them. The killer kills by winking at other players but he must attempt to do so without being seen by other players. If killed, players count to ten and shout "I'm dead" and throw their card into the centre of the circle. If any of the players who are still alive see someone winking at someone else they can challenge that person as the "Killer".

(3) Yes and no

Each player takes a turn to answer questions which are posed by the person designated "Questioner". The aim of the game is to answer questions without saying "Yes" or "No" and also without nodding or shaking the head. Each player has two attempts and the winner is the person who obtains the biggest improvement (in terms of time) between his/her first and second attempt. Different people may be designated "Questioner" at any time.

VI. GENERAL CONCLUSIONS

A. Assessment

The assessments outlined earlier in the chapter give some idea as to the measurement of social inadequacy. One important function of assessment is the evaluation of targets for treatment and thus the assessments selected at the outset are likely to influence treatment to a large extent. However, other important functions would include measurement of treatment benefits (outcome), measurement of the maintenance of these benefits (durability) and measurement of the carry over of these benefits to other situations (generalization). These issues are crucial in order to investigate whether training has been of any *real* benefit to patients, and the assessments used should be selected specifically for the degree to which they attempt to deal with these issues. That is, has the adolescent benefitted from treatment and improved in specific target areas? Have there been any improvements in other areas not targeted? Has the adolescent maintained these improvements over time and has the adolescent successfully generalized these improvements to the social situations in which they are needed? Therefore, assessments should be carried out not only during and at the end of treatment but for some time after treatment until therapists are confident that treatment gains are being maintained. Also, attempts should be made to assess the adolescent's functioning in situations other than the training situation to investigate the extent to which treatment gains have generalized. This is not always easy to do but information from significant others can be valuable. Another consideration is the related problems which may have led to the initial referral. For example, is Muriel still anxious in social situations, can she travel on buses, go shopping and go to public places? Is Stephen still depressed, is he spending less time in bed, going to work regularly and going to football matches? Is Joey still stealing and presenting a management problem at home and at school?

B. Generalization and duration of training benefits

The importance of duration and generalization of benefits and the need to assess these have already been discussed. However, therapists should seriously consider anything which can be included in the treatment package to programme directly for duration and generalization of training. Perhaps the most desirable approach is one which aims to fade out the treatment gradually while fading in appropriate community-based supports, so that changes in the patient's life which were initially brought about by treatment intervention are maintained by changes in the patient's social environment outside treatment. This would include regular peer contact, social integration, social interaction and social reinforcement. Increasing social activities, social contacts and social integration generally would obviously help to achieve this goal.

C. Appropriateness of skills trained

One danger which exists when dealing with the adolescent population is that of imposing inappropriate adult values, and even inappropriate socio-economic values. Research is now being conducted into the validity of various social skills for particular adolescent populations in an attempt to ensure that the skills trained are those which are socially important to the adolescent population concerned (for example, Spence, 1981). There are certain steps, however, which can be taken in the training situation to decrease this danger. Firstly, the adolescent should specify target problems and also have ample opportunity to select goals for treatment. Also, during training the adolescents should be the ones who work out strategies for dealing with these problems. They are, after all, more likely to be familiar with the values appropriate to their particular population. A heterogeneous problem group has already been suggested and this would mean that a whole variety of skills would be available within the group.

In addition, the finding that the most effective models are of the same age as the observer (see Bandura, 1971) indicates that therapists should select group members to model skills rather than model the skills themselves. Generally, therapists should encourage members to be as active as possible in the running of training groups with the adolescents selecting targets, and solutions to these targets, working out strategies for dealing with problems, modelling these strategies, giving feedback on peer performance and giving reinforcement for successful social performance.

D. Motivation

One problem which has been referred to throughout this chapter is lack of motivation. The most direct indication as to the level of motivation amongst members is the attendance rate, and beyond this the extent to which members participate in the group activities. Obviously, unless the therapist can achieve high attendance and participation then little can be achieved in terms of social skills training. Various methods have been described which have been found to increase motivation (see Rowe, 1980 for further details). Over and above this the important issues seem to be the appropriateness of skills trained and the duration and generalization of training benefits. Research is ongoing in these areas and practitioners in the field should be concentrating on ways in which these goals may be achieved most effectively.

VII. REFERENCES

Bandura, A. (1971). A psychotherapy based upon modeling principles. *In* "Handbook of Psychotherapy and Behaviour Change" (A. E. Bergin and S. L. Garfield, *Eds*), pp. 653–708. Wiley, New York.

Bellack, A. S., Hersen, M. and Turner, S. M. (1978). Role-play tests for assessing social skills: Are they valid? *Behav. Ther.* **9**, 448–461.

Christian, C. (1981). The law is vague on video. *On Call* **15 (4)**, 2.

Goldstein, A. P., Sherman, M., Gershaw, N. J., Sprafkin, R. P. and Glick, B. (1977). Training aggressive adolescents in prosocial behaviour. *J. Youth Adol.* **7**, 73–92.

Jackson, M. F. (1981). The investigation of the treatment of adolescent social difficulty in a community based setting. Unpublished Ph.D. Thesis. University of Birmingham, U.K.

Kiff, J. (1980). Adolescent social skills: A comparative study of a group of adolescents referred for social skills training and matched normal controls. Unpublished Masters Thesis. University of Birmingham, U.K.

Marzillier, J. S. (1975). Systematic desensitization and social skills training in treatment of social inadequacy. Unpublished doctoral thesis, University of London.

Rowe, M. F. (1980). The development of a Youth Club for adolescents with social difficulty and the investigation of the application of social skills training in this setting. Unpublished Masters Thesis, University of Birmingham, U.K.

Shepherd, G. (1980). Treatment in natural and special environments. In "The Social Psychology of Psychological Problems" (M. P. Feldman and J. R. Orford, Eds). Wiley, New York.

Spence, S. (1979). Long term generalized effects of SST with adolescent male offenders in an institutional setting. Unpublished Ph.D. Thesis, University of Birmingham, U.K.

Spence, S. H. (1981). The validation of components of social skill with adolescents. *J. Appl. Behav. Anal.* **14**, 159–168.

Spence, A. J. and Spence, S. H. (1980). Cognitive changes associated with social skills training. *Behav. Res. Ther.* **18**, 265–272.

9

Adolescent offenders in an institutional setting

SUE SPENCE

I. INTRODUCTION

The following chapter describes a social skills programme carried out in a Local Authority Community Home School with young male offenders. Before describing the details of the programme it is first worth considering the rationale behind the setting up of this type of a social skills training programme.

The reasons why a young person begins to engage in delinquent activities and continues to do so are numerous. Many different theories of delinquency have been proposed, but in practice, it seems that the aetiological factors vary with different individuals. Factors such as peer pressure to offend, deprived home conditions, truancy from school, opportunity for offending and the effects of financial and material gain are examples of aetiological influences often found to be important in accounting for the development of offence behaviour. Recently, however, theorists and practitioners have begun to emphasize the importance of interpersonal skill deficits in the development and maintenance of offending (Braukmann et al., 1975). If a young person is deficient in social skills they are unlikely to be successful in many aspects of life, such as relationships at home and school, with peers and teachers, in obtaining and keeping jobs and in dealing with encounters with the police and courts. If young people are unable to obtain desirable goals such as friendship, peer status and respect, adult attention and financial gain by socially acceptable means, they may well resort to more delinquent activities as a means of obtaining these goals.

Obviously, this model does not propose that all juvenile offenders are deficient in social skills. Rather, it suggests that this may well be so for many and that any intervention programme should consider the need to remediate social skill deficits. Indeed evidence suggests that many young offenders are deficient in social skills. For example, Freedman et al. (1978) showed that a group of young male offenders responded less skilfully on a series of role-play tests compared to a matched group of non-offenders. The tests involved a series of social situations which, if mishandled, could lead to conflict with the law. A wide range of possible responses were determined for each situation and each response was then rated on a scale of appropriate behaviour by a set of independent judges. This allowed a scale to be produced with which it was possible to score performance on each role-play situation. Freedman et al., 1978 found that institutionalized offenders scored significantly lower on this test than a group of boys without criminal records, who were matched for age, IQ and social background. This study suggests therefore, that in general, young offenders are less socially skilled than their non-offending counterparts.

A more recent study by Spence (1981) investigated differences in micro-level social skills performance between juvenile offenders and non-offenders. Eighteen institutionalized male offenders and a group of 18 boys without criminal records, comparable in terms of age, social background and educational attainment, were videotaped during a 5 minute interview with a previously unknown adult. Each videotape was then subject to a behavioural analysis of 13 measures of specific social skill responses, such as eye contact and latency of response. The tapes were also shown in random order to a group of 6 independent judges (teachers) who rated each tape on 3, 10 point scales of friendliness, social skills performance and probability of being given a part-time job.

The offender group were found to show a significantly lower level of eye contact, head movements (nods and shakes) and total amount spoken, plus a higher level of fiddling and gross body movements, compared to the non-offender group. No differences were found in the use of gestures, smiling, speech dysfluencies, question asking, latency of response and initiations. The teachers ratings showed that the offender group scored significantly lower in terms of social skills performance and judged employability compared to their non-offending counterparts. No difference was found between the groups in terms of friendliness ratings.

Both the studies mentioned above tend to support the suggestion that, in general, young male offenders are less socially skilled than boys of similar age and from similar backgrounds who have not been convicted of offending.

II. PREVIOUS EVALUATIVE STUDIES

Based upon the premise that many juvenile offenders are deficient in social skills and that this may be a causal factor in their persistent delinquent behaviour, several researchers have investigated the potential benefit of teaching social skills to young offenders. The majority of these studies have tended to evaluate the effectiveness of social skills training (SST) over and above the benefits of other ongoing interventions, such as token economies, behavioural contracting or therapeutic communities. It has not generally been proposed that SST should be of dramatic value if used as an isolated technique. Rather it has mostly been considered as an adjunct to other forms of intervention.

For a detailed review of outcome studies related to SST with young offenders, the reader is referred to Spence (1979b). Generally, it can be said that SST has been shown to be effective in producing short-term changes in very specific responses, such as eye contact, or listening skills. Several single case design studies have shown SST to produce positive short-term gains in conversation skills (Minkin et al. 1976; Maloney et al. 1976; Spence and Marzillier, 1979), heterosexual interaction skills (Braukmann et al., 1973), interview skills (Braukmann et al., 1974), police encounter skills (Werner et al., 1975) and specific conflict handling skills (Thelen et al., 1976). These single case design studies however have generally been limited by their failure to investigate whether the benefits were long lasting or whether they generalized beyond the training setting to "real-life" interactions. Despite these limitations it is encouraging to find that improvements in very specific skills can generally be found within the training setting.

Studies which have investigated the training of more complex social skills such as the general handling of conflict situations or making assertive responses have tended to produce varied findings. These studies have typically involved group designs, comparing the benefits of SST with attention or placebo comparison groups or youngsters who did not receive any form of intervention. Several studies report SST to produce positive gains in terms of behaviour within the institution (Ollendick and Hersen, 1979; Shoemaker, 1979) positive attitude change (Sarason and Ganzer, 1973) and a decrease in subsequent re-offending (Sarason and Ganzer, 1973). Although SST was found to be superior to a discussion comparison group by Shoemaker (1979) and Ollendick and Hersen (1979), this was not the case in the Sarason and Ganzer study. It must be concluded that much more research is needed before it can really be said that SST produces long lasting and generalized benefits to young offenders in terms of positive changes in social behaviour in everyday life and prevention of re-offending.

The present chapter describes a SST programme set up within a residential community home for young offenders. The emphasis will be on the practical aspects of the programme rather than the research aspects. Readers interested in details of the research component are referred to Spence and Marzillier (1979; 1981).

III. THE PRESENT STUDY

A. The setting and trainees

The present programme was carried out in a Community Home School with Education on the premises (CH(E)). The boys were resident in two 30 boy open units, divided according to the age of the boys. The regime of the establishment was mainly counselling based. The boys attended daily meetings of the whole unit and weekly, small-group counselling sessions. Weekend leave usually occurred on a fortnightly basis. Boys were required to attend school during the week days.

The age range of the boys was 10–16 years with all boys having been convicted of offences ranging from persistent truancy to arson and assault. Typically they came from deprived home backgrounds and were in care of the local authority. Only those boys who were identified as experiencing difficulty in social situations were considered for the programme. This decision was made from results on a staff questionnaire, self report questionnaire and direct behavioural observation which sampled a variety of basic and complex social skills. Although an attempt was made to pick out boys for training based on identifiable deficits in social skills, it was still necessary to set an arbitrary criteria for defining whether or not deficits were evident. In practice it was found that the vast majority of boys in the school were reported or reported themselves as experiencing problems in interactions with other people. Approximately 80% of the boys in the school were considered to experience social skills problems of some sort and were therefore classed as eligible for the SST programme.

B. Development of assessment methods

The first stage of the project was to develop a series of assessment tools. The creation and collection of a battery of reliable and valid assessment measures is essential when setting up any SST programme and is an area often neglected by trainers. No therapist should ever embark on a SST programme without first having spent time working out an assessment battery that is appropriate for the client population concerned and the environment in which they live.

The assessment process serves 3 main functions:

(1) The assessment process should permit identification of those clients who experience difficulty in social situations and would hence be likely to benefit from SST. This step acts as a filtering process in which those with adequate social skills are filtered away from the programme.
(2) The assessment procedure should also clarify the exact nature of each client's social skill problems, in order to pinpoint the targets for training. In practice, it is hoped that the emphasis of this stage of

assessment will be not just on deficits and excesses in performance, but also on the client's assets. Areas of deficit refer to behaviours which the person is presently performing at an inadequate level and training would aim to increase in frequency, duration or intensity. Areas of excess, on the other hand, refer to behaviours which the person exhibits too frequently, or to too high a level. Training would then aim to decrease the level of performance. The client's assets involve existing skills and resources which the trainer should attempt to enhance or at least maintain as the result of training.

(3) Finally, the assessment procedure should allow evaluation of changes in skill performance over time and in different settings, in order to demonstrate the effectiveness of SST in producing long lasting benefits which generalize to everyday interactions.

Assessment of behaviour needs to consider the clients functioning in as wide a range of settings with as many different people as possible. In order to achieve this goal, the present programme assessed the boys' social skills performance in several different settings with a range of different people. For example:

Settings assessed	People	
School	Parents	
House unit	Teachers	Adults
Home	Police	
Youth club/recreation	Peers	
	Siblings	Children
	Girlfriends	

In order to obtain information in such a large range of social situations, it was necessary to use a variety of information sources. The use of different information sources also made it possible to cross check the data produced and confirm the reliability and generalizability of assessment.

C. Assessment sources

The main assessment tools used in the project involved a staff questionnaire, a self report questionnaire and direct behavioural observations during role-play. Although it was not possible to involve parents in the present study, owing to their unwillingness to participate, it would be desirable to develop parental questionnaires which might provide important information about the boys' behaviour at home. Any assessment measure used must be both reliable and valid, and considerable effort was necessary before measures were eventually produced that met acceptable criteria of both reliability and validity. Unfortunately, at the beginning of the project it was not possible to find existing methods developed by other people that fulfilled the requirements of the assessment. It was therefore necessary to develop new assessment tools, designed for use with adolescent boys. Complete examples of the assessment methods used can be found in Spence (1980) with detailed information regarding the reliability and validity being reported in Spence (1979a) and Spence and Marzillier (1979; 1981).

(1) Staff questionnaire

The first method devised was a staff questionnaire which could be given to the teachers or residential care staff. The final version of the questionnaire involved a 30 item, 5 point rating scale, which focused on both basic and complex interaction skills with adults and peers. Examples of the items were:

	Rating				
Examples of items	1	2	3	4	5
Will ask to join in activities with peers	Never	Rarely	Sometimes	Often	Very often
Becomes aggressive if verbally provoked by peers	Very often	Often	Sometimes	Rarely	Never
Initiates conversation with staff	Never	Rarely	Sometimes	Often	Very often

(2) Self-report questionnaire

The self report questionnaire was designed to be as simple as possible so as to be easily understood by the boys. It involved a list of 60 statements concerning difficulty in social interactions, to which a yes/no response was required. The items were selected from a wide range of situations stated as causing difficulty by several boys in a discussion group. The questions were made as specific as possible and were all checked for reliability and validity. Generally the questionnaire was read out to the boys, many of whom had reading difficulties.

Examples of items to be found in the self report questionnaire include:

Do you find it hard to make friends in a new place?   Yes   No

Do you find it hard to say "no" when your friends
   ask you to join in, to do something wrong?   Yes   No

Do you find it hard to own up to an adult when you've
   done something wrong   Yes   No

(3) *Direct behavioural observation*

One of the most reliable ways of obtaining information about a person's behaviour is to observe them directly. The information can then be stored, either by mechanical means such as video- or audiotape, or transferred to written codings. Fortunately, the school owned a video system so it was possible to film the boys during interactions with others. For the purposes of the research programme, reliable measures of the performance of specific, basic social skills were made from videotaped conversations between each boy and an adult stooge. The content of the conversation was constant, comprising a standard set of conversation topics and questions and then involved a role-play where the boy was asked to return a defective record to a shop. It was then possible to subject each videotape to a detailed analysis. Two main methods were used. Firstly a social skills assessment chart was used in which 32 specific social skills were assessed. Performance on each skill was rated on a 5 point rating scale. The social skills assessment chart can be found in Spence (1980) along with the rating scales used. Areas of social skill considered included:

(a) *Perception of emotions*
   Facial expression
   Posture
   Gestures
   Tone of voice
   (as assessed by specific
   tests—see Spence, 1980)

(b) *Basic non-verbal skills*
   Facial expression
   Posture
   Gestures
   Eye contact

(c) *Non-verbal responses*
   Social distance
   Fiddling movements
   Smiling and laughter
   Head movements

(d) *Voice quality*
   Tone and pitch
   Volume
   Rate
   Clarity

(e) *Quality of speech*
   Dysfluences
   Hesitations and pauses
   Latency of response
   Amount spoken
(g) *Listening skills*
   Acknowledgements
   Reflections
   Question-type feedback
   Personal self-disclosure

(f) *Content of speech*
   Relevancy of conversation
   Interest content
   Interruptions
   Repetitions
(h) *Basic conversation skills*
   Frequency of initiations
   Frequency of question asking
   Information content
   Length of reply to questions

These responses were selected for assessment as they had been suggested to be important components of socially skilled behaviour by other investigators with mainly adult populations (e.g. Marzillier *et al.*, 1976; Minkin *et al.*, 1976; Hersen and Bellack, 1977).

Secondly, in addition to using the 5 point rating scale for each of the above behaviours, the performance of certain social skills responses was actually measured in terms of frequency or duration of response. The level of eye contact, gestures, fiddling movements, smiling, head movements, amount spoken, hesitations and dysfluencies, question feedback responses, initiations and questions asked were all measured for each boy. Such a detailed analysis as the actual measurement of responses may not be practical, nor indeed necessary for many practitioners setting up SST programmes. The present programme was however part of an extensive research project and the complex level of assessment was required.

D. Identifying targets for training: the need for a definition of social skills

Having carried out a detailed assessment of each boy's social skills repertoire, one would imagine that it would be reasonably straight-forward to identify the targets for training. Unfortunately, this was not the case. Several questions remained to be answered. How does the trainer decide whether the performance of a skill is inadequate or excessive, compared to the rest of the population? When should a particular behaviour be considered to be a problem. Exactly which responses are social skills for young boys? These are major questions, to which there seemed to be a noticeable lack of answers. There is a marked lack of information amongst the research literature relating to normative levels of performance and validation of responses as being genuine social skills for adolescents.

It seemed important to clarify exactly what was being meant by socially skilled behaviour, before targets could be identified for the trainees. In the present study, the author eventually incorporated the ideas of others, such as Trower *et al.* (1978) and Combs and Slaby (1977) to produce a working definition of social skills . . . "Social skills are those responses which enable a person to obtain his or her desired outcome from a given social interaction in a manner which is socially acceptable and does not cause harm to others".

This type of definition stresses the need for social skills to lead to successful consequences for individuals. It also implies that the responses that are required for success in interactions will vary depending on the characteristics of those involved and the type of social interaction concerned. Given the lack of data to enable the selection of targets which can be said to be socially valid, it is unfortunately often necessary for the trainer to rely on his or her own clinical intuitions. The same is true in deciding whether or not a particular area can be considered to be problematic and in need of change. Such decisions should also involve the trainees who are in a good position to observe themselves and identify problem areas.

In practice, the targets for training were identified from the assessment tools, by taking any responses that were classed as a problem by the trainee on the self report questionnaire, by the staff or by the trainer on the ratings of the videotaped conversation. Any rating below 3 on the 5 point scale was classed as a problem area. This enabled a list of target areas to be compiled for each trainee.

E. Setting up a SST programme within an institutional setting

(1) *Gaining support from within the establishment*

Before the programme could begin a great deal of planning was required. The first step was to explain the aims and methods of the programme to the senior managers in order to gain their support. In doing so, it was possible to ensure that SST groups became part of the school curriculum—sessions occurred during school hours and were given the same priority as other lessons, to which boys were expected to attend. The groups were not considered to be special in any way, to avoid the connotations of "psychiatric illness" or "abnormality" which often accompanies such groups and for which the boys had a noticeable dread. The priority given to the groups also ensured that boys turned up on time and were not withdrawn suddenly for other purposes, such as to go out to buy new clothes.

Having prepared the way with senior staff, the next stage was to educate the teachers and care staff so that, as far as possible, socially skilled behaviour would be modelled, prompted and reinforced within the school. A series of seminars on the topic was arranged and also served as a means of recruiting interested staff to be trained to take over the running of SST groups at a later date.

(2) Developing trainer skills

Every social skills trainer has to begin somewhere and learn the techniques of SST and group management. One of the easiest ways is to begin with one to one training sessions, at first working on very simple, basic social skills, before moving on to the teaching of more complex responses. Sessions with only one trainee were found to be helpful in that they did not require the trainer to have the additional skills needed to direct and manage a group of very difficult boys. They also allowed the trainer to practice new methods without the critical eye of a co-therapist. The sessions were usually videotaped which allowed the trainer to assess her performance and to ask other practitioners to give their comments. Tapes were usually evaluated in terms of the amount of time the trainer/ trainee were involved in some aspect of SST and whether the trainer managed to incorporate into each session the techniques of instructions/ discussion, modelling, role-play/practice, feedback, social reinforcement and setting homework tasks.

After carrying out individual SST programmes with 6 boys, it was time to consider setting up group sessions. The management of groups of young residents of Community Home Schools is not always an easy task. Basically the skills for running a SST group with young offenders are probably the same as those required for any type of counselling, therapy or drama group. Several points were quickly learned however, which may be worth mentioning here.

It was found to be important to make the emphasis in the groups as positive as possible, providing a great deal of social reinforcement from trainers and other group members. Whenever a trainee attempted a skill, the trainer focused on what was achieved *not* on what was missing, e.g. "Well done Jim, you were looking at Ricky much more often that time, didn't you think so Ricky? Now perhaps you could try again and this time see if you could look at him for a tiny bit longer". Criticisms was found to be much more acceptable if phrased in a positive way.

Similarly, it was found to be better to involve as many group members as possible in any activity, rather than having one or two boys "in the hot seat" while others looked on. This avoided boys becoming bored and also did not mean that any particular boy was the main focus of a problem area at any one time. The boys tended to become more anxious, withdrawn or aggressive if they considered a problem to refer to them specifically. Target behaviours were always discussed therefore in the content of "many boys have this kind of difficulty", rather than "John, you never look at people, so today we're going to concentrate on your problem".

It was found to be useful to use a simple incentive scheme which was very cheap and easy to administer. In order to encourage boys to be on time to their sessions and to stay on task during training, each boy received a point for arriving on time and another point for working during the session. The criteria for earning a point was set by the trainer on an individual basis for each trainee. Those boys who earned a preset number of points by the end of training were then invited to a party in which a videotaped film was shown and fruit juice and biscuits were served. This method was very effective in facilitating punctuality and co-operation and the boys were normally ready outside the training room waiting for the session to begin.

(3) Size of group

A variety of group sizes were tried but in practice it was found preferable to limit groups to between 4 and 6 members. This was mainly for reasons of control in that larger groups were unable to receive enough individual attention and behaviour problems tended to result from boredom. Obviously, larger groups could be used with other client groups who do not present such problems of control.

(4) Number of therapists

After trying various ways of working it was found to be easiest to manage the group with 2 adult trainers, one acting as leader and the other as co-leader. This prevented the 2 trainers competing for the leader role and ensured that a main theme was followed throughout the session. It also became clear that the 2 trainers had to meet before each session to discuss the topics and targets to be covered in order to prevent confusion.

(5) Frequency, duration and number of sessions

At first, sessions were carried out once a week, but it was found that boys had often forgotten the content of the previous session. It was decided therefore to run them twice a week to increase continuity. It may well be preferable to run SST groups everyday for a shorter time than one hour twice a week, but this was not practical in terms of therapist time in the present study.

The boys in the school often had great difficulty concentrating and remaining on task for prolonged periods. Sessions lasting $1^{1}/_{2}$ hours were tried but led to chaos after around one hour. Shorter sessions of half an hour were tried but were impractical as it generally took the first quarter of an hour to get the group going and complete discussion of homework tasks. In the end one hour sessions were used which generally required around three quarters of on task behaviour from the boys.

The decision regarding the number of sessions was difficult to make as the boys tended to vary greatly in terms of the extent of their social skill difficulties. Some would have required a huge number of sessions in order to reach a high level of socially skilled behaviour. Others showed much less severe problems and would benefit greatly from only 5 or 6 sessions. As the research project required a fixed number of sessions, it was decided to make a compromise using 12 sessions over a 6 week period.

(6) Materials

In order to make the groups run more smoothly it was found to be useful to produce a series of modelling videotapes. These did not replace modelling by other group members who were proficient at a particular skill, but were used as an adjunct to live modelling. Adolescent boys from a regular comprehensive school were used to depict a variety of problem social situations often encountered by adolescents, such as dealing with teasing and bullying, attending an interview and making friends. The studio props and content of the scenes were made as realistic as possible and were designed by the boys themselves.

In order to show the modelling tapes and provide videotaped feedback of the trainees performance, a video system was necessary. This was also found to be useful in gaining the boys' interest in the sessions. There was little evidence of anxiety or reluctance to being videotaped and the vast majority of trainees found it great fun. The availability of a video system is not essential, but it was found to be of great value with the young offender group.

Other materials used in the sessions included a series of photographs and audiotapes relating to the assessment and training of perception of other people's non-verbal cues, such as facial expression, posture, tone of voice and gesture. A series of games were also designed that facilitated role-play, such as a converted monopoly board and roulette wheel. Games were played in which specific positions on the board or wheel required the trainees to draw a card on which a set role-play was outlined. A more detailed outline of these games and materials can be found in Spence (1980).

(7) Grouping of trainees

A major question in the running of SST groups is the method of grouping trainees: whether to group boys with similar problems together, or whether to vary the range and severity of problems within a group. The few groups tackled during the initial period did not yield much information to help solve this problem as each group differed so much from the previous one in terms of the presenting problems. In the end it was considered acceptable to group trainees according to the random assignment procedure of the research design, as no contra-indications to suggest otherwise were found. In the actual research phase one group presented problems where one of the boys with mild problems was assigned into a group with a boy with very extreme social skills difficulties. The extreme severity of this boy's problems slowed down the progress of the rest of the group considerably. Perhaps the most that can be said then is that trainers should avoid mixing trainees of extreme opposite levels of difficulty, but within these extremes the mixing of abilities and type of problems did not present as an issue.

(8) Selection of targets: designing the group curriculum

Before the groups began, the trainer collected together all available information on each group member. From this data, it was possible to outline the major targets for training for each trainee. Targets were selected from very simple, basic skills such as use of eye contact, posture, listening skills and also much more complex skill strategies such as dealing with job interviews, making friends, dealing with criticism, teasing or bullying.

An area was considered to be a problem if it was reported as such by either the boy or the staff, or the trainer from the outcome of the videotaped conversation and role-play. Having worked out a set of targets for each group member, it was possible to list the total target areas for the whole group. This list then formed the curriculum for the group. Generally each session focused only on one or two skills: usually a simple skill first and then a more complex skill which incorporated the basic skills already learned.

In the selection of targets for individuals it was important to take several factors into account. For example an attempt was made to select skills that were relevant to the boys' success in everyday life. Consideration was taken of cultural differences, as many of the boys were from West Indian cultures. It was often necessary to ask the boys to observe their more successful peers outside sessions and to ask them to identify what skills and strategies they used in different situations. As far as possible, an attempt was made to avoid selecting targets for training purely on the basis of the trainers clinical intuition. Some type of social validation was attempted to support the social importance to the skills trained, rather than concentrating on "white, middle-class" norms of behaviour. It was also important that targets were selected that were likely to lead to social reinforcement when used in everyday situations, and would not be punished or ignored by the peer group, teachers, care staff or parents. Similarly, it was essential that skills were not trained that would lead to alienation from the boys' sub-cultures.

IV. TRAINING METHODS

The type of training techniques tried out and eventually used were essentially the same as for any traditional SST programme. For example, those reported by Marzillier *et al.* (1976); Argyle *et al.* (1974); and Trower *et al.* (1978). However, several aspects of the training procedure that specifically related to work with young offenders may be worth mentioning.

A. Instructions and discussion

The emphasis in the first part of each session was on trying to encourage the trainees themselves to identify certain responses and strategies as being socially important and work out the implications of such responses for their own social interactions. The trainer tried to avoid a one-way teaching model in which the trainees were told what is important and why. The instruction and discussion phase also allowed trainees and trainer to discuss the way in which a particular skill is performed.

This part of training closely resembles the problem-solving techniques outlined by Spivack and Shure (1978) for younger children. Essentially, their approach teaches children to identify the existence of problem situations, generate a range of alternative courses of action, strategies or responses and identify the likely consequences of each course of action:

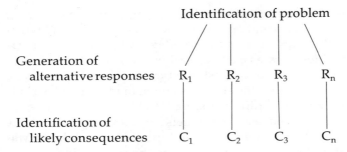

This method is suggested to teach children to think before they act, selecting the response that is most likely to lead to a desirable outcome. This is in direct contrast to the behaviour of many of the boys who typically responded to conflict situations in a very hasty manner, often inappropriately, and without consideration of the consequences.

B. Modelling

Although adolescents may know which course of action and which responses they would like to produce, they may still lack the skills to put these responses into practice in an adequate manner. Further teaching methods are therefore needed to ensure such skills exists.

Modelling provides an example of other people engaging in a particular activity, which allows the trainees to observe and learn from others. There are many different ways in which modelling can be used, but the present programme tended to use peers as models, either live or videotaped. Evidence suggests that learning by the observation is most effective when the model is of similar age, sex and social background to the observer (Bandura, 1977). The situations modelled should also be made as similar and realistic to the trainees own life experience as possible. In addition, research from adult studies has suggested that modelling effects are greatest if the model is shown *coping* rather than giving a perfect, totally proficient performance (Meichenbaum, 1971).

In the present programme, pre-prepared modelling videotapes were used to supplement peer models. The peer models were selected from members of the group who were already reasonably skilled in the target area. Having observed the modelled example the trainer then encouraged discussion within the group about aspects of the performance.

C. Role-play/practice/behaviour rehearsal

Having viewed the model's performance the sessions typically progressed to requiring the trainees to practice the skill observed. During the practice, which normally involved some type of role-play, the trainees were encouraged to imitate the models performance as closely as possible. Although detailed descriptions of role-play are available elsewhere, it may be useful to mention a few practical notes about the role-play aspect of training in the present study. Firstly, whenever a trainee was asked to role-play a particular skill observed in the modelling stage, they were asked to give a verbal description of the setting, characters and situation concerned. Secondly, trainees were encouraged to make their own role-plays as realistic as possible, trying to resemble their own real life situations. Thirdly, as indicated earlier, wherever possible all members of the group were encouraged to become involved in role-playing of each skill, rather the focusing purely on one individual. They tended to take it in turns to role-play then receiving group feedback, but all trainees were required to participate at some time in the session. Fourthly, as the role-plays involved more than one person, it was possible to have trainees taking part in reverse role-plays. For example, the boys frequently found themselves in the role of teachers, policemen, parents and valuable experience was gained through doing so. Quite often the boys would make emphatic statements such as "If I was that teacher I would have really told him off, the way he was cheeky to me". Reverse role-play seemed to allow the boys an opportunity to experience what it feels like to be the "other person" in their interactions. Finally, the trainer tried during role-play to take a passive role as far as possible, only intervening to get the boys to return to the topic when they began to deviate.

D. Feedback and social reinforcement

Generally the role-plays were videotaped and played back to the whole group immediately. Before replay started the trainer would stress points to look out for and emphasize the targets the trainee had been trying to achieve. Having received the video feedback, the trainer then gave some verbal feedback, trying always to make this as positive as possible. Much praise was given for effort and comments were made about any targets reached. The trainer also acted to involve the rest of the group in providing positive feedback to each trainee.

E. Homework tasks

At the end of each session the boys were asked to set themselves a homework task in which to practice the skill/skills learned in the session. The trainer guided the tasks to make them as simple and specific as possible and made a record of each boy's task. For example, tasks tended to state what the boy was going to try, who with, where and when, e.g. "Tomorrow evening at the youth club I will ask Johnny where he lives and when he is going home next".

The outcome of each trainee's homework task was then discussed at the beginning of the next session. If necessary, the boys would role-play any situations that had produced difficulty and practice alternative strategies.

F. Programming for generalization

Several researchers have stressed the need for therapists to actively programme for the generalization of training effects. That is, they need to consider that the benefits produced within a training setting will not automatically carry over into everyday situations. In the case of SST it may be found that the trainees become very socially skilled within the training area and with the trainer but not necessarily in the schoolroom or outside with their families and peers.

In order to make it more likely that the benefits of training carry over into these "real-life" interactions, several methods were tried in this programme which have been suggested to be important in programming for generalization (Goldstein *et al.*, 1977). Firstly, a wide range of trainers were used so that, although the main trainer was constant throughout, a variety of co-trainers were used. Visitors were also invited into the groups when relevant in an attempt to expand the stimulus control of the skills learned. Goldstein *et al.*, also suggest that the training situation should be realistic and created to resemble as closely as possible the physical environment in which the trainees normally live. In order to achieve this, real employers were brought in to role-play interviews, real teachers were involved, real telephones were used and sessions would occasionally move over to the house units or classrooms where possible.

As mentioned elsewhere, an attempt was also made to select targets which were relevant and important to the trainees and which might therefore lead to reinforcing consequences outside sessions. Homework tasks were set to encourage practice outside sessions.

V. CASE ILLUSTRATIONS

A. Case A

(1) Background

John was 14 years old and had been resident in the Community Home School for 9 months. He was in care of the Local Authority as the result of several minor thefts and was generally beyond the control of his mother. John was the youngest child in the family, with 3 older sisters, all living at home. His father had died when he was 6 years old and his mother had not remarried. He had been assessed as being of average intelligence but was almost 2 years behind the level expected for his age on academic attainment skills.

(2) Social skills assessment

John was considered to experience difficulties in interactions with both adults and peers. With adults, he frequently interrupted conversations and made requests in an inappropriate way—demanding immediate action, poking the member of staff and shouting out. In terms of basic social skills with adults John was seen to avoid eye contact and his facial expression was usually inappropriate. His expression generally showed an extreme grin, as if he was laughing. This led to problems in many situations. For example, when told off by staff members, John would continue to grin which was often interpreted by the staff as if John found the situation funny. As a result the staff members would become very angry, making statements such as "take that silly grin off your face". Overall, the situations tended to escalate, resulting in frequent conflicts between John and the care staff and teachers.

In his relationships with his peers, John's social skills performance also showed problems. John was persistently teased and bullied by the other boys, who were mostly taller than him. When teased, John would shout rude retorts (still grinning) until the situation became aggressive, usually resulting in physical attack from the other boy. John made little conversation with his peers, had no friends and was frequently encouraged by the older boys to take part in antisocial activities. For example, both John and the care staff reported that he found it hard to resist peer influence. John's delinquent activities were always carried out when he tagged along at the periphery of a group of youths. When the other boys dared him to misbehave or asked him to join in a delinquent act, John found it very hard to say "no".

(3) Targets for training

From the assessment battery, several targets were identified for John, in terms of both basic and complex social skills:

	Basic skill targets		*Complex skill targets*	
	Eye contact	→ increase	Interrupting appro-priately	
	Fiddling movements	→ decrease	Making requests	
With adults and peers	Listening skills (head movements attention feedback responses)	→ increase	Starting conversations Asking questions Asking for help	Adults
	Facial expression	→ appropriate	Dealing with criticism and reprimands	
	Voice level	→ decrease	Refusing peer influence Dealing with teasing and bullying Starting conversations Maintaining con-versations Making friends	Peers

(4) Responses to training

John attended 12 SST sessions along with 3 other boys of a similar age. The curriculum for the group was based on the targets identified for the 4 boys, many of them being the same as those identified for John. Additional topics were added such as using the telephone, returning articles to a shop, expressing feelings and emotions. It was hoped that in some of these areas John could act as a "coping" model for the other boys.

The 12 sessions took place twice a week in a comfortable room fitted with video equipment. John co-operated in the sessions although he would often become silly and giggly in the role-plays. It was necessary to give him a card on which was written his homework task, to remind him to carry it out. Measures of responses made before, during and after training showed that John improved considerably on his basic social skill targets. He showed an increase in eye contact and listening skills and a decrease in fiddling movements. Both he and the care staff reported fewer problems on the unit related to conflicts with adults and peers. Unfortunately, after training ended, John received no further input and the staff did not attempt to prompt and reinforce appropriate responding. It may come as no surprise then to find that without continued input, John had returned to his old ways at the 3 and 6 month follow ups, in terms of basic and complex social skills. This case example highlights the need for continued support and booster sessions after the initial training sessions end. Without this input, it is less likely that improvements made initially will be maintained. The next case example illustrates how continued support can facilitate effects.

B. Case B

(1) Background

Paul was 15 1/2 years old when admitted to the Community Home School. Over the previous 2 years he had stopped attending school and had taken to roaming the city housing estates with a pack of stray dogs, training them to attack people! Paul was an only child, living at home with his parents.

(2) Social skills assessment

Paul was reported by his teachers and care staff to experience severe difficulties in interactions with both adults and peers. The nature of these difficulties was found to be similar with most people, other than his parents where social interaction was more satisfactory. Whenever Paul was approached by or approached other people his manner was extremely aggressive. His tone of voice, facial expression, posture, and content of speech all conveyed aggressive intent. Paul never smiled, never approached people in a friendly manner and any attempt to converse would circle round his main interests which were Hitler and martial arts.

Paul himself was unaware of his difficulties and interpreted his lack of friends to the hostility of other people. It emerged that his parents had instructed him from an early age that other people were "out to get you" and the best thing was to attack them before they could attack you. Hence, most of Paul's responses to others were hostile. When he approached others it was usually with an aggressive stance, aggressive facial expression and tone of voice, Perhaps, not surprisingly, adults and peers tended to respond to him with either avoidance or hostility—hence creating a self fulfilling prophesy—people really were hostile and aggressive. Interestingly, on tests of emotional perception, Paul was found to judge most facial expressions, postures and gestures as conveying aggressive messages, even those that really depicted friendliness, fear or surprise.

(3) Targets for training

From the assessment battery, a wide range of basic and complex social skill targets were identified.

	Basic skill targets	*Complex skill targets*
Facial expression	→ Less aggressive Friendly when appropriate	Starting conversations Asking questions
Smiling	→ Increase	Selecting topics of conversation
Listening skills	→ Increase	Making friends
Tone of voice	→ Friendly when appropriate	Dealing with peer teasing
Social distance	→ Increase, i.e. not stand so close	Handling criticism for adults
Eye contact	→ Decrease—not excessive glaring	
Posture	→ Decrease agressive stance	
Perception of emotion cues	→ Increase accuracy of judgment	

(4) Response to training

Surprisingly, Paul enjoyed the sessions and attended every one. He was placed in a group with 3 other boys, whose problems were rather different: one boy being very withdrawn and isolated from his peers and the other 2 showing many more excesses of behaviour in terms of verbal abuse in interactions with adults and peers. The boys attended 12 sessions over a 6 week period and showed marked improvements on their target skills within the training sessions. Paul in particular showed considerable improvement on all his target skills, as evident from behavioural measures taken from videotaped conversations and staff questionnaires. The group that Paul attended was an initial pilot group, with 4 boys from a token economy unit. Hence it was possible to request staff to model, prompt and reinforce the target behaviours outside training sessions. The boys in that unit carried target cards and it was possible to set the social skills being taught as his daily targets on the unit. This was suggested to facilitate the generalization process, to increase the likelihood that the benefits of training would carry over to everyday life. On the house unit, Paul made rapid progress, moving off each of his targets as he reached an acceptable criterion of performance. After the training phase ended, the staff on the unit continued to monitor his social skills performance and give the necessary prompting when needed. After 6 months Paul was beginning to make friends and was tolerated within the classroom, attending all his lessons. Shortly after this he was successful in getting a job before leaving the unit.

VI. PROBLEMS ENCOUNTERED

A. The limitations of a research design

As mentioned previously, the programme was part of a research project which involved the use of random allocation of boys to either SST, a discussion companion group (APC), or a group who did not receive any type of intervention other than the ongoing regime of the school (NTC). The research design also required the SST groups to be of a set number (12), over a set time period (6 weeks) and for a set duration (1 hour). This was rather limiting from a practical point of view as it became obvious that to bring about marked changes in a boy's social behaviour after a life time of inappropriate responding would often take many more than 12 sessions. In many cases it was clear that daily input was required, with SST becoming part of the minute-to-minute handling of the boys.

Another great limitation of this programme was that the care staff on the units were not allowed to know which boys were in the SST, APC or NTC groups, as the staff were used as "blind" assessors of the boys behaviour. This ensured that the staff behaved in the same way to all boys, independent of the SST programme and did not bias their evaluation of the boys' behaviour. Unfortunately, this meant that they could not be asked to prompt and reinforce particular responses with the SST boys outside sessions. Programming for generalization of behaviour change to everyday life therefore became much more difficult. It was regularly observed that boys would handle certain situations, e.g. teasing or bullying, extremely well within the sessions and 10 minutes later would be seen swearing and fighting in retaliation to teasing out in the playground.

B. The problem of the "delinquent" sub-culture

If a response taught during SST is to generalize and be maintained, it is important that it leads to reinforcing consequences during day-to-day interactions. Unfortunately, the staff were not the only ones to fail to prompt and reinforce appropriate behaviour, the same was also true of the peer group. Even worse, the peer group was found to actively model, prompt and reinforce anti-social behaviour on many occasions. Attempts by the boys to try out pro-social ways of responding, such as, initiating friendly conversations with staff, or offering to help one of their peers would also frequently be punished by members of the peer group. Patterson (1964) and Furniss (1964) have previously noted that the grouping of young offenders together frequently leads to the development of an anti-social sub-culture with deviant norms of behaviour. Observation studies revealed that the peer group was also more frequent and consistent in the reinforcement of *anti-social* behaviour, than staff were in terms of *pro-social* responding.

For these reasons, it became very difficult to achieve generalization of behaviour change outside the sessions. Perhaps it is unrealistic to expect to produce lasting improvements in social behaviour within a large institution which brings together large groups of juvenile offenders. Indeed several writers have questioned the benefits of any type of intervention that involves the grouping of large numbers of young offenders in isolation from the rest of the community (e.g. Feldman, 1977).

C. The limitations of the institutional setting

The restricted institutional setting also had the limitation that the boys had little opportunity to make use of their skills within the community. Many of the boys had little or no contact with their homes, previous schools and local peer group. This made it very difficult to bring about improvements in social behaviour when the boys did eventually return to the community. Indeed the resarch project found no evidence at 6-month follow ups that SST led to improvements in relationships within the community. Again the lack of generalization of behaviour change from institutional settings to the community has been found for many interventions (Feldman, 1977) and may again stress the futility of institutional regimes for young offenders.

D. Cultural differences

As the project progressed it became increasingly clear that there were marked cultural differences in what is considered to be socially skilled behaviour within different ethnic groups and different social backgrounds. The boys came from Caucasian, Asian and West Indian families and the norms for each culture varied. It was therefore necessary to teach the boys to discriminate between the different cultures in which they interacted and then vary their social skills accordingly.

For example, with boys from West Indian homes it was necessary to teach them to use different responses depending on whether they were responding to their parents or a white, middle class teacher. This obviously was not easy to do as there is very little information relating to cultural differences in social skills. It was often a matter of discussing issues with groups of West Indian and Asian boys in an attempt to identify successful strategies of responding. One example of a marked cultural difference is the use of eye contact. In one case a boy taught to increase eye contact with adults received a severe reprimand from his West Indian father when he looked at him when being criticized. The appropriate response should have been total aversion of gaze and eye contact was interpreted as a sign of impertinence.

Much more research is needed into cultural difference and indeed the validation of social skills *per se*, to help trainers teach appropriate responses to various situations.

E. Teaching the boys to handle policemen

One rather controversial topic within the programme was the teaching of boys to handle meetings with the police. Most of the boys had a very limited and set response to police encounters—usually to swear at them, call them rude names and run away as fast as possible. Many of the boys, being well known to the police were frequently apprehended, often for no crime and ended up in greater trouble because of their response to the policeman. No doubt most people reading this book will have been stopped by the police at sometime and handled the situation with courtesy and respect; making eye contact, with an upright posture, polite tone of voice, perhaps calling the policeman "officer" and so on. This is a very different response strategy to that chosen by the boys and much more likely to lead to a successful outcome.

In teaching the young offender group this set of responses, one may be criticized for teaching the boys to get away with their crimes. Anecdotal evidence did indeed suggest that this was occasionally the case. One morning a local Inspector rang the trainer to ask if two of the SST group were missing, which indeed they were. Stephen and Alec had been picked up the night before carrying their burglary tools. The officer became suspicious when they were extremely polite, stood attentively and called him "officer". His superior, having heard of the SST project checked up on them and his suspicions were confirmed—he reported them to be extremely co-operative and both were let off with a caution. Perhaps this was a victory for SST but less so for the safety of society. It should be remembered that the follow up of the study did not show that SST produced any significant reductions in offending. Further attempts to teach young offenders to handle police encounters should therefore proceed with caution. Undoubtedly the issues surrounding this area are difficult to reconcile.

F. The occasional need for individual sessions

The research project required sessions to be carried out in groups of four. On a few occasions however, this was found to be problematic. The vast majority of boys coped well within the group, but 3 or 4 boys would have benefitted from individual sessions first. These boys showed such extreme deficits in social skills that they had difficulty coping in the group. Initial sessions to develop the skills necessary for them to benefit from the group would have been useful.

VII. CONCLUSIONS

This chapter has tried to give an outline of some of the methods and problems related to carrying out SST with young offenders. One of the major problems appears to be in increasing socially skilled behaviour outside the training setting. The reasons for this have been discussed, mostly the consequence of grouping together young offenders in isolation from the rest of the community. Perhaps we should really be looking to setting up SST programmes with young offenders within the community, for example, in Intermediate Treatment Schemes. Best of all would be to make use of SST as a preventative technique in regular schools, either with all children or those at risk of joining the ranks of juvenile offenders. The trainer is not then in a position of having to remedy, in several sessions, the social skills difficulties developed over a lifetime.

In the meantime, it is encouraging that SST programmes are at least feasible within traditional institutional settings. Hopefully with even greater attempts to programme for generalization than this project was able to offer, it may be possible to produce more lasting and generalized benefits with young offenders.

VIII. REFERENCES

Argyle, M., Trower, P. and Bryant, B. (1974). Explorations in the treatment of personality disorders and neuroses by social skills training. *Br. J. Med. Psychol.* **47**, 63–72.

Bandura, A. (1977). Social Learning Theory. Prentice Hall, London.

Meichenbaum, D. H. (1971). Examination of model characteristics reducing avoidance behaviour. *J. Pers. Soc. Psychol.* **17**, 255–38.

Braukmann, C. J., Maloney, D. M., Phillips, E. L. and Wolf, M. M. (1973). The measurement and modification of heterosexual interaction skills of pre-delinquents at Achievement Place. University of Kansas. (Unpublished)

Braukmann, C. J., Maloney, D. M., Fixen, D. L., Phillips, E. L. and Wolf, M. M. (1974). Analysis of a selection interview training package for pre-delinquents at Achievement Place. *Crim. Just. Behav.* **1**, 30–42.

Braukmann, C. J., Fixen, D. L., Fixen, D. L., Phillips, E. L. and Wolf, M. M. (1975). Behavioural approaches to treatment in the crime and delinquency field. *Criminology* **13**, 299–331.

Combs, M. L. and Slaby, D. A. (1977). Social skills training with children. *In* "Advances in Clinical Child Psychology" (B. B. Lahey and A. E. Kazdin, *Eds*). Vol. 1. Plenum Press, London.

Feldman, M. P. (1977). "Criminal Behaviour: A Psychological Analysis". Wiley, London.

Freedman, B. J., Rosenthal, L., Donahoe, C. P., Schlundt, D. G. and McFall, R. M. (1978). A social behavioural analysis of skill deficit in delinquent and non-delinquent adolescent boys. *J. Consult. Clin. Psychol.* **46**, 1448–1462.

Furniss, J. (1964). Peer reinforcement of behaviour in an institution for delinquent girls. Unpublished masters thesis. Oregon State University.

Goldstein, A. P., Sherman, M., Gershaw, N. J., Sprafkin, R. P. and Glick, B. (1978). Training aggressive adolescent in prosocial behaviour. *J. Youth Adol.* **7**, 73–93.

Hersen, M. and Bellack, A. S. (1977). Assessment of social skills. *In* "Handbook for Behavioural Assessment" (A. R. Ciminero, K. S. Calhoun and H. E. Adams, *Eds*). Wiley, New York.

Maloney, D. M., Harper, T. M., Braukmann, C. J., Fixen, D. L., Phillips, E. L. and Wolf, M. M. (1976). Teaching conversation-related skills to predelinquent girls. *J. Appl. Behav. Anal.* **9**, 127–139.

Marzillier, J. S., Lambert, C. and Kellet, J. (1976). A controlled evaluation of systematic desensitization and social skills training for socially inadequate psychiatric patients. *Behav. Res. Ther.* **14**, 225–238.

Meichenbaum, B. (1977). Cognitive Behaviour Modification: an Integrated Approach. Plenum Press, New York.

Minkin, N., Braukmann, C. J., Minkin, B. L., Timbers, G. D., Timbers, B. J., Fixen, D. L., Phillips, E. L. and Wolf, M. M. (1976). The social validation and training of conversation skills. *J. Appl. Behav. Anal.* **9**, 127–139.

Ollendick, T. H. and Hersen, M. (1979). Social skills training for juvenile delinquents. *Behav. Res. and Ther.* **17**, 547–555.

Patterson, G. R. (1964). The peer group as delinquency reinforcing agents. Unpublished Doctoral Thesis, University of Oregon.

Sarason, I. G. and Ganzer, U. J. (1973). Modelling and group discussion in the rehabilitation of juvenile delinquents. *J. Counselling Psychol.* **5**, 442–449.

Shoemaker, M. E. (1979). Group assertion training for institutionalized male delinquents. *In* "Progress in Behaviour Therapy with Delinquents" (J. S. Stumphauzer, *Ed.*). Charles C. Thomas, Springfield, Illinois.

Spence, S. H. (1979a). The long term generalized effects of social skills training with adolescent, male offenders in an institutional setting. Unpublished Doctoral Thesis, University of Birmingham.

Spence, S. H. (1979b). Social skills training with adolescent offenders: A review. *Behav. Psych.* **7**, 49–57.

Spence, S. H. (1980). "Social Skills Training with Children and Adolescents: A Counsellor's Manual". NFER Publishing Co., Windsor.

Spence, S. H. (1981). Differences in Social Skills performance between institutionalized juvenile male offenders and a comparable group of boys without offence records. *Br. J. Clin. Psychol.* (In press)

Spence, S. H. and Marzillier, J. S. (1979). Social skills training with adolescent, male offenders: 1. Short term effects. *Behav. Res. Ther.* **17**, 7–16.

Spence, S. H. and Marzillier, J. S. (1981). Social skills training with adolescent male offenders. II. Short term, long term, and generalized effects. *Behav. Res. Ther.* **19**, 349–368.

Spivack, G. and Shure, M. B. (1978). "Problem Solving Techniques in Child Rearing". Jossey-Bass Publishers, New York.

Thelen, M. H., Frey, R. A., Dollinger, S. J. and Paul, S. C. (1976). Use of video taped models to improve the interpersonal adjustment of delinquents. *J. Consult. Clin. Psychol.* **44**, 492.

Trower, P., Bryant, B. and Argyle, M. (1978). *Social Skills and Mental Health.* Methuen, London.

Werner, J. S., Minkin, N., Minkin, C. J. and Bonnie, L. (1975). "Intervention Package": An analysis to prepare juvenile delinquents for encounters with police officers. *Crim. Just. Behav.* **2**, 22–36.

SECTION III

New developments and future directions in social skills training

PREFACE BY SUE SPENCE

I. INTRODUCTION AND OVERVIEW OF SECTION III

Early studies of social skills training (SST) were mainly focused on psychiatric patients and recent developments have seen a vast expansion with applications being reported with many different clinical populations. Programmes have now been developed for people presenting with a wide range of behaviour problems such as juvenile or adult offending, peer difficulties at school and both chronic and acute psychiatric disorders. Encouraging results from many research studies suggest that SST could be extended even further and may possible produce benefits for other client groups. For example, with elderly people whose social skills have deteriorated as the result of prolonged institutionalization, or organic brain disorder. Similarly with many mentally handicapped people, where a structured and systematic teaching of social skills is required. Initial reports indicate some success in these areas (Kelley *et al.*, 1979, Rotheram and Corby, 1980) and hopefully further programmes and research will be carried out to investigate these possibilities more extensively.

Recent developments have also seen SST methods applied to an

247

increasing number of non-clinical client groups. An individual's adequacy in social situations will partly be dependent on the type of interactions he or she is required to handle. Today, many jobs and life roles require people to learn very complex and specific social skills which they will not necessarily have acquired as a result of their previous learning experiences. In such cases, it may be possible to teach these skills and SST methods are now being applied to a wide range of interpersonal situations to try to help people to be successful at work and in other social roles. For example, the teaching of specific interpersonal skills to teachers, counsellors and social workers (Ellis and Whittington, 1981). Similarly, the application of SST techniques has been discussed in relation to psychotherapy skills (Trower and Dryden, 1981) and doctor-patient skills (Maguire, 1981). Developments can also be seen in industry, for example in the teaching of selling skills (Poppleton, 1981), negotiation skills (Morley, 1981) and personnel supervision (Georgiades and Orlans, 1981). The techniques of social skills training also therefore seems to have a future with non-clinical populations, but much research is required to determine the effectiveness of such programmes.

The extension of SST methods to non-clinical client groups has not been limited to skills related to job functions. Many people are now seeking help to improve their social skills as they feel dissatisfied with their performance in other areas of their lives. This has been reflected in the increasing interest in skills relating to the changing role of women in society. In Chapter 10, *Lyn Fry* discusses the development of a social skills training programme within a women's group. As the role of women has changed so, many have found it difficult to handle some of the social interactions that they now encounter. Lyn Fry describes how SST approaches can be used within the context of a women's group to teach the skills necessary to handle these difficult situations.

The need to focus specifically on skills related to particular kinds of social situations is highlighted in Chapter 11. *Sue Spence* makes a case for the study of those social skills important for success in sexual interactions with the opposite sex. Methods of assessing and training heterosexual social skills are then outlined. This chapter also describes the need to create individually tailored programmes, setting social skills targets according to the needs of the client. Similarly, it illustrates how SST can be integrated into overall multi-treatment intervention programmes, with clients presenting with problems of sexual deviancy and sexual dysfunction.

In Chapter 12, *Stephen Morley, Geoff Shepherd and Sue Spence* discuss the role of cognitive factors in social functioning and the need to consider these during the assessment and treatment of social difficulties. This is also an important new development of the SST approach and emphasizes the multi-dimensionality of the concept of social adequacy. It stresses the role of cognitive processes in the selection of appropriate responses, the importance of accurate perception of the social behaviour of others and how the person's motivation and goals relate to the interactions. Hence, the way in which a person behaves in a given social situation is not simply dependent upon their behavioural skills. Many cognitive variables intervene and these must be assessed and perhaps changed if possible. This chapter outlines the range of cognitive variables that should be considered and indicates a variety of methods for producing changes. Although such approaches are still in their infancy, techniques of cognitive behaviour change are likely to offer an important adjunct to social skills training programmes in the future.

Finally, it is hoped that much more emphasis will be placed on the potential of SST methods in the prevention of behavioural problems. Much of this book has focused on the reduction of problems once they have become well established. Inadequate social skills during childhood seem to have marked implications for the development of a wide range of psychiatric and psychological problems in later life (Combs and Slaby, 1977). Thus it is possible that many problems could be prevented if social skills could be taught to children in the same way as the skills of reading, writing and arithmetic. Although social skills are just as important as educational skills, perhaps more so, little attention is paid to their development in childhood.

There appears to be an assumption that social skills will develop automatically without specific teaching and yet this is clearly not the case as is evident from the many children who experience difficulty in their social relationships (see Stephen Frosh, Chapter 7). Where children fail to acquire important social skills either as the result of an inadequate learning experience or difficulties in learning, social skills training would be a valuable intervention at an early stage. Indeed, there is much to be said for incorporating SST into the regular school curriculum as a means of preventing further psychological problems which result from or may be exacerbated by inadequate social skills.

II. REFERENCES

Combs, M. L. and Slaby, D. A. (1977). Social skills training with children. *In* Advances in clinical child psychology (B. B. Lahey and A. E. Kazdin, *Eds*), Vol. 1. Plenum Press, London.
Ellis, R. A. and Whittington, D. (1981). "A guide to social skills training". Croom Helm, London.

Georgiades, N. J. and Orlans, V. (1981). The supervision of working groups. *In* "Social skills and work" (M. Argyle, *Ed.*). Methuen, London.

Kelley, J. A., Wildman, B. G., Urey, J. R. and Thuram, C. (1979). Group skills training to increase the conversational repertoire of retarded adolescents. *Child Behav. Ther.* **4**, 323–336.

Maguire, P. (1981). Doctor-patient skills. *In* "Social skills and health" (M. Argyle, *Ed.*). Methuen, London.

Morley, I. (1981). Negotiation and bargaining. *In* "Social skills and work" (M. Argyle, *Ed.*). Methuen, London.

Poppleton, S. E. (1981). The social skills of selling. *In* "Social skills and work" (M. Argyle, *Ed.*). Methuen, London.

Rotheram, M. J. and Corby, N. (1980). Social power and the elderly. *In* "Social competence: interventions for children and adults" (D. P. Rathjen and J. P. Foreit, *Eds*). Pergamon Press, New York.

Trower, P. and Dryden, W. (1981). Psychotherapy. *In* "Social skills and health" (M. Argyle, *Ed.*). Methuen, London.

10

Women in society

LYN FRY

I. INTRODUCTION

Women's role in society has changed rapidly in recent years. They now expect very different satisfactions from their lives and are no longer content to accept their traditional, low power positions. The growth of interest in assertion training has accompanied the growth in the women's movement. Whilst not a new idea (Wolpe outlined the need for assertion training in the 1940s) its extraordinary growth in the 1970s has been demonstrated by the multitude of books which have proliferated over the past 10 years. Most are aimed at the popular press with colourful and provocative titles such as "Woman, Assert Yourself" (Seattle King— County National Organization for Women, 1975). "Don't Say Yes when you want to say No" (Fensterheim and Baer, 1975) or "Stand Up, Speak Out, Talk Back!" (Alberti and Emmons, 1975). Women have thus been quick to see assertion training as one means of achieving their new goals.

Women who would superficially appear to be functioning well in society often express their dissatisfaction with themselves and their ability to fulfil new roles. Some want to be strong and effective, to redefine their personal relationships, change their life styles, job choices and role expectations. But they don't know how to do it. They are frightened of the reactions (real and imagined) of others and they are not sure that if they change they will like what they end up with. These women are now looking for assertion groups as one way of changing their place in society. Recently one glossy magazine mentioned that a Women's Therapy Centre in London was running assertion groups and over 200 women wrote asking for places. This chapter outlines the role of assertion training in women's groups discussing theoretical and practical issues.

Assertion training has its roots firmly in social learning theory. While there may be an emphasis on cognitive restructuring, the focus is primarily on achieving specific, hierarchical goals accomplished by means of constant social reinforcement. Only the content of the sessions would vary from standard social skills instruction. The lesson format and techniques used are the same. Almost without exception, women presenting themselves for assertion groups are from white-collar and professional backgrounds and are highly motivated to change. There is a great variety in age although the majority are between 20 and 40 years old. They frequently appear articulate and questioning and rarely experience assertive problems in all areas of their lives. Rather, they show specific needs in dealing with the family, friends and acquaintances or jobs. It is rare to find someone who is seriously debilitated in all areas. More frequently the problems range from non-existent in some areas to severe in certain aspects of their relationships. The clients attending the women's groups are self-referred and have rarely consulted professional helpers about their assertive problems. They show varying degrees of interest in the women's movement, although many are deeply committed to it, and will be aware of and offended by sexist remarks and assumptions. Some have been to consciousness-raising groups and a few have attended other feminist-oriented groups. Some will also have attended "therapy" groups such as encounter groups, psychodrama groups, or transactional analysis groups.

As a group they are stimulating and rewarding to work with but pose problems for the therapist. They have high expectations that the groups will make an appreciable change in their lives, they expect statements to be backed with evidence, they are highly vocal and sometimes verbose. On the other hand, they are enthusiastic and responsive, they carry out role-plays, keep diaries and can be observed trying to put their learning into practice.

II. ASSESSMENT AND SELECTION OF CLIENTS

Although some selection of suitable clients might take place in psychiatric settings, this would be rare for women already functioning well in society. Women who come to the groups are self-referred, often with vague expectations and in considerable trepidation. They may have talked to someone or read a magazine article and feel it might help but are frightened that they will be expected to become aggressive, selfish, or hurtful to those they love. However, since a minority of women do not appear to profit greatly from the groups, the therapist may want to carry out some selection procedure. For example, some very aggressive women accustomed to having their needs met and unaware of the distress they cause may not change. Others go through a whole course without identifying a specific problem to work on. Others identify problems but do not follow up suggestions, complaining that this is one approach which does not work for them. The therapist may want to take these issues into consideration when selecting the group. However, it seems unwise to exclude women who may not show immediate change (however hard this may be on the therapist) when they may have longer term benefits.

The assessment procedure is typically carried out early in the group, aiming to help women become more specific about their problems. A wide variety of questionnaire-type instruments exist. The majority read like something out of a woman's magazine. For example: (i) Do you generally express what you feel?, (ii) Do you find it difficult to make decisions? (iii) Are you openly critical of others' ideas, opinions, behaviour? (from Alberti and Emmons, 1975). Others look more "scientific", perhaps with the addition of rating scales such as:

	Never	Rarely	Sometimes	Usually	Always
(a) I do my own thinking and make my own decisions	1	2	3	4	5
(b) I can be myself around wealthy, educated or prestigious people	1	2	3	4	5
(c) I am poised and confident among strangers	1	2	3	4	5

(from Osborn and Harris, 1975)

The woman is then told that the higher her score the greater her level of assertive behaviour. A large number of these scales have been published but they are all of doubtful value. What is a *high* score? A *low* score? What is normal? How much change is significant? Does the questionnaire ask the right and relevant questions? These problems often remain unanswered. The scales thus suffer from a wide variety of deficits such as inadequate validation, lack of evidence of reliability, lack of attention to sampling considerations and absence of normative data. In addition, assertive questionnaires usually apply rather specifically to American populations and the reactions of British women to the American assertion literature would suggest that these are unlikely to be directly transferable.

A further limitation of questionnaire assessment concerns the validity of the data produced. A considerable body of literature exists to suggest that correlations between self-report measures and behavioural indices of assertion (e.g. role-play) are often low or non-existent. The same has been shown to apply to questionnaires and independent observations of those knowing the client well. This may be a result of the fact that the questionnaires usually ask generalized questions while the clients have specific problems. A question might be "Can you turn down a request to borrow money?" But who is this talking about? Your mother, an acquaintance, your boss, a beggar, a close friend? Neither reliability nor validity will be high when the questions are as poorly formed as this. These difficulties may arise from a single cause—the lack of an accepted model of assertion. Without agreement on what it means to be assertive as distinct from other forms of behaviour it is impossible to formulate questions or prepare observation schedules which are more than trivial. (For a thorough discussion of this issue, *see* Lineham and Egan, 1979). How, then, does the therapist overcome these problems and arrive at treatment targets? The following is a suggested outline which attempts to overcome the previous difficulties and orient the woman towards her specific deficits.

III. OUTLINE FOR ASSESSMENT AND SELECTION OF TARGETS

(1) Early in the first session use a questionnaire to help the woman begin to understand what areas assertion training is likely to focus on and to begin to think about her own problems. The therapist will also find that the questionnaire is one means of giving relief to what would otherwise become a long didactic session.

(2) Following the questionnaire the therapist discusses a model of assertive behaviour or outlines areas covered in assertion training with lots of examples of assertive and other behaviour. She explains the difference between specific and generalized lack of assertion and asks the women to concentrate carefully on each area bearing in mind the particular circumstances of each situation.

(3) Discuss obstacles to becoming assertive, such as anxiety, and techniques to overcome the anxiety; that is, the use of hierarchies of target behaviours. The therapist now takes another break in the instruction and asks the women to write down 6–10 (or more) specific assertive problems they have and would like to overcome. Once this is done the problems are ranked in order of difficulty of overcoming them. Cotler and Guerra (1976) use a subjective units of discomfort (anxiety) scale at this point to rate the relative degrees of difficulty of each item. The therapist may find this a useful method.

(4) Each woman keeps a diary for the duration of the group. She records:
   (a) Homework task, together with any comments on how to carry it out.
   (b) Success or otherwise on performing the homework task and any particular difficulties found.
   (c) Other assertive actions performed although not previously rehearsed or discussed in the group.
   (d) Difficulties experienced between sessions and either avoided or mismanaged. The difficulties noted in the assertion diary are incorporated into the hierarchy as the sessions proceed.

(5) In general, treatment targets will be selected from the bottom of the hierarchy, the easiest items being chosen first. The exception occurs when a very pressing problem exists. For example, one woman chose to ignore her hierarchy for the first week as she wanted to deal immediately with a solicitor who owed her several thousand pounds and who had been making vague excuses, not answering letters and refusing to talk to her on the 'phone for over 18 months. Her previous experience suggested that she was unlikely to be successful but her annoyance was such that she wanted to tackle him immediately. With careful preparation she did and by the end of the 10 week course had her money.

(6) When particular issues are being discussed the therapist may find it useful to refer to the relevant sections of "The New Assertive Woman" by Bloom *et al.* (1975) which has a number of short questionnaires designed to draw the woman's attention to particular points. The questionnaires are supported by a short discussion on the situation.

(7) It is unlikely that the woman will ever become fully aware of her non-verbal deficits without feedback from the therapist and other group members. Some psychologists have video filming and elaborate scales to measure problems such as eye contact but this is usually unnecessary with groups of women. The therapist will probably find it sufficient to describe non-verbal problems (particularly eye contact, body posture, facial expression) then merely point out deficiencies using her judgment of what is normal and acceptable. The group will also be of help here.

IV. DESCRIPTION OF A "TYPICAL" CLIENT

Jocelyn's problems were typical of many women joining assertion groups. Her reasons for joining the group were vague—wanting to learn voice control—coinciding with her return to work and a sense of dissatisfaction with her life. Although she had many unresolved difficulties with her family, Jocelyn chose to work first on "less risky" areas such as her new job. She had been appointed to work 10 hours as a social worker but wanted this increased to 24 hours. She described herself as "very anxious, insecure, not sure I could cope with the job after the break". Her body posture, voice and face all conveyed this. Her first homework assignment was designed to overcome this by making contact with others at work—making eye contact, smiling, saying "Hello", looking less anxious. Then the job hours were tackled. Vagueness was again a problem and Jocelyn had to decide why it was in her employers best interests to extend her hours. She also wrote a list of her assets which she referred to frequently until she was completely familiar with them. Again she had to work on her non-verbal skills.

Jocelyn was also concerned about her relationship with her mother. The first 2 hours of a visit would be pleasant but arguments soon arose. She decided that visits should cease for a period. She telephoned her mother and said that she wanted a breathing space. It mattered to her that they got on better, she cared about her and would telephone from time to time to see how she was. To her surprise it was all much easier than she had thought. In the next 5 months there was an occasional difficult phone call but when they did meet again Jocelyn felt less dutiful and enjoyed the visit more.

Dealing assertively with her children was also focused on. For example, getting her daughter to clear dishes from the table and her son to turn the television off. After a discussion on parents' rights Jocelyn again worked on making her voice sound firmer and identified consequences which could be applied following non-compliance.

Her relationship with her husband was complicated and she did not start to work on this until a number of other areas had been successfully resolved. Both she and her husband wanted a more "open" marriage permitting both to have sexual relationships with others. Her husband's involvement with another woman led to considerable anguish. Although their own relationship improved immeasurably she found a number of problems. The first was to re-establish contact with the other woman, who had previously been a friend. The next was to rationalize the time her husband spent away from home. An arrangement was negotiated after Jocelyn had role-played exactly what she wanted to say. She learned how to "express my feelings to him, rather than swamp him with criticism, or hold back completely". An unexpected benefit was that her husband learned to speak to her in the same way, making negotiation much easier.

After her 10 week course finished there was considerable generalization particularly in coping with her brother. He came to say for a short period and Jocelyn was able to discuss how he would fit in with their lives, including his excessive use of the telephone. She felt it made a lot of difference to their relationship and he respected her for the first time. She made further progress at work, redefining her position there in relationship to other workers. At follow-up almost a year later Jocelyn role-played a discussion with her husband in which she told him her feelings and asked him to end his relationship with the other woman. Shortly afterwards he did.

V. TECHNIQUES OF ASSERTION TRAINING

The dual emphasis on assertion training from psychologists and the woman's movement has meant that a single approach to the running of groups has not arisen. Psychologists have developed the standard "therapy" approach with one or two knowledgeable leaders. Feminists have tended to support leaderless, self-help groups.

A. The therapy approach

The group size depends on the number of therapists but generally those giving more than an introduction should not exceed 8–10 people. One therapist can cope with 6–8 but if the group exceeds this size another therapist will be needed to give individual attention. A group of less than 6 does not give the variety necessary when rehearsing situations. The larger group is able to give more support and praise and the individual is more likely to find others having similar problems. More than 10 however, becomes unwieldy and makes it difficult for members to identify with and support each other unless the group continues for a long time.

The length of sessions tends to vary according to numbers in the group but are usually of 2–3 hours. Any shorter and it is not possible to deal with everyone's problems; any longer and it is difficult to maintain concentration and vitality for both client and therapist. Groups typically meet once a week but this often becomes less frequent as the group becomes more skilful and the problems less pressing. There may not be sufficient time to carry out the homework if sessions are held more frequently than once a week. However, continuity may not be maintained if the groups are less than weekly at first.

The assertion groups generally meet for a set period—perhaps 6–10 weeks. During this time they focus each week on a specific issue (e.g. saying "No") and at the end of this time most issues are covered and the group finishes. There may be a follow-up a month later where the women discuss further progress and set long-term goals. Alternatively, the group may continue indefinitely so long as assertive problems remain. Even so, this is unlikely to be longer than a year as people will become more satisfied with their performance and drop out. New members are not taken in after the first or second session so the group tends to fade away automatically.

B. The self-help approach

The same issues as those mentioned in relation to therapist conducted groups apply to leaderless groups. However, since maintainance of the group now depends on the members rather than the therapist it is probably more convenient to keep the size smaller. With self-help groups, decision also needs to be made about where to meet. Meeting in the members' homes may help gain an insight into their problems and the group may benefit from the congeniality. There are, however, other issues which need consideration. The running of the home may impinge on the group such as the need to put the children to bed, the television in the background, the phone ringing and so on. The closeness of the problems may also inhibit the person, who might not want to talk about her husband when he is just through the wall. Women also tend to feel a hostess responsibility and even if refreshments are not provided there is still a constraint in ensuring the comfort of the "guests". Self-help groups typically continue on an indefinite scale. They cease when members are satisfied that they no longer have a need for continued support.

There are no fixed rights and wrongs in setting up assertion groups and the therapist or facilitator will usually have to find out what works best for her. The literature can be highly contradictory. Cotler and Guerra (1976) advocate the heterogeneity of the group with regard to "socio-economic status, education, age, marital status and sex" but Lange and Jakubowski (1976) advise homogeneity on these issues, especially age and sex. Cotler and Guerra have also found it useful to have clients from both ends of the assertive spectrum, while Lange and Jakubowski find that aggressive clients can be highly disruptive in a basically passive group. Probably therapists who are less confident or new to the idea of assertion groups will find the Lange and Jakubowski structure easier to manage than that advocated by Cotler and Guerra.

VI. DESCRIPTION OF A TYPICAL SESSION

In either a therapist run or a self-help group there are 3 basic phases to each session. These consist of checking homework, a teaching phase and then setting homework to be checked at the next session. The importance attached to each phase will depend on the time the group has been meeting and on the goals of the group. The first 2 sessions of a therapy group are often oriented to teaching the basic philosophy, assertion terms and a few techniques. On the other hand, women in self-help groups may choose a suitable book covering these issues, read it before the first session and proceed immediately to work on their difficulties.

In either type of group "ground rules" are set during the first session. Two rules are of particular importance. Firstly, *giving advice*. Since a considerable part of assertion training is learning to identify and clarify issues and identify "rights", for this reason there is never the confrontation or pressure to change as there may be in other groups. For example, one woman was working in a large office where no one spoke to her. She was isolated and unhappy. Although many of the group members said afterwards that they thought she should find another job, during the group they concentrated on helping her make her own decisions, weighing up the advantages and disadvantages. She decided that she did not want to leave her job, so the assertive problem was tackled of how she should become less isolated at work. All members of an assertion group are encouraged to help each other identify the best assertive skill, but not to give advice about how to change the situation, unless requested.

Secondly, *giving feedback*. This is an integral part of the training. It needs to be positive and constructive and to describe the effect the assertion had on the observer. Feedback statements should usually start with the word "I". These statements are used throughout the training as women learn to give feedback in a variety of situations where their position and feelings are important. For example:

> "I found it easier to understand what you were saying that time because you kept the statement brief", or "I find it easier to consider your wishes when you tell me what you want".

A. The basic ideas

(1) *The distinction between being assertive, aggressive and passive*

Few books on assertion training, being concerned mostly with a popular press, are concerned with functional definitions. Lineham and Egan (1979) note however that a clear working definition has yet to be achieved in regard to the term "assertive". One possibility is to say that "Assertive behaviour is that in which a person stands up for her rights, expresses preferences or maintains integrity without infringing the rights of others". Passive (or non-assertive) people are those who typically inhibit their spontaneous reactions, feeling manipulated, anxious or angry. They send double messages saying, "I'd be happy to babysit", with tight mouth, weak voice and averted eyes. Aggressive people on the other hand are usually described as those who stand up for their rights while violating the rights of others.

Some women are so concerned with not giving offence that they rarely consider their rights. While Alberti and Emmons (1974, 1975) quote the Universal Declaration of Human Rights, Smith (1979) gives a "Bill of Assertive Rights"; for example, "You have the right to change your mind". Bloom *et al.* (1975) more oriented towards women, give "Every-woman's Bill of Rights". For example, one woman was angry that her lover continually used her toothbrush. He justified himself by saying that since she didn't mind his kissing her why should she object to this. She felt confused as she could rationalize that she shouldn't care but did care very much. As Smith points out, she needed to appreciate that she had the right, both to be illogical in making decisions, and also to offer no reasons or excuses to justify her behaviour. She learned to say "I understand what you are saying, but I still don't want you to use my toothbrush".

(2) *That assertion training is typically concerned with four major areas*

Butler's (1976) rationale is broadly compatible with that of other writers and is summarized below.

(1) *Positive feelings.* These range from thanking someone to telling them you love them.

(2) *Negative feelings.* These vary from "I am annoyed" to "I feel furious" and mainly concern the area of giving criticism.

(3) *Setting limits.* This involves letting someone know "this is where I draw the line" and is usually about time, energy, privacy and money.

(4) *Self-initiation.* Many women find particular difficulty in expressions of competence and authority. For example, taking the lead in sexual relationships, making conversations with strangers, etc.

(N.B. Therapists should be aware that British women may find some of the suggestions in American training manuals culturally inappropriate. For example, in this country few women would dream of telling their boss that he was infringing on their rights. Alternative approaches are therefore necessary with British women).

(3) *That assertion training has five broad aims*

(1) *To increase awareness.* Once the woman is aware that she has assertive problems (possibly by the use of assertive inventories) she needs to develop a belief system to justify acting assertively. The therapist should give numerous examples when discussing the 4 areas above and ask women to think carefully about them with regard to their own problems. Discussion on rights, opinions and beliefs will provide a basis for the building of awareness and is essential when working with women.

(2) *To decrease anxiety.* Women are usually reluctant to act assertively because of the anxiety engendered. Personal hierarchies are used to cope with this. Some women find this a difficult exercise but it is made easier

if the therapist is thorough at each stage of the exposures. The women write down about 10 situations in which they would like to be more assertive. They then rank them in subjective order of difficulty. They now concentrate on overcoming the easier items. These lists are reviewed periodically with new items being added and those which are overcome removed.

Some women will need extra prompting in developing their personal hierarchies. The following questions may make their task easier: Is there something you would like to tell someone? Do you often ask yourself, "Why did I agree to that?" Are you putting off doing something? Have you recently blurted out an angry, sarcastic or bitter remark? Do you feel let down, lack energy or enthusiasm about something? Does your body tell you that you are anxious?—trembling, nail biting, insomnia, stomach cramps, etc.? Despite all this encouragement some still do not come up with a hierarchy.

If this occurs the therapist may wonder why they have come to an assertion group, but it may be overcome if you get them to work on general issues and to role-play parts in other people's scenarios until they produce something of their own. They should also be asked to keep a diary in which they record daily assertive situations and their coping strategies.   Relaxation and desensitization techniques are explained to the group but these are rarely appropriate within the group as the problems are so individualized. Occasionally the therapist may want to give a woman individual sessions or lend out relaxation tapes.

(3) *To correct faulty internal dialogues.* As Butler (1976) points out "the opposition from other people is likely to be minor compared with the opposition from yourself". These ideas are directly attributable to Ellis's (1958) Rational Emotive Therapy. Butler identifies 4 aspects and women rarely have trouble seeing their own inner dialogues.

Firstly, *negative self labelling.* You can't be assertive because you would be "bitchy", "selfish", demanding, etc. Secondly, *setting rigid requirements.* Arbitrary restrictions as to when, where or how are set, e.g. "I will talk to that attractive person if no one else does for 5 minutes". Thirdly, *catastrophising.* A series of disasters following the assertion are visualized, e.g. "If I tell my mother I can't visit her on Sunday she will be terribly hurt and will tell the neighbours how ungrateful and awful I am". Fourthly, *self-punishment.* Following the assertion the person criticizes and censures herself and vows never to do it again.

(4) *To improve non-verbal messages.* Women in society rarely need the concentrated teaching of non-verbal skills needed by clinical and younger groups. Even so therapists will find a valuable exercise in

Osborn and Harris (1975). They have a set of assertive statements, for example, "I would appreciate your not smoking", "Excuse me, there is a queue here and I am next in line". It is useful to add appropriate statements of your own as well. The women select a statement most pertinent to their needs. One by one they then make the statement concentrating on achieving the appropriate eye contact, voice tone, inflection, volume, facial expression and posture. Many women find this both difficult and revealing and require several attempts before satisfying themselves and the group. A tape recorder or mirror may be useful and some women may want to try more than one statement. Avoiding eye contact or inadequate body posture may continue to be problems. The therapist needs to be continually aware and draw these to the woman's attention.

(5) *To improve verbal messages.* Words to cope with specific situations are found in various help-yourself guides. For example, Alberti and Emmons (1975) are good on "put downs"; Baer (1976) is useful on developing a more satisfying social life or sexual relationship. However, good general guidelines concerning verbal skills are rarely found. Butler's (1976) book is possibly the greatest value. She notes that each assertion should be direct, honest and spontaneous.

Thus, an assertive person is not sneaky, subtle or manipulative, they express their feelings *directly*. Feelings should be voiced rather than implied not just leaving the person to guess your emotions. Similarly, the assertion should be addressed to the person with whom you are upset. You don't criticise home at work and work at home, instead you should express your feelings in the place concerned. The importance of "I-talk" is also emphasized, since assertions starting with the word "you" invariably sound aggressive and lead to counter-attack. Butler contrasts the statements; "I disagree" and "You are wrong". The therapist needs to be particularly aware in early sessions of this type of message.

Similarly, you should be *honest*. You should say exactly what you feel, not what you think you should feel, or what your listener wants you to feel or what some role dictates you should feel. Many women are overly aware of others' feelings but need help to label their own feelings. Careful questioning by the therapist may be necessary to identify what is causing the anger or discomfort.

Thirdly, you should also try to be *spontaneous*. Feelings should be expressed immediately the time is appropriate. If someone queue jumps it is of no value to be assertive 30 minutes later. Saying "no" is an area where spontaneity is particularly important. Many women automatically agree to requests because they cannot voice an adequate refusal. A useful technique for this, while the woman is still developing assertive skills and gaining confidence, is to delay. Say "I'll have to think about that" or "I'll let you know in ½ hour/at lunchtime/tomorrow". In the intervening time she formulates what she wants to say; role-plays it covertly and returns with the end product.

(4) *The importance of "protective skills"*

Protective skills are a type of verbal defence commonly used against manipulation, nagging or rudeness. For example, one of the most useful of these skills is the "broken record". Here the woman decides exactly what her views are, e.g. "I don't want to go to the cinema tonight because I need some time to myself". She then makes a statement to this effect and merely keeps repeating this until the message gets across. She must be careful not to be drawn into side issues, e.g. "I appreciate that tonight is the most convenient for you, but I do want time to myself". Another protective skill is known as "fogging". Here the assertive person appears to agree but doesn't change their position, e.g. "You may be right, you could see it that way but . . .". This is often particularly effective against unfair criticism or outright rudeness, e.g. "you look dreadful in jeans"— "Yes, you could be right". The critic is often stunned into silence. Cotler and Guerra (1976) and Smith (1979) give further examples of these protective skills. Butler (1976) also discusses what she calls "metalevel assertion". In this the assertive women, realizing that a solution is unlikely suggests that the whole relationship is considered rather than specific issues. For example, "We are not going to agree about the pictures, but it seems to me that this is just an example of a more general problem that we have". Not all therapists will want to devote too much time to these protective skills in early sessions preferring to leave them until later. However, some group exercises are often helpful, particularly using the "broken record" technique.

B. The use of role-play

It is during the homework and goal setting phases of the session that the typical social skills techniques are used. Behaviour rehearsal is used extensively. The woman role-plays the problem she is having and then practises more appropriate ways of coping until she is satisfied with her performance. Role reversal, in which the woman role-plays the person who will be receiving her assertion while another group member takes her part is frequently employed. The following brief outline gives the steps which are typically used (see also Alberti and Emmons (1975) and Jakubowski-Spector (1973)).

(1) *Identification of the problem situation*

The woman identifies the problem situation and talks briefly about her previous experiences in this area. The situation is discussed until all group members have a clear idea of the problems and issues. Role reversal may need to be used if it is difficult to see what attitude the antagonist is taking.

(2) *Setting the scene for the role-play*

In order to set up the role-play, it is important for the woman to decide when and where will be most convenient to confront the other person. This assertion then generally becomes a homework task. For example, asking the woman to find out her legal or consumer rights in the situation. The discussion of homework is particularly important since careful preparation and foresight are essential. The person should be encouraged to sit quietly for a brief period and covertly role-play the entire scene in order to elicit accurate details about the situation where she will practice her assertion.

(3) *Role reversal*

This is used to give the woman feedback on the effect of her assertion. At other times it is used to point out difficulties in what she has said. Playing the recipient of the assertion enables her to see any danger areas. Role reversal is also used when the woman becomes stuck and doesn't know what to say next. Another woman can volunteer to role-play her while the first woman judges the effect of alternative possible responses.

VII. THERAPIST CHARACTERISTICS

The principal aims of the therapist are: firstly, to act as an educator, teaching the basic framework of the ideas and being able to adequately deal with questions as they arise; and secondly, as a facilitator, keeping the group on the topic, preparing the questions and exercises, watching that one member does not monopolize the group, seeing that everyone has an opportunity to speak, ensuring that the codes of advice giving and feedback are followed.

Therapists are likely to find the homework phase the most difficult as here there is a need to be ready with ideas and suggestions, often very difficult after a dynamic two hours of concentrating and leading. There is also a need to be very well informed and practised on the use of protective skills as there is inevitably a lot of discussion about these. It is also a point where the group may lose momentum if the therapist attempts to have one woman of a pair being offensive while the other practices protective skills. Many British women seem to find it very difficult to be critical and without care the exercise may fizzle out.

There is also need for the therapist to be able to keep all the participants active and to carefully draw in the more retiring women. While no one would ever be forced to participate, some women will need the activities to be very carefully structured before they will take part. All situations should be carefully structured so the women achieve maximum success in their attempts. The therapist should not encourage women to attempt assertions which are likely to lead to failure. If failure does occur then the woman must learn to identify the successful aspects of the assertion.

It is very easy for groups to degenerate into vague discussions where women simply share their experiences of various situations. While many sessions would start with this the therapist needs to be able to stop it and proceed to actually rehearsing the appropriate ways to deal with problems. While some discussion is necessary for group cohesion and scene setting the therapist must therefore endeavour to keep it to a minimum. As in all therapeutic situations the therapist must try to appear completely non-judgmental. Many women expect to be criticized for their attitudes and belief and frequently stammer, blush or cry as they outline the situations in which they find themselves. The role of the therapist is to accept the situation and help the women learn assertive techniques to cope with it to her satisfaction.

Should there be more than one therapist? Certainly the session becomes easier and less intense for the therapist if there is someone else to answer queries and organize role-plays and exercises. There is also the advantage that more women can take part in the group. Assertion groups frequently break into smaller groups of 3 or 4, in order to practice skills and a second therapist ensures that these small groups function better and receive more attention. Alberti and Emmons (1975) claim that with two therapists, they say "the drop-out rate is lower, enthusiasm higher and both self-report and leader observation of growth are greater". If two therapists are decided upon should they both be women, or a woman and a man? Alberti and Emmons point out that co-therapists of opposite sex are best and are able to provide effective models of assertiveness of each sex. This is an undeniable benefit but some women feel they would be more at ease and would function better in a group lead by women. Although their concerns might soon be dispelled in a group with a male co-therapist some might not come to the group in the first place. However, Cotler and Guerra (1976) comment that they find it is "presumptuous for a male therapist to assume that he can fully understand the non-assertive/aggressive feelings of a woman" (and *vice versa*). This seems to be a valid point.

Cotler and Guerra also comment that having a sound knowledge of learning theory is extremely valuable. This is true, particularly with reference to the use of selective and specific social reinforcement as a means of helping people learn. Assertion training has its roots in the social learning theory (although some behaviourists will be horrified to see how far it has come!). Among their other excellent suggestions on therapist requirements and qualities Cotler and Guerra also state that it is essential for the new therapist to have served an apprenticeship or observed others running groups. They suggest that the new therapist should work as a co-therapist with as many group leaders as possible before tackling a group alone. Another method of acquiring the therapist's skill could be to take part in a self-help group, learning to guide others and offer suggestions, while at the same time reading widely in the assertion literature.

VIII. THE OUTCOME OF ASSERTIVE TRAINING PROGRAMMES FOR WOMEN

It must be appreciated that the evaluation of change in the area of assertion training is still in its infancy and several problems exist. Firstly, evaluating progress is extremely difficult when the basic definitions of the behaviour to be learned are unclear. As indicated, the definitions of aggressive, assertive and passive behaviour are equivocal to say the least. Attempts to measure outcomes have been made but they have tended to focus on very specific skills or to teach to authors' particular programmes and have then measured highly specific outcomes often closely related to the programme. These studies have a certain amount of rigour and usually show at least short-term improvements in "assertive" behaviour but do not necessarily have much relevance to the therapist whose group will have an enormous number of different goals. It becomes impossible, then, to assess the progress of the group using tools from most of the research literature. They generally lack importance in daily life. Secondly, the issue of what to measure arises. A difficulty here is that assertion training is not a single therapy but relies on procedures from cognitive therapy, desensitization, social learning theory, covert sensitization and so on. Although these approaches may have been validated on their own accounts, when all are combined into an assertive package individual effects are difficult to isolate. Thirdly, and probably the most serious issue, is one raised by Lineham and Egan (1979) who question the basic premises of assertion training. They suggest that courses may not be teaching appropriate techniques. While skills to achieve particular ends may be learned, effective communication skills such as negotiation and compromise are rarely touched. So when the therapist comes to decide which outcomes should be measured she should be aware that it may be appropriate to question the very model itself.

Despite the difficulties in assessing changes resulting from the assertive training groups, some attempts have been made. Two basic methods of assessing outcomes have been used.

A. Self-reports

The commonest self-report measure is probably a questionnaire. The disadvantages of questionnaires have been discussed earlier and for practical purposes a "diary" is often much more useful. The women are asked to record all homework which they commit themselves to. During the session they make notes about when and where the assertion will be made, suitable words to use and non-verbal traps which may occur. After the assertion they record how effective it was, aspects about which they felt particularly pleased; areas which did not go well and future plans. In addition they are asked to note all unrehearsed assertion situations which occurred between sessions—successes, failures and reasons. These diaries are discussed at the beginning of every session. The aim is to be as objective as possible and the woman is asked to record who, when, where, how and what about the situation. She may also be asked to rate her anxiety (e.g. on a 0–100 scale) when the homework was recorded and when it was actually carried out. While it is important that the woman becomes more aware of her anxiety levels, therapists may find that it takes considerable time and care to train women to rate accurately and this may not be worthwhile in a time-limited group.

The hierarchies drawn up during the first session and added to on subsequent occasions may also be used to show changes. Typically, the first hierarchies have a large number of items; get much longer at the second or third session then gradually dwindle. If subjective anxiety ratings are made for hierarchy items they usually show massive decreases as the items are achieved, and these decreases should be maintained over the period of the group.

B. Behavioural changes

While ratings of behavioural change may be more reliable than self-report measures they are complicated for a therapist to collect if she is not using the group experimentally. In one experiment McFall and Lillesand (1971) had an accomplice telephone members of the group and try to persuade them to do something that would have caused them considerable nuisance. In this assessment method, group members were expected to make assertive responses by refusing the unreasonable request. Despite some criticisms, this type of approach could be an alternative way of assessing behavioural change. It is more common to set up a role-play within the group and assess an increase in an identified behaviour but then the problem of generalization must be faced. That is, development of assertive skills may be shown in the group, but have they also presented in real-life situations? Sometimes, the use of a "permanent product" can be taken as evidence that generalization has occurred. Thus, successful completion of a homework task will result in something tangible such as a cinema ticket or restaurant bill. Women can be encouraged to bring these to the group as evidence of successful performance.

IX. PROBLEMS ENCOUNTERED DURING THE PROGRAMME

Although generalization and maintenance are probably easier to achieve with highly motivated women who come voluntarily to groups and who have ample opportunity to practice new skills in the community, the group must be carefully programmed to accomplish the best effects.

A. Generalization

(1) Across settings

It cannot be assumed that the skills demonstrated in the group will be used in the community and so a number of actions need to be taken.

Firstly, *Shaping*. This is achieved by having the woman firstly choose assertions which she perceives as relatively easy, i.e. low on her hierarchy. The therapist must also ensure that she selects attainable goals. The woman then gradually attempts more difficult items but with growing confidence and less anxiety, thereby making success more likely. Occasionally a woman will have a difficult but important item which she wants to perform. In this case the therapist should rely on "over-learning", i.e. the woman practices numerous times beyond the first correct performance.

Secondly, the use of *Self-reinforcement*. Learning to self-praise is probably one of the best ways of ensuring that the assertion is performed in the community (and in maintaining its use over time). The woman must first identify and discard disruptive inner dialogues. When she pauses in a role-play or appears confused, the therapist should ask her what she is telling herself. Thought stopping has been very useful in stopping the unwelcome intrusion of catastrophizing, self-punishment, etc. As soon as the woman recognizes one of these thoughts she subconsciously shouts "Stop" to herself and concentrates actively on coping with the situation. Alongside the thought stopping, some women have found it useful to have a written list of their positive attributes to which they can refer (or are obliged to refer to) a number of times each day. This is particularly valuable, for example, when asking for a raise or promotion and needing to remember why it is in your boss's best interests to give you the promotion. One woman, who became a stammering, blushing wreck whenever confronted by authority, used such a list to remind herself of the attributes which made her an interesting person, worthy of conversation.

If the women cannot think of any positive idiosyncrases it may be helpful to use self-image exercises, see Seattle-King County National Organisation for Women (1974) pp. 38–43. If used early on these exercises can also seem to build rapport and empathy within the group. Many women also need to learn to notice when others in the community reinforce them, either verbally or non-verbally, or when there is any positive change because of their assertion. Many need to learn to tell themselves how good the results of an assertion are. These should all be recorded in the homework diary so they are not forgotten. It is also useful to encourage the women to elicit reinforcement from the community. A friend can be asked for feedback if the woman is unsure of what she should do or how the assertion went. It is more common for friends to be positive rather than critical. The women within the group are also encouraged to be positive. The therapist models praise and draws attention to the successful parts of the assertion. The others in the group are encouraged to identify with the problem and praise in terms of their own difficulties.

Thirdly, *Role-playing*. Initially the woman is asked to choose a person as an antagonist in her role-play who is as similar as possible to the person whom she will eventually have to confront. Obviously, in all-women groups this can lead to problems if the antagonist is male, but other considerations previously discussed enter into composition of the group. Ideally, once she is happy with this role-play she should repeat it with other antagonists to promote greater generalization. Unfortunately, time limitations on the group will often mitigate against this.

Fourthly, *Homework*. Half of each session is spent either preparing homework or reporting back. There should be gentle pressure to make each woman attempt some goal before the next session, as it is practice in the community which ensures survival of the skills taught. Each woman keeps a homework diary but the therapist will find it useful to make a brief list to remind herself what has been agreed to. The therapist should show enjoyment and enthusiasm for attempts made. Occasionally homework is not carried out. The therapist should then very briefly ascertain why this is so and encourage the woman to try again the following week and if it is still not done, then ignore it. The reasons for the failure (for example, inner dialogue) should be focused on later in a teaching session as part of a different role-play. Some women will want to discuss at great length why they have not done what they agreed to. This should be strongly discouraged, with the group focusing mostly on success.

(2) *Across behaviours*

Although women will learn to apply the skills they have practised in new settings, they also need to develop behaviours which they have not specifically practised in the sessions. The therapist can plan for this by having the woman take part in the role-plays of other women. During these, as part of the role reversal, she will often have to perform assertive behaviours which she does not currently identify as problematic for her. The therapist can also engineer "behavioural traps". This is particularly useful for women who have minor social difficulties and are anxious about forming new relationships. They are taught entry skills to the new group (for example, joining a club, going to a party). Once at the party or club they are encouraged to observe the behaviour of high status members and model their own behaviour on this. Sometimes even this is not necessary and once they are actually in the situation they cope much better than anticipated.

B. Maintenance

Programming so that the woman uses the skills acquired even when the groups have finished is more difficult than generalizing across behaviours or settings. The last session of any series should be devoted to teaching problem-solving skills and planning for the future. Bloom, Coburg and Pearlman (1975) have a "Steps to Assertion" checklist (pp. 175–176) which can be discussed at the last group. This reminds the woman to clarify the situation; look at the gains from being assertive; look for irrational beliefs and anxieties; check that homework is done and so on. The women then look at situations they will have to deal with in the future in terms of this checklist. This gives practice in thinking through their situations using a structured plan. In addition the last homework time is extended so that future goals can be examined, targets set and role-plays performed.

Maintenance is enhanced if the group is gradually faded and a useful technique is to have a follow-up meeting some months after the group finishes. In these following sessions, the homework discussion is made longer so that the women have plenty of time to explain what they have achieved. The therapist may like to spend a brief time reviewing the components of assertive behaviour. The last section of the group is also extended so that there is ample opportunity to practice skills needed in the future.

C. Ethical considerations

It is appropriate for any writers on assertion training to consider ethical issues. Lange and Jakubowski (1974) do give a fair discussion of these, but they do not take issue with the most crucial problem, that of inadequate validation of the whole procedure. Although the teaching techniques (modelling, reinforcement, etc.) have in themselves been carefully researched, the basis for the assertion model is far from adequately validated. Lineham and Egan (1974) suggest that the typical topics in assertion training may not be the best social skills to be taught and are certainly not the only ones which should be focused on. There is a great need for empirical research to determine which responses are the most effective in specific situations. Assertion groups have high face validity—the behaviours taught seem sensible and effective. There is frequently very high consumer satisfaction—at least in the short-term. But there is probably some reversal in behaviours gained as time passes without the group support. Therapists should be aware of the ethical problems involved in explaining these difficulties to the group early on, as this is a time when they are probably hoping to make a good start, building group rapport and capitalizing on any placebo effects. Despite the confidence with which most writers dedicate themselves to "spreading the gospel", there is really no one adequate model of assertion training. There is considerable agreement about what may be taught, but by no means universal support for the varying aspects. The model proposed here relies heavily on Butler's work and while each part is supported by other writers in one way or another, no one gives exactly the same analysis. There is thus a need for further empirical and conceptual analysis.

These problems make it difficult to describe when an "Assertion Training Group" really merits the name. With the proliferation of social skills groups in other areas it has become clear that an enormous number of "Social Skills Groups" exist which bear no relation to those described and validated in the professional literature. They show considerable variety and inventiveness. This should cause concern to those involved in the more usual approach. Probably the only reason this is not a serious problem in Britain is that assertion groups are relatively rare. There is a danger, however, that as groups by this name become more popular those will arise which do not rely on cognitive and behavioural principles and techniques, nor teach within the basic framework outlined here. Lange and Jakubowski are concerned with this issue in the United States and describe one such group as "advanced feminine wiles".

Therapist preparation is an ethical issue which must also be considered. Cotler and Guerra (1976) and Lange and Jakubowski (1976) are both concerned that therapists should be academically qualified, professionally trained people. While they appreciate that this does not guarantee a high standard of leadership they feel that it is a basic requirement because therapists may need to deal with seriously disordered people and those who "play games" with the group and the therapist. They are also concerned that the therapist is a person who is sensitive to a wide range of personal problems and able to identify whether a person is properly placed in an assertion group or needs a different type of therapy. But, this opinion is not shared by all writers. Alberti and Emmons (1974) suggest that there are many advantages to forming groups within the community. They feel that any functioning group "be it a church group, a consciousness raising group, a scouting group, an encounter group, a spiritual awareness group—can benefit from learning about and practicing assertion together". While it is clear that large, commercial or institutional groups almost certainly need an academically trained therapist to deal with more difficult clients it is probably also true that smaller groups (with or without a therapist) can function perfectly well within limited goals and indeed have a number of advantages.

Of course, there are some deep ethical problems involved. As the woman becomes more assertive this may have an impact on her close relationships. While many will enjoy the more open, straightforward communication, others may not. These issues must be discussed and the woman must decide when her fears are justified and when they are not. The central question for her is, on what basis do I want my relationships to continue to exist?

X. REFERENCES

Alberti, R. E. and Emmons, M. O. (1974). "Your Perfect Right" (2nd edition). Impact Publishers, San Luis Obispo, California.

Alberti, R. E. and Emmons, M. O. (1975). "Stand up, Speak out, Talk back!" Pocket Books, New York.

Baer, J. (1976). "How to be an Assertive (Not Aggressive) Woman in Life, in Love and on the Job: A Total Guide to Self-Assertiveness". Signet, New York.

Bloom, L. Z., Coburn, K. and Pearlman, J. (1975). "The New Assertive Woman". Dell, New York.

Butler, P. E. (1976). "Self Assertion for Women". Canfield Press, San Francisco.

Cotler, S. C. and Guerra, J. J. (1976). "Assertion Training". Research Press, Champaign, Illinois.

Ellis, A. (1958). Rational Psychotherapy. *J. Genet. Psychol.* **59**, 35–49.

Fensterheim, H. and Baer, J. (1975). "Don't Say Yes when you want to Say No". David McKay, New York.

Jakubowski-Spector, P. (1973). Facilitating the Growth of Women through Assertive Training. *Counselling Psychologist* **4**, 75–86.

Lange, A. J. and Jakubowski, P. (1976). "Responsible Assertive Behaviour: Cognitive/Behavioural Procedures for Trainers". Research Press, Champaign, Illinois.

Lineham, M. M. and Egan, K. J. (1979). *In* "Research and Practice in Social Skills Training" (A. S. Bellack and M. Hersen, *Eds*), pp. 237–271. Plenum Press, New York.

McFall, R. M. and Lillesand, D. B. (1971). Behavioural Rehearsal with modelling and coaching in assertion training. *J. Abnorm. Psychol.* **77**, 313–323.

McFall, R. M. and Marston, A. (1970). An experimental investigation of behavioural rehearsal in assertive training. *J. Abnorm. Psychol.* **76**, 295–303.

Osborn, S. M. and Harris, G. G. (1975). "Assertive Training for Women". Charles C. Thomas, Springfield, Illinois.

Seattle-King County National Organisation for Women (1974). "Woman, Assert Yourself". Harper and Rowe, New York.

Smith, M. J. (1979). "When I say No I feel Guilty". Dial Press, New York.

11

The training of heterosexual social skills

SUE SPENCE

I. INTRODUCTION

Heterosexual social skills refer to those social behaviours necessary to initiate a social relationship, initiate sexual behaviour and maintain a sexual relationship over a period of time with a member of the opposite sex (Barlow *et al.*, 1977). Although heterosexual interactions concern only one area in the many types of social interactions people need to handle, there seem to be several reasons for including a separate chapter focusing specifically on heterosexual social skills. Firstly, difficulties in interactions with the opposite sex affect a significant percentage of the adult and teenage population (Galassi and Galassi, 1979) indicating a need for specific intervention programmes. Secondly, there is evidence from the factor analysis of social behaviour checklists to suggest that items concerning heterosocial interaction cluster separately from items concerning more general social behaviour (Galassi and Galassi, 1979). Thirdly, the behaviours necessary for success in heterosexual social situations are extremely complex, involving a wide range of behaviours which vary according to the stage of the dating process. Then, finally, there is a need to consider the training of heterosexual social skills as part of an overall treatment approach to a range of client problems, such as sexual deviance or dysfunction.

The following chapter explores in detail the skills involved in various stages of the development and maintenance of heterosexual relationships. The author discusses the importance of heterosexual social skills, their composition and methods of training, providing case examples of the way in which social skills training (SST) can be integrated into an overall treatment programme. Examples involving the treatment of a sexual dysfunction and a deviant sexual behaviour are given.

The training of heterosexual social skills has mainly focused on the modification of dating problems, involving people who experience difficulty in dating the opposite sex as a primary presenting problem. More recently however therapists have shown an interest in extending the concept of heterosexual social skills to the later stages of the process, to include the initiation and maintenance of sexual relationships. This has particularly been so in the treatment of deviant and dysfunctional sexual behaviour, where inadequate heterosexual social skills have been suggested to maintain the problems. Failure to establish an adequate level of heterosexual social functioning has been suggested to limit the long-term effectiveness of the treatment of both deviant and dysfunctional sexual behaviour (Barlow, 1977; Jehu, 1979). For example, Barlow (1977) stresses the need to develop the heterosexual social skills with clients referred for a variety of deviant sexual problems (such as fetish, homosexual or paedophiliac activities), where deficits in interaction with the opposite sex are evident. He argues that it is inadequate to merely increase a person's skill in sexual techniques and re-orient their sexual preferences, if they then do not have the skills necessary to initiate and maintain a social and sexual relationship with an appropriate partner. Jehu (1979) makes a similar case in the treatment of a variety of sexual difficulties such as erectile failure, premature ejaculation, or orgasmic dysfunction. If lasting improvement in sexual performance is to be produced, it is important that the client can both develop and maintain a relationship which allows successful sexual activities to occur.

A therapist may therefore be called upon to carry out heterosexual SST with a variety of client groups; people whose specific problem is in dating the opposite sex, those whose difficulties are limited more to the initiation or maintenance of sexual relations, or those in which SST is just one component of a complex treatment programme. Some clients will be single and others will already have a partner, but be experiencing difficulty in the relationship. The need to ensure the presence of adequate heterosexual social skills applies whether the clients are partnered or single, although the nature of the skills being trained may be slightly different.

In the case of partnered clients, the therapist may need to focus on improving the existing relationship and ensuring that both partners possess the interpersonal skills necessary to allow successful sexual experiences to occur. That is, of course, assuming that both members of the partnership wish to stay together and develop their sexual relationship. Many clients however, will not have partners and may experience great difficulty in developing the type of relationship that allows them to take part in successful sexual activities (Barlow, 1977; Jehu, 1979). The role of the therapist is then to increase the likelihood that such interactions will occur.

The following chapter considers the role played by social skills at each stage of the heterosexual-social process, ranging from initial dating, to initiating sexual activities and finally to the maintenance and termination of sexual relationships. It will emerge that a range of social skills are important at each stage of the process and the trainer must be aware of the need for careful assessment and training of the necessary skills, taking each step separately.

A. Factors influencing success in dating

There has been very little research into dating behaviour with individu-

als who could be classed as either representative of the general population or representative of clients presenting with sexual problems. The
majority of studies have involved college students in the USA and the
extent to which the findings can be extrapolated to individuals seeking
help for sexual problems is obviously limited. However, the data may
provide some idea as to those factors likely to influence success in dating.
The majority of research studies have also tended to focus on the early
stages of dating, which is only one aspect of an extremely complex chain
of events leading up to a regular sexual relationship.

The evidence available however suggests that success in dating is
influenced by 4 major factors (Galassi and Galassi, 1979), namely: (a)
social skills performance, (b) social anxiety level, (c) cognitive distortions,
(d) physical attractiveness.

Studies have shown that high and low frequency daters among college
students differ in terms of self reported social anxiety (Arkowitz et al.,
1975; Martinez and Edelstein, 1977) and cognitive distortion factors, such
as negative self evaluation (Clark and Arkowitz, 1975; Glasgow and
Arkowitz, 1975). Physical attractiveness was also found to be an important factor differentiating between high and low frequency daters
(Glasgow and Arkowitz, 1975; Greenwald, 1978). This seems to be
particularly true for women, where differences in physical attractiveness
accounted for most of the variance between high and low frequency
daters (Greenwald, 1977). Many studies in both analogue and real-life
situations have demonstrated the importance of physical attractiveness
in influencing the likelihood of dating, particularly with women. Physically attractive persons have been found to date more frequently
(Berscheid et al., 1971; Glasgow and Arkowitz, 1975; Greenwald, 1977),
and are rated as more likeable (Curran, 1973; Curran and Lippold, 1975)
and more desirable as a friend or future date (Glasgow and Arkowitz,
1975; Tesser and Brodie, 1971). Similarly, physical attraction seems to
continue to be important during the early stages of dating, influencing
outcome such as the desire to date again (Brislin and Lewis, 1968) and the
liking of a date (Tesser and Brodie, 1971). Physical attractiveness then
appears to become less important in the later stages of the relationship
(Byrne et al., 1968, 1970).

Several studies have identified social skill deficits among individuals
who experience difficulty in heterosexual social interactions. Unfortunately, these studies have been confined again to college students and the
results have frequently been conflicting. Generally, studies have shown
that high and low frequency daters differ in terms of overall global
measures of social skills performance (Galassi and Galassi, 1979).
Attempts to clarify the exact nature of the behaviours which influence

these judgments have been of limited success. Arkowitz *et al.* (1975) showed that high frequency dating male college students talked more, used more eye contact, showed fewer silences and responded quicker in simulated heterosexual situations, compared to their low frequency dating counterparts. They also report that the use of open-ended questions is important to facilitate the smooth flow of conversations with the opposite sex. Differences between high and low frequency dating groups have also been found in terms of frequency of verbal responses to approach cues from females (Curran *et al.*, 1978) and quality of verbal response on the Heterosexual Adequacy Test (Perri *et al.*, 1978). The importance of responses such as ability to extend conversation (Glasgow and Arkowitz, 1975) and make self disclosures (McDonald *et al.*, 1975) have also been suggested by other studies.

An interesting study by Barlow *et al.* (1977) demonstrated differences in a variety of voice quality, conversational and affect skills between two groups of young men who were considered to be adequate or inadequate in terms of their social success with the opposite sex. Differences in performance based on ratings of loudness, pitch and inflection (voice quality), initiation, follow-up, flow and interest (conversation form) and facial expression, eye contact and laughter (affect) were found between the two groups. All subjects were college or high school students, but the inadequate group were selected from a group of clients referred with problems of deviant sexual behaviour.

Studies investigating heterosexual social skills amongst women on the other hand have shown that high frequency daters use significantly more speech (Glasgow and Arkowitz, 1975) and eye contact (Greenwald, 1977). Generally however, studies involving both males and females have produced conflicting results, and there is a general lack of replication among the studies. This failure may partly represent the lack of sophistication in the research methods used and the type of populations usually involved. The subjects normally selected for these studies, namely college students, are unlikely to exhibit such severe deficits in social skills as clinically based populations. Hence, it may be unrealistic to expect to find significant differences in skill performance with non-clinical populations such as college students. It would also be questionable to suggest that the findings of low dating college students should be representative of clinical populations presenting with heterosexual difficulties.

Yet another limitation of existing research is that it has, rather naively, attempted to seek out a common pattern of social skill deficits for low frequency daters in general. A search for common deficits may be unrealistic when one considers that it is more likely that individuals will vary in terms of the pattern of social skill deficits that they experience. Individual differences in patterns of skill deficits may therefore mask overall differences between competent and incompetent groups of subjects.

Other studies which have attempted to validate the importance of specific social skills have concerned conversational skills rather than heterosexual social skills *per se*, or have focused on adolescent populations. Braukmann *et al.* (1973) for example, attempted to identify the important components of heterosexual social interactions with predelinquent adolescents. Four girls and seven boys were asked to complete a questionnaire designed to delineate components of heterosexually friendly behaviour. Smiling, eye contact, listening responses (head nods and attention feedback responses) asking questions, answering questions and sitting close, were all rated as being friendly. In this study however, the data were purely subjective and do not provide experimental validation of the social importance of these responses. The behaviours rated as important may well have been those that the adolescents had been taught to believe were friendly, rather than those which genuinely lead to successful outcomes in heterosexual situations.

A study involving an alternative type of design has been reported by Marzillier (1975). Eighty-one socially inadequate psychiatric outpatients and 13 normal individuals were videotaped in a 5 minute conversation with a previously unknown female stooge. The tapes were then rated by 4 independent judges on 7 point scales of conversation skill, social anxiety and general ability to cope. These ratings were then correlated in a stepwise, multiple regression analysis with 12 behaviour measures obtained from analysis of the videotapes. The outcome suggested that the judges were influenced by a combination of the amount spoken, questions asked, eye contact, fiddling movements, and hesitations, when evaluating social anxiety. The combination of measures of amount spoken, smiling, gestures, eye contact, positional movements and hesitations were found to contribute towards the judgment of conversational skill. Further studies of this type are needed in order to identify the exact nature of those behaviours that determine success in dating. By identifying these responses, it is then possible to say which behaviours should be selected as targets for social skills training with individuals deficient in such skills.

B. Factors influencing the maintenance of heterosexual relationships

The process of forming a relationship with someone of the opposite sex is only one stage in a complex sequence of events involved in the development of a sexual relationship. Having successfully dated a boy or girlfriend, it is then a large step to engaging in sexual activities, and still further to the stage where sexual activities can continue on a regular basis and in a manner considered successful by both members of the partnership. Various authors have stressed the importance of interpersonal skills during sexual activities (e.g. Lobitz and Lopiccolo, 1972; Kaplan, 1974; Barlow, 1977; Jehu, 1979) but there is a noticeable absence of research to clarify the exact nature of such skills. Lobitz and Lopiccolo (1972) stress the need for couples to be able to express affection and emotions, initiate and refuse sexual contact appropriately and assert likes and dislikes for particular sexual activities. Warren and Gilner (1978) suggest that there are 3 important factors in effective interpersonal communication between couples. The first factor they termed "rights assertion", i.e. the ability to stand up for one's own rights and express feelings and needs to the partner in an appropriate way. Secondly, "tenderness expression", i.e. the ability to express positive feelings verbally, making the individual more rewarding, and thirdly, "conflict resolution skills", which enable the individual to resolve interpersonal problems by use of de-escalatory actions.

Although these suggestions have a certain degree of face validity, research is needed to confirm such claims and inform us of other interpersonal skills important during sexual relationships. Unfortunately, the lack of evidence requires the practitioner to fall back on clinical intuitions when dealing with interpersonal skills during the later stages of sexual interactions.

It does seem though that social skills play a very important role in making sexual advances appropriately and in maintaining a lasting sexual relationship. Barlow (1977) stresses that, even when people become heterosexually sophisticated in that they have acquired the sexual knowledge and expertise required for sexual activity, they may still be unable to successfully interact with members of the opposite sex in a way which enables sexual relations to take place. As already mentioned in relation to dating, success depends on a wide range of factors (e.g. anxiety, cognitive distortions, physical attractiveness, opportunity) of which social skills are just one aspect. Similarly, in the later stages of sexual relationships these variables are still important and consideration must be given to factors such as the client's attitudes towards sex, physical attractiveness, orientation of preferences, sexual anxiety, knowledge of sexual techniques and skill in performing these techniques. Heterosexual social skills are again just one variable that can influence a person's success in sexual relationships.

II. THE IMPLICATIONS FOR HETEROSEXUAL SOCIAL SKILLS TRAINING

A. When is heterosexual social skills training appropriate?

So far, a case has been made as to the importance of social skills at various stages of the sexual process. It would seem also that SST methods may be appropriate in enhancing such skills, with clients who have demonstrable social skill deficits in relation to dating or developing a sexual relationship with someone of the opposite sex. However social skill deficits are clearly not the only possible cause of heterosexual difficulties and careful assessment is required in order to clarify the exact causal factors. Before heterosexual social skills training (HSST) is proposed in relation to a client, it is important that the assessment has revealed deficits in the area of heterosexual social skills. There would seem to be little point in pursuing a HSST programme with clients whose skills are considered adequate. Where other causal factors can be identified, such as heterosexual anxiety or lack of knowledge regarding sexual techniques, alternative techniques are appropriate, for example relaxation/desensitization or sexual education. With many clients, a variety of causal factors may be revealed, of which social skills deficits may be one. In such cases, the therapist can develop a multi-faceted intervention programme, considering each of the areas presenting difficulty. Heterosexual social skills training therefore becomes just one component in a multi-method approach.

B. Selecting valid targets for training

When a client has been assessed as experiencing social skill deficits related to dating or handling sexual encounters, the therapist should select for training those target behaviours that are relevant and valid for the individual concerned. Whenever possible, targets for training should be based on more than the therapist's clinical intuitions regarding which behaviours are important. The targets selected for a client should always have some validity in leading to greater success in social-sexual interactions for other people of similar age, sex, status, background, etc.

Heterosexual social skills can be briefly defined as those behaviours that enable a particular individual to engage successfully in interactions with the opposite sex resulting in the opportunity for sexual activities, without causing physical or psychological harm to others. This definition therefore considers that the type of behaviour that is labelled as socially skilled depends on the characteristics of the individuals involved in the interaction (e.g. age, sex, social and cultural background) and of the situation involved (e.g. time and place). Hence, behaviours which are defined as heterosexually socially skilled are situation specific and cannot be generalized to all populations and all situations. For example, the type of response that leads to successful heterosexual-social interactions for a 16 year old boy attending a youth club in a run down city area, are likely to be vastly different from those of a 40 year old business man in an expensive hotel bar.

Part of the therapist's role must therefore be to identify which behaviours are important social skills for a particular client. Unfortunately the lack of available data relating to the validation of specific behaviours as social skills for specific populations makes this a difficult task. Clinical intuitions and information taken from studies which have investigated dating skills with student populations can be backed up to a certain degree by observing individuals from the client's own natural environment engaging in successful heterosexual interactions. For example, it may be necessary for therapists to actually go to the bars, bingo halls, discos and parties that the clients attend, in order to observe individuals of similar age and social background to the client, engaging in "chatting-up" or dating activities. It should then be possible to identify those behaviours and strategies used by individuals who are successful in initiating heterosexual interactions. The responses used may vary greatly from those used by "middle-class" professional therapists! Information from this type of direct observation, combined with data from the few studies that do exist can then provide some guidance in the selection of valid targets for social skills training.

This approach seems fine for the early stages of heterosexual activities but is obviously less practical when it comes to the sexual act itself. It is unpractical and probably unethical for therapists to carry out real-life observations of couples engaging in sexual activities, in order to identify successful interpersonal skills and strategies. At this stage, unfortunately, the therapist is very much left to his/her own clinical intuitions or knowledge based on the suggestions of writers such as Lobitz and Lopiccolo (1972) or Kaplan (1974). As mentioned previously, there is a marked lack of research into this area.

C. Levels of intervention relating to heterosexual social skills training

In addition to ensuring that only valid and relevant targets are selected for training, the therapist must also consider the various levels at which training can be focused. Social behaviour can be broken down into various degrees of complexity. On the one hand social skills can be seen at a micro-behaviour level, such as use of eye contact or social distance. On the other hand the therapist may prefer to focus at a more macro-level of responding, focusing on more complex skills such as strategies for starting conversations or asking for dates. Then, on an alternative level again, the therapist may be more interested in manipulating the person's level of social contacts and likelihood of making potential dates. Previous chapters have discussed the way in which different studies have placed a differing degree of emphasis on each of these three levels. In practice, it is suggested here that the therapist should carefully consider all three areas of basic skill, complex skill and social contact levels in both assessment and intervention.

(1) *Basic (micro) social skills level*

This level concerns very simple, specific behaviours that influence the likelihood of success at a given stage in the heterosexual sequence. The type of behaviour considered to be a skill depends on the characteristics of the individual, situation and stages of the interaction.

Detailed descriptions of a wide range of basic social skills can be found in texts such as Trower *et al.* (1978) or Spence (1980). The assessment and training should focus on both non-verbal skills, such as eye contact, posture, social distance or facial expression, and verbal skills such as tone of voice, amount spoken, or selection of appropriate conversation topics. Consideration should also be given to the perceptual skills of understanding the meaning of other people's social signals such as tone of voice or facial expression.

(2) *Complex (macro) social skill level*

This level of analysis of social skill relates to a more complex level of responding in which a wide range of basic skills are brought into play within an overall strategy of responding. Each complex skill represents a response strategy to a specific situation, in which a combination of basic skills are woven together in order to handle the situation successfully. For example, in starting a conversation with a potential partner, it is important to choose the right time and place to make the approach, appropriate eye contact and facial expression is important, an appropriate conversation topic must be selected, correct listening responses are needed and the reaction of the other person must be correctly assessed. These are only a few of the very many social skills required in the process of starting a conversation and stress the enormous complexity of behaviour involved in these complex social skills. To a large extent the areas of complex social skills mirrors the different stages of the heterosexual social interaction process, a long chain or events progressing from the initial steps of dating up to a lasting sexual relationship. Klaus *et al.* (1977) identify the five most difficult stages of dating for both sexes; initiating contact with prospective dates, initiating sexual activity, avoiding or curtailing sex and ending a relationship. In practice, the therapist should consider a much greater number of complex social skills that the client may find difficult, such as: (*a*) identifying the location of potential dates; (*b*) selecting high probability dates; (*c*) starting a conversation; (*d*) continuing a conversation; (*e*) being a good listener; (*f*) asking for a date; (*g*) dealing with refusals; (*h*) going on a date; (*i*) requesting further meetings; (*j*) initiating sexual contacts/foreplay; (*k*) expressing compliments and affection; (*l*) expressing preferences, likes and dislikes to partner; (*m*) requesting information regarding partners likes and dislikes; (*n*) handling criticism and feedback from partner; (*o*) judging the feelings of others; (*p*) initiating sexual intercourse; (*q*) responding to failure; (*r*) apologizing; (*s*) negotiating further sexual contacts; (*t*) maintaining sexual relationships; (*u*) terminating relationships.

This list provides an indication of just some of the complex social skills necessary to initiate and maintain a successful sexual relationship. The reader can probably identify others that can be considered important. When one considers that each of these skills involves a whole range of basic social skills entwined into an overall strategy of responding it becomes clear just how complicated the whole business is! The social skills trainer needs to be able to breakdown each of these complex skills into its basic social skill components in order to adequately assess and improve performance. However, even after the level of complex skills has been taken into account there is still the third level, that of social contacts, to consider.

(3) Social contact level

At this level of analysis, the therapist is primarily concerned with producing changes in the social activities of single clients, that will increase the likelihood of successful heterosexual social interactions. Examples of possible manipulations could be arranging for friends to take the client out to a social event, encouraging the client to join clubs/social activities or setting up social activities/clubs/support groups to which socially inadequate individuals may attend.

With many clients this level of intervention is important as their opportunity for social contacts with the opposite sex may be very limited. The therapist plays an important role at this stage in guiding the client towards appropriate social activities. Situations should be selected according to the client's characteristics, where members of the opposite sex who are realistic "targets" can be found. The therapist at this stage may need to consider that certain social settings are not realistic situations for some clients to cope with. For example, a very socially incompetent male who is not particularly attractive is unlikely to be very successful in initiating relationships with very attractive girls at an exclusive city night club. In this instance the therapist may need to modify the client's criteria regarding potential dates, so that the most attractive, outgoing partners are not always selected.

III. THE ASSESSMENT OF HETEROSEXUAL SOCIAL SKILLS

A. The aims of assessment

Although many methods have been developed to assess performance in heterosexual social situations, the majority of techniques have been designed for use with college students and have focused on the early stages of dating. An excellent discussion of assessment methods and issues relating to the reliability and validity of particular methods has been produced by Galassi and Galassi (1979). A comparison of various instruments for assessing heterosexual social problems has also been made by Wallander et al. (1980). In practice however, therapists may prefer to design their own assessment tools, but care should be taken to establish the reliability and validity of any methods used.

The assessment process serves three main functions. Firstly, it should identify those clients whose difficulty in heterosexual situations is associated with social skills deficits rather than being purely a function of other factors such as social anxiety, cognitive distortion or lack of physical attractiveness. Secondly, the assessment should identify the exact areas of social skills in which the client is deficient. The targets for social skills training are then determined according to identified deficits in basic and complex social skills or social contact level. Thirdly, the assessment procedure aims to provide a basis against which future performance can be compared in order to determine whether improvements have occurred. Evidence of desirable change serves as an important source of feedback and reinforcement to both client and therapist. Failure to show improvement demonstrates the need for some kind of change in the intervention approach being taken. Unfortunately, many therapists neglect to test out the benefits of their work and seem reluctant to evaluate their own effectiveness as therapists, to the possible detriment of their clients.

B. Assessment techniques

When assessing an individual's performance in heterosexual social situations, it is important not to rely on self reported information from the client. Self report information is notoriously unreliable, particularly with heterosexually anxious individuals who tend to grossly underestimate their own performance (Clark and Arkowitz, 1975). In order to gain reliable and valid information about client performance, it is preferable to obtain information from as wide a range of sources as possible. The following list provides some indication of the type of methods used by the author.

(1) Self report methods

Self report techniques such as structured questionnaires, rating scales, diaries, self monitoring tasks and interviews can be used. Questionnaires such as the Fear of Negative Evaluation (Watson and Friend, 1969), Social Activity Questionnaire (Arkowitz et al., 1975), and Survey of Heterosexual Interactions (Twentyman and McFall, 1975) are perhaps the most well established, but tend to be limited to the early stages of dating.

(2) Reports from significant others

Information from significant others who are able to observe the client's real-life heterosexual social behaviour is a useful source of assessment data. Partners, where available, friends, or relations can easily be used in this respect by completing interviews, questionnaires and rating scales.

(3) Direct behaviour observation

The most reliable and valid method of assessing an individual's heterosexual social performance is to observe directly during real-life interactions. In practice, however, this approach proves to be very time consuming and complex and is generally impractical. As an alternative, several studies have reported the use of simulated role-play and performance tests which can be performed within a clinical setting (e.g. Rehm and Marston, 1968; Perri *et al.*, 1978). Again, this use has primarily been restricted to assessment of dating skills, rather than the later phases of sexual activities. The validity of simulated situations, however, as indicators of real-life performance has been questioned recently by Bellack *et al.* (1978). Perhaps the greatest use of simulated situations is in conjunction with other sources of assessment information which can be used to validate the findings. The opportunity to observe interactions directly, particularly if the response can be videotaped, provides a useful basis from which basic and complex social skills can be assessed, particularly with dating activities. Obviously, the use of video during actual sexual activities is rather more questionable.

In practice, I have found it most useful to make use of a variety of assessment methods, generally involving self report data from interviews and questionnaires, in conjunction with information from significant others and role-play situations set up within the clinic. The information obtained from the various assessment sources is then pooled and used to identify the targets for training for the client.

IV. TRAINING PROCEDURES: PRACTICAL CONSIDERATIONS

A. Designing a curriculum

It is useful to produce a list of targets for training for each client, covering the areas of basic and complex social skills and aspects of the social contact level which require change. This list then acts as the curriculum for training for that person. Similarly, if training is to take place on a group basis, the curriculum would be based on the summed targets of all the group members. It is important to note then that the behaviours trained during HSST are based on the clients' needs and are not based on a "cook-book" approach, with "a bit of eye contact, a few conversation skills and a bit more posture"!

B. Deciding on group versus individual sessions

The decision as to whether a client should take part in either group based or individual sessions depends on the characteristics of the client, the therapist and to a large extent on circumstances. If a client is extremely unskilled socially and extremely anxious or reluctant about participating in a group then individual sessions may be more appropriate. Some therapists may prefer to work on a group basis rather than one-to-one and *vice versa*. Other factors beyond the therapist's control may also influence the decision. For example there may not be enough suitable clients to set up a group within a small clinic, so individual sessions may be necessary. There are however advantages and disadvantages to both approaches and therapists must use their discretion in deciding which to use. Group sessions may be more threatening to some clients, but they have the advantage of providing potential models from within the group, rather than relying on the therapist to model the appropriate response. It is this area I have found most difficult in running one-to-one sessions, particularly being a female therapist with male clients. In order to overcome this I have had to invite adequately skilled males into the sessions to act as models, as it seemed rather unsuitable for a female to model the male role in heterosexual social skills.

C. The content of sessions

(1) *The sequence of skills trained*

The structure of sessions which aim to train heterosexual social skills is essentially the same as in the training of general social skills as described elsewhere in this volume. Normally, one particular skill area is selected from the curriculum, to be worked on throughout a session. I prefer to begin with the very basic skills in the first few sessions and then progress through the complex skill areas in a sequential manner according to their approximate position in the heterosexual social process. Having taught the basic skills, e.g. eye contact and facial expression initially, the trainer can then refer back to these areas in the training of the complex skills required to handle situations such as asking for dates or initiating sexual activities.

There are obviously no fixed rules regarding the way in which training should be carried out and indeed there is a lack of research to help us clarify issues such as what methods to use, how long sessions should be or whether video should be used. In practice therapists must judge for themselves and what follows here only reflects what the author has found useful to date.

(2) *Introducing the notion of social skills*

In the first session, much of the time is spent discussing the notion of social skills and the way in which new skills can be learned during training. The techniques used during training are outlined, particularly video and role-play. Where appropriate, the client then discusses the outcome of the assessment with the therapist, identifying the primary areas of difficulty and targets for training.

(3) *Training methods*

Each session generally begins with a discussion of how the person coped with their homework task. Further role-plays and instructions are given in respect of homework tasks where difficulties were encountered. The session then moves on to introduce the new skill area to be taught. The standard sequence of instructions, discussion, modelling, role-play/ behaviour rehearsal, feedback and setting of new homework tasks is generally followed in the teaching of the target skill. A few practical points may be worth mentioning. Firstly, I have found it helpful to encourage the trainee to take an active part in *discussing* the importance and role-played by a particular skill, rather than merely providing the information myself. Secondly, the *model* used should be of the same sex and similar age, social background and status to the trainee (see Bandura, 1977). Where I have been unable to import someone to act as a model into the session, then it is useful to make up a series of videotapes showing models coping adequately with various situations. In some cases, I have also found it helpful to show videotapes of "how not to do it" scenes in which an unfavourable outcome occurs. Thirdly, in relation to *role-play*, it is important to create as relaxed an atmosphere as possible in order that the client can practice the new skills in a non-threatening environment. This requires considerable encouragement and praise from the therapist, shaping up the trainees attempts so that they gradually become closer to the model's performance. Clients should design their own role-plays based on their real-life experiences. Reverse role-play can also be useful to show the trainee what it feels like to be the other person in the interaction. Fourthly, the feedback phase should be kept as positive as possible, providing a great deal of praise for effort as well as skill. Suggestions to improve the performance can then be gently slipped in amongst the positive comments. Finally, after sufficient attempts at practicing the new skill have occurred, the therapist then works with the trainee to act a homework task. This should state specifically when and where the client is going to practice his new skill outside the session.

(4) *Programming for generalization*

As discussed elsewhere in this volume (see Chapter 1) it is important that the trainee begins to use the skills trained outside the sessions and the improvement is not limited solely to the clinical setting. The transfer of training effects (generalization) is said to be enhanced by setting homework tasks, bringing relevant others (such as a spouse or friend into sessions) and making the training environment as much like the real-life situation as possible (Goldstein *et al.*, 1978). In addition to these methods, I have also found it useful to take the sessions out in the "real-life" situation. So, sessions can be done actually at a disco, pub or club where the trainees can try out new skills in the natural setting under the observation and guidance of the trainer. I have also found this a useful way of directly observing clients' behaviour and the findings are sometimes very revealing. For example, one trainee was found during assessment from self report and information from friends to have some difficulties in heterosexual social skills. After a considerable degree of training the client was still having minimal success with the opposite sex. One session was then actually carried out at a disco and it quickly became obvious that the failure was influenced by two factors other than inadequate social skills. Firstly the trainee tended to select the most tall, beautiful and attractive girls for his potiential partners and he himself was rather short and not particularly attractive. He failed totally to consider whether they would be likely to respond to his advances. Then secondly, he was a terrible dancer and most girls rapidly left the dance floor when they saw him coming. A couple of sessions discussing the merits of selecting realistic "targets" for his efforts and enrolment in a school of dancing produced a much better outcome than the social skills training alone had done. This little anecdote illustrates two points really; the value of actually going into real-life situations if possible and the need to consider alternative explanations for inadequacy in heterosexual situations.

V. CASE ILLUSTRATIONS

Two cases are now described in which deficits in heterosexual social skills were found during the assessment process. Although, in both instances other problems were evident, the cases demonstrate the assessment and training of heterosexual interaction skills and the integration of HSST methods into an overall treatment programme.

A. Case study A

(1) Referral

John was referred to the outpatient department of a psychiatric hospital after an attempted suicide. The attempt followed the recent discovery of his homosexual activities by his parents, after warnings by police for frequent homosexual soliciting in public toilets. On initial interview John stated that his main aim was to have girlfriends and end his homosexual activities.

(2) The client

John was a 26 year old of average intelligence and employed as a hospital porter. He had never had a real girlfriend and had been engaging in regular homosexual contacts with adult males over the past 4 years. He visited public toilets on 4–5 evenings per week to engage in homosexual acts. The sexual acts did not lead on to any further relationship and indeed John could not be said to have "boyfriends" as such. His sexual fantasies were exclusively male orientated. John had frequent contact with women at work but he was treated as rather a joke by them. He rarely initiated conversations with them and he also found it extremely difficult to talk to other men and avoided conversations with them as far as possible.

(3) Interpersonal skills

Assessment of conversations and videotaped interviews revealed that, at least in the interview setting, John's basic skills were quite adequate. The major problem was in the selection of appropriate topics and asking questions during conversation. His posture was also rather poor in that he frequently slouched and lay around in the chair. Unfortunately, his personal appearance was also a problem in that, although he was quite physically attractive, he tended to wear very inappropriate colour combinations.

Information from interview and attempts at role-play revealed that John experienced deficits in most aspects of heterosexual social skills. Indeed his skill deficits were equally applicable to the formation of lasting relationships with his own sex as well as with females. He was only able to initiate sexual contacts in the public toilet setting where sex was the only target of the encounter and verbal communication was not required.

Other than visits to public toilets, John did not take part in any social activities, did not attend any clubs, bars, classes or social functions. His spare time would be spent at home with his parents, watching TV.

(4) *Assessment of other areas*

In addition to the assessment of social skills it is important to mention other areas which influenced the presenting problems, as they provide an indication as to the way in which HSST was integrated into the treatment programme. Firstly, at a cognitive level John's sexual fantasies were exclusively towards males. Discussion with John led us to decide that a programme of covert sensitization (Cautela, 1967) combined with a home-based masturbatory reconditioning (Barlow, 1977) was most appropriate to reorientate his fantasies towards females. Secondly, and perhaps most importantly, John claimed a desire to become heterosexual and was highly motivated to take part in sessions. Little intervention in the area of motivation seemed appropriate. Thirdly, assessment revealed little information to suggest problems of maladaptive thoughts, or lack of sexual knowledge and hence input in these areas was not considered necessary. Finally, some anxiety was evident in relation to conversation with both men and women, for which a relaxation programme seemed appropriate.

(5) *Intervention*

The training of heterosexual interaction skills and sexual reorientation were carried out simultaneously, but in separate sessions. The combination of covert sensitization and home-based masturbatory reconditioning proved very successful within 6 one-hour sessions over a 6-week period. Within this time John reported a marked reduction in homosexual fantasies, no visits to the public toilets and an increased frequency of masturbation to "girlie" magazines.

The HSST programme on the other hand set out to train the following targets:

Basic and complex skill level
(1) Initiating conversations, selecting appropriate topics, asking questions.
(2) Listening skills and continuing conversations with both males and females.
(3) Asking for a date.
(4) Expressing emotions, initiating sexual contacts verbally.

Social contact level
(1) Visit hospital social club twice a week.
(2) Go to the pub once a week with cousin (male).
(3) To ask out a girl from work and take her to cinema.

Heterosexual social skills training was carried out on a one-to-one basis with a female trainer. The training methods consisted of traditional instructions and discussion, modelling, role-playing and practice, feedback and homework assignments. A male colleague was recruited to act as a model on several occasions where it became unsuitable for the female therapist to act as the model. Ten sessions, each lasting half an hour were required before John and the trainer felt an adequate level of skill competency had been reached. Throughout training, targets were also set in the area of social contact, gradually increasing John's social network. As considerable anxiety was evident in relation to initiating friendly conversations, relaxation exercises were taught at the beginning of the programme. John was then able to use these techniques to reduce his anxiety when trying out his new skills in "real-life" situations.

(6) Outcome

Within 4 SST sessions, John was able to visit the work social club, order drinks, enter a group and initiate conversations. By the sixth week he started to visit the local pub with his cousin and also started to go to "bingo" sessions with the ladies from work. During week 10 he invited out a girl from work and took her to the cinema. No sexual activities had taken place. At this point, John requested to end therapy, because of difficulty taking time off work. He claimed he felt confident to continue his heterosexual attempts and was no longer visiting the public toilets.

After 3 months however, John returned to the clinic for a follow-up appointment. He reported that he was now much happier, was regularly engaging in social activities and had gone to live with his new boyfriend. Although he had returned to his homosexual orientation he was now able to form relationships on a permanent basis. He no longer wanted to change his sexual orientation and had not returned to visiting the public toilets.

(7) Discussion

Although the outcome of the treatment programme was not exactly what would have been predicted at the outset one cannot regard it as a failure. Initially John had been certain that his aim in therapy was to work towards a heterosexual life but clearly this was not really the case and he may, to a large extent, have been succumbing to the pressures of his parents and society. What SST may have achieved was to provide John with the chance to interact more successfully with people in general and to develop lasting relationships with others. He was then able to form friendships and sexual relationships with others, which he previously had been unable to do. He was then in a position to choose whether these relationships were with men or women. As far as John was concerned, the outcome of intervention had been a great success. This case highlights one of the main ethical issues which arise in working with homosexual clients. How should the therapist respond to referrals in which a re-orientation in sexual preference is requested? Caution is necessary in ensuring that the targets for treatment are really what the client wants and therapists should not allow themselves to become "puppets", responding to the pressure of the clients parents, friends, colleagues or society in general to move towards a heterosexual outcome.

B. Case study B

(1) *The referral*

Mr. and Mrs. P. were referred to the outpatients' department of a psychiatric hospital by their General Practitioner. They had jointly visited his surgery to ask for help regarding sexual difficulties.

(2) *The couple*

Mr. and Mrs. P. were both 41 years old and had 3 children aged 18, 16 and 13. They had been married for 21 years, lived in a modern, well furnished house and were both working, bringing in an adequate income. Mr. P. reported a persistent failure to obtain an erection during intercourse with his wife. This had developed 10 years previously, after he had returned from an overseas visit where he had visited a local brothel with a friend. His wife was unaware of his extra-marital activities on this visit and Mr. P. experienced considerable guilt about the event. No medical cause could be identified, nocturnal emissions and masturbatory erections were normal, with the problem only being evident in his wife's presence.

(3) *Interpersonal skills*

Although both Mr. and Mrs. P. were certain they wanted to stay together, many aspects of their relationship were causing problems, which they attributed to the sexual difficulty. The couple did not go to social occasions together and indeed rarely went out in the evenings or weekends. They frequently rowed over minor incidents and the matter of sex was never discussed. Neither partner made any sexual initiations for fear of rejection or failure. Several areas of heterosexual social skills were identified as problematic from self report and role-played situations. These mainly referred to complex interpersonal skills and both Mr. and Mrs. P. were quite skilled in terms of basic response components. The main complex skill areas identified as leading to problems in their relationship were related to communication. Over the 10 years of sexual difficulties much of their communication had become negative. They frequently criticized each other, argued about minor events, rarely expressed positive feelings to each other and spent minimal time conversing in a friendly manner. Perhaps not surprisingly they no longer attempted sex and the matter was rarely discussed for fear of arguments developing.

(4) Intervention

It seemed that treatment needed to focus on 3 main areas, not only tackling the sexual dysfunction directly using a Masters and Johnson (1970) approach but also focusing specifically on the teaching of communication skills within the couple. In addition it seemed important to reduce Mr. P.'s guilt feelings regarding the incident with the prostitute (while at the same time respecting his initial request for confidentiality of the matter with regard to his wife).

It was found feasible to continue the training of interpersonal skills into the same sessions as applying the Masters and Johnson approach. Indeed the two approaches fit together nicely as many of the Masters and Johnson methods bring in the teaching of communication skills. It was therefore easy to expand this component of the approach to include a more specific focus on particular heterosexual social skills. Therapy began with an initial ban on intercourses and brought in sensate focus tasks (Stages I and II), leading eventually in later sessions to instructions in the use of the female superior position. Within the teaching of the sex therapy techniques (e.g. touching exercises) the sessions also involved the teaching of ways of initiating sexual contacts verbally, reading the feelings of the partner, asking for feedback regarding preferences, expressing emotions and preferences, giving instructions, giving feedback and refusing sexual contacts in a positive way. These areas were discussed in turn, with the female therapist modelling where appropriate. The couple were required to role-play each skill within the sessions and homework assignments were set for practice outside sessions. Eight sessions lasting one hour were required over a 10 week period.

(5) Outcome

Mr. and Mrs. P. conscientiously carried out their homework tasks in relation to both the sensate focus and the heterosexual social skills. Any problems of communication that became evident during the sensate focus exercises at home were brought back to the sessions to role-play (e.g. how to say "no" when you really don't feel like it, without upsetting your partner). Improvements in the couple's interpersonal communication in relation to sex rapidly occurred, as seen within session role-plays and as reported by the couple at home. By the sixth session sensate focus exercises I and II had been completed and were being enjoyed. Mr. P. was now able to obtain an erection in response to his wife's caressing and graded periods of insertion using the female superior position began. When they arrived for the seventh session 2 weeks later, the couple reported successful intercourse, being satisfactory for both partners. No further erectile difficulties were reported by Mr. and Mrs. P. at the 6 month follow-up, although a 3 month contact session was used as a booster in order to facilitate certain heterosexual social skills, such as giving instructions to the partner regarding preferences. Interestingly, before the eighth session Mr. P. told his wife about the affair in the brothel who although obviously upset was understanding and the disclosure did not have an adverse effect upon their relationship. This also seemed to reduce the husband's guilt feelings and there no longer appeared a need to work on this area.

(6) Discussion

As mentioned in previous sections heterosexual social skill deficits often play an important part in the development and maintenance of sexual problems. This was clearly so with this couple and this case provides a nice example of the way in which HSST can be integrated into a sex therapy programme. The two methods can easily be brought together within the same session, with the one following on from the other. The following section discusses in greater detail the integration of the two approaches when considering the outcome evidence.

VI. OUTCOME STUDIES

Having made a case for the use of SST procedures in the teaching of heterosexual social skills it is important to consider whether such an approach really is of value in practice. The majority of research studies into the effectivenes of training heterosexual social skills have been focused on work with college students who experience difficulty in dating the opposite sex.

Extensive reviews of the literature relating to dating behaviour among college students have been produced by Curran (1977) and Galassi and Galassi (1979). Both reviewers conclude that the evidence available supports the view that SST procedures can produce beneficial changes in the treatment of minimal dating and dating anxiety. Curran (1977) however, suggests that the "results should be interpreted with a certain degree of cautious optimism because many of the reviewed studies suffered from several methodological and procedural problems". As with research in other areas of SST, the studies have been limited by the frequent use of inadequate or invalid assessment measures and failure to investigate the transfer and durability of training effects. They have also varied tremendously in terms of the components of the procedures used, the length of training and the criteria for client selection. Galassi and Galassi (1979) acknowledge these limitations but suggest that the results obtained are promising as they frequently surpass those obtained by alternative treatments, attention placebo and no-treatment controls. Briefly, the results support the value of practice in dating (Christensen and Arkowitz, 1974; Martinson and Zerface, 1970), behaviour rehearsal (McDonald et al., 1975) and a combination of modelling, behaviour rehearsal, feedback and task assignment (Curran, 1975; Curran et al., 1978). Much more research investigating the long term, generalized effects of SST in the treatment of dating difficulties is required before valid conclusions can be drawn.

The majority of research into the training of the social skills involved in the later stages of sexual interactions, has involved clients presenting with sexual dysfunction. For example, Obler (1973) reported the use of a SST procedure in conjunction with relaxation training and systematic desensitization in the treatment of a variety of sexual dysfunctions with both males and females. Although the approach was described as more successful in eliminating sexual dysfunctions and reducing associated sexual and social anxieties compared to a psychoanalytic group treatment or no treatment, there was no attempt to assess the relative contribution of the SST approach. Munjack et al. (1976) also report the use of a similar approach to the training of assertive responding in sexual situations, as part of a package treatment for female orgasmic dysfunction. Again there was no attempt to explore the value of the SST component. Yulis (1976) on the other hand found a statistically significant association between participation in an assertion training component of a multi-treatment programme and successful generalization of therapeutic gain to successful sexual intercourse with a partner not involved in the therapy. The assertion training component focused on teaching expression of desires, needs and preferences and interaction skills related to both dating and sexual contact. It seems likely that, although the short-term value of HSST procedures remains to be shown, the training of heterosexual social skills may facilitate greater generalization and maintenance of improved sexual performance with clients who present deficits in heterosexual social skills. Research along these lines would be extremely useful.

Finally, in a more recent study, Tullman *et al.* (1981) investigated changes in effective interpersonal communication during a traditional Masters and Johnson (1970) procedure. The authors proposed that a major component in the Masters and Johnson approach to the treatment of sexual dysfunctions is the improvement of couple communication. Although there is no attempt to focus on this area directly, it is an important outcome from the sensate focus exercises. Indeed, their research showed that positive improvements in assertion responses during sex and positive expression of feelings were found with 43 couples attending a 2 week course at the Masters and Johnson clinic, as measured by a variety of self-report questionnaires. There was some evidence however that these improvements were not maintained in the 3 months follow-up. It does seem likely though from this study that an important factor in the success of Masters and Johnson's approach is in the improvement of those interpersonal skills important in sexual interactions. Much more research into this area would be valuable. Indeed it would be interesting to investigate whether the clients showing greatest improvements in sexual behaviour were also those showing greatest improvements in heterosexual social skills.

Although several authors have stressed the need for therapists working with sex offenders to consider the client's ability to develop and maintain adequate heterosexual relationships, there has been a marked lack of evaluative research in this area. In clinical practice many therapists working with sex offenders in both the prison and health services report the use of heterosexual social skills training, but details are rarely published. Similarly there has been a general failure to investigate whether long-term, generalized improvements in heterosexual social skills can be produced with sex offenders and whether these have any influence on future offending. This is obviously an area wide open to researchers and evaluative studies would be of great value.

VII. CONCLUSIONS

A case has been made for training heterosexual social skills with a variety of client groups ranging from those who experience difficulty in dating to those whose deficits reflect an inadequacy in interpersonal skills important in the later stages of sexual interactions. Particular emphasis was placed on the need to consider the assessment and training of heterosexual social skills with clients referred with problems of deviant or dysfunctional sexual behaviour. Failure to ensure an adequate level of heterosexual social skills is likely to impair the long-term effectiveness of treatment with both these client groups.

An approach to the assessment and training of heterosexual social skills was outlined, indicating some of the basic and complex skill areas that are likely to be important during sexual interactions. However, it is clear that there is a need for research to identify the social importance of specific behaviour at various stages of interactions with the opposite sex. Generally, the evidence available to date has been limited to student populations who may not necessarily be representative of the type of person likely to seek help from a professional therapist. Similarly, research has mainly focused on the assessment and training of behaviours early on in the sequence (i.e. dating behaviour). In clinical practice, it is likely that therapists will need to put greater emphasis on interaction skills during the initiation of and participation in sexual activities. Hence, much more research is needed in this area.

There also seems to be a need to identify whether SST methods can be effective in training both basic and complex heterosexual skills with sexually dysfunctional and deviant clients. Although the importance of such skills is frequently stressed in the literature (e.g. Barlow, 1977) it remains to be demonstrated whether SST can produce effective changes in heterosexual social skills and whether this adds anything to the long term effectiveness of the treatment package. Much more development is also required in the area of assessment. There is a lack of reliable and valid assessment measures which limits the value of research and practice in this area.

On a final note, it is clear that the area of heterosexual social skills training is still in its infancy but the limited evidence available does suggest that SST procedures offer some promise in the modification of heterosexual social problems.

VIII. REFERENCES

Arkowitz, H., Lichtenstein, E., McGovern, K. and Hines, P. (1975). The behavioural assessment of social competence in males. *Behav. Ther.* **6**, 3–13.

Bandura, A. (1977). "Social Learning Theory". Prentice-Hall, Englewood Cliffs, New Jersey.

Barlow, D. (1977). Assessment of sexual behaviour. *In* "Handbook of Behavioural Assessment" (A. R. Ciminero, K. S. Calhoun and H. E. Adams, *Eds*). Wiley, New York.

Barlow, D. H., Abel, G. G., Blanchard, E. B., Bristow, A. R. and Young, L. D. (1977). A heterosocial skills behaviour checklist for males. *Behav. Ther.* **8**, 229–239.

Beck, A. T. (1976). "Cognitive Therapy and the Emotional Disorders". International Universities Press.

Bellack, A. S., Hersen, M. and Turner, S. M. (1978). Role-play tests for assessing social skills: Are they valid? *Behav. Ther.* **9**, 448–461.

Berscheid, E., Dion, K., Walster, E. and Walster, G. W. (1971). Physical attractiveness and dating choice: A test of the matching hypothesis. *J. Exp. Soc. Psychol.* **7**, 173–189.

Braukmann, C. J., Maloney, O. M., Phillips, E. L. and Wolf, M. M. (1973). The measurement and modification of heterosexual interaction skills of pre-delinquents at achievement place. Unpublished Master Thesis, University of Kansas.

Brislin, R. W. and Lewis, S. A. (1968). Dating and physical attractiveness. *Psychol. Reps.* **22**, 976.

Byrne, D., London, O. and Reeves, K. (1968). The effects of physical attractiveness, sex and attitude similarity on interpersonal attraction. *J. Personal.* **36**, 259–271.

Byrne, D., Ervin, C. R. and Lamberth, J. (1970). The continuity between the experimental study of attraction and "real life" computer dating. *J. Pers. Soc. Psychol.* **16**, 157–165.

Cautela, J. R. (1967). Covert sensitisation. *Psy. Rev.* **20**, 459–468.

Clark, J. V. and Arkowitz, H. (1975). Social anxiety and self evaluation of interpersonal performance. *Psychol. Rep.* **36**, 211–221.

Christensen, A. and Arkowitz, H. (1974). Preliminary report on practice dating and feedback as treatment for college dating problems. *J. Couns. Psychol.* **21**, 92–95.

Curran, J. P. (1973). Correlates of physical attractiveness and interpersonal attraction in the dating situation. *Soc. Beh. Personal.* **1**, 153–157.

Curran, J. P. (1975). An evaluation of a skills training programme and a systematic desensitisation programme in reducing dating anxiety. *Behav. Res. Ther.* **13**, 65–68.

Curran, J. P. (1977). Skills training as an approach to the treatment of heterosexual-social anxiety: A review. *Psychol. Bull.* **84**, 140–157.

Curran, J. P. and Lippold, S. (1975). The effects of physical attraction and attitude similarity on attraction in dating dyads. *J. Personal.* **43**, 528–538.

Curran, J. P., Little, I. M. and Gilbert, F. S. (1978). Reactivity of males of differing heterosexual social anxiety to female approach and non-approach. Conditions. *Behav. Ther.* **9**, 961.

Ellis, A., and Grieger, R. (*Eds*) (1977). "Handbook of Rational Emotive Therapy". Springer Publishing Co., New York.

Galassi, J. P. and Galassi, M. D. (1979). Modification of heterosocial skills deficits. In "Research and Practice in Social Skills Training" (A. S. Bellack and M. Hersen, Eds). Plenum Press, New York.

Glasgow, R. E. and Arkowitz, H. (1975). The behavioural assessment of male and female social competence in dyadic heterosexual interactions. Behav. Ther. 6, 488–498.

Glass, C. R., Gottman, J. M. and Shmurak, S. H. (1976). Response acquisition and cognitive self-statement modification approaches to dating-skills training. J. Counsel. Psychol. 23, 520–526.

Goldstein, A. P. (1973). Structured Learning Therapy. "Towards a Psychotherapy for the Poor". Academic Press, New York.

Goldstein, A. P., Sherman, H., Gershaw, N. J., Sprafkin, R. P. and Glick, B. (1978). Training aggressive adolescents in prosocial behaviour. J. Youth Adol. 7, 73–93.

Greenwald, D. P. (1977). The behavioural assessment of differences in social skill and social anxiety in female college students. Behav. Ther. 8, 925–937.

Greenwald, D. P. (1978). Self-report assessment in high- and low-dating college women. Behav. Ther. 9, 297–299.

Jacobson, N. S. (1977). Problem solving and contingency contracting in the treatment of marital discord. J. Consult. Clin. Psychol. 45, 92–100.

Jacobson, N. S. (1978). A stimulus control model of change in behavioural couples' therapy: Implications for contingency contracting. J. Marriage Family Counselling 4, 39–35.

Jehu, D. (1979). "Sexual Dysfunction. A behavioural approach to causation, assessment and treatment". Wiley, New York.

Kaplan, H. S. (1974). "The New Sex Therapy: Active Treatment of Sexual Dysfunctions". Bailliere Tindall, London.

Kramer, S. R. (1975). Effectiveness of behaviour rehearsal and practice dating to increase heterosexual social interactions. Diss. Abs. Inter. 36, 913B–914B.

Klaus, D., Hersen, M. and Bellack, A. S. (1977). Survey of dating habits of male and female college students. A necessary precursor to measurement and modification. J. Clin. Psychol. 33, 369–375.

L'Abate, L. (1981). Skill training programmes for couples and families. In "Handbook of Family Therapy" (A. S. Gurman and D. P. Kniskern, Eds). Brunner/Hazel, Inc., New York.

Lindquist, C. V., Kramer, J. A., McGrath, C. A., MacDonald, M. and Ryne, I. D. (1975). Social skills training: Dating skills. JSAS Catalogue of Selected Documents 5, 279.

Lobitz, W. C. and Lopiccolo, J. E. (1972). New methods in the behavioural treatment of sexual dysfunction. J. Behav. Ther. Exp. Psychiat. 3, 265–271.

MacDonald, M. L., Kramer, J. A., Lindquist, C. V. and McGrath, R. A. (1975). Social skills training: Behaviour rehearsal in groups and dating skills. J. Couns. Psychol. 22, 224–230.

Margolin, G. and Weiss, R. L. (1978). Communication training and assessment: A case of behavioural marital enrichment. Behav. Ther. 9, 508–520.

Martinez, J. A. and Edelstein, B. A. (1977). Heterosocial competence: A validity study. Paper presented at the annual meeting of the Association for the Advancement of Behaviour Therapy. Atlanta.

Martinson, W. D. and Zerface, J. P. (1970). Comparison of individual counselling and a social programme with non-daters. J. Couns. Psychol. 17, 36–40.

Marzillier, J. S. (1975). Systematic desensitization and social skills training in the treatment of social inadequacy. Unpublished doctoral thesis, University of London.

Masters, W. H. and Johnson, V. E. (1970). "Human Sexual Inadequacy". Little, Brown and Co., Boston.

Munjack, D., Cristol, A., Goldstein, A. and Kanno, P. (1976). Behavioural treatment of orgasmic dysfunction: A controlled study. *Br. J. Psychiat.* **129**, 497–502.

Obler, M. (1973). Systematic desensitisation in sexual disorders. *J. Behav. Ther. Exp. Psychiat.* **4**, 93–101.

Patterson, G. R., Hops, H. and Weiss, R. L. (1975). Interpersonal skills training for couples in early stages of conflict. *J. Marriage Family* **37**, 295–303.

Perri, M. G., Richards, C. S. and Goodrich, J. D. (1978). The heterosexual adequacy test (HAT): A behavioural role-playing test for the assessment of heterosocial skills in male college students. *JSAS Catalogue of Selected Documents in Psychology.* **8**, 16 (MS. No. 1650).

Priestley, P., McGuire, J., Flegg, D., Hemsley, V. and Welham, D. (1979). "Social Skills and Personal Problem Solving: A Handbook of Methods". Tavistock Publications, London.

Rehm, L. P. and Marston, A. R. (1968). Reduction of social anxiety through modification of self-reinforcement: An instigation therapy technique. *J. Consult. Clin. Psychol.* **32**, 565–574.

Spence, S. H. (1980). "Social Skills Training with Children and Adolescents: A Counsellor's Manual". NFER Publishing Co., Windsor.

Tesser, A. and Brodie, M. (1971). A note on the evaluation of a "computer date". *Psychonomic Sci.* **23**, 200.

Trower, P., Bryant, B. and Argyle, M. (1978). "Social Skills and Mental Health". Methuen and Co. Ltd., London.

Tullman, G. M., Gilner, F. H., Kilodny, R. C., Dornbush, R. and Tullman (1981). The pre- and post-therapy measurement of communication skills of couples undergoing sex therapy at the Masters and Johnson Institute. *Arch. Sex. Beh.* **10**, 95–109.

Twentyman, C. T. and McFall, R. M. (1975). Behavioural training of social skills in shy males. *J. Consult. Clin. Psychol.* **43**, 384–395.

Vincent, J. P., Weiss, R. L. and Birchler, G. R. (1975). A behavioural analysis of problem solving in distressed and non-distressed married and stranger dyads. *Behav. Ther.* **6**, 475–487.

Wallander, J. L., Conger, A. J., Mariotto, M., Curran, J. P. and Farrell, A. D. (1980). Comparability of selection instruments in studies of heterosexual-social problem behaviours. *Behav. Ther.* **11**, 548–560.

Warren, N. J. and Gilner, F. H. (1978). Measurement of positive assertive behaviours. The behavioural test of tenderness expression. *Behav. Ther.* **9**, 178–184.

Watson, D. and Friend, R. (1969). Measurement of social-evaluative anxiety. *J. Consult. Clin. Psychol.* **33**, 448–457.

Yulis, S. (1976). Generalization of therapeutic gain in the treatment of premature ejaculation. *Behav. Ther.* **7**, 335–358.

12

Cognitive approaches to social skills training

STEPHEN MORLEY, GEOFF SHEPHERD AND SUE SPENCE

I. INTRODUCTION

Cognitive theories of behaviour and behaviour change are still controversial and some critics have questioned a fundamental assumption of cognitive therapies: that cognitions can "cause" behaviour (Eysenck, 1979; Wolpe, 1978). These authors argue that the behaviour can best be understood by recourse to conditioning principles and that cognitions are by-products of these more basic processes. We do not intend to discuss the epistemological status of cognitive therapies here and the interested reader is referred to the writings of Bandura (1977), Erwin (1978), Marzillier (1980), Mahoney (1974) and Rachlin (1977). Notwithstanding this, we should make our own prejudices clear. We are persuaded that much human behaviour cannot be adequately understood without reference to cognitive events and processes. Furthermore, we believe there is sufficient evidence to suggest that modifying cognitive activity directly has distinct advantages over behavioural treatments which leave cognitive variables to change fortuitously as a by-product of behavioural change.

Schwartz and Gottman (1976) have provided an elegant demonstration of the importance of cognitive variables in assertive behaviour. They divided 101 subjects into 3 groups by means of a questionnaire representing high, medium and low degrees of assertiveness. The subjects were then asked to role-play a series of situations requiring them to refuse an unreasonable request. They were also asked to provide a model response in writing and a verbal response which they might advise a friend to give. These 2 situations assessed their knowledge about what to say and their actual performance in a hypothetical situation. Further measures were taken by recording heart-rate and ratings of how nervous they felt before, and after, their role-playing exercise. Finally, subjects completed a rating scale, the Assertiveness Self Statement Test which was especially designed for the study and consisted of a list of positive (e.g. "I was thinking that I am perfectly free to say no") and negative (e.g. "I was worried about what the other person would think of me if I refused") thoughts related to the preceding assertive situations.

The data showed that the low assertive group performed less well than medium and high assertive groups during the role-play test. However, there were no differences between the groups in either their knowledge of what an appropriate assertive response entailed, or their actual performance in a hypothetical situation. There were also no differences in heart-rate responses, but the low assertive group reported themselves as being more nervous during baseline and the role-play tests. When the positive and negative statements were analysed it was clear that low assertive subjects reported more negative and fewer positive self-statements than did either the medium, or the high, assertive groups. Low assertive subjects tended to endorse statements reflecting concern about a negative self image, i.e. a fear of being disliked and a concern for other person's position, feelings and needs. Low assertive subjects also tended to endorse roughly equal numbers of positive and negative statements whereas more assertive individuals endorsed more positive and fewer negative statements. Schwartz and Gottman thus suggest that high assertive individuals have little doubt about the appropriate course of action but low assertive people are characterized by an "internal dialogue of conflict". Their problems lie not in a lack of knowledge about what to do, or in their performance in a hypothetical situation, but in their uncertainty about what will happen if they do behave assertively and their tendency to assume that this will lead to being disliked and rejected by others.

Another demonstration of the effect of cognitive processes on social behaviour is provided in a study by Mandel and Shrauger (1980). They asked their subjects, who were male college students, to read and try to "experience" either self enhancing, e.g. "I have the energy and ability to do anything", or self critical, e.g. "I have little faith in my abilities", statements. The subjects then tried to produce their own self enhancing or self critical statements. Following this, their interaction with an attractive female confederate was unobtrusively observed. Subjects who had read self critical statements took longer to initiate a conversation, spent less time in conversation, had less eye contact, smiled less and had less facial expressiveness. They also reported more negative mood feelings during their interactions with the confederate. Thus, the effect of this simple manipulation of cognitive activities was to produce quite marked changes in behaviour.

Although these cognitive activities are considered by many psychologists to be crucial to our understanding of human behaviour (see Kelvin, 1969; Neisser, 1976) nevertheless, until recently, social skills training (SST) has focused on trying to change the behavioural component of social behaviour. Typically the targets have been improvements in posture, eye contact, voice control, etc., and therapists have tended to neglect what people think or feel in problematic social situations. If one refers back to Argyle's social skills model discussed by Geoff Shepherd in Chapter 1 (see pp. 1–19) it is clear that social skills trainers have focused on the motor responses and relatively little attention has been paid to the cognitive mediation components of the model. In practice, it seems that many cognitive processes are operating to determine exactly how a person behaves in a given social interaction. Thus, when a client seeks help in order to improve his or her social performance it is essential that the therapist clarifies the exact reason for the problem. Treatment can then involve modification of either cognitive, or behavioural, components as appropriate. How then can cognitive events influence the way in which we are seen to behave socially? Although there is a marked lack of direct research into the way in which our thoughts influence our behaviour, some initial suggestions can be made by expanding the original social skills model. As indicated in Chapter 1 (pp. 1–19) there are a number of important cognitive components, viz. goals, plans and motivation, the perception of others and the translation and selection of responses.

Goals and plans may be many and various but particular problems may arise when an individual's goals are in conflict. For example, the teenage boy in the classroom who is reprimanded by his teacher for not completing his homework. The boy's goal may be to leave the interaction with as little trouble as possible and he is aware that this could be achieved by apologizing and making a believable excuse. At the same time he has come to believe that all teachers pick on boys, school is a waste of time, that boys should never lose face to a teacher, and that teachers should generally be told to "get lost". As a result of this conflict many boys would choose the response that led to further trouble rather than the "easier" and more socially acceptable course of action even though they were perfectly aware of it.

Social perception relates to the individual's accuracy in interpreting the social behaviour of others. Throughout an interaction, people give out a great deal of information from a range of verbal and non-verbal cues, regarding their aims in the situation and their reactions to those involved. It is therefore important to be able to accurately interpret the cues given out by others: is he/she angry or friendly? Is she/he responding in the way I want them to, or do I need to change my behaviour in order to change theirs? Social interactions often involve extremely complex chains of events which require considerable skills of social perception in monitoring the behaviour of others. Only if the person correctly perceives the cues given out by others can he make the necessary adjustments to his own behaviour required to bring about the desired outcome. Inadequate or distorted social perception can result in extremely inappropriate social behaviour. For example, if a person misinterprets the social cues emitted by others as being aggressive, then he or she is likely to respond in an unfriendly manner or with avoidance. Similarly, problems may arise if a person does not monitor the response of others and does not therefore make the necessary changes in their own behaviour. For example, when a person continues with a friendly advance, or a boring conversation, when it has been made clear that the other person is not interested. Not only must a person be able to perceive accurately the responses of others, but they must also be accurate in their evaluation of their own performance. Although a person's overt social behaviour may be quite adequate, they may not think it to be so, for example thinking "I was awful. I made a mess of that". Clearly such distorted self perception is likely to inhibit further attempts at social interaction and indeed create a "self fulfilling prophecy" (see Trower, 1980a; 1980b; and Chapter 1, pp. 1–19). Although a complete analysis of social perception is beyond the scope of this book, it is clearly an important skill and has marked influences upon social behaviour. Much more research is needed into the difficulties produced by inaccurate perception and into methods of teaching such essential skills.

Finally, in any social interaction the person may choose to behave in a variety of ways. The response which is actually selected is generally that which seems most likely to lead to the desired goal. In order to select the optimal response choice, the person must be able to predict the likely outcome of a range of alternatives. Obviously this is a complex cognitive process and problems may arise at a variety of stages. For example:

At the perception stage
(a) accurately judging the behaviour of others and the nature of the interaction;
(b) correctly interpreting the feedback from others and judging own performance;

At the "translation" stage
(c) ability to generate a range of alternative responses;
(d) ability to predict likely outcomes and select accordingly;
(e) planning the component responses to carrying out the response selected.

Recently, more attention has been paid to the translation phase, with the development of problem-solving techniques (Spivack and Shure, 1974). This area would seem to be an essential part of SST, bringing together the two aspects of response selection and response performance. Indeed many programmes teaching more complex social skills such as interview skills or heterosexual social skills appear to take a more problem-solving approach to training (see Chapter 11).

Although much of the behavioural literature indicates that changing behaviour can, and often does, lead to secondary changes in cognitive measures, these changes are by no means guaranteed. Clearly people whose behavioural performances have changed but who still feel unhappy or uncertain about their capabilities are incompletely treated. Thus, if methods can be developed which can change behaviour *and* related cognitive variables then this is to be desired. A further reason for developing the cognitive therapies for social skills is that these procedures may help to solve the ubiquitous generalization problem (Shepherd, 1980). A tacit assumption of the cognitive therapies is that changing general cognitive mediating processes will be superior to treatments aimed at modifying behaviour alone (Rachman and Wilson, 1980). This assumption is open to empirical investigation and there are indeed a number of experiments which report that the results achieved by cognitive therapy are often better than those achieved by traditional social skills methods (Alden *et al.*, 1978; Carmody, 1978; Thorpe, 1975; Wolfe and Foder, 1977). But these results are by no means conclusive and further research in this area is needed. However, the promise of a direct attempt to modify cognitions is clear and we shall now therefore go on to describe three approaches under this general heading of "cognitive therapies".

II. COGNITIVE THERAPY AND SOCIAL SKILLS TRAINING

The three approaches to cognitive therapy are those associated with Ellis (1977), Beck (1976) and Meichenbaum (1977). We will illustrate these approaches with case studies in which we have attempted to apply the clinical methods advocated by these clinicians. There are differences between these 3 workers, but they do all share certain common assumptions, viz. (1) That thoughts, attitudes and feelings are important and need to be considered in addition to the behavioural component of any presenting problem. (2) That these thoughts, attitudes and feelings "exist", or at least can be made to exist, i.e. they can be uncovered. (We prefer to think of them as hypothetical constructs developed by the client and therapist as explanations for behaviour). (3) That these cognitive events can be considered as internal, verbal statements. (4) That these cognitions exert some kind of controlling influence on behaviour and mood. (5) That they can be changed and it is the goal of cognitive therapies to change them (hence the methods are sometimes called "cognitive restructuring" techniques). (6) That when these cognitions are changed there will be a corresponding change in the behaviour and mood of the client.

The theories which we will describe share these core assumptions and it is difficult to provide clinical examples of one approach which are not closely related to the other theories. Nevertheless, we believe that they are sufficiently different to warrant separate presentations.

A. Rationale-emotive therapy (RET)

(1) *An introduction to the approach*

Rational emotive therapy is a form of cognitive restructuring pioneered by Albert Ellis (1958, 1977). Ellis stresses that we do not have direct emotional reactions to most situations but that our emotional reactions depend on the way in which we perceive the event. Thus, it is not the events which worry, upset, annoy or anger us, but the way in which we interpret and ascribe meaning to them. Indeed it is not surprising that a child is upset when his father shouts at him but that the next door neighbour who hears the same "objective stimulus" is completely untouched by the father's outburst. Ellis proposes that people can have maladaptive and irrational ways of interpreting events which produce emotional disturbance to a degree which is unwarranted by the actual rational appraisal of the event. Ellis organizes his description of emotional behaviour into a sequence easily remembered by a simple ABC mnemonic where: A = Activating events and situations; B = Beliefs, rational and irrational, which the person has and uses to interpret A; C = Consequences both emotional and behavioural which follow from the person's interpretation of A.

The relationship between A and C is not predictable unless we know B. Thus, if a person interprets the situation in an inappropriate way then the consequences are also likely to be inappropriate. This sequence of events can be sketched diagrammatically:

Acting event	Beliefs	Consequences
	may be *Rational*(RB)	may be *Rational* (RC)
thus, Event ↗ ↘		
	or *Irrational* (IB)	and *Irrational* (IC)

For example, an adolescent girl has been invited to a party. Her emotional reaction to this and the decision about whether she goes or stays at home are governed by her beliefs about the situation viz.

Activating event	Belief	Consequences
	Rational "Oh good that's a chance to meet new people. It might be a bit scary at first but I expect I'll find someone to talk to"	*Rational* Feels a bit nervous. Goes to party. Enjoys party.
Being invited to party ↗ ↘		
	Irrational "I can't go. Everyone will stare at me. I won't know what to say. I will say the wrong thing. Everybody will think I am stupid and no-one will like me."	*Irrational* Very anxious. Does not go to party.

(2) *Types of irrational beliefs*

Ellis has classified irrational beliefs into 4 major categories:

(1) *"Mustabatory"*. Beliefs which indicate that somebody or something must differ from the way they actually are, e.g. "I must win the game", "He must be nice to me", etc.

(2) *"Awfulising" beliefs.* Beliefs that things are awful, terrible and catas-
    trophic because they are not the way they should be, e.g. "It will be
    awful if I don't thoroughly clean the house before the guests arrive".
(3) *"Shoulds and oughts".* Statements that relate to the person not being
    able to stand or tolerate the world if it differs from the way it "should"
    be.
(4) *Damning statements.* Beliefs which degrade the person or another if
    they cause the situation to differ from the way it "should" or "ought"
    to be, e.g. "He is a terrible person and should be punished because
    he didn't turn up on time".

In addition to these 4 categories of belief Ellis has, at various times,
identified common "core" irrational ideas which he asserts are at the root
of most emotional disturbance. A list of these 12 basic irrational ideas is
shown in Table 12.1. (Marzillier (1980) has noted that these 12 core beliefs
have now been extended to 27).

TABLE 12.1
Twelve basic irrational ideas (Ellis 1958)

---

1. That it is a dire necessity for an adult to be loved by everyone for everything
   he does.
2. That certain acts are wrong or wicked and that people who perform these acts
   should be severely punished.
3. That it is catastrophic when things are not the way one would like them to be.
4. That unhappiness is externally caused and forced on one by outside people
   and events.
5. If something is fearsome or dangerous one should be terribly concerned
   about it.
6. That it is easier to avoid than to face difficulties and responsibilities.
7. One needs something either stronger or greater than oneself on which to rely.
8. That one should be thoroughly competent, adequate, intelligent and achieving in all possible respects.
9. That because something once strongly affected one's life it should always
   affect it.
10. That it is important for our happiness what other people do and we should
    make great effort to change them in the direction that we want them to go.
11. That happiness can be achieved by inertia and inaction.
12. That one has no control over one's emotions and that one cannot help feeling
    certain things.

The process of therapy is clearly described by Ellis (1958). The first aim of
the therapist is to persuade the client of the validity of RET. This is done
by describing the theoretical basis of RET and providing examples. A
second step is taken when the therapist persuades the client to look for
their own irrational beliefs. This adds a D to the ABC sequence, the D

refers to the *detecting* of the irrational beliefs held by the client. The third phase follows with the therapist *debating* and *disputing* the client's irrational beliefs. The client is then encouraged to develop and rehearse his own arguments against the irrational beliefs and to substitute more suitable appraisals of activating events. This stage is the *Effect* (E) whereby the client develops new rational and realistic beliefs about events.

We will now describe in more detail how these ideas might work out in practice with clients referred with social problems. The examples have been culled from our own experience and the methods from a number of sources including Ellis (1977); Goldfried *et al.* (1974); Lange (1977) and Lange and Jakubowski (1976). All these sources provide useful information for the would-be practitioner but we should emphasize that there is very little research in this area and it would be premature to attempt to provide definitive guidelines on precisely when RET should be employed as an adjunct to an SST programme. Our own approach has been to introduce cognitive methods gradually into already established behavioural programmes. This also seems to be the case in studies which have attempted to evaluate RET applied to social skills problems (Alden *et al.*, 1978; Carmody, 1978; Linehan *et al.*, 1979). Lange and Jakubowski (1976) tend to bring in RET procedure at around the 10–14th session of an SST package and couple it with further behavioural rehearsal. The following outline is therefore intended only as a basis from which therapists may develop their own ideas and procedures depending on their experience, client population and training setting.

(3) A suggested outline

Stage 1
(1) Introduce the ABC model and present the rationale of treatment to the client. Set up an example of irrational and rational thoughts relating to a social event which has some relevance for the client. Discuss how these beliefs can be followed by rational and irrational behavioural and emotional consequences.
(2) Present the list of irrational statements (Table 12.1) and discuss with the client why these statements are irrational and what rational statements could replace them (good examples of these are given in Lange and Jakubowski, 1975, Ch. 5). It is a good idea to write out the rational statements.
(3) Ask the client to identify a common problem situation of their own. Discuss what irrational thoughts occur in this situation and what consequences of the situation usually prevail. Write these thought

consequences down and ask the client to generate and record more rational thoughts.

Homework. Ask the client to identify two more real-life problems and discover his ABC sequence. Once he has done this she/he should try and generate more rational beliefs and explore their consequences.

Stage 2

(1) Encourage the client to identify irrational thoughts, feelings and actions occurring in specific problem situations. The situations must be specific and not vague. For example, statements like, "When I meet an attractive girl and think . . . 'what if I don't know what to say' . . . I just stand there looking daft with my mouth open" (irrational beliefs numbers 3 and 8 in Table 12.1 might be implied by this statement) are preferred to more general statements such as, "When I am with people I have no confidence". To help clients capture the full impact of problem situations we have used a simple imagery technique. Clients are asked to close their eyes, relax and imagine recent problem situations and to report on their thoughts and feelings in that situation.

(2) Once a number of situations have been elicited they are ordered in a hierarchy of difficulty or stressfulness using the same principles of hierarchy construction as in systematic desensitization. At this stage no attempt is made to "uncover" or develop a set of irrational beliefs, although one might often have a good guess at what is the most likely predominant belief(s).

Stage 3

(1) The therapist then presents each of the problem situations in an hierarchical order, starting with the least problematic. The situations can be presented either in discussion, in imagination, or in real-life. The latter two methods of presentation often allow the full flavour of the disturbing emotion to be captured by the therapist. During each presentation the client is instructed to describe his feelings and to recount his thoughts. The aim of this exercise is to establish the emotional feeling as a cue for the person to search for his irrational thoughts. At this stage the thoughts will not appear neatly parcelled and labelled as in Table 12.1. It is the therapist's job to assimilate and probe the client's reports. When the therapist judges he can formulate the client's thoughts he might either ask the client to summarize what the predominant irrational belief is, or provide the summary himself.

(2) As each irrational belief is exposed it is challenged by the therapist who then gradually encourages the client to take over the role of disputation. The challenge is polemical and one asks the client if his

beliefs are 100% true, inevitable and based on incontravertible fact. Counter instances are presented and the client is encouraged to think of more rational appraisals of the activating event and what the consequences of these rational beliefs might be.

(3) The client is asked to rehearse the rational alternatives while exposed to the activating event (via imagery, role-play or real-life) in the presence of the therapist. The therapist teaches the client how to monitor his emotional reaction (a simple 0–100 "fear thermometer" method is most convenient) and during the early stages the therapist also acts as prompter and shaper for rehearsing rational appraisals. Each activating event is rehearsed and monitored until it no longer provokes intense emotion.

Homework. The client is instructed to practise the process in real-life situations. A record of his practice and improvement can be kept in diary.

(4) A case example

Jane was an 18 year old hairdresser who lived at home with her parents. When she was first seen she was away from work following an admission to a psychiatric hospital after she had attempted suicide by overdosing with sleeping pills. Jane was an only child and reported having no friends. She never went out with her colleagues from work and had never had a boyfriend. At work Jane found it difficult to talk to her colleagues and customers but she reported no difficulty in getting on with her parents and was able to talk to them relatively easily. She was an attractive looking girl and was occasionally invited out by her work mates but she invariably refused these invitations. Her spare time was spent at home reading, watching TV and dressmaking. During a course of interviews the therapist established a number of problem situations and skills deficits:

Problem situations
(a) accepting invitations; (b) starting conversations; (c) maintaining conversation; (d) replying to questions; (e) returning articles to shops; (f) refusing unreasonable requests; (g) asking questions.

Skills deficits
(a) excessive fiddling with buttons and bits of clothing; (b) infrequent eye contact; (c) voice volume too quiet; (d) lack of head movement and a bent posture; (e) social distance too far; (f) miserable facial expression; (g) no smiling.

An initial treatment programme was set up to focus purely on teaching

Jane the basic and complex social skills in which she was known to be deficient. She learnt these skills but it became obvious that there was no lasting change in her emotional state or in her social activities. The therapist then proposed RET as a suitable treatment and explained the rationale and discussed some examples. Jane agreed to try this therapy and each problem was examined. The following is a condensed account of a session in which Jane examined what happened when she was asked out by her colleagues. She was asked to imagine a situation where she was invited out for a drink. The session went like this:

T.   What are you thinking when they ask you to join them for a drink?

J.   At first I think I'd like to go but then I quickly change my mind. I become scared that things might go wrong.

T.   What are you worried might be wrong?

J.   Well, I'm afraid that I will not be able to think of things to say to them.

T.   And what will happen if you can't think of things to say?

J.   Well, I suppose everyone would stare at me and think I'm stupid. Then they probably won't invite me again as I'm boring to be with.

T.   So, you feel that if you can't think of things to say then the others will notice this and think less of you?

J.   Yes, I suppose so.

T.   And it also seems that if your friends thought you were stupid, that would be really awful, so you'd rather not go in the first place?

J.   Mm.

T.   Now, there are several counts where your thinking really doesn't seem very logical. Perhaps we can go through these together and see where they go wrong. First of all, you said that you were afraid because you wouldn't know what to say to them. Now, is this one hundred per cent true? You've had plenty of practice in choosing topics to talk about so is it really correct that you won't know what to say?

J.   Well, I don't suppose so really.

T.   And also, you then start "catastrophising".* "What if I can't think of something to say, they'll stare at me and think I'm stupid". Now how true and accurate is that? Do people stare when others don't say anything? Do they think they are stupid?

J.   When you put it like that, they wouldn't really.

T.   And even if they did think you were stupid, is that so awful?

J.   Well it seems so at the time.

T.   But what's so terrible about the possibility that some of your friends think you are stupid?

J.   Well they wouldn't like me and ask me again.

T.   And does everyone have to like you all the time?

J.   Well I suppose not.

T.   What rational and more positive thoughts could you say to yourself instead in this situation?

J.   I could say that I should be able to think of some things to say and even if I don't it's unlikely that the others will notice that much.

---

* Catastrophising is also a term used by Beck, see p. 320.

T.   And what about if any of them did notice and think you are stupid?
J.   Well, I suppose everyone can't like me and it wouldn't be the end of the world if they didn't ask me again.
T.   Right, so why don't you imagine your way through the situation again now. This time thinking it through rationally and positively and seeing the positive consequences.
J.   O.K.
T.   Then the next time you come to face it in real-life, you'll think it through this way and not let those irrational thoughts get in the way, O.K.?

After a number of sessions examining problem situations it was possible to summarize Jane's predominant beliefs about herself. These are listed below with the numbers in parenthesese indicating the corresponding irrational beliefs described by Ellis (Table 12.1).

(1) I am a failure (8).
(2) If I say anything it will sound stupid (8, 1).
(3) Unless everyone likes me life isn't worth living (1).
(4) I can never change. I'll always be miserable and a failure (12).
(5) I can't make a mistake in front of people (1, 3, 8).
(6) I would rather not take a chance but stay at home (6).
(7) I can't stand being a failure. I'd rather die (3).

Each of these beliefs was debated and more rational beliefs were developed. Jane was encouraged to expose herself to problem situations and use the procedure she had learned in therapy sessions.

B. Beck's cognitive therapy

(1) An outline of the theory

Beck's Cognitive Theory (Beck, 1972; Beck *et al.*, 1979) has been most extensively applied to the problems of depressed patients (*see* Rush *et al.*, 1977; Taylor and Marshall, 1977). Like Ellis, Beck believes that an individual's mood and behaviour are largely determined by the way in which he construes or interprets the world. Beck refers to these constructions as negative cognitive patterns or "schema". These schema are like filters, "conceptual spectacles", with which we view the world and select certain aspects of the events we experience and interpret them in particular ways. Beck's approach is to focus on these selective, interpretive processes and to ask the client to consider carefully really what evidence he or she has for these particular interpretations. Together with the client, Beck discusses the rational basis for his or her beliefs and helps the client to set up real-life tests of these beliefs. Beck is emphatic that to be a good cognitive therapist, one first needs to be a good psychotherapist. He argues that a good psychotherapist is able to create a good relationship with the client and shows the characteristics of warmth, concern, interest and the capacity to listen without expressing hasty judgment or criticism. The therapist should also show a high degree of empathic understanding and be sincere, not hiding behind a professional facade. All these qualities are crucial for establishing the relationship without which the therapy cannot take place. The therapy itself takes the following basic form.

(2) *A suggested outline*

Stage 1—providing a rationale. As with Ellis' RET it is important to prepare the client for cognitive therapy by explaining the rationale of the treatment. A key element in Beck's technique is to obtain the client's account of his problem and the steps he/she has already taken to solve it. The therapist then builds his rationale into the account given by the client, presenting it as an alternative way of construing the problem. Beck provides (Beck *et al.*, 1979) excellent accounts of this process.

Stage 2—identifying the negative thoughts. This is a difficult and subtle process because the underlying cognitive "schema" are often automatic and almost unconscious. They are the person's habitual way of construing the world. The therapist will provide a definition of a cognition ("either a thought or a visual image that you may not be very aware of unless you focus your attention on it", Beck *et al.*, 1979, p. 147) and begin to examine with the client what cognitions predominate. There are a number of ways of "capturing" these automatic thoughts. The client may simply be asked what thoughts most frequently come into his mind. More precise information may be obtained by the client using a diary to log the thoughts which occur in problem situations. These situations may also be sampled by using imagery in the therapy session. It is thus the task of the therapist to work out with the client what particular negative thoughts characterize their thinking. The therapist achieves this by asking a lot of questions, "So you believe that . . . is the case? Is that right? Now, what makes you think that?" The questioning is not done in an attacking fashion, but in a gentle, empathic manner, "Now, have I got this right? You say you believe . . . because of . . . is that right?"

The negative thoughts that are identified may be very much like Ellis' "Irrational Beliefs", only in the case of Beck's approach he recommends negotiating these with the client directly and phrasing them in the client's own words. In contrast, Ellis has established a set of irrational beliefs which he believes are common in the culture he works in. Thus, reading some of the RET literature one is left with an impression that the RET therapist's main job is to match the client with a number of irrational beliefs, while Beck approaches the problems of discovering the client's cognitive activity with an emphasis on the idiosyncratic nature of the cognitions. Nevertheless, Beck does list a number of the most common types of "negative thoughts", viz.:

(1) Having negative opinions of self based on unfavourable comparisons with others, e.g. "I have failed as a worker or parent".
(2) Feelings of self-criticism and worthlessness, e.g. "Why should anyone bother with me?"
(3) Having consistent negative interpretations of events (making mountains out of molehills), e.g. "Because X has gone wrong, everything is a mess".
(4) Having negative expectations about the future, e.g. "It will never be any good. I'll never be able to get on with people".
(5) Feeling overwhelmed by responsibilities and the enormity of the task, e.g. "It's too difficult. There's just too much to think about".

As these thoughts are identified the therapist begins to demonstrate with the client how they are associated with emotional disruption. He may begin by asking the client to imagine an unpleasant scene unconnected with the client's dysfunction. He might describe other scenes which are remote from the client's experience in order to demonstrate that the way one thinks about the world determines how one feels about it. The therapist will also point out the habitual, automatic quality of these thoughts and the rapid, profound, and apparently inexplicable effects that they have.

Stage 3—examining faulty cognitions. Once the negative thoughts have been identified the therapist encourages the client to "distance" himself from them in order to try to "objectify" their problem. Many clients have difficulty in examining their cognitions in a detached manner so that they are unable to separate what is factual from what is a belief. In order to help the client the therapist might ask him to describe himself in the third person, for example, "Well, there's this guy and he meets this new bloke at work, immediately he says to himself, now I've got to impress this bloke, how can I make him think well of me?". By describing himself in the third person in this way, the client may begin to see his own thinking in a more objective light.

Stage 4—challenging faulty cognitions. Once it is established that the client can "objectify" his thoughts the process of challenging can begin. There are two ways to do this, cognitive and behavioural.

(1) Cognitive challenges. The cognitive challenge consists of examining the logical basis for each thought. As indicated earlier the therapist can ask the client whether he really has sufficient reason for his beliefs. Beck lists a number of common errors and alternative interpretations which can be applied to them. These are shown in Table 12.2.

TABLE 12.2
Common cognitive errors and their alternative interpretations

Error	Alternative
Over-generalizing If it is true in one case it is true in every case which is even slightly similar	Are the cases really similar? Establish criteria to evaluate their similarity
Selective abstraction Recalling only "bad" experiences and failures	Recalling all the good instances which the person forgot
Excessive responsibility Feeling personally responsible for all the bad things that happen	Challenging the person's attribution. Generating other causes of events
Predicting from the past If it has been true in the past then it will always be true	Challenge whether the situation is identical. Is the situation actually the same?
Excessive self reference I am the centre of everybody's attention. Everybody sees my poor performances. I cause misfortunes	Establish criteria to decide whether this is true. Examine other possible causes
Catastrophising The worse is always likely to happen	Estimate the real likelihood that something awful will happen. Cite instances when it didn't happen
All or nothing Things are either good or bad, wonderful or awful	Show that there is usually a continuum of events

As each automatic thought is examined the therapist teaches his client how to test its reality. He does not aim to discredit the thought completely but to establish with the client a number of ways in which the thought may be tested against reality. Examples of the counter arguments or alternatives for each class of thought are also shown in Table 12.2. The therapist will then aim to point out the selective way in which the individual perceives the world and attributes meaning and causality to events, consistently emphasizing that there are a number of alternative explanations which the client could choose to test out. This procedure is very much a dialogue with the client who is encouraged to set up his own realistic criteria for testing faulty cognitions. These tests are often behavioural.

(2) Behavioural challenges. The therapist and client thus set out to test whether the faulty cognitions or the alternative interpretations are closer to reality. These tests are usually assigned as "homework", although it may often be useful for the therapist and client to do a trial run together. For example, a young man who was avoiding social situations because he said others looked at him (excessive self-reference) was asked to go into a pub and note how many people looked at him on entering it. He was then to sit there for 30 minutes and note how many people looked at others who entered the pub. In this way he was able to demonstrate to himself that newcomers are almost always examined by others, but that the interest wanes and there is therefore nothing unusual about people looking at him when he entered social situations. As the client continually challenges his faulty cognitions he should begin to replace them with more appropriate appraisals of his world and the degree of emotional distress and behavioural disability should therefore be reduced.

(3) *A case example*

Paul was 29. He shared a flat with another man but still saw a lot of his widowed mother with whom he was somewhat over-involved. He had had 2 fairly long in-patient admissions when aged 23 and 25, and one day-hospital admission for 15 months, aged 26. The diagnoses made were of social anxiety and paranoid personality. He had never felt comfortable mixing with people and had few friends. At the beginning of treatment he rarely went out socially but was working as a clerk in an insurance office. The presenting problem was a fear of being attacked while out in the street. (He was actually "mugged" about a year previously). Although he recognized this fear as not being entirely rational it had reached such proportions that he was thinking of giving up work and staying at home entirely.

Assessment of problem areas. At the initial interview he did not seem too nervous but his behaviour gave the appearance of some tension. When speaking about his fears he twiddled his fingers and covered his mouth, but generally his social skills were not a problem. He talked freely about his desire to avoid all social contact outside the house. When asked about his problem he reported that whenever he was outside the house and saw 2 or 3 youths who might threaten him, he thought, "Oh, no, it's going to happen again. One of them is bound to come up and be violent towards me. I won't know what to say and I'll reveal my weakness. Then they'll start on me". Paul was instructed to begin a social diary, recording every excursion outside his home every day. He recorded the situations when he felt anxious and noted down any automatic thoughts that appeared. Examination of his diary showed that there were 4 thoughts occurring whenever he saw 2–3 youths in the street.

Thought 1. "This is like the last time".
Thought 2. "One of them is bound to come up to me".
Thought 3. "I won't know what to say or do".
Thought 4. "I'll reveal my weakness".

Treatment programme. At this point the therapist introduced the idea of cognitive errors and taking one thought each week he and Paul worked out ways of testing the reality of the thought. Paul wrote down each thought and some ideas about how to test it. He was then told to try out his new skill whenever possible. Paul was also asked to rate how strongly he felt each thought was true by using a simple 0–100 rating scale. Paul's notes for testing each thought are shown here:

Thought 1. Is it *really* like last time? This thought is an *overgeneralization* and a possible false *prediction from the past.* Ask yourself, "Is it really like the last time when it was dark and you were alone? Is there anybody about anywhere?"

Thought 2. Why should they pick on you? This is an example of *excessive self-reference.* Aren't there others around? What is special about you?

Thought 3. But you can learn what to do and say. Is it true you don't know what to do? Aren't you *catastrophising*? If they do come towards you you could do a number of things, e.g. shout for help, run, talk to them. (Paul also role-played this situation of being approached by and talking to a stranger).

Thought 4. What makes you think you are weak? You are putting yourself in an *all or nothing* category of being weak or strong. What evidence have you got that you are strong? Don't *selectively abstract* evidence to the contrary.

As Paul rehearsed these alternative cognitions his fears of going out gradually decreased. As his confidence increased so his general feelings of inadequacy declined dramatically. (Other details of his treatment are given in Shepherd, 1982, in press).

C. Stress innoculation training: a coping skills technique

(1) An introduction to the approach

The final cognitive approach to be considered is associated with the name of Donald Meichenbaum. He has written extensively about cognitive-behaviour modification (Meichenbaum, 1975, 1976, 1977). His major emphasis is on the idea that talking to oneself can help develop and regulate appropriate behaviour. The use of language as a guide for behaviour is most readily observed in young children, as they play, especially if they are carrying out complicated manoeuvres, they talk to themselves about what they are doing. Adults use this trick too when they are learning new motor skills, often the skill is broken up into small sequences each of which has a precise instruction. One of the authors recalls being taught to change gear by a driving instructor who insisted that the author speak the whole sequence as he was changing gear in strict rhythmic time. In this case the sequence of instructions was:

(1) *Foot* off throttle.
(2) Depress *clutch* quickly.
(3) Put gear into *neutral*.
(4) Move *gear* to appropriate ratio (change up or down).
(5) Slowly *release* clutch and depress throttle.

Skilled drivers may repeat this sequence flawlessly many times in a journey without the need to verbalize their actions. Indeed the skill may be so well learned that the driver can carry out other activities, usually talking to someone else, without any deleterious effect on his performance. Although this phenomenon is not well understood, there is a growing literature on its natural history and the development of individual differences in "self talk" (*see* Zivin, 1979). In the last decade there have been a number of successful attempts to apply this phenomenon to the improvement of deficient cognitive and motor performances. For example, teaching hyperactive children to improve their academic skills, improving creativity in college students and improving schizophrenics' performance on a number of cognitive tests similar to those used in intelligence tests (Meichenbaum, 1977). These treatments are generally known as "self-instructional training". What follows is an account of a particular form of self instructional training known as "Stress Innoculation Training".

Meichenbaum conceives this form of therapy as being analogous to being immunized against biological disease. An immunization procedure is one which deliberately exposes the subject to a small dose of the infection so that the natural defences of the individual are activated in such a way that subsequent exposure to larger doses of the infection can be satisfactorily managed. Thus Meichenbaum's stress innoculation training (SIT) deliberately exposes individuals to particular stresses and attempts to train them to tolerate and manage the stresses by altering their behavioural and cognitive reactions. Various elements of SIT are present in other behavioural and cognitive treatments such as anxiety management training (Suinn and Richardson, 1971), and problem solving (D'Zurilla and Goldfried, 1971). We have chosen Meichenbaum's procedure as being illustrative of a general approach to training coping skills and the technique can be an important adjunct to social skills training. Meichenbaum describes 3 major phases of SIT, each of which contains a number of separate components.

(2) An outline of the procedures

Stage 1—education, assessment and formulation. Meichenbaum places great emphasis on the necessity for the therapist to educate the client. By this he means that the therapist should provide the client with a conceptual framework by which he may understand the nature of his behaviour in problem situations. Meichenbaum and his associates aim to help the client understand his problem in terms of contemporary experimental cognitive psychology. Thus, phobic and anxious clients are introduced to Schacter's theory of emotion which highlights the inter-dependence of cognitive attributions and physiological arousal in the experience of emotion (Schacter and Singer, 1962; Strongman, 1978). Similar conceptualization can be developed for clients with problems of aggression and pain (Novaco, 1978; Turk, 1978). A treatment "package" has yet to be developed for people with social anxiety but a suitable conceptualization can be developed by using Schacter's ideas and applying an analysis of social anxiety such as that reported by Nichols (1974). The conceptualization developed by the therapist aims to be plausible and acceptable to the client, while its scientific validity is of secondary importance. The purpose of this conceptualization is 3 fold. Firstly, it aims to get the client to regard his problem as being an understandable, and therefore controllable, phenomenon. It thus helps to reduce the feelings of hopelessness present in so many clients. This should also induce a positive therapeutic expectation and motivate him into activity likely to reduce his distress. Meichenbaum summarizes this as getting the client to talk to himself differently about his problem. Secondly, it provides the client with a rationale to monitor and record information about his own behaviour in problem situations. This facilitates the assessment of the problem and the development of an individually-centred treatment plan. Thirdly, it introduces the client to considering the importance of what he says to himself as a precipitating factor of his emotional problems and as a determinant of his response to them.

The assessment component runs in parallel with the development of the conceptualization of the client's problem. During the initial interview the client is asked to describe his experience and behaviour. The therapist may use imagery to facilitate the client's reporting. A real-life exposure to the problem situation might also be arranged so that the therapist can observe the client's behaviour and the client can report on his subjective experiences and thoughts. As with most clinical behaviour therapy the client is instructed to keep a diary to record his daily confrontations with problem situations. In addition to recording information about the situation and his behaviour the client is asked to note his thoughts which occur just prior to, and at the initiation of, the stressor. Thoughts may be conveniently categorized into those concerning what the stressful event will do to the client, thoughts about how the client will behave and thoughts about how he thinks others will behave and think towards him.

The therapist uses the information reported by the client for 2 main purposes. Firstly, to confirm and develop the initial conceptualization, in particular the relationship between the client's appraisal of the stressful situation and his subsequent emotional reaction is emphasized. Second, the therapist can assess what the client knows about how to behave in problem situations. With regard to social situations it is not uncommon to find that the client has a very limited understanding of what is appropriate. Nichols (1974) describes this as the client having a rigid concept of appropriate social behaviour and an anxiety that he should not depart from the presumed set of rules for that situation or he will meet with overwhelming disapproval. One of the roles of the therapist is therefore to enlighten the client about what is appropriate behaviour.

The therapist then proposes a formulation of the client's problem which encompasses suggestions about possible therapeutic interventions. This formulation typically contains a number of elements based on a refined conceptualization of the client's problem. Thus, the client's stress reactions are described, these consist of increased physiological activity (raised heart rate, muscle tension, dry mouth, sweating, etc.) and the presence of anxiety inducing and maintaining thoughts. The appropriate treatment is aimed at reducing each of these components. An additional step is made by presenting the client with an analysis of his stress reaction which develops the notion that it should be regarded as a series of interlocking steps, rather than as a single event of overwhelming proportions. The 4 steps described by Meichenbaum are: (1) preparing for the stressor, (2) confronting and handling the stressor, (3) coping with the possibility that one might be overwhelmed emotionally with the stressful event, (4) evaluating one's coping activity after the stressor has passed. A set of self-instructional coping statements can then be developed for each of these steps and the client can be taught to use them and the associated behavioural skills such as relaxation. At this point the stage of rehearsal begins.

Stage 2—rehearsal. In this stage of treatment the details of the coping skills to be used by the client are worked out and learnt. There may be a number of skills to be learnt depending on the conceptualization arrived at in the initial stage. Usually strategies are worked out for managing both the physiological and cognitive components of the problem. Progressive relaxation training (Bernstein and Borkovec, 1973) is easily taught and after reasonable practice most clients can learn to identify slight levels of increased muscle tension and relax accordingly. Details about procedures for relaxing and controlling specific muscle groups can be found in Bernstein and Borkovec (1973) and Cautela and Groden (1978). Meichenbaum also emphasizes the role of controlling breathing. Learning how to pace and maintain a regular even breathing rate of around 8–10 inhalations per minute can help to reduce some of the physical signs of anxiety such as sweating and increased heart rate.

The rationale for cognitive coping stems from the idea that the emotional response of the person is determined in part by what he says to himself. So, if the person thinks about himself as being unable to cope, expecting disastrous consequences and being unable to control his reactions, he will probably perform in this way. Most people have these and similar thoughts when faced with stressful circumstances. If they can be replaced by more adaptive ones the degree of discomfort experienced can be reduced. At this stage the client is probably well aware of the negative thoughts which he has when confronting a stressor so he is now taught to use these thoughts as cues for producing a series of positive statements which serve to block out the negative thoughts and to direct him to carry out coping behaviour. The positive self statements are developed in consultation with the client, the therapist giving some initial examples and then helping the client to generate his own statements. The statements can be placed in each of the 4 steps mentioned at the end of the first stage.

For example, statements about *preparing for the stressor* would be concerned with generating a plan of action to deal with it, such as, "What do I have to do?", "What are my options?", "Don't think negative thoughts", "Make a realistic appraisal". *Confronting and handling* the stressor might produce statements like, "Use the relaxation", "Keep breathing evenly", "Just try and concentrate on the task at hand", "Think about the next thing to do not about what could happen in 10 minutes time". Typical statements for *coping with the feeling of being overwhelmed* might be, "OK don't fight it", "It will rise then go away", "Just accept that it will come and go", "Focusing on it and thinking about it will just prolong it". Finally, the client can produce statements for *evaluating his performance* such as, "Good, I stayed on task", "I can cope with being anxious and performing OK", "Good, I spotted the negative thoughts quickly enough". Once these statements are prepared it is useful to type them on cards so that the person can carry them around and memorize them. He is then ready to try them out under controlled stressful conditions.

Stage 3—application training. Meichenbaum has his clients practice their coping skills under a number of different conditions such as watching films, or doing experimental tasks in which electric shock is threatened. In clinical practice one might not have access to technical facilities and simpler ways of exposing the person to the stressor must be used. The two most suitable procedures are role-play with initial modelling by the therapist and imagery. These procedures are very simple and convenient to use but it also possible to use videotape facilities for practice in applying the coping skills. A more detailed account of this stage is given in the following case example.

(3) *A case example*

Lynne was a 27 year old housewife with 2 young children aged 4 and 6. She had had one previous contact with the psychiatric services 2 years before the present referral. At that time she was diagnosed as agoraphobic and she had been treated using a standard exposure method in a small group. This treatment had apparently helped her and she and her husband reported that she had made some progress. However, she was still markedly handicapped and found it difficult to complete a number of daily tasks such as taking her small son to school. During the initial interview it became clear that Lynne's anxiety was not invariably connected with being outside. She was just as likely to experience panic feelings in relatively safe places such as her own or a friend's home. She could not offer any explanation for this, she said that she didn't think that she had any social problems, she lived in an area where she knew many people from her childhood and had a large number of friends. She also acted as an agent for a company selling clothes and household articles and frequently gave parties as promotions for these products.

Lynne was asked to keep a diary in which she recorded the events and thoughts preceding each panic attack and noted how she coped. At the third session the diary was discussed and each panic episode was considered. At this point it became clear that the panic attacks often occurred when Lynne was in conflict or frustrated by a social situation. For example, she might be having a coffee in a neighbour's house and at the same time be wishing that she could get home to make lunch or get on with her own work. Her mind would become filled by the thought that she must get out and escape from the situation. This would produce typical feelings of anxiety such as palpitations, sweating and a dry mouth. She was unable to leave because she felt that in her state of anxiety she would be likely to faint. She also expressed the fear that were she to leave she would be disappointing her friend who would then reject her. Lynne said that she now realized that she found it extremely difficult to say no and express her own wishes and needs in social situations.

During the third session a simple account of emotion based on Schacter's model was explained to her. She was also taught simple relaxation and breathing exercises and was instructed to practice daily with the aid of an audio cassette. In the following session a series of self instructional statements were prepared and typed onto cards for Lynne to carry with her and rehearse in her spare moments. These statements are shown in Table 12.3.

TABLE 12.3
A sample of Lynne's self instructional coping statements

Preparing for the stressor

O.K. what do I have to do?

Identify the reason for being jittery
Do I have to leave
Do I want to leave
I've got a right to go if I want to
Remember the ways of saying good-bye

Confronting and handling the stressor

Relax—especially shoulders and head.
Breathe properly.
Don't try and rush out it will only increase panic.
Pay attention to what is going on outside.
Get ready to say "I'm leaving".
Be truthful—tell them you've got other things to do.

Coping with the possibility of being overwhelmed
Don't think about escaping—it will just make it worse.
Stay with it—the symptoms will die down soon.
Get involved in a conversation.

Evaluating/Reinforcing the outcome
Well done. I left that feeling pretty calm.
Nobody objected to my leaving.
If people don't like me because I leave are they really worth knowing?

Following this a single session was held during which Lynne rehearsed the self instructions while imagining a number of situations which had caused her anxiety in the past. These situations were drawn from her diary and included scenes such as: sitting at home with a friend and wishing that she would go home, wanting to get home quickly from shopping but being intercepted by a neighbour, etc. In addition to the straight rehearsal of the self instructions Lynne also carried out covert modelling (Kazdin, 1980) where she imagined herself being assertive and expressing her wishes to others. She was instructed to use her imagination to try out several ways of refusing requests and leaving people. She was also encouraged to elaborate her responses so that she had a good range of things to say to people. The therapist helped her to generate a number of replies. Lynne rapidly became used to rehearsing her skills in imagination and the anxiety which this procedure had initially provoked rapidly disappeared. At this stage she decided that it was no good waiting for difficult situations to arise and she would actively seek opportunities to assert herself even when a conflict was not aroused. She therefore set out to visit a series of friends with the expressed intent of leaving them within 20 minutes of arriving. Until this time the average time spent with friends and neighbours was well over 1 hour. She soon discovered that her assertiveness did not result in rejection by others and that she actually enjoyed her social life more than she had done before. Six months after the end of treatment Lynne had only experienced one or two minor attacks of panic. She had taken a part-time job in a shop and her diaries showed that she was going out more. She was also doing tasks which she had never previously contemplated doing such as visiting a distant park with her children.

D. Discussion

In this chapter we have described 3 approaches to cognitive therapy.

Each approach has assumed that cognitive events can cause, or influence, emotional and behavioural dysfunctions, but there are a number of differences in the ways in which the therapies attack the cognitive element. Ellis' RET and Beck's cognitive therapy both aim to change the content of the person's thought. Ellis writes that the goal of RET is to produce a new psychological "set" in clients so that they will bring a "radically revised outlook to all *new*, present and future situations that will semi-automatically help them to stop disturbing themselves" (Ellis, 1980, p. 327). In contrast to this, Meichenbaum's SIT does not primarily focus upon destroying the person's maladaptive beliefs. These beliefs may well change as a function of therapy, but the aim of treatment is to train the client to use the presence of the thought as a cue for engaging in more appropriate coping thoughts and behaviour.

The therapies also differ in the emphasis placed on the development of a planned behavioural intervention. RET does not exclude behavioural procedures but its main thrust is a highly polemical and didactic attack by the therapist on the client's irrational beliefs. On the other hand, Beck quite explicitly links cognitive and behavioural components together as challenges to the person's automatic thoughts. In Beck's therapy behavioural tasks are an integral part of the treatment package and a principal technique in getting the patient to test out the reality of his thought pattern. The behavioural tasks are unique for each person and depend entirely on the content of the automatic thought under scrutiny. It is only the inventiveness of the therapist which restricts what a behavioural task will be. Although Meichenbaum' SIT also concentrates on idiosyncratic behavioural tasks during the Application stage, the form of the behavioural component is more fixed than in Beck's therapy. Thus, Meichenbaum focuses on reducing physiological arousal, via breathing regulation and relaxation, and graded exposure to stressful situations. There is one other notable difference between the therapies of Beck and Ellis. Ellis is very specific about the actual content of peoples' faulty beliefs. He suggests that the beliefs found in Table 12.1 (p. 312) represent a core of irrational ideas found in neurotic patients. In contrast to this Beck's description of faulty cognition concentrates on the common errors of reasoning found in patients. These differences between therapies may well reflect their different origins. Ellis' RET was developed from his experience with neurotic New Yorkers, whereas Beck's therapy comes from his experience in treating depressed patients and Meichenbaum's SIT reflects elements of a contemporary psychological theory of emotion and behaviour therapy.

Which of these approaches should be used in social skills training? Unfortunately, there are no firm rules which could help us decide. On balance we suspect that RET requires clients of above average intelligence and articulateness. The typical argumentative style of treatment would certainly not be recommended for chronic psychiatric patients or for those with histories of major affective or psychotic disorders. Beck's approach is psychologically gentle and his insistence that the therapist possess the ability to be warm, empathic and genuine makes this approach more acceptable for those clients who have pervasive emotional distress. Meichenbaum is perhaps the most directive of all the treatments and, because it does not require a detailed intellectual examination of the faulty cognitive component, it is easier to adapt to group settings and to use with less articulate clients. Although there are some reports of controlled experimental studies of RET and SIT applied to social skills problems (Rachman and Wilson, 1980) it should be emphasized that there is little known about the type of client who responds to the introduction of a cognitive component to treatment. We can only recommend that therapists experiment with the approaches described in this chapter to find the most suitable combination of techniques for their own client group. Thus, careful description and the measurement of outcome in a number of single cases is probably the safest way to proceed (see Hersen and Barlow, 1976; Shepherd, 1982, in press).

III. REFERENCES

Alden, L., Safran, J. and Weideman, R. (1978). A comparison of cognitive and skills training strategies in the treatment of unassertive clients. *Behav. Ther.* **9**, 843–846.

Bandura, A. (1977). Self efficacy: Toward a unifying theory of behaviour change. *Psychol. Rev.* **84**, 191–215.

Beck, A. T. (1972). "Depression: Causes and treatment". University of Pennsylvania Press, Philadelphia.

Beck, A. T. (1976). "Cognitive Therapy and the Emotional Disorders". International Universities Press, New York.

Beck, A. T., Rush, A. J., Shaw, B. F. and Emery, G. (1979). "Cognitive Therapy of Depression". Guildford Press, New York.

Bernstein, D. A. and Borkovec, T. D. (1973). "Progressive Relaxation Training". Research Press, Champaign, Illinois.

Carmody, T. P. (1978). Rational-emotive, self instructional and behaviour assertion training: Facilitating maintenance. *Cognitive Ther. Res.* **2**, 241–254.

Cautela, J. R. and Groden, J. (1978). "Relaxation: A comprehensive manual for adults, children and children with special needs". Research Press, Champaign, Illinois.

D'Zurilla, T. and Goldfried, M. (1971). Problem solving and behaviour modification. *J. Abnorm. Psychol.* **78**, 107–126.

Ellis, A. (1958). Rational psychotherapy. *J. Gen. Psychol.* **59**, 36–49.

Ellis, A. (1977). The basic clinical theory of rational emotive therapy. *In* "Handbook of Rational Emotive Therapy" (A. Ellis and R. Grieger, *Eds*). Springer, New York.

Ellis, A. (1980). Rational-emotive therapy and cognitive-behaviour therapy: Similarities and differences. *Cognitive Ther. Res.* **4**, 325–340.

Erwin, E. (1978). "Behaviour Therapy: Scientific, Philosophical and Moral Foundations". Cambridge University Press, Cambridge.

Eysenck, H. J. (1979). Behaviour therapy and the philosophers. *Behav. Res. Ther.* **17**, 511–514.

Goldfried, M. (1977). The use of relaxation and cognitive relabelling as coping skills. *In* "Behavioural Self-Management" (R. B. Stuart, *Ed.*). Brunner/Mazel, New York.

Goldfried, M. R. and Davison, G. C. (1976). "Clinical Behaviour Therapy". Holt, New York.

Goldfried, M. R., Decenteceo, E. T. and Weinberg, L. (1974). Systematic rational restructuring as a self control technique. *Behav. Ther.* **5**, 247–264.

Hersen, M. and Barlow, D. H. (1976). "Single Case Experimental Designs: Strategies for Studying Behaviour Change". Pergamon Press, Oxford.

Hersen, M. and Bellack, A. S. (1976). Social skills training for chronic psychiatric patients: Rationale, research findings and future directions. *Comprehensive Psychiatry* **197**, 559–580.

Kazdin, A. E. (1980). Covert and overt rehearsal and elaboration during treatment in the development of assertive behaviour. *Behav. Res. Ther.* **18**, 191–202.

Kelvin, P. (1969). "The Social Basis of Behaviour". Routledge and Kegan Paul, London.

Lange, A. J. (1977). Cognitive behavioural assertion training. *In* "Handbook of Rational Emotive Therapy" (A. Ellis and R. Greiger, *Eds*). Springer, New York.

Lange, A. J. and Jakubowski, P. (1976). "Responsible Assertive Behaviour". Research Press, Illinois.

Linehan, M. M., Goldfried, M. R. and Goldfried, A. P. (1979). Assertion therapy, skill training or cognitive restructuring? *Behav. Ther.* **10**, 372–388.

Mahoney, M. J. (1974). "Cognition and Behaviour Modification". Ballinger, Cambridge, Massachusetts.

Mandel, N. M. and Shrauger, J. S. (1980). The effects of self evaluative statements on heterosexual approach in shy and non-shy males. *Cognitive Ther. Res.* **4**, 369–381.

Marzillier, J. S. (1978). Outcome studies of skill training: a review. *In* "Social Skills and Mental Health" (P. Trower *et al.*, *Eds*). Methuen, London.

Marzillier, J. S. (1980). Cognitive therapy and behavioural practice. *Behav. Res. Ther.* **18**, 249–258.

Meichenbaum, D. (1975). Self-instructional methods. *In* "Helping People Change: A Textbook of Methods" (F. H. Kanfer and A. P. Goldstein, *Eds*). Pergamon Press, New York.

Meichenbaum, D. (1976). Toward a cognitive theory of self-control. *In* "Consciousness and Self-Regulation: Advances in Research" (G. E. Schwartz and D. Shapiro, *Eds*), Vol. 1. Plenum Press, New York.

Meichenbaum, D. (1977). "Cognitive-Behaviour Modification: An Integrative Approach". Plenum Press, New York.

Neisser, U. (1976). "Cognition and Reality". W. H. Freeman and Co., San Francisco.

Nichols, K. (1974). Severe social anxiety. *Br. J. Med. Psychol.* **47**, 301–306.

Novaco, R. W. (1978). Anger and coping with stress: Cognitive-behavioural interventions. *In* "Cognitive Behaviour Therapy: Research and Application" (J. P. Forejt and D. P. Rathjen, *Eds*). Plenum Press, New York.

Rachlin, H. (1977). A Review of M. J. Mahoney's Cognition and Behaviour Modification. *J. Appl. Behav. Anal.* **10**, 369–374.

Rachman, S. J. and Wilson, G. T. (1980). "The Effects of Psychological Therapy". Pergamon, Oxford.

Rush, A. J., Beck, A. T., Kovacs, M. and Hollon, S. (1977). Comparative efficacy of cognitive therapy and imipramine in the treatment of depressed outpatients. *Cognitive Ther. Res.* **1**, 17–37.

Schacter, S. and Slinger, J. (1962). Cognitive, social and physiological determinants of emotional state. *Psychol. Rev.* **69**, 378–399.

Schwartz, R. M. and Gottman, J. M. (1976). Towards a task analysis of assertive behaviour. *J. Consult. Clin. Psychol.* **44**, 910–920.

Shepherd, G. (1980). The treatment of social difficulties in special environments. *In* "The Social Psychology of Psychological Problems" (P. Feldman and J. Orford, *Eds*). Wiley, Chichester.

Shepherd, G. W. (1982). Assessment of cognitions in social skills training. *In* "Cognitive Perspectives in Social Skills Training" (P. Trower, *Ed.*). Pergamon Press, Oxford. (In press)

Spivack, G. and Shure, M. B. (1974). "Social Adjustment of Young Children". Jossey Bass, San Francisco.

Strongman, K. T. (1978). "The Psychology of Emotion" (2nd Edition). Wiley, Chichester.

Suinn, R. and Richardson, F. (1971). Anxiety management training: A non-specific behaviour therapy programme for anxiety control. *Behav. Ther.* **2**, 498–510.

Taylor, F. G. and Marshall, W. L. (1977). Experimental analysis of a cognitive-behavioural therapy for depression. *Cognitive Ther. Res.* **1**, 59–72.

Thorpe, G. L. (1975). Desensitisation, behaviour rehearsal, self-instructional training and placebo effects on assertive-refusal behaviour. *Eur. J. Behav. Anal. Mod.* **1**, 30–44.

Trower, P. (1980a). How to lose friends and influence nobody: An analysis of social failure. *In* "The Analysis of Social Skills" (W. Singleton *et al., Eds*). Plenum Press, New York.

Trower, P. (1980b). Situational analysis of the components and processes of behaviour of socially skilled and unskilled patients. *J. Consult. Clin. Psychol.* **48**, 327–339.

Turk, D. C. (1978). Cognitive behavioural techniques in the management of pain. *In* "Cognitive Behaviour Therapy: Research and Application" (J. P. Forejt and D. P. Rathjen, *Eds*). Plenum Press, New York.

Wolfe, J. L. and Foder, I. G. (1977). Modifying assertive behaviour in women: A comparison of three approaches. *Behav. Ther.* **8**, 567–575.

Wolpe, J. (1978). Cognition and causation in human behaviour and its therapy. *Am. Psychol.* **33**, 437–436.

Zivin, G. (*Ed.*) (1979). "The Development of Self Regulation Through Private Speech". Wiley, Chichester.

SECTION IV

Concluding comments

GEOFF SHEPHERD AND SUE SPENCE

We have tried in this volume to focus on the problems and pitfalls of the SST approach. Our contributors have been concerned with a wide range of client groups in a variety of settings. In these final comments we will attempt to summarize the main themes that have emerged and to draw out some of the implications for future research and practice.

I. CONCLUSION 1—THE OUTCOME EVIDENCE REGARDING THE EFFECTIVENESS OF SST IS STILL EQUIVOCAL

It is clear that various methodological problems, notably poor definition of samples, inadequate dependent measures and lack of follow-up data, preclude one from drawing any very firm conclusion regarding the effectiveness of SST, either in a general or in a specific sense. This means that each would-be practitioner has a responsibility to evaluate his/her effectiveness with whatever client group they are concerned with and in whatever setting they are working. The use of SST cannot be justified by an appeal to "the evidence" and it should be viewed as an experimental procedure in the sense that its outcome is somewhat uncertain. The burden of proof regarding its use must thus still rest with its advocates, rather than its detractors.

II. CONCLUSION 2—THERE IS VERY LITTLE CONSENSUS REGARDING MANY OF THE BASIC PARAMETERS OF THE TREATMENT APPROACH

This point has been made before (e.g. Curran, 1979) and while it is clear that there is good agreement as to what techniques comprise SST, i.e. goal-setting, modelling, practice (role-play), feedback and homework, there are very few clear guidelines as to how these techniques should be combined and deployed in practice. To a certain extent this is inevitable as it reflects the use of SST with widely different client groups, different aims, different settings, etc. However, it poses problems if one is concerned with the scientific replication of research findings. We need to consider very carefully how such a complex and flexible approach can be standardized such that some comparison of results between different investigators becomes possible. This problem has also been raised with regard to other multiple-technique approaches and in the past we considered using a flow-chart analysis to try to solve it (Shepherd and Durham, 1977). The problem with this method, and it would be the same in the case of SST, is that we lack the basic information to move through the choice points of the flow chart, e.g. when to choose modelling as opposed to verbal instructions?, when to work on eye-contact rather than speech volume?, etc. These difficulties lead us into conclusions 3 and 4.

III. CONCLUSION 3—THERE IS A CLEAR CONSENSUS REGARDING THE NEED TO INDIVIDUALIZE TREATMENT PACKAGES AS MUCH AS POSSIBLE

While it may not be possible to specify exactly *how* to individualize treatment procedures, there does seem to be a very clear agreement that it is at least necessary to try. Clearly, some clients seem to benefit a great deal from the approach, while others do not. Similarly, some techniques work very well with some populations, but not others. This need to strive for the best fit between client characteristics and treatment technique seems absolutely central to the whole question of the effectiveness of the approach. While it would be splendid if we could specify such parameters *a priori*, at the moment this is not possible. Thus, for the present it may be that the most productive research strategy is to focus on the outcomes of individual cases rather than use large, group-based studies where random allocation deliberately obscures the effects of individual differences (*see* Marzillier and Winter, 1978; Shepherd, 1981). These individually-tailored programmes will need to be based on the outcome of a detailed assessment of each client's social difficulties.

IV. CONCLUSION 4—THAT IDENTIFYING THE CHARACTERISTICS OF EFFECTIVE THERAPISTS IS A CRUCIAL, BUT NEGLECTED, AREA

The need to individualize treatment, and to match client characteristics and treatment technique, underlines the need to identify much more clearly what makes a good social skills therapist. Therapists must not only be technically proficient, they must also be able to select relevant and feasible treatment goals, negotiate these with the client, have a knowledge of subcultural norms, etc. Our contributors were quite unanimous that this involved much more than simple "book-learning". Nearly everyone agreed that what makes a good social skills therapist is probably not very different from what makes a good therapist with any other kind of psychological technique. They should be open, genuine, warm, empathic, able to distance themselves, concerned, non-judgmental, etc. (*see* Beck *et al.*, 1979). To achieve this they must have the opportunity to practice their therapeutic skills and to receive clear and constructive feedback upon them. A period of training followed by close working with a co-therapist seemed to be the favoured method for doing this. Further research which examines in detail what therapists actually do in treatment sessions and then relate this directly to outcome (e.g. Alexander *et al.*, 1976) would be useful.

V. CONCLUSION 5—SST IS NOT A PANACEA, IT IS ONLY EFFECTIVE AS PART OF AN OVERALL TREATMENT STRATEGY

Our contributors were often at great pains to emphasize that SST should not be seen as the cure-all for every client and every problem. The approach should be integrated within a comprehensive treatment strategy based on a detailed examination of each individual's problems. It seems to be most effective if clients are selected specifically because their social difficulties are prominent and if their other problems are also receiving therapeutic attention (e.g. as in Chapter 10 where sexual problems were also being treated). SST is thus an important element in treatment but it cannot stand alone. In a similar way, SST is most effective if it can be integrated within the overall goals and aims of the particular setting. Several contributors stressed the importance of trying to reconcile the aims of an SST programme with other organizational pressures within the settings and this leads us on to the broader questions of generalizing and maintaining therapeutic change.

VI. CONCLUSION 6—THE PROBLEMS OF GENERALIZING AND MAINTAINING THERAPEUTIC CHANGE DEPEND UPON A CLEAR APPRECIATION OF THE CONTEXT IN WHICH THE CLIENT'S PROBLEMS EXIST

SST is clearly effective in producing limited changes, in specific targets, evaluated over short periods of time. Whether it is also effective in producing rather wider, more "clinical" changes, which are generalized and stable, seems more doubtful. This problem is not, of course, confined to SST (see Goldstein and Kanfer, 1979) however, unless it can be overcome then the clinical appeal of the approach will remain limited. Our contributors suggested a number of ways in which these problems might be tackled. These included technical improvements so as to improve the efficiency of the treatment itself (e.g. better matching of techniques to individual differences, c.f. conclusion 3). Also, improvements in the methods of training so as to maximize the similarity between training conditions and the conditions which prevail in the settings into which one hopes that the improvements will transfer and be maintained. As a general "rule of thumb", the more dissimilar and artificial the treatment is the less one can expect generalization or maintenance. However, the crucial point is to be able to understand the client's social context sufficiently well so that one can ensure that realistic goals can be achieved and once achieved that these will be maintained. This means understanding the institution, the family, the school, or the peer group and then trying to influence it (*see* Shepherd, 1980). In practice, the degree to which this can be achieved will often be limited, nevertheless it is important to be aware of this limitation as one may then wish to pursue alternative strategies. For example, to try and involve the client in some longer term social context which will maintain their social functioning while not aiming at directly improving it (e.g. in a day centre, workshop, or social club). In many cases the problems of generalizing and maintaining improvements, may thus be more realistically redefined as problems of maintaining functioning given the presence of certain, relatively fixed, disabilities. This may seem like a modest aim, but at least it gives one a clear strategy for dealing with "failures" and an alternative solution to the very difficult problems of generalization and maintenance.

VII. CONCLUSION 7—THAT THE FULL IMPORTANCE OF THE COGNITIVE PROCESSES IN SST HAS YET TO BE APPRECIATED

Another approach to dealing with the problems of generalizing and maintaining change which was suggested by several of our contributors was to rely on cognitive changes to bridge the "gap" across settings and across time. The importance of cognitive processes both in terms of the assessment of social difficulties and in terms of their treatment has been noted by several writers (e.g. Bellack, 1979; Yardley, 1979; Trower, 1981) and attempts are now being made to develop suitable assessment measures and effective treatment interventions (*see* Shepherd, 1982; Morley *et al.*, Chapter 11). It may seem contradictory that a treatment approach which is very much associated with the identification of deficits in skilled *behaviour*, should now be continually emphasizing the importance of cognitive processes in determining difficulties and influencing the course of treatment. However, as indicated in the Introduction there is nothing in Argyle's original model that would necessarily lead one to focus exclusively, or even initially, on the behavioural components of the model. This renewed preoccupation with unobservable thoughts and feelings is therefore perhaps predictable, but it represents possibly the single most important challenge to the SST approach. If cognitions are really what is important, then why use a skills training approach to change them? This brings us to the question of mechanism.

VIII. CONCLUSION 8—IN GENERAL, THE MECHANISMS THROUGH WHICH SST WORKS ARE NOT WELL UNDERSTOOD

SST can certainly be effective in the narrow sense described above, however why and how it is effective is not clear. Does it work by teaching clients new skills, or does it work by producing certain cognitive changes, e.g. reduction in fear or changes in expectancies? Of course, these two kinds of explanations are not mutually exclusive. It could be the case that the elaborate procedure of "training" new skills is actually the most effective way of producing changes in expectancies or other aspects of cognitions. But, to be clearer about this would be a considerable advantage. Certainly, on theoretical grounds, it is difficult to account for how any kind of treatment improvement could generalize or be maintained *without* involving cognitive changes. In addition to lacking an adequate general understanding of how the treatment works, we also lack a more specific understanding of how to change each component of social difficulties and how they interact with one another (*see also* conclusion 3). For example, it was suggested in the Introduction that we might get much better results if we focused simply on changing role performance (or cognitions) rather than by focusing on behaviour. Further elucidation of these mechanisms would certainly be very useful.

IX. CONCLUSION 9—THAT PREVENTION OF LATER DIFFICULTIES THROUGH SST REMAINS A POSSIBILITY RATHER THAN A REALITY

Prevention remains one of the glittering prizes in mental health. One of the major attractions of the SST approach is that it purports to offer a technology for preventing later psychological and behavioural distress. But to be effective in prevention at a primary level (i.e. to prevent new cases from arising) demands that: (a) there is a direct causal relationship between early social problems and subsequent mental disturbance, and (b) that we can intervene effectively to treat social difficulties in a meaningful and enduring way. From everything that has been said so far, it is clear that as far as SST is concerned the evidence in support of both these propositions is unconvincing to say the least. This is not to say that prevention at a secondary or tertiary level might not be feasible, i.e. it may be possible to identify clients "at risk" earlier than tends to be the case and possibly increase the likelihood that treatment will be effective. Similarly, an effective and efficient treatment intervention might minimize the accumulation of secondary handicaps. A preventive model perhaps has most to offer regarding children (*see* Chapter 7) but until much stronger evidence is forthcoming we have to conclude that it remains more of a hope than a reality.

X. CONCLUSION 10—SST MAY BE A SENSIBLE PLACE TO START, BUT IT ISN'T NECESSARILY WHERE WE ARE GOING TO END UP

Oscar Wilde said that a pessimist is an optimist in full possession of the facts. In this sense we are pessimistic about the future of SST. We see it as a plausible starting point for thinking about social difficulties and perhaps effectively treating them. We do not view it as a panacea. We are aware of its limitations and recognize that it may be necessary to go well beyond the original model and approach in order to improve its effectiveness. The field of mental health is littered with the remains of dead treatment approaches which were once the very latest fads and fancies and if SST is not to befall a similar fate it must be able to move and grow and change. Our hope is that it will be able to do this. We feel that it is a good beginning: it is sensible, practical and has high "face validity". If it can progress and through careful research build on what is useful and reject what is not, then it surely must have an important future. Perhaps this book will mark a small milestone along the way.

XI. REFERENCES

Alexander, J. F., Barton, C., Schiavo, R. S. and Parsons, B. V. (1976). Systems behavioural intervention with families of delinquents: Therapist characteristics family behaviour and outcome. *J. Consult. Clin. Psychol.* **44**, 656–664.

Beck, A. T., Rush, A. J., Shaw, B. F. and Emery, G. (1979). "Cognitive Therapy of Depression". Guildford Press, New York.

Bellack, A. S. (1979). Behavioural assessment of social skills. *In* "Research and Practice in Social Skills Training" (A. S. Bellack and M. Hersen, *Eds*). Plenum Press, New York.

Curran, J. (1979). Social skills: Methodological issues and future directions. *In* "Research and Practice in Social Skills Training" (A. S. Bellack and M. Hersen, *Eds*). Plenum Press, New York.

Goldstein, A. P. and Kanfer, F. H. (1979). "Maximizing Treatment Gains". Academic Press, New York.

Marzillier, J. S. and Winter, K. (1978). Success and failure in social skills training: Individual differences. *Behav. Res. and Ther.* **16**, 67–84.

Shepherd, G. (1980). The treatment of social difficulties in special environments. *In* "Psychological Problems: The Social Context" (P. Feldman and J. Orford, *Eds*). Wiley, Chichester.

Shepherd, G. (1981). Social Skills Training: The Way Backwards? Paper presented at the Annual Conference of British Association for Behavioural Psychotherapy, Bristol, July.

Shepherd, G. (1982). Assessment of cognitions in social skills training. *In* "Cognitive Approaches in Social Skills Training" (P. Trower, *Ed.*). Pergamon Press, Oxford. (In press)

Shepherd, G. and Durham, R. (1977). The multiple techniques approach to behavioural psychotherapy: A retrospective evaluation of effectiveness and an examination of prognostic indicators. *Br. J. Med. Psychol.* **50**, 45–52.

Trower, P. (1981). Social skill disorder: Mechanisms of failure. *In* "Personal Relationships in Disorder" (R. Gilmour and S. Duck, *Eds*). Academic Press, London.

Yardley, K. (1979). Social skills training: A critique. *Br. J. Med. Psychol.* **52**, 55–62.

Index